KEY FEATURES

MARKETING: CONCEPTS AND STRATEGIES
Tenth Edition
William M. Pride and O. C. Ferrell

Marketing: Concepts and Strategies, Tenth Edition, includes an exceptional, comprehensive package of learning and teaching materials that are described briefly in the following list:

For Instructors

INSTRUCTOR'S RESOURCE MANUAL This ancillary is a complete teaching tool. Each chapter includes the following elements:

> Teaching Resources Quick Reference Guide
> Purpose and Perspective
> Guide for Using Color Transparencies
> Lecture Outline
> 2 Class Exercises (in transparency master format)
> Debate Issue (in transparency master format)
> Chapter Quiz (in transparency master format)
> Answers to Discussion and Review Questions
> Comments on the Cases (including video teaching materials)

In addition, the *Instructor's Resource Manual* includes a transition guide for users who are moving from the ninth to the tenth edition, special notes for teachers using our Pride/Ferrell Instructional Center on the Internet, sample syllabus, video easy-reference table, comments on the part-ending strategic cases, and answers to text Appendix B: Financial Analysis in Marketing.

TEST BANK The *Test Bank* provides a total of more than 3,000 items, including true/false, multiple-choice, and essay questions for each chapter. Each objective test item comes with the correct answer, a main text page reference, and a key to whether the question tests knowledge, comprehension, or application. This completely revised tenth edition also provides difficulty and discrimination ratings derived from actual class testing for more than one-half of the multiple-choice questions.

Lists of author-selected questions have been developed that facilitate quick construction of tests or quizzes. These questions are representative of chapter content and of each question type.

COMPUTERIZED TEST BANK This program is designed for use on IBM and IBM-compatible computers. With this program, the instructor can select questions from the *Test Bank* and produce a test master for easy duplication. The program gives instructors the option of selecting their own questions or having the program select them.

ON-LINE TESTING AND GRADEBOOK These features, which come with the *Computerized Test Generator,* allow instructors to administer tests via a network system, modem, or personal computer; set up records for a new class; record grades from tests or assignments; analyze grades; and produce class and individual statistics.

CALL-IN TEST SERVICE This service lets instructors select items from the *Test Bank* and call our toll-free number to order printed tests.

COLOR TRANSPARENCIES A set of nearly 250 color transparencies offers the instructor visual teaching assistance. About half of these are illustrations from the text; the rest are figures, tables, and diagrams that can be used as additional instructional aids.

VIDEOTAPES This series is to be used in conjunction with the video cases at the end of every chapter. Specific information about each video is given in the Comments on the Cases section in this *Instructor's Resource Manual.*

POWERPOINT SLIDES The Power Connection is a unique classroom presentation program consisting of over 400 PowerPoint slides relating to the learning objectives for each chapter in the text. The slides, created by Milton Pressley of the University of New Orleans, are completely original representations of the concepts in the book, providing additional insights, examples, and humor to reinforce learning. In addition, embedded within the program are lecture notes relating to each of the slides, which instructors can use or adapt as they wish.

For Students and Instructors

One of the most exciting developments related to this revision is the creation of an entire Web site for students and instructors. The site includes

- *Chapter 24, "Marketing and the Internet."* This chapter explores the world of online marketing and will be updated at least once every semester to incorporate the latest developments that influence marketing on the Internet.

- *Internet Exercises for Chapters 1–23.* These exercises reinforce chapter concepts by guiding students through specific Web sites and asking them to assess the success of the site and its information from a marketing perspective.

- *The Research Center.* This comprehensive list provides links to a variety of marketing information resources on the Internet and will be continually updated.

- *The Idea Exchange.* The Idea Exchange is a forum where students can share their perspectives about online marketing and the Internet.

For Students

STUDY GUIDE This book includes the following review material for each chapter of the text: a chapter outline, matching exercises, true-false questions, multiple-choice questions, a minicase with multiple-choice questions, and answers.

PC STUDY This disk provides additional review and self-test material (different from that in the printed *Study Guide*) for each chapter. Matching and multiple-choice questions are also included.

MARKETER: A SIMULATION This tool is a dynamic computer-based simulation prepared by Jerald R. Smith and Peggy Golden. *Marketer* creates a realistic business environment characterized by many of the opportunities and decisions real marketers face. Students, acting as management teams, make a variety of decisions that will have an impact on their company's operations. The computer evaluates students' decisions and produces the results of those decisions that will have an impact on their company's operations in easy-to-read printouts. Complete instructions for running this simulation are contained in the instructor's disk.

THE POWER CONNECTION In this custom-published version of the PowerPoint slides, printed representations of the slides are provided in a workbook format, with plenty of space next to each slide for notetaking. The workbook can then be used by students as a study aid.

Instructor's Resource Manual

MARKETING

Concepts and Strategies

TENTH EDITION

William M. Pride
Texas A & M University

O. C. Ferrell
University of Tampa

HOUGHTON MIFFLIN COMPANY   BOSTON   NEW YORK

Sponsoring Editor: Jennifer B. Speer
Associate Sponsoring Editor: Joanne M. Dauksewicz
Senior Manufacturing Coordinator: Priscilla J. Bailey
Marketing Manager: Michael B. Mercier

Copyright © 1997 by Houghton Mifflin Company. All rights reserved.

Houghton Mifflin Company hereby grants you permission to reproduce the Houghton Mifflin material contained in this work in classroom quantities, solely for use with the accompanying Houghton Mifflin textbook. All reproductions must include the Houghton Mifflin copyright notice, and no fee may be collected except to cover the cost of duplication. If you wish to make any other use of this material, including reproducing or transmitting the material or portions thereof in any form or by any electronic or mechanical means including any information storage or retrieval system, you must obtain prior written permission from Houghton Mifflin Company, unless such use is expressly permitted by federal copyright law. If you wish to reproduce material acknowledging a rights holder other than Houghton Mifflin Company, you must obtain permission from the rights holder. Address inquiries to College Permissions, Houghton Mifflin Company, 222 Berkeley Street, Boston, MA 02116-3764.

Printed in the U.S.A.

ISBN: 0-395-83685-9

123456789-PO-00 99 98 97 96

CONTENTS

TRANSITION GUIDE
A Guide for Instructors Who Are Switching to the Tenth Edition of
MARKETING: CONCEPTS AND STRATEGIES

To help with your course preparation, we have compiled the following list of major text changes and a list of chapter-by-chapter changes.

MAJOR TEXT CHANGES FOR THE TENTH EDITION

- The concept of relationship marketing is emphasized in this new edition.

- Many of the changes that we have made relate to the use of technology in marketing. Topics such as telecommuting, the Internet, and online marketing are addressed. We also focus on the use of new technologies in marketing research, including database research, electronic bulletin boards, single-source data, online information services, the Internet, and E-mail surveys.

- The distribution chapters have been reorganized to include the concept of supply chain management, which emphasizes long-term partnerships among channel members working together to reduce inefficiencies, costs, and redundancies in order to heighten customer satisfaction.

- New sections have been added to this edition that deal with brand equity and brand loyalty.

- A complete new section has been included in this edition that focuses on public relations.

- All of the chapter opening vignettes are new to this edition or have been updated.

- Over half of all the cases are new to this edition.

- Nearly all of the boxed features are new to this edition.

CHAPTER-BY-CHAPTER REVISIONS

Chapter 1 An Overview of Strategic Marketing

- The chapter opens with a discussion of the launch of BMW's new Z3 sportster and the importance of creating a successful marketing strategy with a product that satisfies consumers' needs.

- The chapter now introduces and defines the concept of relationship marketing to emphasize the importance of customer value and customer relationships in marketing.

- A new boxed feature describes how a nonbusiness organization, the Texas Parks and Wildlife Department, is using marketing activities to achieve its goals and improve relationships with customers. A second new boxed feature discusses Olympic sponsorships used to promote companies and their products and to create goodwill with their customers.

- Both of the end-of-the-chapter cases are new to this edition. The video case describes AutoZone's efforts to develop a marketing mix that satisfies the needs of do-it-yourself customers. The Microsoft case covers the launch and marketing strategy of the firm's Windows 95 operating system.

Chapter 2   The Marketing Environment

- A new chapter-opening vignette describes how companies are responding to changing consumer values and needs by creating new low- and no-fat snacks.

- Many of the federal laws that affect marketing decision are now summarized in a new table, Table 2.5.

- New to this edition is a section addressing how the new Federal Sentencing Guidelines for Organizations encourages companies to obey the law and create effective compliance programs to ensure that their employees act in accordance with society's wishes.

- A new Ethical Challenges box focuses on the issue of breast implant litigation to illustrate the complexities and expenses associated with legal and regulatory issues of the marketing environment. A second new boxed feature describes how the Rainforest Cafe restaurant chain is capitalizing on changes in sociocultural forces of the marketing environment.

- A new end-of-chapter case on Archer Daniels Midland focuses on that company's legal and ethical problems associated with allegations of price fixing by the company.

Chapter 3   Marketing Ethics and Social Responsibility

- This chapter begins with a discussion about the controversial issue of hot-beverage lawsuits, asking students to consider who bears responsibility when a consumer is injured by a product.

- A new Ethical Challenges box summarizes a dispute between the rock band R.E.M. and Hershey Foods to illustrate that ethical disputes are often resolved through the court system.

- A section has been added on the importance of ethics compliance programs, codes of conduct, and ethics officers in creating ethical organizations and deterring unethical and irresponsible conduct in marketing.

- A second new Ethical Challenges box discusses the Calvin Klein jeans advertising scandal and asks students to ponder where to draw the line when using sex in advertising.

- Social responsibility and ethics success stories are provided in a discussion of the *Business Ethics* Award.

- A new end-of-chapter case profiles Eli Lilly & Co., with a focus on the ethical issues associated with the marketing of the controversial drug Prozac.

Chapter 4 Global Markets and International Marketing

- A new opening vignette features Procter & Gamble's experience in selling consumer products in Latin America.

- A new Global Perspectives box discusses international marketing by Brother Industries to expand despite increasing product obsolescence. A second new boxed feature indicates that some U.S. firms are successfully marketing their products in Japan despite the widespread perception that breaching Japanese trade barriers is nearly impossible.

- Sections on international environmental forces and regional trade alliances, markets, and agreements have been updated and strengthened to promote discussion of current issues in marketing and focus on changing relations with countries such as Mexico, China, Japan, Vietnam, and Russia.

- The end-of-chapter cases are new to this edition. The Nike video case explores the importance of international marketing to that company's success. The second case profiles KLM and describes how the airline is taking advantage of changing legal forces to expand its global reach through international partnerships and alliances. Additionally, a new strategic case on Kentucky Fried Chicken, with a focus on the firm's international marketing and changes in the firm's domestic markets, completes Part 1 of the text.

Chapter 5 Information Systems and Marketing Research

- A new opening vignette highlights how Frito-Lay used marketing research to develop its new Baked Lay's Potato Crisps.

- The discussion of information systems has been revised to focus on how markcters can capitalize on new tcchnologies for marketing research. This section now includes databases, electronic bulletin boards, online information systems (such as CompuServe), and the Internet, including the World Wide Web. New tables describe Internet use in North America and provide World Wide Web page addresses useful in marketing research.

- The survey methods section has been expanded to include E-mail surveys. In addition, a new Ethical Challenges box addresses issues associated with using electronic mail for marketing research.

- A new boxed feature describes recent trends in focus-group interviewing.

- A new end-of-chapter video case describes how Campbell's, Maidenform, and AT&T used marketing research to solve problems and learn more about consumers' needs.

Chapter 6 Consumer Buying Behavior

- A new opening vignette features Boston Market, a company that has made major changes in order to satisfy its customers' needs.

- A definition and explanation of evaluative criteria have been added to the section on the evaluation of alternatives.

- The new Technology in Marketing box discusses consumers' purchasing habits for high-tech entertainment products.

- The discussion of the information search stage of the consumer buying decision process has been refined to communicate more concisely.

- The discussion of postpurchase evaluation now includes techniques used to reduce cognitive dissonance.

- The section on the psychological factors that influence the buying decision process has been streamlined to allow for more focused discussions of perception and learning.

- A definition and explanation of consumer socialization has been added to the roles and family influences section.

Chapter 7 Organizational Markets and Buying Behavior

- The chapter begins with an example of an organizational marketer, Emerson Electric, that has achieved long-term success through effective planning and its commitment to customer satisfaction.

- Several definitions, including value analysis and vendor analysis, have been added to the section on the stages of the organizational buying decision process.

- The new Inside Marketing box looks at Breed Technologies' struggle to develop and gain acceptance of airbag technologies.

- The new Technology in Marketing box focuses on how an organizational marketer improved customer service by using a centralized database.

- The WMX Technologies, Inc., case has been updated to include the current performance of WMX and the factors contributing to the company's recent rebound and success.

Chapter 8 Target Markets: Segmentation and Evaluation

- The chapter begins with a discussion of the changing cable TV industry and how cable networks segment television viewers.

- The new Inside Marketing box discusses Playtex's new high-tech bra aimed at the 35–49 age group.

- A new Ethical Challenges box looks at ethical issues associated with the practice of targeting vulnerable groups.

- A new table (Table 8.2) provides an illustration of market segment profiles. Based on data from the PGA, this table profiles segments of golfers.

- The new Ryka athletic shoes video case features a socially responsible shoe manufacturer that uses unique marketing approaches.

Chapter 9 Product Concepts

- The chapter-opening vignette discusses the success of low-fat and non-fat snacks such as RJR Nabisco's SnackWell's line and traces Nabisco's development of this new line based on changes in customers' preferences.

- The section covering the introduction stage of the product life cycle has been streamlined.

- The new Global Perspective box focuses on Frito-Lay's practice of adjusting the product mix of Chee-tos to fit the unique tastes of different cultures.

- The new Ethical Challenges box discusses the increasing tendency of U.S. consumers to file frivolous product liability lawsuits.

- The product design and features section has been expanded to include a discussion of how information can be used to better serve customers.
- The new Schwinn case deals with the company's product management efforts to regain market share in the bicycle industry.

Chapter 10 Developing and Managing Products

- The new chapter-opening vignette features AM General, a manufacturer of unique vehicles that is modifying an existing product in an attempt to enter new markets.
- A new section has been added on the topic of managing existing products. In this section, line extension and product modification are discussed as methods of improving a product mix. The coverage of product modification appeared near the end of this chapter in the previous edition.
- The new Inside Marketing box features Prison Blues, a unique producer of denim goods that hopes to increase sales through increased marketing efforts.
- A new table on selected approaches for managing products in the maturity stage has been added to the subsection on marketing strategy for mature products.
- A new Global Perspective box discusses Gillette's commitment to developing new products and entering new markets.
- Both cases at the end of the chapter are new. The video case focuses on product management at Outboard Marine Corporation. The other case examines Pepsi's commitment to new-product development.

Chapter 11 Branding and Packaging

- The new opening vignette looks at Frito-Lay's decision to change the packaging of Doritos, the best-selling snack in the United States.
- The section on branding has been expanded considerably. A subsection on brand loyalty has been added, which discusses brand recognition, brand preference, and brand insistence. A new subsection on brand equity focuses on the major components of brand equity.
- A new table (Table 11.1) indicates the values of the top ten brands in the world.
- The new Inside Marketing box discusses the licensing success of Nickelodeon.
- New to this chapter is a table (Table 11.4) showing the top ten spenders on packaging.
- The new Ethical Challenges box discusses the effectiveness of laws regulating the information shown on product labels.
- Evian's new package is the focus of a new end-of-chapter case.

Chapter 12 Services

- The new opening vignette examines the intense competition among online service providers.
- The new Inside Marketing box focuses on USAA's dedication to customer service.
- The new Technology in Marketing box discusses the challenges of marketing of high-tech eye surgery.

- Many of the discussion and review questions are new.
- Both cases at the end of the chapter are new. The Grucci video case focuses on a company that creates world-renowned fireworks shows. The second case considers several marketing issues faced by marketers at Harrah's Casinos.

Chapter 13 Marketing Channels

- A new chapter-opening vignette examines the importance of distribution in the success of Electronics Boutique, a software, video games, and computer accessories retailer.
- The section on the nature of marketing channels has been streamlined.
- This edition introduces the concept of supply chain management to emphasizes the importance of cooperative partnerships among marketing channel members. Several sections of the chapter have been reorganized and subordinated to supply chain management to show their relationship with that concept.
- A new boxed feature describes a dispute between Rubbermaid and Wal-Mart to illustrate channel conflict.
- Both the end-of-chapter cases are new to this edition. The video case discusses CUTCO Cutlery's use of direct sales to market its products. The second case describes the evolution of new marketing channels for automobiles and the effect of these new channels on members of more traditional vehicle marketing channels.

Chapter 14 Wholesaling

- A new boxed feature profiles wholesaler Super Valu and its role in supply chain management of grocery products.
- The final section of the chapter has been reworked to include the importance of productivity and quality in wholesaler success.

Chapter 15 Retailing

- A new Technology in Marketing box focuses on Best Buy Co. A second new boxed feature explores how nonbusiness organizations (the U.S. Postal Service and various states' departments of motor vehicles) are using retailing strategies to improve service to their customers.
- The section on nonstore retailing has been expanded to cover online marketing. A new table (Table 15.2) provides World Wide Web page addresses for a sample of retailers.
- The second end-of-chapter case, on Walt Disney Co., is new to this edition. It includes descriptions of retail strategy issues such as positioning and atmospherics of several Disney operations.

Chapter 16 Physical Distribution

- A new chapter-opening vignette describes the importance of physical distribution to Weight Watcher's new strategy of selling weight-loss food products.
- The section on the importance of physical distribution has been combined with physical distribution objectives and streamlined; a discussion on reducing cycle time has been added.

The sequencing of some chapter topics has been changed, with inventory management moving closer to the front because most elements of physical distribution stem from order processing and inventory management.

- A new Global Perspectives box discusses the complexities of transporting perishable products around the world.

- A new Technology in Marketing box describes changes in warehousing technology that are improving the efficient movement of goods.

- A new end-of-chapter case profiles The Home Depot and its leadership role in supply chain management.

Chapter 17   Promotion: An Overview

- The promotion mix used by Columbia Sportswear is described in the new opening vignette.

- The new Global Perspective boxed feature looks at the international appeal of celebrity endorsers in several international markets.

- The Inside Marketing box, also new to this edition, discusses the increasing amount of licensed merchandise that is tied to movies.

- The introduction section under selecting promotion mix elements has been expanded to include word-of-mouth communications.

- A new case examines the efforts of Anheuser-Busch to promote messages and programs aimed at combating underage drinking and alcohol abuse.

Chapter 18   Advertising and Public Relations

- The new chapter-opening vignette discusses the public relations efforts of the Beverly Hills Hotel.

- The new Technology in Marketing box examines the use of online advertising.

- The new section on public relations discusses this topic in detail. This section examines why public relations is important to organizations, the various public relations tools that are available, and the ways to evaluate the effectiveness of public relations.

- The discussion of publicity has been integrated into the discussion of public relations.

- The new Global Perspective box features Greenpeace's effective use of public relations.

- A new case highlights Marvel Entertainment's use of public relations.

Chapter 19   Personal Selling and Sales Promotion

- IBM's re-engineering of its sales force is the focus of the new opening vignette for this chapter.

- The prospecting section includes an expanded discussion of the use of commercial databases.

- The new Technology in Marketing box examines the use of technology to improve customer service.

- The section on compensating salespeople has been streamlined.

- The new Inside Marketing box looks at the sales force of Invacare, a company that markets medical equipment.

- A subsection on scan-back allowances, which are becoming widely used by manufacturers, has been added to the trade sales promotion methods section.

- Both cases at the end of the chapter are new. The video case focuses on Chili's practice of improving customer service in order to increase sales. The second case examines Nintendo's use of sales promotion to regain market share in a highly competitive industry.

Chapter 20 Pricing Concepts

- The new chapter-opening vignette highlights the use of price competition by cereal companies.

- The new Global Perspective box looks at the variability of the price of certain foods in different countries.

- The Inside Marketing box, also new to this edition, examines how new cars can be bought through the Internet at lower, no-haggle prices.

- The Southwest Airlines case at the end of the chapter has been revised. This case now includes updated information on the price competition taking place in the airline industry. The second case, which is new to this edition, discusses the new pricing strategy at Denny's.

Chapter 21 Setting Prices

- Pricing of Lamborghini automobiles is discussed in the new opening vignette.

- The new Global Perspective box discusses GE's success in the Japanese market, which the company achieved by marketing larger refrigerators at competitive prices.

- The new Ethical Challenges boxed feature looks at a situation in which Bausch and Lomb sold identical contact lenses at different prices.

- Both cases at the end of the chapter have been updated.

Chapter 22 Strategic Market Planning

- A new chapter-opening vignette profiles the King Ranch, the largest ranch in continental United States, and describes changes in that organization's marketing plans and strategies to position itself for a new century of ranching history.

- The chapter includes mission statements for FedEx and Lockheed Martin.

- The corporate strategy section has been streamlined to focus on product portfolio analysis.

- A new boxed feature discusses how MCI is taking advantage of market opportunities created by changes in the legal environment and the Internet. A new Technology in Marketing box explores Packard Bell's acquisition of Zenith Data Systems.

- Both the end-of-chapter cases are new to this edition. The video case explores marketing strategies at PETsMART. The second case profiles Anheuser Busch and changes in that firm's marketing plans and strategies.

Chapter 23 Marketing Implementation and Control

- A new chapter-opening vignette discusses Neiman Marcus and its implementation of marketing plans.

- The sequence of some topics in the chapter has been changed, with sections on the marketing implementation process and approaches to marketing implementation combined and moved to the front of the chapter.

- A new Global Perspective box focuses on changes to PepsiCo's cola operations.

- A new Technology in Marketing box considers how Deluxe Corp. is adjusting to a changing marketing environment.

- The section on marketing cost analysis has been revised to include the latest terminology.

- Both the end-of-chapter cases are new to this edition. The video case explores the trend of casual clothes at work and how companies are modifying their marketing strategies to take advantage of this trend. The second case looks at Denny's problems in the wake of a racial-discrimination scandal and how the chain is restructuring to avoid such problems in the future. Finally, a new strategic case exploring Apple Computer's problems, with a focus on its struggle to maintain a consistent marketing strategy, completes Part 7.

TO THE INSTRUCTOR

The *Instructor's Resource Manual* contains a variety of teaching aids for *Marketing: Concepts and Strategies,* Tenth Edition, by William M. Pride and O. C. Ferrell. We designed the manual to assist instructors as much as possible in teaching basic marketing courses.

CHAPTER TEACHING AIDS

For each chapter there is a teaching resources quick reference guide, a purpose and perspective section, a guide for using color transparencies, a lecture outline, teaching transparency masters, suggested answers to text discussion and review questions, and comments on the cases.

The **quick reference guide** that opens each set of chapter materials in the *Instructor's Resource Manual* will help you easily identify and locate the resources available to aid you in presenting the chapter material to your class.

The **purpose and perspective** section gives an overview of the major topics covered in this chapter. We state why the chapter is included and how it fits into the total framework. This section is an introduction, not a summary.

The **guide for using color transparencies** gives suggestions for appropriate ways to use the transparencies while presenting chapter materials in class. The transparencies are identified to show whether they appear within the textbook or are additional illustrations. For example, transparencies that repeat illustrations from the text will be identified according to the double-number label provided in the textbook (such as Figure 2.1). Illustrations that are new to the transparency program will be labeled with a chapter number reference and alphabet label (such as Figure 2A).

For each chapter, we also include a **lecture outline** that can be used in a variety of ways. Besides basing lectures on the outlines, you may want to supplement or correlate the outlined topics with your own lecture materials. Outlines are spaced to allow room for the instructor's notes. The lecture outlines also can be used for a quick review of the topics covered in the chapter.

Several teaching **transparency masters** (two class exercises, a debate issue, and a chapter quiz) are included for every chapter. The primary intent of the class exercises is to encourage students to apply key terms from the text in actual business settings. A secondary intent is to provide students with opportunities to participate in classroom discussion, which will enhance their communication and social skills. Instructors who grade participation in the classroom may find these particularly useful. This manual contains the exercise objectives and possible answers. You may approach these exercises in at least the following three ways or some combination thereof:

1. **Small groups.** The class may be separated into groups of three to five students to discuss questions among themselves. After allowing time for small group discussion, call for representatives from the small groups for their conclusions. Debate or differences of opinion will facilitate students' learning the material. Requiring students to generate responses forces them to internalize the concepts. This method may be used with small or large classes and may be a useful way of creating involvement in larger classes where you cannot personally interact with all students.

2. **Class discussion.** When classes are small enough, or time is limited, these exercises can lead individual students to respond in class discussion. Depending on the makeup of the class and your instructional preferences, some questions may be geared for more individual responses.

3. **Class lectures.** Enough background material and suggestions are provided in the instructor's manual for these exercises to constitute full lectures. The discussion questions may be used to provoke thought and do not necessarily require verbal responses from students.

The key benefits of using these exercises are (1) variety in classroom experiences, (2) better learning and internalization of marketing concepts, and (3) enhancement of communication and social skills of students.

The suggested **answers to discussion and review questions** are not intended to be the *only* acceptable answers. We tried to develop the questions to encourage creative thinking, so some of the answers should be based on students' judgments and personal insights. Because many of our suggested answers are short and concise, you may want to examine additional dimensions in class.

Comments on the cases present additional information and suggestions that could be helpful when discussing the cases in class. We did not attempt to provide singular, optimal solutions to these cases. In fact, at times we discuss incorrect marketing decisions to help clarify the concepts covered in the text. In some instances it is easier to point out what went wrong than to formulate a strategy that guarantees success. The purpose of the questions at the end of the cases is to direct class discussions to relevant areas. For the video cases, information about the videos is provided.

The need for students to develop creativity and critical thinking is discussed, but seldom are there devices to encourage the development of decision skills. The **application questions** at the end of each text chapter are designed to help students develop critical thinking, creativity, and decision-making skills. They are structured to give students an appreciation of how the concepts and frameworks presented in the text are used in marketing decision making. The application questions require students to consider business situations in their community as well as nationally known businesses. Each question is developed from concepts or frameworks from the chapter in the text. They are general in nature but are specific in application to the specific location. Some of the questions involve problem solving in that they ask the student to "help" a manager make a marketing decision using the information available or using a "real world" business. This may require some analysis and observation of local business, or it may require that the student research a business or type of organization at the library. Other questions can be answered through group discussion or brainstorming exercises.

The process of answering these questions provides the opportunity for application of the text content. There are no specific "right" answers, but you can determine the degree to which the student has "correctly" applied the concepts and frameworks from the text. The answer should include an explanation of the marketing concept or framework, a brief description of the problem, alternative solutions, and a discussion of what "should be done." Students should be allowed to explore conventional solutions as well as unconventional methods so long as they support their reasoning. Provide support for their answers in either instance. Remember that this is an exercise that encourages the students to think and be creative. Avoid looking for only one correct answer. You may remind them before assigning the questions that the methods developed in the text have been tested and proven to be effective, but that there may be better solutions or answers to the problems or questions presented.

The application questions may be assigned to be turned in at the beginning of the following class, in which case you can take the opportunity to evaluate the answers and provide written feedback. Provide more time as you deem necessary for these questions.

The questions could be assigned so that students present the answers in class. Presentation or discussion at the beginning of the class provides the students an opportunity to participate in class and promotes discussion in general. The more involved students are in the class, the more they will probably learn. This is also another opportunity for other students to be exposed to different approaches to solving a problem. Discussion at the beginning of class may also allow the students to talk more freely about different answers. The student should be encouraged to become involved without the threat of being wrong. Focus on the logic and use of concepts in the text to reach a solution.

Another possible use of the application questions is to assign a question to different groups of students, instructing each to approach the question from a different perspective and support the approach. This allows you to set up a class debate on different marketing concepts or methods of solving problems. An in-class debate promotes participation by all and encourages critical evaluation of answers.

These are several possible uses of the application questions, and we encourage you to consider other uses as well. If a unique and effective use is discovered, please let us know, and we will share the ideas in future editions of the text.

OTHER TEACHING AIDS

This manual also includes a number of other teaching aids. In the beginning of the manual, we provide a transition guide to help instructors who are switching from the ninth to the tenth edition. There is a sample quarter syllabus, listing the chapters we recommend assigning on a quarter or shortened time-frame basis. We have also included a Video Easy-Reference Table providing key information about the videos that are available for each chapter.

In addition, there is a brief guide to using the Pride/Ferrell Marketing Learning Center on the World Wide Web. Each element in the Learning Center is described: Chapter 24, "Marketing and the Internet," Internet Exercises, Research Center, Idea Exchange, and PC Study. Tips for getting started and special teaching suggestions for using the Web site are also provided.

At the end of this manual, we have provided two Appendixes. Appendix A presents comments on the end-of-part strategic cases. Appendix B provides answers to the discussion and review questions that follow the financial analysis appendix in the text.

This manual is provided to help you teach from *Marketing: Concepts and Strategies,* Tenth Edition. Because we realize that instructors use many different approaches to teach basic marketing, we provide a comprehensive package of materials that satisfies a wide variety of instructional needs. Although you may not use all these materials, we hope this manual is of value to you. Your comments and suggestions are always welcome; they can help us significantly in developing a better set of instructional materials.

William M. Pride
O. C. Ferrell

QUARTER SYLLABUS

As authors who teach the basic marketing course on a regular basis, we recognize that it is difficult for some professors to cover every chapter in the text. We view the 23 chapters as a menu for you to select from, based on your personal teaching philosophy for this course. For example, we customarily assign between 18 and 20 chapters for in-house lecture and discussion. Chapters not assigned as part of regular class meetings can be used as outside reading or reference. Because many professors have asked us what chapters we would assign on a quarter or shortened time-frame basis, we provide the following selection. These chapters are considered the most fundamental to understanding the basics of marketing if there is time for only 18 chapters to be covered in a term.

Chapter	Title
1	An Overview of Strategic Marketing
2	The Marketing Environment
3	Marketing Ethics and Social Responsibility
5	Information Systems and Marketing Research
6	Consumer Buying Behavior
8	Target Markets: Segmentation and Evaluation
9	Product Concepts
10	Developing and Managing Products
11	Branding and Packaging
13	Marketing Channels
15	Retailing
17	Promotion: An Overview
18	Advertising and Public Relations
19	Personal Selling and Sales Promotion
20	Pricing Concepts
21	Setting Prices
22	Strategic Market Planning
23	Marketing Implementation and Control

VIDEO EASY-REFERENCE TABLE

Chapter	Case and Video Title	Length	Tape Number	Segment Number
1	*Case Title:* AutoZone: Where the Customer Is Boss *Video Title:* The AutoZone Success Story	24:10	1	1
2	*Case Title:* AT&T: Working Toward a Safe and Green Tomorrow *Video Title:* A Safe and Green Tomorrow	10:10	1	2
3	*Case Title:* Hershey Foods; Ethics and Social Responsibility *Video Title:* Hershey Foods Philosophy and Values	21:12	1	3
4	*Case Title:* 20 Years of Innovation: There Is No Finish Line for Nike *Video Title:* International Marketing Featuring Nike	10:06	1	4
5	*Case Title:* Marketing Research for V-8 Vegetable Juice, Maidenform, and AT&T's 800 Service Advertising *Video Title:* Goodbye Guesswork	27:02	1	5
6	*Case Title:* In Japan, an End to All Work And No Play *Video Title:* The Newest Wave of Japanese Consumers	25:12	1	6
7	*Case Title:* Intel Builds Brand Awareness From the Inside Out *Video Title:* Intel Inside Market Development Program	8:00	2	7
8	*Case Title:* Ryka Athletic Shoes: By Women, For Women, Helping Women *Video Title:* Ryka Sales Training	10:40	2	8

Chapter	Case and Video Title	Length	Tape Number	Segment Number
9	*Case Title:* The Positioning of the New *American Heritage Dictionary*			
	Video Title: The New *American Heritage Dictionary*	11:00	2	9
10	*Case Title:* Product Management at Outboard Marine Corporation			
	Video Title: Managing the Product	8:57	2	10
11	*Case Title:* Labeling Requirements in the Red Meat Industry			
	Video Title: The Meat Consumer 1992	16:11	2	11
12	*Case Title:* Fireworks by Grucci Entertains America			
	Video Title: Grucci: The First Family of Fireworks	9:08	2	12
13	*Case Title:* CUTCO Cutlery: Differentiation via Direct Sales			
	Video Title: Direct Selling on the Global Frontier	12:53	2	13
14	*Case Title:* Fleming: Success Through Service			
	Video Title: The Fleming Companies Incorporated Overview	7:00	2	14
15	*Case Title:* The Container Store: The Definitive Place to Get Organized			
	Video Title: The Container Store—Wrap It Up	13:00	2	15
16	*Case Title:* Airborne's Competitive Dogfight			
	Video Title: Airborne Express Delivering Satisfaction Worldwide	5:39	2	16
17	*Case Title:* National Pork Producers Promote "The Other White Meat"			
	Video Title: The Retail Battle	7:43	2	17

Chapter	Case and Video Title	Length	Tape Number	Segment Number
18	*Case Title:* The Advertising Council: Advertising for Good, Not for Gain			
	Video Title: The Advertising Council Historical Reel	16:00	3	18
19	*Case Title:* Chili's Restaurants Take Training Seriously			
	Video Title: Suggestive Selling	12:22	3	19
20	*Case Title:* Low Prices and Fun: The Winning Combination at Southwest Airlines			
	Video Title: The Lone Star Flying Society's Good Time Band	28:15	3	20
21	*Case Title:* Steinway: Price Supported by Over 140 Years of Quality			
	Video Title: It's a Steinway	15:12	3	21
22	*Case Title:* PETsMART: Looking to Be Man's Second-Best Friend			
	Video Title: Where Pets Are Family	7:00	3	22
23	*Case Title:* Marketing Casual Clothes at Work: Dressing Down, Productivity Up			
	Video Title: Levi's Casual Business Wear	4:35	3	23

GUIDE TO USING THE PRIDE/FERRELL MARKETING LEARNING CENTER

This edition of Pride/Ferrell *Marketing: Concepts and Strategies* is unique in that it offers the Pride/Ferrell Marketing Learning Center, a one-stop guide to the world of online marketing. The objective of this material is twofold: (1) to get students to use the Internet for research and (2) to give students an opportunity to see how marketing can be conducted online. The Learning Center provides dynamic materials about marketing on the Internet, including a virtual Chapter 24, "Marketing and the Internet"; Internet Exercises for Chapters 1–23; links to marketing organizations, publications, and other information resources; a place to share perspectives on marketing and the Internet; and study software that students can download at no charge. The content of the Web page will be updated regularly to ensure that it keeps pace with the rapidly evolving Internet and continues to provide strong examples of the Internet as a marketing medium. As such, the Marketing Learning Center represents a unique opportunity to give students hands-on insight into this exciting medium.

GETTING STARTED

The Marketing Learning Center is available as a "page" on the World Wide Web at http://www.hmco.com/college/PridFerr/home.html. Accessing this site requires a computer with a modem, Web-browsing software (such as Netscape), and access to the Internet. Most university computer labs can satisfy the first two requirements, and faculty and student computer accounts fulfill the third. Your college or university's computer systems administrator can provide the specifics about logging on to your system and navigating the World Wide Web with the software available. The Marketing Learning Center can also be accessed through accounts on America Online, CompuServe, and other national computer information services, as well as local Internet service providers. Systems administrators for those services can provide specific information about logging on to their services and getting to the Marketing Learning Center Web page.

For additional information about the Internet and using basic software for navigating the World Wide Web, you may wish to consult and/or recommend to your students *Using the Internet,* by Mary Micco and Therese D. O'Neil (Houghton Mifflin Co., 1996), and *The Business Student's Guide to Using the Internet,* by Glenn Owen (Houghton Mifflin Co., 1996). These books provide a solid overview of the Internet, describe how to use the most common software for navigating the World Wide Web, and provide useful exercises for learning to get around. If many students in your class are not familiar with the Internet, you might even require the latter text as supplemental reading and exercises. Information on these books is available from your Houghton Mifflin college textbook sales representative.

THE MARKETING LEARNING CENTER

The Marketing Learning Center consists of five elements.

Marketing and the Internet. This is Chapter 24 of the Pride/Ferrell text. This unique online chapter explores how marketers are incorporating the Internet into their strategies to improve their relationships with customers. The content will be updated at least once every semester to integrate the latest developments that affect marketing on the Internet.

Internet Exercises. The second section of the Marketing Learning Center provides Internet-related exercises for each of the twenty-three chapters of the text. These exercises reinforce chapter concepts by guiding students to specific World Wide Web sites and asking them to evaluate the sites and their information from a marketing perspective. For example, students may be invited to go online with the American Marketing Association, read recent articles in *Business Ethics* magazine, observe online retailers, and use *American Demographics* Power Tools, learn about the goods and services of firms as diverse as FedEx, Kodak, Southwest Airlines, and Apple, all while expanding their knowledge of marketing. The Web sites will be updated regularly, so the exercises will change as dictated by the content of the Web pages chosen. A guide to the answers of current exercises can be found in "The Faculty Lounge," an instructor-related section of Houghton Mifflin Company's home page at `http://www.hmco.com/college/PFinstruct/home.html`.

The Research Center. The Research Center contains links to a variety of marketing information resources, including marketing organizations, publications, and other information sources. This section will be continually updated.

The Idea Exchange. The Idea Exchange is a dynamic, interactive "bulletin board" where students can share their perspectives about online marketing and the Internet. From time to time, the site may also include surveys and contests. Users of the Idea Exchange will also be able to offer feedback about the Marketing Learning Center and recommend new Web sites that illustrate marketing principles. This area will evolve through user participation and current events.

PC Study. The final section of the Marketing Learning Center enables students to download a MicroStudy version of the Study Guide to administer their own self-tests on computers in a computer lab or at home. Directions for downloading the MicroStudy will be included.

Additionally, as mentioned, Houghton Mifflin's home page will offer a section entitled "The Faculty Lounge," which will offer resources for instructors, teaching suggestions, and more specific answers for the student exercises; these will change regularly to match updated exercises.

SUGGESTIONS FOR USING THE MARKETING LEARNING CENTER

Instructors can use the Pride/Ferrell Marketing Learning Center in a variety of ways. Many instructors have indicated that they plan to devote class time to the topic of marketing on the Internet. We suggest that students be assigned to read "Marketing and the Internet," the online Chapter 24 of the text, and to explore the hotlinks contained in the chapter. You may even wish to devote a class period to discuss this material early in the semester. Students can then be assigned to complete Internet Exercises for each chapter you cover over the course of the semester. The exercises may be completed individually, with students handing in their answers on paper or E-mailing them to your university E-mail box. Classes can also be divided into groups, with each group assigned an Internet Exercise as a group project to be presented to the rest of the class or prepared as a written or E-mail report. In lieu of assigning the exercises, students may be required to write a paper evaluating one or more Web sites as to how they illustrate the marketing concepts described in the assigned chapter. Students should also be directed to use the materials in the Research Center for class work and research and to participate in the Idea Exchange area of the Web page.

If your class includes a number of students who lack computer and/or Internet experience, you may wish to ask your college or university's computer systems administrator to speak to the class about using their student accounts, the computer labs, accessing the Internet and the World Wide Web, Web-browsing software, and "Netiquette." Other teaching suggestions for using this material may be available in "The Faculty Lounge" area of Houghton Mifflin's Web page.

Instructor's Resource Manual

MARKETING

Concepts and Strategies

1 AN OVERVIEW OF STRATEGIC MARKETING

TEACHING RESOURCES QUICK REFERENCE GUIDE

Resource	Location
Purpose and Perspective	IRM, p. 2
Guide for Using Color Transparencies	IRM, p. 2
Lecture Outline	IRM, p. 2
Class Exercises, Debate Issue, and Chapter Quiz	IRM, p. 12
Class Exercise 1	IRM, p. 14
Class Exercise 2	IRM, p. 15
Debate Issue: Is the marketing concept short-term oriented?	IRM, p. 16
Chapter Quiz	IRM, p. 17
Answers to Discussion and Review Questions	IRM, p. 18
Comments on the Cases	IRM, p. 20
Case 1.1	IRM, p. 20
Video	Tape 1, Segment 1
Video Information	IRM, p. 20
Multiple-Choice Questions About the Video	IRM, p. 21
Case 1.2	IRM, p. 21
Transparency Acetates	Transparency package
Examination Questions: Essay	TB, p. 1
Examination Questions: Multiple-Choice	TB, p. 2
Examination Questions: True-False	TB, p. 15
Author-Selected Multiple-Choice Test Items	TB, p. 446

PURPOSE AND PERSPECTIVE

The purpose of this chapter is to give students an overview of marketing and provide a general framework for studying the field of marketing. First, we present a definition of *marketing* and introduce some basic terminology. Next, we show why the study of marketing is relevant to students. Because we believe that an understanding of the marketing concept is fundamental, we devote several pages to this area, including its basic components, development, and implementation. Then we provide an overview of strategic marketing management and describe in general what a marketing strategy is. We examine four basic marketing management tasks: target market selection, marketing mix development, market environment analysis, and the management of marketing activities. Finally, we give an overview of a marketing plan.

GUIDE FOR USING COLOR TRANSPARENCIES

There are two groups of color transparencies. The transparencies identified by a double number are the same as the figures in the text. The transparencies labeled with a number and a letter are illustrations that do not appear in the text, but they can be used as additional examples of concepts discussed.

Part 1 Opener	Marketing and its environment
Figure 1.2	Exchange between buyer and seller
Figure 1.5	Methods consumers use to request information and express opinion
Figure 1.7	Marketing strategy tasks
Figure 1.8	Components of the marketing mix and marketing environment
Figure 1A	Chapter 1 outline
Figure 1B	Relationship marketing
Figure 1C	Marketing to a calorie-conscious target market
Figure 1D	Use of pricing variable in promotion
Figure 1E	Marketing and profit costs
Figure 1F	Target markets for selected products
Figure 1G	Target markets by age most likely to use frequent purchase cards

LECTURE OUTLINE

I.   Marketing defined

We define **marketing** as the process of creating, distributing, promoting, and pricing goods, services, and ideas to facilitate satisfying exchange relationships in a dynamic environment. An **exchange** is the provision or transfer of goods, services, or ideas in return for something of value.

A.   Marketing deals with products, distribution, promotion, and pricing.

1. Marketing involves developing and managing a product that will satisfy customer needs.

2. Marketing focuses on making products available in the right place and at acceptable prices.

B. Marketing focuses on goods, services, and ideas.

   1. A **product** can be a good, service, or idea.

      a. A *good* is a physical entity that can be touched.

      b. A *service* is the application of human and mechanical efforts to people or objects to provide intangible benefits.

      c. *Ideas* include concepts, philosophies, images, and issues.

C. Marketing facilitates satisfying exchange relationships.

   1. Individuals and organizations—both business and nonprofit—engage in marketing activities to facilitate exchanges.

   2. Figure 1.2 (text, p. 5) depicts the exchange process. For an exchange to occur, four conditions must exist.

      a. Two or more individuals, groups, or organizations must participate.

      b. Each party must possess something of value that the other party desires.

      c. Each party must be willing to give up something of value to receive something of value held by the other party.

      d. The parties to the exchange must be able to communicate with each other and to make their somethings of value available.

3. An exchange will not necessarily take place just because these four conditions exist, but marketing activities have still occurred.

4. Marketing activities should attempt to create and maintain satisfying relationships for both buyers and sellers.

5. Maintaining positive relationships with buyers is an important goal for a seller.

D. Marketing occurs in a dynamic environment.

1. Marketing occurs in an environment of changing forces such as competition, economic conditions, political pressures, laws, regulations, technological advances, and sociocultural factors.

2. The effects of these forces can be dramatic and difficult to predict; they can create threats to marketers and generate opportunities for new products and new methods of reaching customers.

II. Why study marketing?

A. Marketing is used in many organizations.

1. From 25 to 33 percent of all civilian workers in the United States perform marketing activities.

2. Whether a person earns a living through marketing activities or performs them voluntarily in nonbusiness projects, marketing knowledge and skills are valuable assets.

B. Marketing is important to businesses and the economy.

1. Businesses must sell products to survive and grow, and marketing helps sell their products.

2. Marketing activities help produce the profits essential not only to the survival of individual businesses but also to the health and ultimate survival of the whole economy.

C.   Marketing knowledge enhances consumer awareness.

   1.   Marketing activities help improve the quality of our lives.

   2.   Studying marketing activities allows us to weigh their costs, benefits, and flaws more effectively and to evaluate corrective measures that could stop unfair, damaging, or unethical marketing practices.

D.   Marketing costs consume a sizable portion of buyers' dollars.

   1.   About one-half of a buyer's dollar goes to pay the costs of marketing.

   2.   Because marketing expenses consume such a significant portion of our dollars, we should know how this money is used.

III.   The marketing concept

According to the **marketing concept,** an organization should try to provide products that satisfy customers' needs through a coordinated set of activities that also allows the organization to achieve its goals.

A.   Basic elements of the marketing concept

   1.   Customer satisfaction is the major focus of the marketing concept.

      a.   An organization must determine what customers want and use this information to create satisfying products.

      b.   The firm must continue to alter, adapt, and develop products to keep pace with customers' changing desires and preferences.

   2.   The marketing concept is not a second definition of marketing, but, rather, is a management philosophy guiding an organization's overall activities.

   3.   The marketing concept is not a philanthropic view; a firm that adopts the marketing concept must satisfy not only its customers' objectives, but also its own, or it will not survive.

4. Marketers must consider not only their current customers' needs but also the long-term needs of society.

B. The evolution of the marketing concept

1. The production era

    a. During the second half of the nineteenth century, the Industrial Revolution came into its own in the United States.

    b. As a result of new technology and new ways of using labor, products poured into the marketplace, where consumer demand for the new manufactured goods was strong.

2. The sales era

    a. Between the mid-1920s and the early 1950s, businesspeople viewed sales as the major means of increasing profits.

    b. During this era, businesspeople believed that the major marketing activities were personal selling, advertising, and distribution.

3. The marketing era

    a. By the early 1950s, some businesspeople recognized that they must first determine what customers want and then produce it, rather than make products and try to persuade customers that what they need is produced.

    b. Today, businesses want to satisfy customers and build meaningful, long-term buyer-seller relationships. **Relationship marketing** refers to long-term, mutually beneficial arrangements in which the buyer and seller focus on value enhancement through the creation of more satisfying exchanges.

C. Implementing the marketing concept

To implement the marketing concept, an organization must accept some general conditions and recognize and deal with several problems. Consequently, the marketing concept has yet to be fully accepted by all American businesses.

1. To implement the marketing concept, management must first establish an information system that will enable the firm to learn about customers' needs and use the information to create satisfying products. Without an adequate information system, an organization cannot be customer-oriented.

2. Management's second major task for implementing the marketing concept is to coordinate all activities. This may require restructuring operations and objectives.

3. Effective implementation of the marketing concept also requires a **market orientation**—the organizationwide generation of market intelligence pertaining to current and future customer needs, dissemination of the intelligence across departments, and organizationwide responsiveness to it.

4. Achieving the full profit potential of each customer relationship should be the fundamental goal of every marketing strategy. At the most basic level, profits can be obtained through relationships in the following ways:

    a. Acquiring new customers

    b. Enhancing the profitability of existing customers

    c. Extending the duration of customer relationships

IV. Marketing strategy

A **marketing strategy** is a plan of action for developing, distributing, promoting, and pricing products that meet the needs of specific customers. To develop and manage marketing strategies, marketers focus on selecting a target market, developing a marketing mix, assessing environmental forces, and managing marketing efforts effectively (Figure 1.7; text, p. 12).

A. Marketing strategy: target market selection

1. A **target market** is a specific group of buyers on whose needs and wants a company focuses its marketing efforts.

2. Marketers may define a target market as a vast number of people or as a relatively small group. They may target multiple target markets, with different products, promotion, prices, and distribution systems for each market.

3. Marketing managers evaluate possible target markets to determine the following:

    a. How entry into a market would affect the firm's sales, costs, and profits

    b. Whether the firm has the resources to develop the right mix of product, price, promotion, and distribution to meet the needs of the target market

    c. If satisfying the target market's needs will be consistent with the firm's overall objectives

    d. Whether the size and number of competitors already serving the market are of concern

4. A **marketing opportunity** exists when the right combination of circumstances and timing permit an organization to take action to reach a particular target market.

    a. Marketers need to be able to recognize and analyze market opportunities because an organization's survival depends on developing products that satisfy its target market(s).

    b. A company can choose among several options for continued product development that will achieve its objectives and satisfy buyers:

        (1) Modify existing products.

        (2) Introduce new products.

        (3) Delete some products that customers no longer want.

5. Accurate target market selection is crucial to productive marketing efforts.

B. Marketing strategy: marketing mix development

1. The **marketing mix** consists of four marketing activities—product, distribution, promotion, and pricing—that the firm can vary by type and amount in order to meet the needs of customers within its target market.

2. Marketing mix variables are often viewed as controllable variables because they can be changed; however, there are limits to how much they can be altered.

3. Marketing managers must develop a marketing mix that precisely matches the needs of people in the target market. This requires the collection of in-depth, up-to-date information about those needs.

4. The marketing mix decision variables

    a. The *product variable* is the aspect of the marketing mix that deals with researching consumers' wants and designing a good, service, or idea that satisfies those wants.

        (1) Product variable decisions include creating and modifying packaging and brand names and decisions regarding warranty and repair services.

        (2) Product variable decisions are important because they are involved directly with creating products that satisfy consumers.

    b. In dealing with the *distribution variable,* marketing managers seek to make products available in the quantities desired to as many customers as possible and to hold total inventory, transportation, and storage costs as low as possible.

    c. The *promotion variable* relates to activities used to inform individuals or groups about an organization and its products. Promotion can be used to

        (1) Increase public awareness of the organization and of new or existing products.

(2)   Educate consumers about a product's features.

(3)   Urge people to take a particular stance on a political or social issue.

(4)   Maintain interest in an established product.

(5)   Associate the firm or its products with things that make consumers feel good.

d.   The *price variable* relates to decisions and actions associated with establishing pricing objectives and policies and determining product prices.

(1)   Price is a critical component of the marketing mix because consumers are concerned about the value obtained in an exchange.

(2)   Price is often used as a competitive tool.

C.   Marketing strategy: influence of the environment

1.   The **marketing environment**—competitive, economic, political, legal and regulatory, technological, and sociocultural forces—surrounds the buyer and the marketing mix.

2.   The forces of the marketing environment affect a marketer's ability to facilitate exchanges in three ways:

a.   They influence customers by affecting their lifestyles, standards of living, and preferences and needs for products.

b.   They help determine whether and how a marketing manager can perform certain marketing activities.

c.   They may affect a marketing manager's decisions and actions by influencing buyers' reactions to the firm's marketing mix.

3.   Environmental forces can fluctuate quickly and dramatically.

4. Marketing environment forces are closely interrelated, so a change in one may cause changes in others.

5. Changes in the marketing environment produce uncertainty, but they also create opportunities.

D. Marketing management

1. **Marketing management** is the process of planning, organizing, implementing, and controlling marketing activities to facilitate exchanges effectively and efficiently.

    a. *Effectiveness* is the degree to which an exchange helps achieve an organization's objectives.

    b. *Efficiency* refers to minimizing the resources an organization must spend to achieve a specific level of desired exchanges.

2. Planning is a systematic process of assessing opportunities and resources, determining marketing objectives, and developing a marketing strategy and plans for implementation and control.

3. Organizing marketing activities involves developing the internal structure of the marketing unit to direct activities.

4. Implementing the marketing plan involves coordination of marketing activities, employee motivation, and effective communication with the marketing unit.

5. The marketing control process consists of establishing performance standards, comparing actual performance with established standards, and reducing differences between desired and actual performance.

V. The marketing plan: an overview

A **marketing plan** is a written document that specifies an organization's resources, objectives, marketing strategy, and implementation and control efforts planned for use in marketing a specific product or product group.

1. The marketing plan describes the firm's current situation, establishes marketing goals or objectives for the product or product group, and specifies how the organization will attempt to achieve these objectives.

2. Marketing plans may be short-term (covering less than one year), moderate-range (covering two to five years), or long-term (covering more than five years).

3. Developing a clear, well-written plan is time consuming but important.

    a. It is used internally for communication.

    b. It covers the assignment of responsibilities, tasks, and schedules for implementation purposes.

    c. It presents objectives and specifies how resources are to be allocated in order to achieve these objectives.

    d. It helps marketing manager to monitor and evaluate the performance of a marketing strategy.

CLASS EXERCISES, DEBATE ISSUE, AND CHAPTER QUIZ

On the following pages, you will find two class exercises, a debate issue, and a chapter quiz. These are formatted in large-size type so that you can use them as class handouts or for making transparencies. Below are the authors' comments on the class exercises, the debate topic for this chapter, and the answers to the chapter quiz.

Class Exercise 1: The objective of this class exercise is to help students understand how the marketing concept works and to be able to apply the marketing concept to the implementation of marketing strategy.

Question 1. To generate interest, you might ask, "Why are some local firms doing poorly or going out of business?" or "What bad experiences have you had with local companies?" The causes for business failure or bad experiences can then be traced back to weak need satisfaction and poor coordination (e.g., lack of market orientation). You may also want to cover the implementation of the marketing concept (acceptance by top management, need for information systems, and reorganization).

Question 2. Customer satisfaction/seller satisfaction: An exchange must be satisfying to both the buyer and the seller. Some firms offer products that few people want and thus do not satisfy customers. Other firms offer what people want, but not at a price that will allow the firms to stay in business. Cover the four conditions required for an exchange to take place when explaining this point.

Maintaining long-term, positive relationships: Students will likely have examples of car dealers or others who are more concerned with making the immediate sale than they are with building customer relationships. Mercedes dealerships and salespeople, on the other hand, make it a point to know their customers and maintain contact after the sale.

Recognizing and responding to environmental forces: Marketing occurs in a dynamic environment—including laws, regulations, political activities, societal pressures, changing economic and competitive conditions, and technological advances.

Selecting and clearly defining target markets: Organizations that try to be all things to all people typically end up not satisfying the needs of any customer group very well.

The marketing mix: product, distribution, promotion, price: Examples of problems with the marketing mix might include poorly prepared food or small portion sizes at restaurants; banks or campus offices that have inconvenient hours; overpricing PCs in undifferentiated segments; or new stores with low customer awareness levels.

Question 3. Most students can distinguish between goods and services. In addition to political and religious organizations, you as an instructor are marketing ideas to your students.

Question 4. Some firms are still operating as if they were in the production or sales era, when businesspeople emphasized technology, personal selling, or advertising rather than customers. The case of General Motors, with losses of more than $5 billion in 1991, illustrates the failure associated with operating under a production or sales orientation.

Class Exercise 2: The objective of this class exercise is to help students understand the meaning of a "product" and differentiate between a good, a service, and an idea. Answers:

1.	Overnight stay in a hotel	service
2.	VCR	good
3.	This marketing course	service
4.	Dry cleaning	service
5.	Political party platform	idea
6.	Advice from a marriage counselor	idea/service
7.	Utilities, such as electricity	service
8.	Meal at Red Lobster	good/service
9.	Pair of jeans	good
10.	A movie at a theater	service
11.	Candy bar	good
12.	Airplane flight	service

Debate Issue: Is the marketing concept short-term oriented?

Chapter Quiz: Answers to multiple-choice questions are

1. c	3. c
2. a	4. d

CLASS EXERCISE 1

1. **Of all the organizations and companies in your area, which ones do not appear to be implementing the marketing concept?**
   - **Are they trying to satisfy their customers' or their own needs?**
   - **Are their efforts coordinated?**
   - **Are all employees working together to satisfy customers?**

2. **With what areas of marketing are these organizations or companies having difficulty? Why are they failing in these areas?**
   - **Customer satisfaction/seller satisfaction**
   - **Maintaining long-term, positive relationships**
   - **Recognizing and responding to environmental forces**
   - **Selecting and clearly defining target markets**
   - **The marketing mix: product, distribution, promotion, price**

3. **Which of these organizations' or companies' "products" are primarily goods? Services? Ideas?**

4. **Would you place these organizations or companies in the marketing era? Why or why not?**

CLASS EXERCISE 2

A PRODUCT CAN BE A GOOD, A SERVICE, OR AN IDEA. HOW WOULD YOU CLASSIFY THE FOLLOWING PRODUCTS?

1. Overnight stay in a hotel
2. VCR
3. This marketing course
4. Dry cleaning
5. Political party platform
6. Advice from a marriage counselor
7. Utilities, such as electricity
8. Meal at Red Lobster
9. Pair of jeans
10. A movie at a theater
11. Candy bar
12. Airplane flight

DEBATE ISSUE

IS THE MARKETING CONCEPT SHORT-TERM ORIENTED?

YES

- Marketers learn the immediate wants of customers and develop products to satisfy those wants

- Studying the long-term needs of customers entails considerable time and expense

- Companies are producing products with minor modifications rather than assessing latent or unseen needs

- Marketers are merely responding to the marketplace rather than striving for revolutionary or innovative products

NO

- No component of the marketing concept requires that it be used on a short-term basis

- If managers focus on short-term objectives and performance, it is not the fault of the marketing concept

- Japanese marketers have a reputation for having a long-term focus; yet they are very successful at embracing the marketing concept

- Being long-term oriented does not mean that a marketer cannot follow the marketing concept

CHAPTER QUIZ

1. Marketing is best defined as
   a. developing a product and matching it with its market.
   b. advertising and selling products.
   c. creating marketing mixes to facilitate satisfying exchange relationships.
   d. transferring goods to stores to make them available.
   e. a process of bringing buyers and sellers together.

2. If IBM offered cash to any user of its software products who could find a flaw, this cooperative problem solving would illustrate
   a. relationship marketing.
   b. supply chain management.
   c. Internet marketing.
   d. interactive marketing.
   e. network marketing.

3. A Panasonic CD player has average marketing costs and sells for $100. Approximately how many of the buyer's dollars go to marketing costs?
   a. $25   d. $75
   b. $35   e. $85
   c. $50

4. The two components of a marketing strategy are
   a. marketing objectives and promotion.
   b. promotion and distribution.
   c. marketing mix and marketing objectives.
   d. target markets and marketing mix.
   e. target markets and promotions.

ANSWERS TO DISCUSSION AND REVIEW QUESTIONS

1. What is marketing? How did you define marketing before you read this chapter?

   The text defines *marketing* as the process of creating, distributing, promoting, and pricing goods, services, and ideas to facilitate satisfying exchange relationships in a dynamic environment. The second part of this question can be used to stimulate class discussion about how the average person views marketing.

2. Why should someone study marketing?

   The study of marketing is important because marketing costs consume a sizable portion of buyers' dollars and a knowledge of how such money is used helps consumers understand why products cost as much as they do. As a result, consumers may be able to stretch their dollars more effectively in the marketplace. Many organizations other than businesses use marketing activities, and approximately 25 to 33 percent of all U.S. civilian workers perform marketing activities. Whether or not a person is directly employed in marketing functions, the knowledge of such functions is beneficial.
   Our society depends on marketing activities to generate profits that are essential for economic survival. Marketing activities also affect our everyday lives. Many of the improvements we desire in the quality of our lives can be achieved through an understanding of marketing activities.
   Studying marketing activities also enables consumers to weigh the costs, benefits, and flaws associated with marketing activities and to evaluate laws, regulations, and industry guidelines intended to stop unfair, misleading, and unethical marketing practices.

3. Discuss the basic elements of the marketing concept. Which businesses in your area use this philosophy? Explain why.

   The marketing concept is an organizational philosophy that states that an organization should try to provide products that satisfy customers' needs through a coordinated set of activities that also allows the organization to achieve its goals. The major focus is consumer satisfaction. If the firm coordinates its activities to achieve customer satisfaction, it is practicing the marketing concept.
   The answers to the other parts of this question are based on local examples.

4. Identify several business organizations in your area that obviously have *not* adopted the marketing concept. What characteristics of these organizations indicate nonacceptance of the marketing concept?

   Students' answers to this question will vary based on local examples and their personal experiences.

5. Describe the major components of a marketing strategy. How are the components related?

   A marketing strategy is a plan of action for developing, distributing, promoting, and pricing products that meet the needs of specific customers. A marketing strategy is the core of successful marketing efforts: the means for accomplishing the marketing objectives.

6. Identify the tasks involved in developing a marketing strategy.

   Developing a marketing strategy requires selecting a target market, preparing a marketing mix, assessing environmental forces, and managing marketing efforts.

7. Why is the selection of a target market such an important issue?

   Target market selection is crucial to generating productive marketing efforts. If management does not identify the specific customer group to which it is directing its products and marketing efforts, the business may fail. The identification and analysis of a target market form a foundation for developing a marketing mix.

8. What are the primary issues that marketing managers consider when conducting a market opportunity analysis?

   The marketing manager must consider various alternatives through which the organization can grow and sustain itself. This can be done through product modification, introduction of new products, and deletion of products consumers no longer want. An organization's very survival depends on its ability to develop products that satisfy its target market(s).

9. Why are the elements of the marketing mix known as variables?

   The marketing mix is the combination of marketing variables used to perform various activities to facilitate and expedite exchanges. These variables are product, distribution, promotion, and price. They are called *variables* because marketing managers can vary the type and amounts of these components used in developing and maintaining a marketing mix.

10. What are the variables in the marketing environment? How much control does a marketing manager have over environmental variables?

    The marketing environment surrounds both consumers and the marketing mix. The variables in the marketing environment include competitive, economic, political, legal and regulatory, technological, and sociocultural forces. All these variables affect marketing activities and decisions. These forces are sometimes called "uncontrollables," but they are not totally uncontrollable. Marketers have little control over these environmental forces, but they must be aware of them, adapt to them, and capitalize on the opportunities they provide.

11. What types of management activities are involved in the marketing management process?

    Managing marketing activities involves planning, organizing, implementing, and controlling. Planning is a systematic process that focuses on assessing opportunities and resources, determining marketing objectives, developing marketing strategy, and developing plans for implementing and controlling. Organizing marketing activities involves developing the internal structure of marketing units. Implementing entails coordinating marketing activities, motivating marketing personnel, and effectively communicating within the marketing unit. Controlling consists of establishing performance standards, evaluating actual performance by comparing it with these standards, and reducing the difference between desired and actual performance.

12. Describe the contents of a marketing plan. How does a good marketing plan benefit an organization?

A marketing plan is a written document that specifies an organization's resources, objectives, marketing strategy, and implementation and control efforts planned for use in marketing a specific product or product group. In a clear and specific way, it outlines communication, assignment of responsibilities, scheduling, objectives, resource allocation, and evaluation. Without such clear guidance, marketers have difficulty making marketing decisions that help an organization achieve its objectives.

COMMENTS ON THE CASES

Case 1.1   AutoZone: Where the Customer Is Boss

To introduce this case, you may wish to ask students how many work on their own vehicles and whether they have patronized AutoZone. Ask those who have to compare their experiences with the company to those described in the video and case.

The first question asks what types of customers make up AutoZone's target market and invites students to speculate as to why the firm has chosen to concentrate on this one segment of customers. Based on the information provided in the case, students should be able to recognize that AutoZone's primary target market includes people (men and women) who do their own automobile maintenance work, whether to save money or because they enjoy working on their own vehicles. AutoZone may have chosen to target this group because of the growing number of people working on their own cars. Additionally, the company may have felt it had the resources to serve this target market properly and as well as or better than competing firms.

Question 2 asks how AutoZone implements the marketing concept. AutoZone provides a full selection of auto parts and accessories, competitive prices, clean stores, and premium customer service from knowledgeable store personnel in order to satisfy do-it-yourself mechanics' needs. By satisfying customers, AutoZone has experienced strong growth, which has allowed it to reach sales of more than $1.8 billion.

Question 3 asks whether AutoZone is a market-oriented organization. AutoZone's practices appear to be consistent with the description of a market orientation, described in the text as the organizationwide generation of market intelligence pertaining to current and future customer needs, dissemination of the intelligence across departments, and the organizationwide responsiveness to it. Without determining what DIY mechanics need and want from an auto parts store and creating a marketing mix that satisfies those needs and wants, AutoZone could not be as successful as it has become today.

Video Information

Video Title: The AutoZone Success Story
Location: Tape 1, Segment 1
Length: 24:00
Video Overview: In an industry often characterized by low-service retail operations and intimidating service personnel, AutoZone has successfully set itself apart by building its marketing policies and programs around serving the specific and diverse needs of the DIY customer. AutoZone stands as a high-service provider of high-quality auto parts and accessories at low everyday prices. By treating its employees—"AutoZoners"—with the utmost respect, they in turn offer the same to the company's growing number of loyal, satisfied customers. All

marketing activities at the company are built around customer needs, including the level of service provided.

Multiple-Choice Questions About the Video

c   1. Which of the following is *not* a reason for the growing DIY market?
      a. More people are driving more cars.
      b. Rising new-vehicle prices mean more older, out-of-warranty cars on the road.
      c. Auto repair costs are low.
      d. Auto repair costs are high.

b   2. "GOTCHA" refers to
      a. AutoZoners' practice of dropping whatever they are doing to wait on customers before they've been in the store for 30 seconds.
      b. AutoZone's practice of going out to customers' cars to help install parts or resolve problems.
      c. Whatever It Takes to Do the Job Right.
      d. AutoZone's flexible parts inventory system.

a   3. How does AutoZone differentiate itself from the competition?
      a. Premium customer service
      b. An almost exclusive focus on foreign car replacement parts
      c. High prices
      d. Cheap, low-quality parts

d   4. On average, how often does AutoZone open a new store?
      a. Once a year
      b. Once a week
      c. Every day
      d. Every other day

Case 1.2   Windows 95: Start Me Up

Many students have their own personal computers or have access to one through school or work, and consequently, many are likely to be familiar with Windows and other Microsoft products. Others may have been exposed to the product through advertising. How Microsoft markets Windows may therefore interest them, and through this case, their knowledge of the software can enhance their understanding of the concepts introduced in Chapter 1. The purpose of this case is to provide students with a situation in which they are asked to consider fundamental strategic issues such as marketing mix, target market, and environmental forces.

For the first question, students must describe Microsoft's marketing strategy for Windows 95. Microsoft's target market includes all home and business users of IBM-based personal computers. From the case, students should also be able to describe the basics of Microsoft's marketing mix for Windows 95, including the product itself, distribution, promotion, and price.

The second question asks what aspects of Microsoft's activities foster relationship marketing. Microsoft's relationship marketing is evident from the long-term partnership developed with its customers who buy software. Microsoft will continue to conduct research and development and monitor customer usage of its software to make continuous improvements. It is also evident that Microsoft wants Windows 95 to be a high-involvement experience and even fun. The use of the Rolling Stones in television ads and Windows 95 launch parties for customers in forty cities indicate a desire to develop strong relationships with customers.

Question 3 asks which marketing environment forces Microsoft has to monitor to ensure success with Windows 95 and its other software products. Microsoft must monitor the technological environment to ensure that Windows continues to maximize the technology currently available and to be able to upgrade the program to meet the hardware and software technologies currently coming online. It must also monitor the legal environment so as to comply with the law and abide by society's wishes with regard to business practices. Moreover, its current legal problems may result in criminal or civil charges (although no charges have been filed as of this writing), which may affect its ability to do business. Other environmental forces—economic and sociocultural, for example—may determine consumers' ability and desire to purchase Microsoft products and therefore must be watched closely as well.

2 THE MARKETING ENVIRONMENT

TEACHING RESOURCES QUICK REFERENCE GUIDE

Resource	Location
Purpose and Perspective	IRM, p. 24
Guide for Using Color Transparencies	IRM, p. 24
Lecture Outline	IRM, p. 24
Class Exercises, Debate Issue, and Chapter Quiz	IRM, p. 35
Class Exercise 1	IRM, p. 37
Class Exercise 2	IRM, p. 38
Debate Issue: Is self-regulation an effective way to control and maintain good business practices?	IRM, p. 39
Chapter Quiz	IRM, p. 40
Answers to Discussion and Review Questions	IRM, p. 41
Comments on the Cases	IRM, p. 45
Case 2.1	IRM, p. 45
Video	Tape 1, Segment 2
Video Information	IRM, p. 46
Multiple-Choice Questions About the Video	IRM, p. 47
Case 2.2	IRM, p. 47
Transparency Acetates	Transparency package
Examination Questions: Essay	TB, p. 19
Examination Questions: Multiple-Choice	TB, p. 20
Examination Questions: True-False	TB, p. 34
Author-Selected Multiple-Choice Test Items	TB, p. 446

PURPOSE AND PERSPECTIVE

In this chapter we examine competitive, economic, political, legal and regulatory, technological, and sociocultural forces in the marketing environment. First we discuss environmental scanning, environmental analysis, and two general approaches firms use to respond to environmental forces: a passive approach and an aggressive approach. Next we discuss competitive forces, focusing on the types of competitive structures and competitive tools. Then we consider the effect of general economic conditions, consumer demand, and spending behavior. Next we define political forces—how they influence business decisions and how businesses may react to them. In our presentation of legal forces, we cover two broad categories: procompetitive laws and consumer protection laws. Then we explore the problems marketers experience when interpreting laws and consider the effect of compliance programs. In dealing with regulatory forces, we describe the potential effects of federal, state, and local government and nongovernment regulatory units on marketing decisions and discuss specific ways legal and regulatory forces affect marketers' decisions. We then describe technology and consider the impact of technology on society and on marketing decisions. We also look at more specific effects of technology on marketing decision making and examine several factors that influence marketers' adoption and use of technology. Finally, we define sociocultural forces and discuss diversity, demographic factors, cultural values, and consumer movements.

GUIDE FOR USING COLOR TRANSPARENCIES

There are two groups of color transparencies. The transparencies identified by a double number are the same as the figures in the text. The transparencies labeled with a number and a letter are illustrations that do not appear in the text, but they can be used as additional examples of concepts discussed.

Figure 2.7	Projected U.S. population by age and race for the year 2010
Figure 2A	Chapter 2 outline
Figure 2C	TV viewers shift to the Internet
Figure 2D	New legislation thwarts product counterfeiting
Figure 2E	Market potential for women's purchase of selected products
Figure 2F	This ad campaign demonstrates sociocultural values for preserving the environment.

LECTURE OUTLINE

I.   Examining and responding to the marketing environment

The marketing environment consists of dynamic external forces that directly or indirectly influence an organization's acquisition of inputs (human, financial, and natural resources and raw materials, and information) and creation of outputs (goods, services, or ideas). These influences can create opportunities and threats for marketers.

A.   Environmental scanning and analysis

1. **Environmental scanning** is the process of collecting information about forces in the marketing environment.

   a. Scanning involves observation, secondary sources such as business, trade, government, and general-interest publications, and marketing research.

   b. Environmental scanning can give marketers an edge over competitors in taking advantage of current trends.

2. **Environmental analysis** is the process of assessing and interpreting the information gathered through scanning.

   a. Marketers evaluate the information for accuracy, try to resolve inconsistencies in the data, and assign significance to the findings.

   b. Environmental analysis enables marketers to identify potential threats and opportunities linked to environmental changes.

B. Responding to environmental forces

   1. Some marketers view environmental forces as uncontrollable and remain passive and reactive to the environment.

   2. Other marketers believe that environmental forces can be shaped (through psychological, political, or promotional skills), and these marketers are, to a certain extent, proactive.

   3. Which approach is most appropriate for a particular firm depends on its managerial philosophies, objectives, financial resources, customers, human skills, and other environmental forces.

II. Competitive forces

An organization's **competition** is generally defined as other firms marketing products that are similar to or can be substituted for its products in the same geographic area.

A. Types of competitive structures

The number of firms that supply a product may affect the strength of competition.

1. A **monopoly** exists when a firm offers a product that has no close substitute, making it the sole source of supply.

2. An **oligopoly** exists when a few sellers control the supply of a large proportion of a product.

3. **Monopolistic competition** exists when a firm with many potential competitors attempts to develop a marketing strategy to differentiate its product.

4. **Pure competition,** if it existed, would entail a large number of sellers, no one of which could significantly influence price or supply.

B. Competitive tools

1. To survive, a firm uses one or more available tools to deal with competitive economic forces.

2. Price is probably the first competitive tool used, but many firms use noncompetitive tools based on markets, product offering, distribution, promotion, or enterprise.

C. Monitoring competition

1. Marketers need to be aware of the actions and strategies of major competitors and determine how those strategies affect their own.

2. It is not enough to analyze available information; the firm must develop a system for gathering ongoing information about competitors.

III. Economic forces

Economic forces in the marketing environment influence both marketers' and customers' decisions and activities.

A. General economic conditions

Changes in general economic conditions affect (and are affected by) supply and demand, buying power, willingness to spend, consumer expenditure levels, and the intensity of competitive behavior. Fluctuations in the economy follow a general pattern often referred to as the *business cycle*.

1. **Prosperity** is a stage of the business cycle characterized by low unemployment and relatively high total income, which together cause buying power to be high. Marketers often expand their product offerings to take advantage of increased buying power.

2. **Recession** is a stage of the business cycle during which unemployment rises and total buying power declines, stifling both consumer and business spending.

    a. Marketers should focus on marketing research during a recession to determine precisely what functions buyers want and integrate these functions into their product.

    b. Promotion efforts should emphasize value and utility.

3. **Depression** is a business cycle stage in which unemployment is extremely high, wages are very low, total disposable income is at a minimum, and consumers lack confidence in the economy.

4. **Recovery** is a stage of the business cycle in which the economy moves from depression or recession to prosperity. Marketers should be as flexible as possible to be able to adjust their strategies as economic gloom subsides and buying power increases.

B. Buying power

1. The strength of a person's **buying power** depends on the size of the resources—money, goods, and services that can be traded in an exchange—that enable the individual to purchase and on the state of the economy.

2. Major sources of buying power are income, credit, and wealth.

    a. **Income** is money received through wages, rents, investments, pensions, and subsidy payments for a given period.

(1) **Disposable income,** or after-tax income, is used for spending or saving. It is affected by wage levels, rate of unemployment, interest rates, dividend rates, and tax rates.

(2) **Discretionary income** is disposable income available for spending and saving after an individual has purchased the basic necessities of food, clothing, and shelter.

b. Credit enables people to spend future income now or in the near future, but it increases current buying power at the expense of future buying power.

c. **Wealth** is the accumulation of past income, natural resources, and financial resources.

3. Information about buying power is available from government sources, trade associations, and research agencies. One comprehensive source is *Sales & Marketing Management* magazine's *Survey of Buying Power.*

4. The most direct indicators of buying power are effective buying income and buying power index.

a. **Effective buying income (EBI)** is similar to disposable income; it includes salaries, wages, dividends, interest, profits, and rents, less taxes.

b. The **buying power index (BPI)** is a weighted index consisting of population, effective buying income, and retail sales data.

(1) Marketers use buying power indexes to compare the buying power of one area with the buying power of another.

(2) Marketers also use BPIs to analyze trends for a particular area by comparing its buying power indexes for several years.

5. Marketers need to be aware of current levels of and expected changes in buying power because it directly affects the types and quantities of goods and services that consumers purchase.

C. Willingness to spend

1. People's **willingness to spend** (their inclination to buy because of expected satisfaction from a product) is, to some degree, related to their ability to buy.

2. Willingness to spend is affected by several factors:

    a. Buying power

    b. A product's absolute price and its price relative to the price of substitute products

    c. The amount of satisfaction currently received or expected in the future from a product already owned

    d. Expectations about future employment, income levels, prices, family size, and general economic conditions

IV. Political forces

Political, legal, and regulatory forces of the marketing environment are closely interrelated.

A. Marketing organizations must maintain good relations with elected political officials because

    1. Political officials well disposed toward particular firms or industries are less likely to create or enforce laws and regulations unfavorable to these companies.

    2. Political officials can influence how much a government agency purchases and from whom.

    3. Political officials can play key roles in helping organizations secure access to foreign markets.

B. Although some marketers view political forces as beyond their control and simply adjust to conditions arising from those forces, other firms seek to influence political forces through public protests or campaign contributions.

V.   Legal and regulatory forces

A.   Procompetitive legislation

Procompetitive legislation refers to laws designed to preserve competition; Table 2.5 (text, p. 34) describes some of the most important of these.

1.   The **Sherman Antitrust Law** was passed to prevent businesses from restraining trade and monopolizing markets. It applies to firms operating in interstate commerce and to U.S. firms engaging in foreign commerce.

2.   The **Clayton Act** limits specific antitrust activities such as price discrimination, tying and exclusive agreements, and the acquisition of stock in another corporation "where the effect may be to substantially lessen competition or tend to create a monopoly."

3.   The **Federal Trade Commission Act** created the Federal Trade Commission (FTC), which regulates the greatest number of marketing practices.

4.   The **Wheeler-Lea Act** outlaws unfair and deceptive acts or practices, regardless of whether they injure competition, and specifically prohibits false and misleading advertising of foods, drugs, therapeutic devices, and cosmetics.

5.   The **Robinson-Patman Act** directly influences pricing policies; it prohibits price discrimination among different purchasers of goods of similar grade and quality where the effect of such discrimination reduces competition among the purchasers or gives one purchaser a competitive edge.

B.   Consumer protection legislation

Federal and state consumer protection laws deal with consumer safety, hazardous materials, information disclosure, and specific marketing practices.

1.   Because laws are often vague, marketers are forced to rely on legal advice rather than their own understanding and marketing ethics.

2.   Some organizations operate in a legally questionable way to see how far they can get with certain practices before being prosecuted.

3. Other firms interpret laws and regulations strictly and conservatively to avoid violating a vague law.

D. Encouraging compliance with the law

1. Legal violations may occur when marketers "push the envelope" of standards and develop programs that unknowingly or unwittingly overstep legal bounds.

2. Marketers may lack experience in dealing with complex legal actions and decisions and therefore may not recognize that certain activities may be unacceptable or illegal.

3. To ensure that marketers comply with the law, the federal government is increasing organizational accountability for misconduct through detailed guidelines that regulate the sentencing of companies convicted of breaking the law.

   a. The basic philosophy of the Federal Sentencing Guidelines for Organizations is that companies are responsible for crimes committed by their employees.

   b. These guidelines hold companies accountable for the illegal actions of their employees (previously, laws punished only those employees directly responsible for an offense, not the company).

   c. The guidelines focus on crime prevention and detection by mitigating penalties for firms that have chosen to develop compliance programs should one of their employees be involved in misconduct.

D. Federal regulatory agencies

Federal regulatory agencies influence many marketing activities, including product development, pricing, packaging, advertising, personal selling, and distribution, and they often have the power to enforce specific laws.

1. The **Federal Trade Commission (FTC)** influences marketing activities the most.

a.   It regulates a variety of business practices and focuses in particular on curbing false advertising, misleading pricing, and deceptive packaging and labeling.

b.   It can issue complaints and cease-and-desist orders, and can require companies to run corrective advertising.

c.   It also assists businesses in complying with laws.

2.   Other regulatory units are limited to dealing with specific products, services, or business activities (see Table 2.6; text, p. 37).

F.   State and local regulatory agencies

All states, as well as many cities and towns, have regulatory agencies that enforce laws and regulations regarding marketing practices within their states or municipalities.

G.   Nongovernmental regulatory forces

1.   In the absence of governmental regulatory forces and in an attempt to prevent government intervention, some businesses try to regulate themselves.

2.   A number of trade associations have developed self-regulatory programs that may include ethics codes.

a.   Self-regulatory programs have the advantage of being less expensive to establish and implement, having more realistic and operational guidelines, and reducing the need to expand government bureaucracy.

b.   Self-regulatory programs are limited because they are not mandatory for nonmembers, may lack the tools or authority to enforce guidelines, and may be less strict than those established by government agencies.

3.   The best-known nongovernmental regulatory group is the **Better Business Bureau,** a local agency supported by local businesses that aids in settling problems between specific business firms and customers.

    a. The Council of Better Business Bureaus is a national organization composed of all local Better Business Bureaus.

    b. The National Advertising Division of the Council of Better Business Bureaus operates a self-regulatory program that investigates claims of alleged deceptive advertising.

    4. The **National Advertising Review Board** is a self-regulatory entity that considers cases in which an advertiser challenges issues raised by the National Advertising Division about an advertisement. Though it has no official enforcement powers, the NARB can publicize questionable practices and file complaints with the FTC.

VI. Technological forces

    Technology is the application of knowledge and tools to solve problems and perform tasks more efficiently.

    A. Impact of technology

        1. Technology determines how society satisfies its physiological needs, such as improving communication.

        2. Technology can help marketers and consumers become more productive.

    B. Adoption and use of technology

        1. It is important for firms to determine when a technology is changing an industry and to define the strategic influence of the new technology.

        2. The extent to which a firm can protect inventions stemming from research also influences its use of technology.

        3. Through **technology assessment,** managers try to foresee the effects of new products and processes on the firm's operations, on other business organizations, and on society in general.

VII. Sociocultural forces

Sociocultural forces are the influences in a society and its culture(s) that bring about changes in attitudes, beliefs, norms, customs, and lifestyles.

A.   Demographic and diversity characteristics

Changes in a population's demographic characteristics—age, gender, race, ethnicity, marital and parental status, income, education—have a significant bearing on relationships and individual behavior because they lead to changes in how people live and consume products.

1.   One demographic change affecting the U.S. marketplace is the increasing proportion of older consumers.

2.   The number of singles is also on the rise, and they have different spending patterns than couples and families with children.

3.   The United States is about to enter another baby boom, and these children are more diverse than previous generations.

4.   Immigration is increasing the multicultural nature of U.S. society.

5.   These and other changes bring unique problems and opportunities for marketers.

B.   Cultural values

Changes in values have dramatically influenced people's needs and desires for products; these values change at varying speeds.

1.   Cultural changes are veering away from materialism and conspicuous consumption, a trend that affects not only the types of products consumers desire, but also how these products are branded, priced, promoted, and distributed.

2.   Issues of health, nutrition, and exercise have increased in importance, affecting behavior, lifestyles, and product choices.

3.   The concept of family is changing, though children remain important.

4.   Today's consumers are more concerned about the environment.

C.   Consumer movement

1.   The **consumer movement** is a varied array of independent individuals, groups, and organizations seeking to protect consumers' rights.

2.   They achieve their objectives by writing letters to companies, lobbying government agencies, broadcasting public service announcements, and boycotting companies whose activities they deem irresponsible.

CLASS EXERCISES, DEBATE ISSUE, AND CHAPTER QUIZ

On the following pages, you will find two class exercises, a debate issue, and a chapter quiz. These are formatted in large-size type so that you can use them as class handouts or for making transparencies. Below are the authors' comments on the class exercises, the debate topic for this chapter, and the answers to the chapter quiz.

Class Exercise 1: The objective of this class exercise is to identify environmental forces that may affect marketing strategy and to illustrate the importance of environmental scanning and analysis.

Question 1. Defining the competitive structure requires that the relevant product or market be defined. If we are referring to the distribution of basic cable services, then the structure is a monopoly in most metropolitan markets. However, if we are referring to the offering of recently released movies, then the structure is most likely an oligopoly. In addition to premium cable services such as HBO, Cinemax, and The Movie Channel, video rental stores and theaters compete for the same entertainment dollar.

Question 2. The state of the economy affects the buying power of the consumers and thus influences how they view price. Cable companies should emphasize different marketing mix variables depending on the state of the economy: prosperity (expand product mixes to take advantage of increased buying power); recession or depression (promotion should emphasize value and utility); recovery (maintain flexibility, which allows moving from restraint to freedom; e.g., from an economical and reliable car to a reliable and luxurious car).

Question 3. In part (a), a typical chain of events might be this: consumers get upset → form consumer activist groups → activist groups contact politicians and regulating agencies → politicians and/or regulatory agencies take action.

In part (b), students will naturally side with the consumers, who want to keep low prices. However, when asked if they would want the government to control their own marketing practices, most students will recognize that the *proactive* approach used by the cable companies is a logical response to environmental uncertainty.

In part (c), the FTC regulates a variety of business practices, including curbing false advertising, misleading pricing, and deceptive packaging and labeling. Possible actions include (1) the FTC issues a complaint to the offending cable company, (2) a cease-and-desist order is issued, or (3) civil penalties against the offending company may be sought in court.

Question 4. This question asks students to perform an informal technology assessment, wherein managers try to foresee the effects of new products and processes on their firm's operation, on other business organizations, and on society in general. Some students may be familiar with high-definition television (HDTV), fiber optics, Direct Satellite Systems, or other forthcoming advancements. One day we may be able to obtain cable TV through our phone company. In addition, future programming may come to us entirely on a pay-per-view basis, effectively making programming schedules obsolete.

Class Exercise 2: The goal of this exercise is to help students realize the differences among the six marketing environmental forces. Answers:

1.	Prosperity	**economic**
2.	Federal Trade Commission	**regulatory**
3.	Personal computers without keyboards	**technological**
4.	Development and widespread use of facsimile machines	**technological**
5.	People's willingness to spend	**economic**
6.	Contributions to campaign funds	**political**
7.	A society's high material standard of living	**sociocultural**
8.	Sherman Antitrust Act	**legal**
9.	Better Business Bureau	**regulatory**
10.	Consumer movement	**sociocultural**
11.	Buying power index	**economic**
12.	Food and Drug Administration	**regulatory**
13.	A monopoly	**competitive**
14.	Government purchases of goods and services	**political**
15.	Group of people threatening to boycott the sponsors of a television program that they believe contains too much sex and violence	**sociocultural**

Debate Issue: Is self-regulation an effective way to control and maintain good business practices?

Chapter Quiz: Answers to multiple-choice questions are

1.	a	3.	b
2.	b	4.	a

CLASS EXERCISE 1

BECAUSE CABLE TELEVISION SERVICE PRICES INCREASED 61 PERCENT DURING THE PREVIOUS FOUR YEARS, THE FCC IN 1991 APPROVED REGULATIONS THAT ALLOW COMMUNITIES WITH FEWER THAN SIX TELEVISION STATIONS TO REGULATE BASIC CABLE RATES.

1. What type of competitive structure exists for cable systems?

2. How do current economic conditions affect consumers' views of cable prices? How should cable companies respond?

3. Anticipating the FCC proposal, cable companies redefined basic programming into tiers of "basic" and "extended basic." Rates for extended basic (which adds channels like CNN, ESPN, and MTV) have continued to increase.

   a. If prices continue to increase under tiering formats, how might consumers, politicians, and regulators react?

   b. If you were the manager of a cable company, would you have maintained basic cable packages and allowed the local government to control prices?

   c. Over the telephone, customers are only told the prices of premium tiers so very few people ever subscribe to just basic cable. If this misleading practice continues, what federal agency might intervene?

4. How might future technological advances affect the way programming is transmitted and received? How will we use television in the twenty-first century?

CLASS EXERCISE 2

SIX ENVIRONMENTAL FORCES ARE COMPETITIVE, ECONOMIC, POLITICAL, LEGAL AND REGULATORY, TECHNOLOGICAL AND SOCIOCULTURAL FORCES. WITH WHICH FORCE IS EACH OF THE FOLLOWING MOST DIRECTLY ASSOCIATED?

1. Prosperity
2. Federal Trade Commission
3. Personal computers without keyboards
4. Development and widespread use of facsimile machines
5. People's willingness to spend
6. Contributions to campaign funds
7. A society's high material standard of living
8. Sherman Antitrust Act
9. Better Business Bureau
10. The consumer movement
11. Buying power index
12. Food and Drug Administration
13. A monopoly
14. Government purchases of goods and services
15. Group of people threatening to boycott the sponsor of a television program that they believe contains too much sex and violence

DEBATE ISSUE

IS SELF-REGULATION AN EFFECTIVE WAY TO CONTROL AND MAINTAIN GOOD BUSINESS PRACTICES?

<u>YES</u>	<u>NO</u>
• Self-regulation is less expensive and less restrictive than governmental regulation	• Participation in self-regulation programs is voluntary in most industries
• Failure to implement self-regulation may lead to government intervention	• The industry trade associations that establish self-regulation guidelines have no authority to enforce the regulations
• Self-regulation leads to fewer complications within an industry	
• Self-regulation is a means of encouraging socially responsive behavior that enhances consumer goodwill	• Companies that follow self-regulation guidelines are often at a competitive disadvantage relative to companies that do not
	• Industry-established regulations may not be as stringent as those established by the government

CHAPTER QUIZ

1. If M&M Mars Candies found a magazine article that provided key information on the television viewing habits of major candy consumer groups, this would be an example of information obtained through environmental
   a. scanning.
   b. forces.
   c. analysis.
   d. strategizing.
   e. management.

2. Sally Jones was recently hired as a salesperson by a large national hospital supply firm. She has received total authority to set the prices charged for her products to the various hospitals in her territory. Which one of the following acts would it be most important for her to remember from her basic marketing class at State University?
   a. Sherman Act
   b. Robinson-Patman Act
   c. Wheeler-Lea Amendment
   d. Federal Trade Commission Act
   e. Unfair Trade Practices Act

3. To move toward greater organizational accountability, the United States Sentencing Commission introduced guidelines that mitigate penalties for developing compliance programs called the
   a. Organizational Compliance Guidelines.
   b. Federal Sentencing Guidelines for Organizations.
   c. Federal Trade Guidelines.
   d. Antitrust Guidelines.
   e. Consumer Protection Guidelines.

4. Mixed concrete cannot be shipped farther than twenty-five miles because the concrete might harden in the truck. Citrus County Concrete Company is the only supplier of mixed concrete to customers within a thirty-mile radius. Citrus County Concrete is an example of which one of the following competitive structures?
   a. Monopoly
   b. Oligopoly
   c. Monopolistic competition
   d. Pure competition
   e. Monopsony

ANSWERS TO DISCUSSION AND REVIEW QUESTIONS

1. Why are environmental scanning and analysis so important?

   Understanding the current state of the marketing environment and recognizing the threats and opportunities arising from changes within it help marketing managers assess the performance of current marketing efforts and develop marketing strategies for the future.

2. In what ways can each of the business cycle stages affect consumers' reactions to marketing strategies?

   Prosperity. Assuming a low level of inflation, total buying power is high because unemployment is low and aggregate income is high. Thus customers have the ability to purchase.

   Recession. Total buying power declines because unemployment rises. The lack of buying power coupled with the general pessimism that often accompanies recession causes consumer spending to decline. Buyers become more conscious of price and value, desiring products that are basic and fundamental.

   Depression. Total disposable income is at a minimum because wages are very low and unemployment is extremely high. Because of low disposable income and a total lack of confidence in the economy, consumers cut their spending to a minimum.

   Recovery. Disposable income increases as the high unemployment rate declines. Customers become more optimistic about the state of the economy. Consumer spending levels increase.

3. What business cycle stage are we experiencing currently? How is this stage affecting business firms in your area?

   This question is designed to prompt students to analyze the current state of our economy and to evaluate the effects of these economic conditions on local businesses. One major issue to consider is the degree to which the state of the national economy affects local businesses.

4. Define income, disposable income, and discretionary income. How does each type of income affect consumer buying power?

   Income is the amount of money an individual receives through wages, rents, investments, pensions, and subsidy payments for a given time period. Disposable income is income remaining after paying taxes and is used for spending and/or saving. Discretionary income is disposable income that is available for spending and/or saving after an individual has purchased the basic necessities of food, clothing, and shelter. Each income measure relates to consumers' buying power because the size of each may affect the degree of buying power.

5. How is consumer buying power affected by wealth and consumer credit?

   As current credit use increases, so does current buying power. By allowing persons to spend future income now, credit increases current buying power but reduces future buying power. Wealth also increases buying power. Wealthy persons can use their wealth not only for current purchases but also to generate additional income and to acquire large amounts of credit.

6. How is buying power measured? Why should it be evaluated?

The buying power for a geographic unit usually is measured on the basis of one or more of the following factors: population, effective buying income, or retail sales. *Sales Management's Buying Power Index* consists of a weighted average of all three factors. When using a buying power index, a marketer is concerned not only with the current index for a geographic unit but also with how this changes from one time period to another.

A marketer measures buying power because buying power determines customers' ability to make purchases. Such measurements are used in assessing marketing opportunities, forecasting sales, establishing sales quotas, and budgeting marketing expenditures.

7. What factors influence a consumer's willingness to spend?

Factors that influence a consumer's willingness to spend are the product's price, the individual's level of satisfaction obtained or expected in the future from currently used products, family size, and the consumer's expectations about future employment, income, prices, and general economic conditions.

8. How are political forces related to legal and governmental regulatory forces?

Marketers are concerned with political and legal forces because of their potential control of business practices. Persons in government positions create regulatory agencies, enact legislation, and interpret laws through the courts. The effects of these forces can be favorable or unfavorable to marketers, depending on political attitudes or public feelings toward the business sector. When political officials have favorable attitudes toward a specific industry, they are less likely to create or enforce laws and regulations that will negatively affect organizations in that industry.

9. Describe marketers' attempts to influence political forces.

Firms attempt to influence the political structure by helping to elect officials who are or will be favorable toward business interests. The help sometimes takes the form of campaign contributions, both legal and illegal. Such support may be simply to protect against unfavorable legislation rather than to prompt favorable legislation. Elected officials are expected to respond by supporting the business during their terms of office.

10. What types of procompetitive legislation directly affect marketing practices?

Procompetitive laws were created to preserve competition. The Sherman Antitrust Act was enacted in 1890 to prevent businesses from restraining trade and monopolizing markets. It applies to firms operating in interstate commerce and to U.S. firms operating in foreign commerce. Because this law was written in very general terms, the Antitrust Division of the Department of Justice has had some difficulty enforcing its provisions; in some cases, the courts have interpreted the law in ways that its creators did not intend. Because of these weaknesses, additional legislation has since been passed.

In 1914, the Clayton Act was passed to supplement the Sherman Act. It prohibits price discrimination, tying and exclusive agreements, certain stock acquisitions of other corporations, and interlocking directorates. It also exempts farm cooperatives and labor organizations from antitrust legislation. The penalty for violation of the Clayton Act is usually a fine, which in most cases is minimal.

Also enacted in 1914 was the Federal Trade Commission Act, which established the FTC. This act regulates the greatest number of marketing practices and deals with unfair methods of competition. The FTC has investigatory powers. The Wheeler-Lea Act of 1938 amended the FTC act. It prohibits false advertising of foods, drugs, therapeutic devices, and cosmetics, imposes penalties for violations, and establishes procedures for enforcement.

All these laws have had a broad impact on marketing activities and thus are of considerable concern to marketers.

11. What was the major objective of most procompetitive laws? Do the laws generally accomplish this objective? Why or why not?

The primary objective for creating procompetitive laws was to preserve a competitive environment. These laws have helped achieve this objective, in some respects, by diminishing the use of monopolistic practices. However, to some degree, procompetitive laws have also stifled competition by restricting the use of competitive tools such as pricing, advertising, and sales promotion.

12. What are the major provisions of the Robinson-Patman Act? Which marketing mix decisions are influenced directly by this act?

The Robinson-Patman Act was passed because of popular support for additional legislation dealing with price discrimination. The act prohibits price discrimination among purchasers of commodities of like grade and quality when the effect of such discrimination may substantially reduce competition or tend to create a monopoly. It also deems price differentials legal when they can be justified on the basis of cost savings or meeting competition in good faith. Also, it is unlawful to knowingly induce or receive discriminatory prices where such prices are prohibited by this law. Finally, furnishing services or facilities to purchasers on terms not accorded to all purchasers on proportionately equal terms is illegal. Marketers are directly affected by this law because it affects pricing decisions and activities.

13. What types of problems do marketers experience as they interpret legislation?

Many laws and regulations that affect marketers are written in vague terms, and marketers must resort to legal counsel rather than rely on their own interpretations. Because the laws are sometimes ambiguous, a marketer may choose to operate in a legally questionable way to determine the extent to which it can function before being prosecuted under the law. Or, to ensure compliance with a law that is vaguely worded, a marketer may take a very conservative stand. New sentencing guidelines hold both companies and employees accountable in the event of a violation.

14. What are the goals of the Federal Trade Commission? List the ways in which the FTC affects marketing activities. Do you think a single regulatory agency should have such broad jurisdiction over so many marketing practices? Why or why not?

The underlying goals of the FTC are to (1) prevent the free enterprise system from being stifled by monopoly or anticompetitive practices, and (2) protect consumers directly from unfair or deceptive trade practices.

To achieve its goals, the FTC enforces laws and establishes guidelines and operating procedures. A major goal is to assist and inform businesses so that they may comply with the laws. The FTC explains to businesses what is considered unfair, deceptive, or illegal and considers each case on its own merits rather than strictly applying a single set of guidelines for all firms. The agency may encourage firms in an industry to establish their own trade practices voluntarily, but it also has the power to set guidelines. The FTC's actions affect marketing decisions and activities such as pricing, advertising, labeling, packaging, product development, and distribution.

Because marketing involves continuous change, new marketing practices must be evaluated by the FTC each year. As new commissioners are appointed, FTC rulings regarding what is illegal or unfair also change. To do their job effectively, marketers must constantly review FTC decisions to discern the agency's current attitudes and positions.

15. Name several nongovernmental regulatory forces. Do you belief that self-regulation is more or less effective than governmental regulatory agencies? Why?

Although governmental regulatory forces are of primary concern to marketers, marketers must also deal with various nongovernmental agencies that influence marketing decisions. Some businesses attempt self-regulation, often through trade associations. Many of these programs are designed to stop or stall the development of laws and governmental regulatory groups that would regulate marketing practices. Some programs deal with ethical or social issues. Businesspeople generally view self-regulation as a preferable alternative to further governmental intervention, but self-regulation may be unenforceable or less strict.

One well-known nongovernmental agency is the Better Business Bureau (BBB), a local unit supported by local businesses. The BBB is concerned primarily with providing aid in settling problems that arise between consumers and businesses.

16. What does the term *technology* mean to you?

As the chapter states, spacecraft, computers, automobiles, the Internet, superconductors, lasers, and heart transplants are applications or outgrowths of technology, but none of them *is* technology. As defined in this chapter, technology is the application of knowledge and tools to accomplish tasks and solve problems. Students should be aware of this distinction.

17. How does technology affect you as a member of society? Do the benefits of technology outweigh its costs and dangers?

Technology determines whether we are born, how we live, and how we die. Students should discuss aspects of their lives affected by technology, such as working, playing, learning, eating, drinking, sleeping, and other areas. In discussing the favorable and unfavorable aspects of technology, factors such as improved productivity, improved goods and services, increased leisure time, and improvements in education, communication, transportation, and entertainment should be weighed against the unfavorable technological effects of polluted air and water, health hazards, unemployment, and any other factors that students view as unwanted effects of technological applications.

18. Discuss the impact of technology on marketing activities.

    Because technology affects people's desires for goods and services, it affects marketing activities. Technology influences the types of products that marketers can offer for sale; the production process, which affects the quality and price of products; the ways marketers reach consumers to communicate about products; and the way products are transported and stored.

19. What factors determine whether a business organization adopts and uses technology?

    A business organization's use of technology is determined by the firm's ability to use it, consumers' ability and willingness to buy technologically improved products, the perceived long-run effects of applying technology, the extent to which the firm is technologically based, the degree to which technology is used as a competitive tool, and the extent to which the business can protect resulting technological applications through patents or other means.

20. What is the evidence that diversity is increasing in the United States?

    Statistics indicate immigration has increased, resulting in a greater population of minorities in the United States. These statistics suggest that blacks and Hispanics will comprise 12.6 percent and 13.5 percent, respectively, of the U.S. population by the year 2010. Additionally, the percentage of older Americans is increasing, as is the number of people under age 18. Such changes may have a profound effect on marketing activities.

21. In what ways are cultural values changing? How are marketers responding to these changes?

    Among the cultural changes occurring are an increased emphasis on health, nutrition, fitness, the family, and the environment, and a shift away from conspicuous consumption. Marketers are responding by researching these changing values and developing new products to address them.

22. Describe the consumer movement. Analyze some active consumer forces in your area.

    The consumer movement is a social movement that offers consumers means for expressing dissatisfaction and correcting some of the conditions that have caused it. Examples of forces in the students' area might include the Better Business Bureau, government agencies, independent consumer groups, or individual consumer activists.

COMMENTS ON THE CASES

Case 2.1   AT&T: Working Toward a Safe and Green Tomorrow

This video and case illustrate how companies can apply technology to address sociocultural issues, particularly public demand for more environmentally sound production and marketing activities, and create satisfying marketing exchanges.

The first question asks students to evaluate the legal and regulatory forces that AT&T must monitor. Obviously, AT&T must ensure that it obeys all laws and regulations, such as the Sherman Antitrust Act, and complies with federal regulatory agencies such as the Federal Communications Commission. Additionally, AT&T must monitor the legal environment to determine whether any legislation that may affect its ability to conduct business is being considered in federal or state capitols. The company may respond to such potential legislation by lobbying elected officials or by creating new programs to satisfy the law. In Arizona, for example, a state mandate to reduce the number of commuter miles encouraged AT&T to set up a telecommuting program that allowed some Phoenix employees to work at home.

Question 2 concerns the influence of competition, technology, and economics on the development of AT&T's marketing strategy. AT&T must carefully monitor the marketing efforts of MCI, Sprint, and other competitors, and it may need to modify its marketing mix or even introduce new products to match the efforts of competitors. As a technology company, AT&T is certainly affected by technological advancements, which are often created in AT&T's own research facilities. AT&T must constantly research and develop new communications technologies to remain competitive and continue to satisfy the needs of its target customers. The state of the economy affects AT&T's marketing strategies by influencing consumers' buying power and willingness to spend; during a recession, for example, consumers may reduce their long-distance calling to family members.

The final question requires students to evaluate AT&T's efforts to improve the environment and to judge whether these efforts foster relationships with customers. AT&T has spent much time and millions of dollars working to reduce waste, minimize harmful emissions, and develop recycling efforts to minimize the impact of its activities on the environment. While some of AT&T's efforts have been prompted by new laws and regulations, others have been instigated to help the company save money and develop better relationships with the public. By trying to create an image of an environmentally concerned organization, AT&T hopes to build long-term relationships with customers who have environmental concerns. The firm's environmental stance may give it a competitive advantage if rivals do not take steps to develop a similar image.

Video Information

Video Title: A Safe and Green Tomorrow
Location: Tape 1, Segment 2
Length: 10:10
Video Overview: AT&T uses Total Quality Management principles to meet its environmental safety goals profitably. Examples of the company's socially responsible programs are seen at corporate facilities worldwide. The company is an innovative leader in recycling, reducing production-related toxic emissions, reducing automobile pollution, and applying its product technologies to assist in the achievement of its environmental safety goals. AT&T considers social responsibility an investment in the future of humanity and will continue to strive to be at the forefront of environmentally conscious technology.

Multiple-Choice Questions About the Video

c   1. AT&T's first CFC-free facility is in
    a. Milan.
    b. Tokyo.
    c. Singapore.
    d. Atlanta.

a   2. AT&T views socially responsible corporate behavior as
    a. environmentally sound and economically practical.
    b. environmentally sound but unprofitable.
    c. economically practical but not environmentally sound.
    d. not environmentally sound but desired by consumers.

b   3. AT&T first experimented with telecommuting to minimize environmental problems in
    a. Albuquerque.
    b. Phoenix.
    c. Atlanta.
    d. Philadelphia.

d   4. By developing an array of technologies designed to eliminate ozone-depleting emissions, it not only succeeded, but also estimates that it saves
    a. nothing.
    b. $5 million annually.
    c. $250 million annually.
    d. $25 million annually.

Case 2.2   Legal Issues at Archer Daniels Midland

This case highlights how legal issues have affected one company's marketing efforts. Although this case is quite complex (and unresolved as of this writing), it provides great detail about the legal issues Archer Daniels Midland faces and gives students an opportunity to witness how competitive, technological, and legal issues can create ethical and legal problems within a company.

The first question, which asks what top management can do to prevent price fixing by marketing managers, helps students appreciate the role top management plays in developing a law-abiding, ethical organization. The top management of Archer Daniels Midland needs to emphasize that price fixing is illegal by stating so in corporate policies and employee manuals. It should also establish and publicize to employees the punishment for violating company policies and federal laws on price fixing, and it should carefully enforce the rules. Finally, top management needs to implement a program to detect and punish price fixing and other infractions, and corporate executives should set an example for other employees to follow.

The second question asks students what marketing managers need to know about price fixing in developing marketing strategies. Clearly, marketing managers need to be aware of what constitutes price fixing, the legality of various pricing practices, and the penalties for violating the law, in order to avoid acting illegally when developing marketing strategy.

Question 3 asks how a compliance program could be used to avoid legal problems in the development and implementation of a marketing strategy. If top management develops and implements a program that precisely defines price fixing and other questionable illegal or unethical practices, clearly states the company's policy on such practices, imposes punishments for violations of company policy, and establishes a mechanism for detecting illegal practices, marketing managers will be less likely to include such activities in marketing strategies. Moreover, if the company institutes such a compliance program, it may face lesser penalties in the future should another price fixing incident occur.

3 MARKETING ETHICS AND SOCIAL RESPONSIBILITY

TEACHING RESOURCES QUICK REFERENCE GUIDE

Resource	Location
Purpose and Perspective	IRM, p. 50
Guide for Using Color Transparencies	IRM, p. 50
Lecture Outline	IRM, p. 50
Class Exercises, Debate Issue, and Chapter Quiz	IRM, p. 58
Class Exercise 1	IRM, p. 60
Class Exercise 2	IRM, p. 61
Debate Issue: Can ethics be taught?	IRM, p. 62
Chapter Quiz	IRM, p. 63
Answers to Discussion and Review Questions	IRM, p. 64
Comments on the Cases	IRM, p. 66
Case 3.1	IRM, p. 66
Video	Tape 1, Segment 3
Video Information	IRM, p. 66
Multiple-Choice Questions About the Video	IRM, p. 67
Case 3.2	IRM, p. 67
Transparency Acetates	Transparency package
Examination Questions: Essay	TB, p. 41
Examination Questions: Multiple-Choice	TB, p. 42
Examination Questions: True-False	TB, p. 43
Author-Selected Multiple-Choice Test Items	TB, p. 446

PURPOSE AND PERSPECTIVE

This chapter surveys the role of ethics and social responsibility in marketing decision making. First, we define marketing ethics and discuss the factors that influence ethical decision making in marketing. Then we address specific ethical issues in marketing. Finally, we discuss the concept of social responsibility and examine several important social responsibility issues.

GUIDE FOR USING COLOR TRANSPARENCIES

There are two groups of color transparencies. The transparencies identified by a double number are the same as the figures and tables in the text. The transparencies labeled with a number and a letter are illustrations that do not appear in the text, but they can be used as additional examples of concepts discussed.

Figure 3.2	Factors that influence the ethical decision-making process in marketing
Figure 3.6	The pyramid of corporate social responsibility
Table 3.3	A method to create ethical relationships in marketing
Table 3.4	Seven steps to ethical compliance
Figure 3A	Chapter 3 outline
Figure 3B	The use of sex in advertising can be considered an ethical issue.
Figure 3C	The Rock the Vote organization promotes social responsibility.
Figure 3D	Telephone fraud: An ethical issue
Figure 3E	Should the liquor industry advertise on television?
Figure 3F	Social responsibility's interface with improved profits
Figure 3G	Pizza Hut's social responsibility focus
Figure 3H	What social responsibility actions gain favorable publicity?
Figure 3I	Toyota acts socially responsible through its donation of over $12 million a year to organizations such as the National Science Teachers Association and the United Negro College Fund.
Figure 3J	The ethical compliance audit

LECTURE OUTLINE

I.   The nature of marketing ethics

Though misunderstood and controversial, ethics needs to be examined in order to support marketing decisions that are acceptable and beneficial to society.

A.   Marketing ethics defined

Marketing ethics refers to principles that define acceptable conduct in marketing.

1. The most basic ethical issues have been codified as laws and regulations.

2. Some marketers engage in ethical behavior because of enlightened self-interest, the expectation that "ethics pays," or the belief that if they do not act in the public interest, the public and customers will strike back with restrictive regulations and legal action.

3. Marketers must be aware of ethical standards and acceptable behavior from several viewpoints—company, industry, and society.

4. When marketers deviate from accepted standards, the exchange process can break down, resulting in customer dissatisfaction, lack of trust, and lawsuits.

5. Ethical conflict occurs when it is not clear whether to apply one's personal values or the organization's in a decision situation.

B. Why study marketing ethics?

1. Studying marketing ethics can help you to better recognize, understand, and resolve ethical conflicts.

2. Ethical issues in marketing can include difficult questions, and most marketers will need experience within a specific industry to understand how to operate in gray areas or handle close calls.

C. Marketing ethics and the role of the legal system

1. The distinction between legal and ethical issues is often blurred in decision making.

    a. Marketers operate in a marketing environment in which overlapping legal and ethical issues color many decisions.

    b. The legal system provides a formal venue for marketers to resolve ethical as well as legal disputes.

2. Marketing strategy decisions involve complex and detailed discussions in which correctness may not be clear-cut.

a. Because all members of an organization are not trained as lawyers, identifying ethical issues and implementing codes of conduct comprise the best approach to preventing violations and avoiding civil litigation.

b. Without proper ethical training and guidance, it is impossible for the average marketer to understand the exact boundaries for illegal behavior.

II. Understanding the ethical decision-making process

A. Individual factors

1. Ethical conflict arises when people encounter situations they cannot control or resolve in the privacy of their own lives; in such situations, people base their decisions on their own concepts of right or wrong and act accordingly.

2. Moral philosophies—the principles or rules that individuals use to decide what is right or wrong—are often cited to justify decisions or explain behavior.

a. There are two major types of moral philosophy associated with marketing decisions, each with its own concept of ethicalness and rules for behavior.

(1) *Utilitarianism* is concerned with maximizing the greatest good for the greatest number of people; utilitarians judge an action by the consequences for all people affected.

(2) *Ethical formalism* focuses on the intentions associated with a particular behavior and on the rights of the individual; ethical formalists develop specific standards of behavior by determining whether an action can be taken consistently as a general rule, without considering alternative results.

b. There is no universal agreement on the correct moral philosophy to use.

(1) Research suggests that marketers may use different moral philosophies in different situations.

(2) Marketers may sometimes change their value structure or moral philosophy when making decisions.

B. Organizational relationships

1. Marketers learn to resolve ethical issues from their individual backgrounds and from people with whom they associate in work groups and in the marketing organization.

    a. **Significant others** include superiors, peers, and subordinates in the organization who influence the ethical decision-making process.

    b. Organizational structure and culture operate through significant others to influence ethical decisions.

2. **Organizational, or corporate, culture** can be defined as a set of values, beliefs, goals, norms, and rituals that members or employees of an organization share. An organization's culture gives its members meaning and suggests rules for how to behave and deal with problems within the organization.

3. Top management sets the ethical tone for the entire organization, and the interaction between corporate culture and executive leadership helps determine the ethical value system of the firm.

4. The more a person is exposed to unethical activity by others in the organizational environment, the more likely it is that he or she will behave unethically.

5. Organizational pressure plays a key part in creating ethical issues.

    a. Nearly all marketers face difficult issues where solutions are not obvious or where organizational objectives and personal ethical values may conflict.

    b. Research suggests that many employees feel pressure to violate company policy in order to achieve business objectives or say they have observed unethical actions by others.

6. Because organizational culture, relationships, and pressures influence ethical behavior, the management of marketing ethics should focus on designing and developing organizations for marketers, who display a range of personal ethical variations and the tendency sometimes to take advantage of opportunities.

C.   Opportunity is a favorable set of conditions that limit barriers or provide rewards.

   1.   If a marketer takes advantage of an opportunity to act unethically and is rewarded or suffers no penalty, he or she may repeat such acts as other opportunities arise.

   2.   The larger the rewards and the milder the punishment for unethical behavior, the greater is the probability that unethical behavior will be practiced.

III.   Ethical issues in marketing

An **ethical issue** is an identifiable problem, situation, or opportunity requiring an individual or organization to choose from among several actions that must be evaluated as right or wrong, ethical or unethical.

A.   Product-related issues may arise when marketers fail to disclose risks associated with the product or fail to provide information regarding the function, value, or use of a product, or when marketers fail to inform customers about changes in product quality.

B.   Ethical issues related to promotion include false and misleading advertising and manipulative or deceptive sales promotion, tactics, or publicity efforts. Other issues are linked to advertising, personal selling, and bribery.

C.   In pricing, typical ethical issues are price fixing, predatory pricing, and failure to disclose the full price associated with a purchase.

D.   Ethical issues in distribution involve relationships among producers and marketing middlemen (wholesalers and retailers).

IV.   Organizational approaches to improving ethical behavior

A.   It is possible to improve ethical behavior in an organization by eliminating unethical persons and improving the organization's ethical standards.

B.   If top management develops and enforces programs to encourage ethical decision making, they become a force to help individuals make better ethical decisions.

C.   Marketers can never fully abdicate their personal ethical responsibility in making decisions.

D.   Promoting ethical conduct requires teamwork and initiative, which often result in higher-quality products; this, in turn, leads to the potential for an ethical advantage: better reputation, sales, market share, and profits.

E.   A proactive ethical approach to marketing should consider at least four fundamental values of interpersonal communication: respect, understanding, caring, and fairness.

V.   Ethics compliance programs

A.   The Federal Sentencing Guidelines for Organizations established by the United States Sentencing Commission encourage organizations to develop ethics and legal compliance programs before infractions occur.

B.   Without compliance programs and uniform standards and policies on conduct, it is hard for employees to determine what behavior is acceptable within a company.

C.   To improve ethics, many organizations have developed **codes of conduct,** which are formalized rules and standards that describe what the company expects of its employees.

1.   Codes of conduct promote ethical behavior by eliminating opportunities for unethical behavior because employees know both what is expected of them and what kind of punishment they face if they violate the rules.

2.   Codes of conduct do not have to take into account every situation, but they should provide guidelines that are capable of achieving organizational ethical objectives in an acceptable manner.

D.   Marketing compliance programs must be overseen by high-ranking persons in the organization known to abide by legal and common ethical standards; this person is usually referred to as an ethics officer.

E.   To foster ethical behavior in marketing, open communication and coaching on ethical issues are essential. This means providing employees with ethics training, clear channels of communication, and follow-up support throughout the organization.

F. It is important that companies consistently enforce standards and impose penalties or punishment on those who violate codes of conduct.

G. The company must also take reasonable steps in response to violations of standards and, as appropriate, revise the compliance program to diminish the likelihood of future misconduct.

VI. The nature of social responsibility

A. **Social responsibility** in marketing refers to an organization's obligation to maximize its positive impact and minimize its negative impact on society.

1. Whereas ethics relates to doing the right thing in making individual and group choices, social responsibility is a broader concept that is achieved by balancing the interests of all stakeholders in an organization.

2. Four dimensions of social responsibility are economic, legal, ethical, and philanthropic concerns.

3. In enlightened companies, social responsibility is a vital factor in marketing strategy decisions; when marketers deviate from socially acceptable activities, they can be held legally responsible and possibly be damaged in terms of economic success.

B. Impact of social responsibility on marketing

1. Recognition is growing that the long-term value of conducting business in a socially responsible manner far outweighs short-term costs.

   a. Consumers are increasingly expressing a preference to buy from socially responsible firms.

   b. Ethicalness and social responsibility are being rewarded by industry as well as consumers.

2. Marketers must determine what society wants, although this is very difficult because society is made up of many diverse groups; balancing societal demands to achieve the satisfaction of all members and groups is equally difficult, if not impossible.

3.   Because there are costs associated with many of society's demands, marketers must evaluate the extent to which members of society are willing to pay for what they want.

C.   Social responsibility issues

1.   The consumer movement refers to the efforts of independent individuals, groups, and organizations to protect the rights of consumers.

a.   Consumer activism has resulted in consumer safety and protection legislation.

b.   Consumers have four basic rights as spelled out by John F. Kennedy:

(1)   The right to safety

(2)   The right to be informed

(3)   The right to choose

(4)   The right to be heard

2.   Individual communities expect marketers to participate as members of the community, often through philanthropic contributions to civic projects and educational and other institutions.

3.   **Green marketing** refers to the specific development, pricing, promotion, and distribution of products that do not harm the environment.

4.   Marketers who successfully integrate and utilize the increasingly diverse work force experience increases in creativity and motivation and reductions in turnover.

VI.   Social responsibility and marketing ethics

A.   Although the concepts of marketing ethics and social responsibility are interrelated and often used interchangeably, they are different.

B.   To evaluate whether a specific behavior is ethical and socially responsible, a decision maker can ask members of the organization, the industry, consumer groups, or government agencies if they approve of the behavior.

C.   A rule of thumb for ethical and social responsibility issues is that if they can withstand open discussion and result in agreements or limited debate, then an acceptable solution may exist.

CLASS EXERCISES, DEBATE ISSUE, AND CHAPTER QUIZ

On the following pages, you will find two class exercises, a debate issue, and a chapter quiz. These are formatted in large-size type so that you can use them as class handouts or for making transparencies. Below are the authors' comments on the class exercises, the debate topic for this chapter, and the answers to the chapter quiz.

Class Exercise 1: The objective of this class exercise is to help students identify ethical issues and understand the importance of codes of ethics.

Question 1. In part (a), ask students to apply the moral philosophy of utilitarianism, which seeks to maximize the greatest good for the greatest number of people. A distribution manager who accepts a gift of any magnitude may make a decision that is not necessarily in the best interest of the company (e.g., selecting a higher-cost trucking company because it provides box seats to ball games).

In part (b), ask students to apply ethical formalism, which focuses on the intentions associated with a particular behavior and the rights of the individual. Specifically, if an action is acceptable for you, it must be acceptable for everyone else. Students might change their minds about acceptable gifts if asked, "What if everyone did it?"

Question 2. You might ask students if they know of instances in their own jobs where organizational relationships have had a negative or positive effect on ethical decision making. For instance, how does seeing a boss file inaccurate expense reports (to cover unauthorized expenditures) affect others in the firm? How might people react when peers take supplies or merchandise home?

Question 3. The role of opportunity may determine whether a person will behave ethically. You might also want to ask, "What if I gave an exam and left the classroom for the hour—would you be more likely to cheat?" Opportunity may be a better predictor of unethical activities than personal values.

Question 4. An effective code of ethics should let employees know both what is expected of them and the punishment for violating the rules. For instance, a firm may have a policy against accepting any gifts valued over $25. The penalty for accepting anything over that amount may be dismissal. However, simply having a policy or code will be ineffective if top management and superiors do not support and enforce it.

Class Exercise 2: The main objective of this exercise is to discuss the complex issues in defining ethical behaviors. Have the class discuss the ethical issues in each situation and determine whether the action described is ethical or unethical. You could also have the students discuss what it means to be ethical or unethical. Can a manager be truly ethical across all situations? What is the role of understanding the circumstances in ethical decision making? Try not to moralize by telling the students the right answer (if there is one). Encourage the students to reach a group consensus.

Debate Issue: Can ethics be taught?

Chapter Quiz: Answers to multiple-choice questions are

1. b
2. e
3. e
4. c

CLASS EXERCISE 1

YOU ARE THE DISTRIBUTION MANAGER FOR A LARGE CONSUMER PRODUCTS FIRM. YOUR COMPANY IS ABOUT TO RELEASE A VERY LARGE SHIPMENT OF PRODUCTS. AS MANAGER, YOU MUST DECIDE AMONG SEVERAL COMPETING TRANSPORTATION COMPANIES THAT ARE SEEKING YOUR BUSINESS. SALES REPRESENTATIVES FROM RAILROAD AND TRUCKING COMPANIES OFTEN MAKE CALLS TO YOUR OFFICE. YOUR DECISION WILL MEAN THE LOSS OR GAIN OF MILLIONS OF DOLLARS OF REVENUE FOR THESE COMPANIES.

1. Which of the following gifts would you be willing to accept from sales representatives of the transportation companies?
   - Pen and pencil set (with the company's logo)
   - Five-year supply of scratch pads (with logo)
   - Dinner for four at an exclusive restaurant
   - Season tickets to a professional football team
   - Fruits and nuts delivered to you each Christmas
   - Three-day, all-expense-paid golfing vacation
   - $500 in cash
   - Bag of groceries delivered to your home each week
   - Lavish trip to the Cayman Islands

   a. Would the acceptance of any of these gifts lead to personal gain at the expense of others?

   b. Would it be acceptable if everyone else in your firm received the same types of gifts?

2. What role would top management, superiors, and peers play in your decision on accepting these gifts?

3. If you had the chance to take some of the gifts on the list without anyone knowing, would you?

4. Would a code of ethics or an ethical corporate culture help you in making your decision?

CLASS EXERCISE 2

HOW ETHICAL ARE THE FOLLOWING BEHAVIORS?

1. The manufacturer of a leading insect spray changes the formulation of its product to eliminate problems with some people being allergic to one of its ingredients. The manufacturer does not inform consumers. The change in the formula will make the product less effective.

2. A bribe is paid to a company official in the island country of Kocomo to facilitate the movement of a product in that country. Bribes are a normal and expected business practice in Kocomo.

3. A beer company engages in an advertising campaign that is targeted to undergraduate college students, many of whom are under the legal drinking age.

4. A rental car company strongly advises customers to purchase insurance when renting a car. Although most personal car insurance covers the insured motorist when driving a rental car, most rental car customers are not aware of it.

5. *Consumer Reports* publishes the results of a study on shampoos that provides strong evidence that all shampoos are basically the same. In fact, the results suggest that a mild dishwashing liquid will do the same job for a lot less money. After the study is published, a leading shampoo marketer claims that its latest product will remove oil, add body, condition, and replenish hair better than any competing shampoo and do it all in one step.

DEBATE ISSUE

CAN ETHICS BE TAUGHT?

YES

- Courses on business ethics can teach students how to analyze ethical dilemmas

- By focusing on those factors that influence marketing decisions (individual beliefs/values, peer pressure, and opportunity), students can understand why decision makers behave as they do

- Many companies and colleges are instituting ethical training programs to teach the principles of ethical decision making

- Once the training is complete, students can apply what they have learned to the ethical dilemmas they face

NO

- An individual's beliefs, values, and morals are developed long before he or she enters school or begins a career

- Every person's morality is shaped by his or her social experiences with family, friends, school, and church

- No course or training session in marketing ethics can change a person's deep-rooted and long-held beliefs and values

- Learning ethical principles does not guarantee that they will be used

CHAPTER QUIZ

1. Marketing ethics
   a. refers to laws and regulations that govern marketing.
   b. refers to moral principles that define acceptable conduct in marketing.
   c. does not vary from one person to another.
   d. is most important for advertising agencies.
   e. applies well-defined rules for appropriate marketing behavior.

2. Which of the following is *not* one of the four dimensions of social responsibility as presented in your text?
   a. legal
   b. philanthropic
   c. ethics
   d. economic
   e. green marketing

3. Which of the following *best* identifies an ethical issue?
   a. Disagreements over peer evaluations
   b. Several middle managers are in conflict with upper management
   c. A company employee is convicted of a white-collar crime
   d. Disagreements on where to build a new manufacturing plant
   e. Conflicts between individual moral values and organizational values

4. Karen believes that her personal philosophy on honesty and fairness is enough for her to avoid misconduct in marketing decisions. Which of the following is the *best* evaluation of her belief?
   a. Personal values will always keep her from making ethical mistakes in marketing decisions.
   b. Being honest and fair is a virtue that anyone can successfully apply in marketing.
   c. Marketing decisions are complex, and correct ethical and legal correctness may not be so clear.
   d. Marketing managers have no right to provide direction to people like Karen on ethical issues.
   e. In reality, personal ethics has nothing to do with ethical marketing decisions.

ANSWERS TO DISCUSSION AND REVIEW QUESTIONS

1. Why is ethics an important consideration in marketing decisions?

    Because of the many publicized incidents in marketing relating to manipulation, corruption, and objectionable marketing activities, today's marketers have placed top priority on improving their ethics. It is important for marketers to go beyond legal issues and foster mutual trust among individuals and in marketing relationships. Consumers generally regard unethical marketing activities, such as deceptive advertising, misleading selling tactics, price collusion, and marketing of harmful products, as unacceptable and often refuse to do business with marketers who engage in such practices.

2. How do the factors that influence ethical or unethical decisions interact?

    Individual factors, organizational relationships, and opportunity are the three factors that interact to determine ethical decisions in marketing. While individuals in organizations should have personal moral philosophies that are socially acceptable, an employee assumes some measure of moral responsibility by agreeing to abide by the organization's rules and standard operating procedures. If an organization has limited ethical leadership and guidance, the individual may feel free to operate by his or her own standards. When opportunities are available, individuals can act according to their own best interests if the organization has provided limited direction.

3. What ethical conflicts could exist if business employees fly certain airlines just to receive benefits for their personal "frequent flier" programs?

    The potential for ethical conflicts would depend on each company's policy. If a company has a policy that frequent flier mileage belongs to the company, then no ethical conflict would exist. If the company allows its employees to keep all frequent flier mileage, however, then it would depend on whether the employee chose the better value for the company. If the employee chooses a higher-priced airline just to get the frequent flier miles, then the company is being injured and the employee's action would be unethical. If the employee's airline happens to be the best value, then both parties benefit. A company could eliminate the potential for ethical conflicts by making airline reservations for all employees.

4. List the components of the marketing mix and an example of how each can be affected by ethical issues.

    Answers for these will vary, but students should be able to cite appropriate examples.

    Product: The brand name can be misleading. Citrus Hill Fresh Orange Juice was changed due to the controversy over its being made from concentrate—not fresh orange juice. The product can be dangerous—General Motors mounted fuel tanks of some pickup trucks outside the frame, even though they were found to be involved in fiery crashes twice as often as other trucks.

    Promotion: False or misleading advertising claims. Mobil agreed to stop making claims of biodegradability of its trash bags. Aggressive telemarketing of questionable products (worthless securities, vacations with strings attached, and so on) over the phone.

Pricing: Inflating prices during peak sales periods and/or manipulating the supply of the product. Nintendo allegedly raised its prices by 20–30 percent during the Christmas season and then limited the supply of the games.

Distribution: Distributing counterfeit products. Some record stores distribute bootleg recordings, and some computer software retailers are making unauthorized copies of software.

5. How can ethical decisions involved in marketing be improved?

Ethical decisions in marketing organizations can be improved by eliminating unethical persons through screening techniques and enforcement of the firm's ethical standards and by improving the organization's ethical standards. Establishing codes of conduct and other corporate policies on ethics help eliminate the opportunity to act unethically. However, such codes and policies must be enforced in order to be effective. Establishing and enforcing codes of ethics and effective ethical compliance programs can also help minimize penalties to an organization should one of its employees break the law.

6. How can people with different personal values join together to make ethical decisions in an organization?

By sensitizing marketers to ethical issues and potential areas of conflict, it is possible to eliminate or defuse some of the ethical pressures that occur in daily marketing activities. Awareness of, and sensitivity to, ethical issues can eliminate the risk of making unethical decisions. Individuals must join together and establish standards or codes of ethics and agree on what the ethical issues are and how to resolve them. While individuals may define ethics differently and not agree on personal ethical standards, they should be able to join together and agree on standards of acceptable behavior to guide all marketing decisions within the organization.

7. What is the difference between ethics and social responsibility?

Ethics refers to principles that define acceptable conduct in marketing, whereas social responsibility is an organization's obligation to maximize its positive impact and minimize its negative impact on society. Ethics relates to doing the "right thing" when making individual and group choices; social responsibility requires balancing the interests of all stakeholders within and outside an organization. Although the terms do not mean the same thing, they are interrelated, and ethics can be considered one dimension of social responsibility.

8. What are major social responsibility issues?

Among major social responsibility issues is the consumer movement, which includes the activities undertaken by independent individual, groups, and organizations to protect their rights as consumers. Community relations is a social responsibility issue that relates to marketers' attempts to contribute to the well-being of communities, including solving social problems and participating in community activities. Green marketing is becoming a major social responsibility issue; it relates to environmental issues such as conservation, water pollution, air pollution, and land pollution. Finally, successfully integrating and utilizing the increasingly diverse work force can increase creativity and motivation while reducing turnover.

COMMENTS ON THE CASES

Case 3.1 Hershey Foods: Ethics and Social Responsibility

The primary objective of this case is to illustrate how a company, particularly one as large and well-known as Hershey Foods, can be both profitable and socially responsible. Several examples of socially responsible behavior on the part of the company are cited, such as Milton Hershey's founding of the Milton Hershey School orphanage, as well as specifics of how Hershey tries to maintain an ethical and socially responsible culture. You may want to ask students to find and present examples of other companies similarly exhibiting socially responsible behavior.

Question 1 asks students to describe the impact of Milton Hershey's personal values on his company's corporate philosophy of ethics today. Milton Hershey believed that his company should not only make superior candy but also be a superior company with integrity, honesty, and respect. He built an ethical and socially responsible culture as a foundation for Hershey, which the company has relied on and built upon over the years.

The second question asks how social responsibility at Hershey has contributed to the company's success. Hershey's ethical and socially responsible culture guides the company today in all aspects of its operations. People want to work for Hershey because they know they will be respected and treated fairly; this favorable impression makes recruiting new employees easier. Suppliers and intermediaries (wholesalers and retailers) want to work with Hershey because they know they can trust the company in exchange situations. Additionally, some consumers may express a preference for Hershey products over competitors' because of the firm's reputation.

For question 3, students must identify what they believe is the most significant ethics or social responsibility program at Hershey Foods and to explain their choice. Many answers are possible—some students will cite the company's sponsorship of the Milton Hershey School, for example—but students should be able to defend their choice based on their understanding of the text as well as their own personal feelings about the alternatives.

Video Information

Video Title: Hershey Foods Philosophy and Values
Location: Tape 1, Segment 3
Length: 21:12
Video Overview: This video explores Hershey Foods Corporation's commitment to ethics and social responsibility and how that commitment translates into daily corporate activities. Milton Hershey, the company's founder, built his firm with high standards of fairness, integrity, honesty, and respect. It is often said that Hershey was more concerned with benevolence than with profits, but the company has been very successful for nearly a century. Milton Hershey's values and standards still permeate the company's daily activities today. The video addresses Hershey Foods' corporate philosophy, which shows concern for customers, employees, and stockholders. At Hershey, ethics and social responsibility are an important part of the corporate culture. Employees are well aware of the company's commitment to quality, value, and fairness and know their decisions will be supported by Hershey as long as they maintain those standards. Every job at Hershey is considered important, and the company takes great pride in its commitment to participative management and employee involvement. In this organization, business means more than just making a dollar; it also involves maintaining a corporate philosophy and value system. Hershey Foods is a good example of a company that is able to maintain its ethical standards while remaining profitable.

Multiple-Choice Questions About the Video

b   1. Hershey Foods started out as the
    a. Milton Hershey Company.
    b. Lancaster Caramel Company.
    c. Hershey Foods Corporation.
    d. Nestlé Company.

d   2. All of the following are attributes Milton Hershey tried to incorporate into the company *except*
    a. honesty.
    b. respect.
    c. integrity.
    d. irresponsibility.

a   3. One of the majority owners of Hershey Food Corporation today is
    a. the Milton Hershey School trust.
    b. Nestlé.
    c. M&M Mars.
    d. Milton Hershey.

c   4. If a Hershey Foods employee has a question about proper conduct, he or she should first
    a. contact the firm's legal department.
    b. call the 800-number employee concern line.
    c. consult his/her immediate supervisor, unless the supervisor is the problem.
    d. do nothing and hope the problem goes away.

Case 3.2   Eli Lilly & Co.: Inventing a New Corporate Culture

The objective of this case is to demonstrate how a major organization can strive to be an ethical and socially responsible organization but still struggle with specific issues associated with its industry. Although some students may argue that Eli Lilly has always been socially responsible because of its role in developing life-saving drugs, the company has experienced negative publicity and lawsuits over some of those drugs. The company is trying to build a new culture to foster ethical and socially responsible decisions.

Question 1 asks what ethical and social responsibility issues are associated with the antidepressant Prozac. Students' answers will vary widely according to their own opinions and experiences with the antidepressant. However, most will probably cite concerns about the safety of the drug, the degree of testing Prozac underwent, Eli Lilly's promotion of Prozac (both to doctors and to counter negative publicity), and how Lilly encourages doctors to prescribe Prozac only for purposes for which it is approved. Some students may argue that the company should withdraw the drug from the market pending further testing, but others may believe that Prozac's benefits for some patients outweigh the potential for misuse. There are no "correct" answers, but this debate may give some students food for thought on this issue and help them see the gray area that clouds many ethical situations.

The second question asks what ethical and social responsibility obligations a pharmaceutical company owes its patients and society. Like the first question, this should prompt a lively debate as students realize such issues cannot be viewed as black or white. Many students will cite Kennedy's bill of consumer rights (the right to safety, to be informed, to choose, and to be heard) in their response to this question. Certainly, all firms have an obligation not knowingly to market products that are harmful to consumers or the environment, but in the pharmaceutical industry, the issue of side effects complicates this principle. At what point do harmful side effects outweigh the potential benefits of a drug? Students may argue that a pharmaceutical firm has an obligation not to release any medicines before testing has revealed them to be perfectly safe. (However, as devil's advocate, you might ask the class how an AIDS patient might feel if he or she had to wait years for a promising new treatment to be tested and approved for sale.)

The third question asks how Lilly's recent actions illustrate its commitment to be more socially responsible. In recent years, Lilly has reduced the emissions of harmful substances from its facilities, implemented recycling programs, and responded appropriately (perhaps above and beyond the expected) when faced with a product-tampering crisis. Moreover, the company handled a recent layoff with more benevolence than might be expected from such a large firm.

4 GLOBAL MARKETS AND INTERNATIONAL MARKETING

TEACHING RESOURCES QUICK REFERENCE GUIDE

Resource	Location
Purpose and Perspective	IRM, p. 70
Guide for Using Color Transparencies	IRM, p. 70
Lecture Outline	IRM, p. 70
Class Exercises, Debate Issue, and Chapter Quiz	IRM, p. 77
Class Exercise 1	IRM, p. 79
Class Exercise 2	IRM, p. 80
Debate Issue: Are the criticisms leveled against Japanese businesses justified?	IRM, p. 81
Chapter Quiz	IRM, p. 82
Answers to Discussion and Review Questions	IRM, p. 83
Comments on the Cases	IRM, p. 85
Case 4.1	IRM, p. 85
Video	Tape 1, Segment 4
Video Information	IRM, p. 85
Multiple-Choice Questions About the Video	IRM, p. 86
Case 4.2	IRM, p. 86
Transparency Acetates	Transparency package
Examination Questions: Essay	TB, p. 59
Examination Questions: Multiple-Choice	TB, p. 60
Examination Questions: True-False	TB, p. 72
Author-Selected Multiple-Choice Test Items	TB, p. 446

PURPOSE AND PERSPECTIVE

This chapter examines the increasing importance and unique features of global markets and international marketing. We show how target market selection in foreign countries is structured by the environment (we cover the basic environmental variables). Several regional and global trade agreements, alliances, and markets are considered. Finally, we examine the levels of commitment American firms have to international marketing.

GUIDE FOR USING COLOR TRANSPARENCIES

There are two groups of color transparencies. The transparencies identified by a double number are the same as the figures in the text. The transparencies labeled with a number and a letter are illustrations that do not appear in the text, but they can be used as additional examples of concepts discussed.

Figure 4.2	Levels of involvement in global marketing
Figure 4A	Chapter 4 outline
Figure 4B	International marketing
Figure 4C	International Häagen-Dazs ad
Figure 4D	This ad demonstrates the cross-cultural meaning of certain symbols.
Figure 4E	U.S. enforces trade embargo against Cuba
Figure 4F	International blunders or near blunders
Figure 4G	U.S. and China trade
Figure 4H	Comparative consumption activities in different regions of the world

LECTURE OUTLINE

I.   Global markets and international marketing

International marketing means developing and performing marketing activities across national boundaries. Many U.S. firms are finding that international markets provide tremendous opportunities for growth.

A.   International involvement

Marketers engage in international marketing activities at several levels of involvement covering a wide spectrum (Figure 4.2; text, p. 81).

1.   Domestic marketing involves marketing strategies aimed at markets within the home country, while, at the other end of the continuum, global marketing means developing marketing strategies for major regions or for the entire world.

2. Regardless of the level of involvement, marketers must choose either to customize their marketing strategies for different regions of the world or to standardize them for the entire world.

B. Customization versus globalization of international marketing strategies

1. Traditional international marketing strategies customize marketing mixes according to cultural, regional, and national differences.

2. In contrast, **globalization** involves developing marketing strategies as though the entire world (or its major regions) were a single entity; a globalized firm markets standardized products in the same way everywhere.

3. For years, organizations have attempted to globalize the marketing mix as much as possible by employing standardized products, promotion campaigns, prices, and distribution channels for all markets.

4. The degree of similarity between the various environmental and market conditions determines the feasibility of globalization.

5. International marketing demands some strategic planning by the firm to incorporate foreign sales into its overall marketing strategy.

II. Environmental forces in international markets

Before a company enters a foreign market, it must analyze the environment thoroughly and understand the complexities of all environments involved.

A. Cultural and social forces

1. Culture refers to concepts, values, and tangible items, such as tools, buildings, and foods, that make up a particular society.

2. When products are introduced from one nation into another, acceptance is far more likely if there are similarities between the two cultures.

3. Product adoption and use are influenced by consumers' perceptions of other countries.

4. Culture may affect marketing negotiations and decision-making behavior on the part of marketers, industrial buyers, and other executives.

5. Marketing activities are primarily social in purpose and are therefore influenced by the institutions of family, religion, education, health, and recreation.

B. Economic forces

1. Many trade restrictions affect international marketing and must be considered when analyzing global markets.

   a. An import tariff is any duty levied by a nation on goods bought outside its borders and brought in. They are designed either to raise revenue for the country or to protect domestic products.

   b. Quotas set limits on the amount of goods the importing country will accept for certain product categories in a specific time period.

   c. Embargoes occur when a government suspends trade in a particular product or with a given country. They may be imposed for political, health, or religious reasons.

   d. Countries may also limit imports to maintain a favorable balance of trade, which is the difference in value between a nation's exports and imports.

   e. Exchange controls are restrictions on the amount of a particular currency that can be bought or sold.

2. Economic differences in standards of living, availability of credit, discretionary buying power, income distribution, national resources, and conditions that affect transportation may dictate adjustments in international marketing strategies.

   a. **Gross domestic product (GDP)** is an overall measure of a nation's economic standing in terms of the market value of the total output of goods and services produced in a nation for a given period of time.

b.   Opportunities for international marketers are not limited to countries with the highest incomes.

C.   Political and legal forces

1.   A country's political system, national laws, regulatory bodies, special interest groups, and courts all have great impact on international marketing, as do its policies toward public and private enterprise, consumers, and foreign firms.

2.   A government's attitude toward cooperation with importers has a direct impact on the economic feasibility of exporting to that country.

3.   Differences in political and governmental ethical standards abound; for example, some foreign firms and governments engage in practices prohibited in U.S. firms, such as payoffs and bribes.

D.   Technological forces

Marketing technology used in North America and other industrialized regions of the world may be ill-suited for developing countries.

III.   Regional trade alliances, markets, and agreements

A.   **The North American Free Trade Agreement (NAFTA),** which went into effect on January 1, 1994, effectively merged Canada, Mexico, and the United States into one market of about 374 million consumers.

1.   NAFTA makes it easier for U.S. businesses to invest in Mexico and Canada, provides protection for intellectual property, expands trade by requiring equal treatment of U.S. firms in both countries, and simplifies country-of-origin rules.

2.   Canada's 29 million relatively affluent consumers represent a significant market for U.S. marketers.

3.   The growth of Mexico's economy represents a significant opportunity for U.S. marketers, and, despite some economic turmoil, provides an opportunity to reach other Latin American countries while strengthening NAFTA.

4. Although NAFTA is politically controversial, it is expected to be a positive factor for U.S. firms wishing to engage in international marketing.

B. The European Union (EU), which consists of Belgium, France, Italy, Germany, Luxembourg, the Netherlands, the United Kingdom, Spain, Denmark, Greece, Portugal, and Ireland, was officially formed as a single world trade market with 340 million consumers in 1993.

1. To facilitate free trade among members, the EU is working toward the standardization of business regulations and requirements, import duties, and value-added taxes; the elimination of customs checks; and the creation of a standardized currency for use by all members. These changes have not been without controversy.

2. Although the EU nations are trying to function as one large market and consumers in the EU may become more homogeneous in their needs and wants, markets must be aware that cultural differences among the twelve nations may require modifications in the marketing mix for consumers in each nation.

C. Pacific Rim nations

1. Companies of the Pacific Rim nations—Japan, China, South Korea, Taiwan, Singapore, Hong Kong, the Philippines, Malaysia, Indonesia, Australia, and Indochina—have become increasingly competitive and sophisticated in global business in recent years.

2. Despite the high volume of trade between the U.S. and Japan, the two nations continually struggle with cultural and political differences and are, in general, at odds over how to do business with each other.

3. South Korea has become remarkably successful in world markets with familiar name brands such as Samsung, Daewoo, and Hyundai. Before that, many of their products prospered under U.S. company labels.

4. The People's Republic of China represents a huge potential market opportunity with its 1.2 billion people, but there are many risks associated with doing business in China.

5. Less visible Pacific Rim nations such as Singapore, Taiwan, and Hong Kong are also experiencing economic growth.

D.   Changing relations with Eastern Europe and the former Soviet Union

    1.   The countries of the former Soviet Union and other Eastern European nations are experiencing great political and economic changes. While these changes may prove beneficial in the long run, the short-term result has been serious economic distress.

    2.   The changing conditions in these countries are creating many marketing opportunities.

E.   The **General Agreement on Tariffs and Trade (GATT),** based on negotiations among member countries to reduce worldwide tariffs and increase international trade, provides a forum for tariff negotiations and a place where international trade problems can be discussed and resolved.

    1.   The most recent Uruguay Round (1988–1994) reduced trade barriers for most products and provided new rules to prevent **dumping,** the selling of products at unfairly low prices.

    2.   Each of the previous GATT rounds has reduced trade barriers and introduced a period of strong economic growth.

IV.   Developing organizational structures for international marketing

The level of commitment to international marketing is a major variable in deciding what kind of involvement is appropriate.

A.   Exporting is the lowest level of commitment to international marketing and the most flexible approach.

    1.   Export agents bring together buyers and sellers from different countries.

    2.   Foreign buyers from companies and governments provide a direct method of exporting and eliminate the need for an intermediary.

B.   A **trading company** links buyers and sellers in different countries but is not involved in manufacturing or owning assets related to manufacturing.

1. An important function of trading companies is taking title to products and performing all the activities necessary to move the products from the domestic country to a foreign country.

2. Trading companies reduce risk for firms interested in getting involved in international marketing.

C. **Licensing** is an arrangement in which a licensee pays commissions or royalties on sales or supplies used in manufacturing. It is an alternative to direct investment when the political stability of a foreign country is in doubt or when resources are unavailable for direct investment.

D. A **joint venture** is a partnership between a domestic firm and a foreign firm or government.

1. Joint ventures are especially popular in industries that call for large investments, such as natural resources extraction or automobile manufacturing.

2. Joint ventures are often a political necessity because of nationalism or governmental restrictions on foreign ownership.

3. **Strategic alliances** are partnerships formed to create competitive advantage on a worldwide basis; they are very similar to joint ventures.

    a. The partners forming international strategic alliances often retain their distinct identities, and each brings a distinctive competence to the union.

    b. International strategic alliances differ from other business structures in that member firms in the alliance may have been traditional rivals competing for market share in the same product class.

E. **Direct ownership,** the purchase of subsidiaries or other facilities overseas, is a possibility when a company makes a long-term commitment to marketing in a foreign nation.

1. The term **multinational enterprise** refers to firms that have operations or subsidiaries located in many countries.

2. A wholly owned foreign subsidiary may be allowed to operate independently of the parent company so that its management can have more freedom to adjust to the local environment.

CLASS EXERCISES, DEBATE ISSUE, AND CHAPTER QUIZ

On the following pages, you will find two class exercises, a debate issue, and a chapter quiz. These are formatted in large-size type so that you can use them as class handouts or for making transparencies. Below are the authors' comments on the class exercises, the debate topic for this chapter, and the answers to the chapter quiz.

Class Exercise 1: The objective of this class exercise is to point out how various environmental forces may influence a company's marketing strategy. The information contained in the examples came from an actual in-class discussion among students, many of whom were from European countries. The text offers numerous other examples that students can use if they have not been to Europe.

a. In the EuroDisney situation, students may point out that Disney's advertising would definitely be affected. Not only would the language in an ad have to be changed, but the availability of media would also affect Disney's strategy. In addition, the increased use of public transportation in Europe might change how Disney builds the facility (i.e., parking lots, shuttle buses).

b. In the McDonald's situation, some students may question whether a fast-food restaurant makes sense in Europe. Fast food is popular in America because we greatly value our time. Likewise, the conversion to a metric system would require changes in all of McDonald's portion sizes (i.e., a 20-ounce soft drink equals .59 liters).

c. When the NFL expands into Spain, it must obviously convert all measurements to the metric system. In addition, the new team should be concerned over the actions of excited sports fans and plan accordingly.

d. Federal Express would be concerned about the availability of transportation and communication networks in Hungary. Additional concerns might include changes in weights and measurements, pricing, and advertising.

e. If Procter & Gamble begins to sell Ivory soap in France, the company has a unique problem: How do you convince people who are not concerned about body odor to buy soap? This problem will force many changes in the company's advertising.

In addition to these specific changes, students should recognize other changes. Will bribes or payoffs be required to establish business in these foreign countries? How will inflation rates affect the prices these companies must charge for their products and services? Can the people of these countries even afford to buy the products and services? McDonald's is having this problem in Moscow, where a Big Mac costs as much or more than many Muscovites make in an entire month.

Class Exercise 2: This exercise asks students to match each factor with its corresponding environmental force, but it should not end there. Ask your students to explain their own customs, such as handshaking, the use of color, or behavior at sporting events. Chances are they take these things for granted in their lives and will have some difficulty explaining them to the class. Then correlate this difficulty to the challenge of understanding the environmental forces affecting international marketing activities. Most likely answers:

Characteristic	Environmental Force
1. Handshaking	**cultural**
2. Religion	**cultural**
3. Transportation networks	**economic**
4. Computer literacy	**social/technological**
5. Sporting events	**social**
6. Color preferences	**cultural**
7. Standard of living	**economic**
8. Role of children in the family	**social/cultural**
9. Communication equipment	**technological**
10. Touching	**cultural**
11. Import restrictions	**political/legal**
12. Government stability	**political/legal**
13. Climate	**economic**
14. Language	**cultural/social**
15. Payoffs and bribes	**cultural/political/legal**

Debate Issue: Are the criticisms leveled against Japanese businesses justified?

Chapter Quiz: Answers to multiple-choice questions are

1.	b	3.	a
2.	b	4.	d

CLASS EXERCISE 1

THERE ARE MANY DIFFERENCES BETWEEN EUROPEAN COUNTRIES AND THE UNITED STATES. THE FOLLOWING ARE JUST SAMPLES:

CULTURAL: Advertising in many European countries often contains nudity. Some Europeans are not as concerned with body odor and cleanliness as are people in the United States.

SOCIAL: People in the United States are often more serious and aggressive about religion than in some European countries. Sports fans (particularly soccer) in Europe are much more fanatic and violent; in some cases, large fences are needed to separate the fans of different teams.

ECONOMIC: European countries in general place a greater emphasis on public transportation (train and bus) than does the United States. Many European countries face much higher inflation rates than does the United States.

POLITICAL/LEGAL: In some European countries, bribes and payoffs are common business practices. Other countries allow the sale of addictive drugs without prosecution. Prostitution is legal in some countries.

TECHNOLOGICAL: Most countries outside the United States use the metric system. Television and radio stations are often not as widespread as they are in the United States.

BASED ON YOUR UNDERSTANDING OF DIFFERENCES BETWEEN EUROPEAN COUNTRIES AND THE UNITED STATES, HOW MIGHT A U.S. COMPANY'S MARKETING STRATEGY BE AFFECTED IN EACH OF THE FOLLOWING SITUATIONS?

a. The Walt Disney Company opens EuroDisney in Paris, France.

b. McDonald's opens a fast-food restaurant in Berlin, Germany.

c. The National Football League forms a team in Barcelona, Spain.

d. Federal Express begins overnight package delivery to Hungary.

e. Proctor & Gamble begins to sell Ivory soap in France.

CLASS EXERCISE 2

THE FOLLOWING ENVIRONMENTAL FORCES AFFECT INTERNATIONAL MARKETS: CULTURAL AND SOCIAL, ECONOMIC, TECHNOLOGICAL, AND POLITICAL/LEGAL. WITH WHICH FORCE IS EACH OF THE FOLLOWING MOST CLOSELY ASSOCIATED?

1. Handshaking
2. Religion
3. Transportation networks
4. Computer literacy
5. Sporting events
6. Color preferences
7. Standard of living
8. Role of children in the family
9. Communications equipment
10. Touching
11. Import restrictions
12. Government stability
13. Climate
14. Language
15. Payoffs and bribes

DEBATE ISSUE

ARE THE CRITICISMS LEVELED AGAINST JAPANESE BUSINESSES JUSTIFIED?

YES

- The United States carries an extremely large trade imbalance with Japan

- Japanese direct investment in the United States continues to escalate

- Japanese firms are increasing capacity, reducing costs, and developing new technologies faster than U.S. firms

- The Japanese unfairly restrict U.S. imports

- American consumers are becoming increasingly dependent on Japanese products

- The entire world economy is becoming dominated by the Japanese

NO

- The total of all foreign investment in the U.S. economy (including Japanese) is only about 4 percent

- The British and Canadians have more investment in the United States than do the Japanese

- Foreign investment in other countries is becoming a typical business practice as globalization becomes a reality

- Many U.S. companies, like Ford and Chrysler, own substantial portions of some Japanese companies, like Mitsubishi and Mazda

- Foreign investment in the United States is good because it is being directed at permanent assets like plant and equipment—this stimulates American industry by providing jobs and stabilizing the economy

CHAPTER QUIZ

1. The Shelby Company plans to export expensive consumer gift items to Germany. The best overall economic measure of market potential would be Germany's
   a. gross domestic product.
   b. gross domestic product per capita.
   c. gross national product.
   d. balance of trade.
   e. unemployment rate.

2. Japan's Sony Corporation is a prime example of a multinational enterprise. With this in mind, which of the following would most accurately characterize Sony's operations?
   a. Sony follows a strategy of market globalization.
   b. Sony has operations or subsidiaries in many different countries.
   c. Sony places most of its emphasis on profits generated in foreign countries.
   d. Sony would not expect its foreign operations to share the same goals as the parent firm.
   e. Sony does not concern itself with differences in markets around the world.

3. Which of the following is *true* about NAFTA?
   a. It remains politically controversial.
   b. It will increase the total output of goods and services in foreign markets.
   c. It will decrease the total number of jobs in the U.S.
   d. It eliminated all tariffs on goods traded between the U.S., Canada, and Mexico.
   e. It will reduce the number of illegal aliens in the U.S.

4. The IBC Corporation—a U.S.-based watch maker—recently entered into a partnership agreement with the Australian government to make watches. What type of partnership agreement does this situation most likely represent?
   a. A trading company
   b. A licensing arrangement
   c. A direct ownership arrangement
   d. A joint venture
   e. A combination in restraint of trade

ANSWERS TO DISCUSSION AND REVIEW QUESTIONS

1. How does international marketing differ from domestic marketing?

   International marketing differs from domestic marketing in that exchange occurs across national boundaries. When marketing occurs across national boundaries, decisions should take into account differences in the marketing environment and the unique needs of customers in other countries.

2. What factors must marketers consider as they decide whether to become involved in international marketing?

   International marketing involvement relates to the firm's goals and the perceived opportunity from serving foreign markets. To develop desired profits and growth, marketers sometimes consider it necessary to cross national boundaries.

3. Why are the largest industrial corporations in the United States so committed to international marketing?

   The largest industrial corporations in the United States are committed to international marketing because their resources and market opportunities can be optimized in serving foreign markets. The profit bases of such companies as Exxon and Cola-Cola have been increased tremendously by increasing the size of the world markets these companies serve.

4. Why was so much of this chapter devoted to an analysis of the international marketing environment?

   The environment is a major consideration in analyzing international marketing. If a marketing strategy is to be effective across national boundaries, the complexities of all environments must be understood. The cultural, social, technological, economic, and political/legal environments of many foreign countries differ considerably from those in the United States.

5. A manufacturer recently exported peanut butter with a green label to a nation in the Far East. The product failed because it was associated with jungle sickness. How could this mistake have been avoided?

   By using a marketing intelligence system or conducting marketing research, the selling firm could have understood the culture, taboos, and attitudes of the nation in the Far East. The green label should have been market tested in the foreign country; the results would have indicated that green had inappropriate connotations for a food label.

6. How do religious systems influence marketing activities in foreign countries?

   Religious systems structure international marketing processes by helping form a society's ethics and value structure. All societies have some philosophy for explaining the unknown and supernatural. Religious factors can affect what products consumers buy or don't buy, and can influence exchange negotiations as well.

7. If you were asked to provide a small tip (or bribe) to have a document approved in a foreign nation where this practice was customary, what would you do?

   This question relates to the values and ethical standards of the individual involved. There is no right or wrong answer in this situation, but such tips should be avoided if possible. In the United States, this type of payment is considered a bribe and therefore is unethical and probably illegal.

8. In marketing dog food to Latin America, what aspects of the marketing mix need to be altered?

   Extensive research should be conducted to determine how the marketing strategy should be altered. The target market should be defined properly. The product, price, promotion, and distribution will have to be developed to match the needs of dog owners in the country to be served.

9. What should marketers consider as they decide whether to license or to enter into a joint venture in a foreign nation?

   A decision to license or to enter into a joint venture in a foreign country depends on the nature of the product and the political and economic stability of the nation being served. Licensing is not as risky as a joint venture because the licensee pays commissions or royalties on the sales of supplies used in manufacturing in a foreign country. This technique is an alternative to direct investment. The joint venture is a partnership between a domestic and a foreign firm and/or government. In a joint venture, there is always the possibility that the domestic and foreign firms will disagree, and the foreign firm can be at a disadvantage. There is always the possibility of expropriation—the foreign country may take over all control of a joint venture. On the other hand, a joint venture often guarantees that a firm will gain a foreign market, and it may help develop local support for the firm's products.

10. Discuss the impact of strategic alliances on marketing strategies.

    Strategic alliances, partnerships formed to create competitive advantage on a worldwide basis, are the newest form of international business structure. The number of strategic alliances is growing at an estimated rate of about 20 percent per year, and in some areas they are becoming the predominant means of competing. For example, Chrysler and Mitsubishi have formed Diamond Star Motors in Normal, Illinois, to produce Plymouth, Eagle, and Mitsubishi nameplates. All three cars are basically the same except for minor steel metal and nameplate changes. This plant is owned 50 percent by Chrysler and 50 percent by Mitsubishi and helps to strengthen each company's product mix. Through the efficiency of joint manufacturing, each company is able to share in the lower costs of production. The impact of strategic alliances such as this on marketing strategies is that the companies can offer high-quality products at the lowest competitive price available and focus on their unique approaches to promotion and distribution.

COMMENTS ON THE CASES

Case 4.1   20 Years of Innovation: There Is No Finish Line for Nike

This case focuses on Nike's marketing efforts in China. The case provides a brief history of Nike, explains some of the challenges of marketing in China, and describes Nike's determination to satisfy the Chinese market in the face of intense competition from Reebok and other firms. Many students will be familiar with Nike either through purchase of its products or observation of television and printed advertisements. Seeing how a well-known firm markets to consumers in another country should be interesting to them.

The first question asks students why athletic shoes are ideal for global marketing. Consumers everywhere purchase athletic shoes for sports, recreation, and general use. Moreover, athletics play some role in all cultures, as indicated by participation in and television ratings for the Olympics. Consequently, the market for athletic shoes is more or less global, although consumers in different countries may have different needs and preferences with regard to athletic shoes. China, in particular, represents a market opportunity because its 1.2 billion consumers are becoming more affluent and more aware of Western culture.

Question 2 asks what advantages Nike has in its competition with Reebok to obtain leadership in the Chinese athletic shoe market. One significant Nike advantage is its manufacturing base: 30 percent of Nike's products are already manufactured in China, allowing the firm to respond quickly to changes in local markets. For example, Nike has been able to take advantage of the growing popularity of basketball in China through new products and promotions featuring popular American basketball stars. Nike also sponsors China's national basketball and tennis teams, some Olympic athletes, and various professional and semiprofessional soccer teams. Such sponsorships and celebrity associations give Nike great exposure to Chinese consumers.

The third question asks what risks Nike faces in investing its resources in manufacturing and marketing athletic shoes in China. There are many risks to doing business in China, including a poor transportation infrastructure, burglars, pirates, uncooperative customs agents and trade officials, and a casual attitude toward contracts. Additionally, China's political instability of the last few years may also present problems. Nike must carefully monitor the environment in China in order to respond to these issues as necessary.

Video Information

Video Title: International Marketing Featuring Nike
Location: Tape 1, Segment 4
Length: 10:06
Video Overview: This video shows how Nike's corporate culture and organization are at the core of its success. The founders of Nike were involved in track running and wanted to create shoes that would help athletes perform at their highest potential. The general goal of Nike was passed on to the employees of the company. Thus, innovation, competitiveness, and flexibility to meet each customer's needs are central values at Nike.

Innovation is fostered by employee stimulation and involvement. At Nike, every new idea is welcome, whether it will end up being a good or a bad idea. Also, employees whose product ideas are accepted have the opportunity to become a project manager for the new product. The challenge of competitiveness is accentuated by the sponsorship of sport champions such as Michael Jordan.

The organization of Nike facilitates openness, communication, and teamwork. The firm is divided into several independent business units. Each of these units is composed of small teams of designers, technicians, and marketers. The teams regroup employees with different qualifications. Overall, Nike can be seen as an organization that has developed the adequate culture and structure to meet its objectives.

Multiple-Choice Questions About the Video

a 1. Nike was founded by
   a. Phil Knight.
   b. John McEnroe.
   c. Michael Jordan.
   d. Bill Gates.

d 2. One reason for Nike's success is the philosophy,
   a. "Winning is everything."
   b. "There are no losers."
   c. "It's not whether you win or lose but how you play the game."
   d. "No idea is a stupid idea here at Nike."

c 3. China accounts for _____ percent of all Nike manufacturing worldwide.
   a. 0
   b. 10
   c. 30
   d. 50

Case 4.2   KLM Flies High with Global Alliances

This case discusses international marketing from the perspective of a non-American firm. It highlights the efforts by one foreign airline to use joint ventures and strategic alliances to enter and achieve success in new global markets. The case also provides a history of KLM and describes how certain environmental factors have affected the airline's success.

Question 1 asks how KLM is using strategic alliances to expand internationally. KLM has formed numerous ventures and alliances, such as ownership stakes in Covia Partnership, which owns and operates United Airlines' Apollo computer reservation system; Transavia, a Dutch charter airline; Air Littoral, a French regional airline; and ALM Antillean Airlines. One of the firm's most significant alliances is its partnership with U.S.-based Northwest Airlines. These partnerships have helped KLM enter new markets and expand its presence in others, and together with Northwest Airlines, KLM has become the world's third-largest carrier in terms of revenues.

The second question asks what environmental forces have affected KLM's ability to expand and its partnership with Northwest. World War II and Hitler's occupation of Holland stifled KLM's growth in the early part of the century. However, relaxing political barriers and the increasing importance of international marketing have propelled KLM's strong growth in the years since. KLM has taken advantage of political forces, in particular. For example, KLM's alliance with Northwest was possible largely because of a Dutch-American "open skies" treaty that permits airlines of both countries to fly unrestricted into each other's markets. Although trade barriers prevent Northwest from flying into Rome, KLM, with its European Union advantages, serves Rome on behalf of Northwest's customers.

For question 3, students must determine what strategy KLM seems to be using in world markets. Based on the information provided in the case, students should recognize that KLM is expanding largely through strategic alliances and joint ventures that expand its presence in specific markets. The carrier also adjusts its marketing mixes to cater to the needs of customers in certain countries and to specific types of flyers (for example, it gives tiny china houses filled with Dutch gin to some business-class passengers).

5 INFORMATION SYSTEMS AND MARKETING RESEARCH

TEACHING RESOURCES QUICK REFERENCE GUIDE

Resource	Location
Purpose and Perspective	IRM, p. 89
Guide for Using Color Transparencies	IRM, p. 89
Lecture Outline	IRM, p. 89
Class Exercises, Debate Issue, and Chapter Quiz	IRM, p. 98
Class Exercise 1	IRM, p. 101
Class Exercise 2	IRM, p. 102
Debate Issue: Does marketing research (surveys, telephone interviewing) invade a respondent's privacy?	IRM, p. 103
Chapter Quiz	IRM, p. 104
Answers to Discussion and Review Questions	IRM, p. 105
Comments on the Cases	IRM, p. 107
Case 5.1	IRM, p. 107
Video	Tape 1, Segment 5
Video Information	IRM, p. 107
Multiple-Choice Questions About the Video	IRM, p. 108
Case 5.2	IRM, p. 108
Transparency Acetates	Transparency package
Examination Questions: Essay	TB, p. 77
Examination Questions: Multiple-Choice	TB, p. 78
Examination Questions: True-False	TB, p. 94
Author-Selected Multiple-Choice Test Items	TB, p. 446

PURPOSE AND PERSPECTIVE

This chapter focuses on the ways of gathering information needed for marketing decisions. It distinguishes between managing information within an organization (a marketing information system) and conducting marketing research. We discuss how marketers can capitalize on new technologies, such as the Internet, to improve data collection. Then, we discuss the role of marketing research in decision making and problem solving. We identify a set of steps to follow in conducting a marketing research project. The steps are (1) defining and locating problems, (2) designing the research project, (3) collecting data, (4) interpreting research findings, and (5) reporting research findings. Then we turn to the methods of gathering marketing research data. We describe primary data collection methods, focusing on survey methods and observation methods, and various sources of secondary data. Then we examine sampling and experimentation. The discussion of sampling includes most of the sample designs used in marketing research.

GUIDE FOR USING COLOR TRANSPARENCIES

There are two groups of color transparencies. The transparencies identified by a double number are the same as the figures in the text. The transparencies labeled with a number and a letter are illustrations that do not appear in the text, but they can be used as additional examples of concepts discussed.

Part 2 Opener	Buyer behavior and target market selection
Figure 5.3	Five steps of the marketing research process
Figure 5A	Chapter 5 outline
Figure 5B	American Business Information provides customers with secondary data including demographic information on business in a CD-ROM format.
Figure 5C	To change consumers' images of milk, the American Dairy Association needed to link marketing research and analysis.
Figure 5D	Internet uses
Figure 5E	An example of a perceptual map for displaying data analysis

LECTURE OUTLINE

I.   Marketing research and marketing information systems

    A.   **Marketing research** is the systematic design, collection, interpretation, and reporting of information to help marketers solve specific marketing problems or take advantage of marketing opportunities.

        1.   It is a process for gathering information not currently available to decision makers.

        2.   It is conducted on a special-project basis, with the research methods adapted to the problems being studied and to changes in the environment.

B. **A marketing information system (MIS)** is a framework for the day-to-day management and structuring of information gathered regularly from sources both inside and outside an organization.

1. An MIS provides a continuous flow of information about prices, advertising expenditures, sales, competition, and distribution expenses.

2. In the MIS, the means of *gathering* data receive less attention than do the procedures for expediting the *flow* of information.

C. Marketing research is an information-gathering process for specific situations, whereas an MIS is a system that provides continuous data input for an organization.

D. The real value of marketing research and marketing information systems lies in improving a marketer's ability to make decisions.

II. Capitalizing on new technologies for marketing research

A. **A database** is a collection of information arranged for easy access and retrieval.

1. Databases allow marketers access to an abundance of information useful for making marketing decisions.

2. Marketing researchers may use commercial databases developed by information research firms to obtain useful information for marketing decisions; examples include databases supplied by CompuServe, DIALOG, NEXIS, and Dow Jones News Retrieval.

3. Marketers may also obtain information from a single firm on household demographics, purchases, television viewing behavior, and response to promotions such as coupons and free samples; this is referred to as **single-source data.**

4. Many marketers develop their own databases, and some firms can sell their databases to other organizations.

B. Electronic bulletin boards (BBSs) are a method of communicating through computer networks; they allow users to post messages for other participants to read and discuss.

1. Many business computer networks include a BBS for employees to pose questions, discuss work issues, and air grievances.

2. Many firms are also installing BBSs accessible by customers to generate information for the marketing information system.

C. Online information systems—services such as CompuServe, America Online, and Prodigy—offer subscribers access to E-mail, discussion groups, files for downloading, chat rooms, news, databases and related research materials, and other services, such as airline reservations and the ability to subscribe to mailing lists.

D. The Internet is a network of business, university, government, and other networks (yes, literally, a network of networks).

1. The Internet permits the exchange of E-mail, global discussion through newsgroups, access to databases, and much more.

2. With the development of the World Wide Web (WWW or Web), the Internet has become a significant medium for obtaining marketing information.

3. The Internet has evolved as the most powerful communication medium, linking customers and companies around the world via computer networks.

4. Many large companies are developing internal Web pages, called "intranets," accessible only by employees needing internal data such as customer profiles and product inventory.

5. Relationship marketing can be facilitated by giving customers access to non-proprietary information through the Internet or World Wide Web, as FedEx does.

6. The U.S. Census Bureau also employs WWW pages to disseminate information that may be useful to marketing researchers.

III. The marketing research process

Marketing research is a systematic process that includes five steps.

A.   Defining and locating problems

B.   Designing the research project

C.   Collecting data

D.   Interpreting research findings

E.   Reporting research findings

IV.   Defining and locating problems

Problem definition focuses on uncovering the nature and boundaries of a negative, or positive, situation or question.

A.   The first sign of a problem is usually a deviation from some normal function, such as conflicts between or failures in attaining objectives.

B.   To pinpoint the specific causes of the problem through research, marketers must define the problem and its scope in a way that requires probing beneath the superficial symptoms. The result should be a clear definition of the problem.

C.   The research objective specifies what information is needed to solve the problem.

V.   Designing the research project

A.   Once the problem has been defined, an overall plan for obtaining the information needed to address it must be formulated.

B.   Researchers must ensure that research techniques are both reliable and valid.

1.   A research technique has **reliability** if it produces almost identical results in successive repeated trials.

2.   A technique has **validity** if it measures what it is supposed to measure, not something else.

C. The objective statement of a marketing research project should include hypotheses drawn from both previous research and expected research findings. A **hypothesis** is an informed guess or assumption about a certain problem or set of circumstances based on all the insight and knowledge available about the problem or circumstances from previous research studies and other sources.

D. The kind of hypothesis being tested determines which approach will be used for gathering general data.

   1. **Exploratory studies** are conducted when marketers need more information about a problem or want to make a tentative hypothesis more specific.

   2. **Descriptive studies** are used when marketers need to understand the characteristics of certain phenomena to solve a particular problem.

   3. In **causal studies,** it is assumed that a particular variable x causes a variable y, and the study is designed to prove or disprove that assumption.

VI. Collecting data

A. Marketing researchers make use of two types of data.

   1. **Primary data** are observed and recorded or collected directly from respondents.

   2. **Secondary data** are compiled inside or outside the organization for some purpose other than the current investigation.

B. Secondary data collection

   1. Marketers often begin the marketing research process by gathering secondary data.

   2. Internal sources of data, such as an organization's marketing database and accounting records, can contribute to research.

   3. Secondary data can also come from periodicals, government publications, unpublished sources, and online databases.

C.   Primary data collection

1.   **Survey methods** include interviews by mail, telephone, E-mail, and personal interviews.

    a.   Selection of a survey method depends on the nature of the problem, the data needed to test the hypothesis, and the resources available to the researcher, such as funding and personnel.

    b.   Gathering information through surveys is becoming more difficult because response rates are declining.

    c.   Mail surveys

        (1)   A mail survey is the least expensive survey method as long as the response rate is high enough to produce reliable results.

        (2)   Disadvantages of mail surveys include the possibility of a low response rate or misleading results if respondents differ significantly from the population being sampled.

    d.   Telephone surveys

        (1)   Advantages of telephone surveys over mail surveys include a higher rate of response, speed, and the opportunity for interviewers togain rapport with respondents and ask probing questions.

        (2)   Disadvantages include the fact that many people do not like to participate or feel indifferent toward them, they are limited to oral communication and preclude the use of visual aids or observation, and researchers must make adjustments for subjects who are not at home or who do not have telephones.

        (3)   To be effective, telephone surveys require some adjustment for groups of respondents that may be undersampled because of smaller-than-average incidence of telephone listings.

        (4)   Voice mail allows researchers to ask simple questions and obtain quick responses.

(5) Telephone surveys, like mail and personal interview surveys, are sometimes used to develop panels of respondents who can be interviewed repeatedly to measure changes in attitude or behavior.

e. E-mail surveys are evolving as an alternative as more people gain access to computer networks.

(1) The potential advantages of E-mail interviewing are quick response and lower cost than traditional mail and telephone surveys.

(2) However, limited access to respondents and unreliable response rates have kept researchers from achieving the potential of this survey method.

(3) As more households obtain computers and online access, and as negative attitudes toward telephone surveys render that technique less representative and more expensive, the integration of E-mail, fax, and voice mail functions into one PC-based system provides a promising opportunity for survey research.

f. Personal interview surveys, long favored by marketing researchers for their flexibility, permit more in-depth interviewing, may yield more information, and allow respondents to be selected more carefully.

(1) The in-home (door-to-door) interview offers an advantage when thoroughness of self-disclosure and the elimination of group influence are important.

(2) Focus-group interviewing permits observation of group interaction when members are exposed to an idea or concept.

(3) Most personal interviews today are shopping mall intercept interviews, whereby a percentage of persons passing by certain "intercept" points in a mall are interviewed.

(a) Advantages of mall interviewing include the opportunity to recognize and react to respondents' nonverbal indications of confusion; the ability to observe respondents' reactions to prototypes and other visual materials; the ability to deal with complex situations such as taste tests; and lower costs and greater control.

       (b) On-site computer interviewing allows respondents to complete a self-administered questionnaire displayed on a computer.

2.   Questionnaire construction

    a. Questions must be designed to elicit information that meets the study's data requirements, and they must be clear, easy to understand, and directed toward a specific objective.

    b. Questions can be of three kinds:

        (1) Open-ended

        (2) Dichotomous

        (3) Multiple choice

3.   Sampling

    a. Because the time and the resources available for research are limited, it is almost impossible to investigate all members of a **population,** or "universe"—all the elements, units, or individuals of interest to researchers.

    b. By systematically choosing a **sample**—a limited number of units to represent the characteristics of a total population—marketers can project the reactions of a total market or market segment.

    c. The objective of **sampling** in marketing research is to select representative units from a total population.

    d. Sampling techniques

(1) In **random sampling,** all the units in a population have an equal chance of appearing in the sample.

(2) In **stratified sampling,** a population is divided into groups according to a common characteristic or attribute, and then a probability sample is conducted within each group.

(3) **Area sampling,** a variation of stratified sampling, involves selecting a probability sample of geographic areas, and then selecting units or individuals within the selected geographic areas for the sample.

(4) **Quota sampling** is judgmental because the final choice of respondents is left to the interviewers.

4. When using **observation methods,** researchers record respondents' overt behavior, taking note of physical conditions and events.

a. Observation methods may be combined with interviews.

b. Data gathered through observation can be biased if the respondents are aware of the observation process.

c. Observation is straightforward and avoids the problem of motivating respondents to state their true feelings or opinions; however, observation tends to be descriptive and may not provide insight into causal relationships.

VII. Interpreting research findings

A. Interpretation of research findings is easier if marketers plan their data analysis methods early in the research process and allow for continual evaluation of the data during the entire collection period.

B. The first step is often tabulating the data.

C. Next, researchers conduct **statistical interpretation,** which focuses on what is typical or what deviates from the average.

D.   If the results of a study are valid, the decision maker should take action; however, if a question has been incorrectly worded, the results should be ignored.

VIII.   Reporting research findings

A.   The marketer must take a clear, objective look at the findings to see how well the gathered facts answer the research question or support or negate the hypotheses posed in the beginning.

B.   The report presenting the results is usually a formal, written document.

C.   When marketers have a firm grasp of research methods and procedures, they can better integrate reported findings and personal experience.

D.   A major problem comes from bias and distortion because the researcher wants to obtain favorable results.

E.   Marketers who cannot understand basic statistical assumptions and data gathering procedures may misuse research findings.

IX.   The importance of ethical marketing research

A.   Professional standards in marketing research are necessary because of the ethical and legal issues that develop in gathering data.

B.   The ethical and legal considerations of some aspects of marketing research, such as telephone and Internet privacy, are taking shape slowly.

C.   Ethical conflict typically occurs because the parties involved in the marketing research process often have different objectives. Without clear understanding and agreement, including mutual adoption of standards, ethical conflict will lead to mistrust and questionable research results.

CLASS EXERCISES, DEBATE ISSUE, AND CHAPTER QUIZ

On the following pages, you will find two class exercises, a debate issue, and a chapter quiz. These are formatted in large-size type so that you can use them as class handouts or for making transparencies. Below are the authors' comments on the class exercises, the debate topic for this chapter, and the answers to the chapter quiz.

Class Exercise 1: The objective of this class exercise is to apply the marketing research process to solving a marketing problem.

Question 1. The answers to this question will depend on how the students view the opportunity on your campus. Typical problem statements might include "We don't know if a sizable, profitable market exists for Fluff-and-Fold" or "We don't know which dorms at what times offer good opportunities for our service." You might suggest that *focus groups* could help define the problem more clearly.

Question 2. Most students will take the example and adapt it. However, you might push them further by asking, "Can you be any more specific about the target market? For instance, do you expect more underclassmen will use the service? More males or females?" Other typical hypotheses might involve service expectations (one-day pick-up and delivery) and daily operation issues (primary demand on weekends versus weekdays).

Question 3. This may be a good time to explain how a focus group can help resolve or clarify research problems. You may even want to set up a focus group discussion in class. After students have developed a few open-ended questions (for example, "How much would you be willing to pay for Fluff-and-Fold service?"), you might want to allow time for students to gather from one another information related to the questions. You might also point out that inexpensive data collection such as focus groups or polling customers can ensure better marketing decisions.

Question 4. Observation, combined with interviews, may be an efficient way to determine what times students will need the service. However, observation alone will not assess true feelings or opinions.

In part (a), perhaps the best way to select a sample is through the use of stratified sampling, especially if demand is likely to vary by classification (freshmen, etc.). The student directory should provide this information. However, quota sampling, which is nonprobabilistic, may suffice for exploratory research.

In part (b), mail surveys may be the cheapest (because of campus mail) and may be suitable to the short surveys most students will develop. However, response rate may be low. Phone surveys might increase the response rate, but finding students at home may be problematic. Personal interviews conducted at central meeting points on campus might help overcome refusals but might also introduce interviewer and sample bias.

In part (c), you may want to illustrate the problems associated with double-barreled, leading, nonmutually exclusive, and exhaustive questions, among others. You might even have students collect data by using these questions.

Class Exercise 2: This exercise is designed to prompt students to think about how to solve data collection problems. Students should discuss the merits of alternative data collection methods as they solve each problem. Obviously, each problem can be solved by more than one collection method. The students should decide which data collection procedure is *best* for each situation and be able to defend their choices. Possible answers:

1. Telephone interviews or possibly focus-group interviews
2. Mall intercept interviews
3. Telephone interviews
4. This information can be obtained most easily in a census report. However, if census information is too dated to be useful, the next best source might be the U.S. Department of

Housing. Overall, this type of data is usually available in secondary form from government or industry sources.

5. A mail survey of Sears, Roebuck's charge customers

Debate Issue: Does marketing research (surveys, telephone interviewing) invade a respondent's privacy?

Chapter Quiz: Answers to multiple-choice questions are

1.	b	3.	b
2.	c	4.	c

CLASS EXERCISE 1

YOU ARE CONSIDERING OPENING A NEW "FLUFF & FOLD" LAUNDRY PICK-UP, CLEANING, AND DELIVERY SERVICE FOR STUDENTS. YOU ARE UNCERTAIN WHETHER SUFFICIENT DEMAND EXISTS, AND YOU HAVE QUESTIONS ABOUT WHEN STUDENTS WILL NEED YOUR SERVICE MOST AND WHAT LEVEL OF SERVICE THEY WILL REQUIRE. YOU REALIZE THAT MARKETING RESEARCH CAN HELP SOLVE YOUR INFORMATION NEEDS. YOU MUST NOW DECIDE HOW TO BEST ANSWER THESE QUESTIONS.

1. Define the problem.

2. Design the research project.

3. After consulting any secondary data available, you decide to conduct an *exploratory study* with students in your classes. Develop open-ended questions to ask other students that will provide information regarding your hypotheses.

4. Having gained some insight into the problem, you are now ready to conduct a *descriptive study.* You decide to conduct a survey to further test your refined hypotheses. However, you have several decisions to make regarding this study.

   a. What type of sampling approach (random, stratified, area, quota) will you use and why?

   b. What survey method (mail, telephone, personal interview) will you use and why?

   c. How will you construct the questionnaire? Develop open-ended, dichotomous, or multiple-choice questions that will test your hypotheses. Remember to remain impartial and inoffensive.

CLASS EXERCISE 2

WHAT IS THE MOST APPROPRIATE DATA COLLECTION METHOD FOR EACH OF THE FOLLOWING RESEARCH QUESTIONS?

1. How do consumers in South Dakota feel about Christmas shopping?

2. How do JC Penney customers feel about Penney's customer service?

3. What is the opinion of U.S. consumers toward a Chrysler advertisement that questions the quality of Japanese cars?

4. How many people nationwide currently live in apartments?

5. How do Sears, Roebuck's charge customers view that company's new pricing policy?

DEBATE ISSUE

DOES MARKETING RESEARCH (SURVEYS, TELEPHONE INTERVIEWING) INVADE A RESPONDENT'S PRIVACY?

YES

- A great deal of marketing research asks questions that are too personal

- Some marketing research, especially telephone and personal interviews, is nothing more than a disguise for sales presentations

- The information obtained from marketing research is often used to develop mailing lists that are used to sell consumers products that they may not want

- Sometimes the true nature of the research is disguised to get consumers to respond

NO

- The right to privacy deals with an individual's ability to restrict personal information

- Individual respondents must decide for themselves how much of their personal lives they will share with others

- What constitutes private information and public information is ultimately up to the individual respondent

- As long as the researcher obtains the consent of the respondent, the research does not invade the respondent's privacy

CHAPTER QUIZ

1. Marketing information systems and marketing research have changed rapidly because customers and companies around the world have been linked by
   a. the computer.
   b. the Internet.
   c. the Interactive Network.
   d. electronic online services.
   e. telecommunications.

2. Dan was given the task of conducting a research project for his firm, and proceeds with the following steps. He asks questions to determine the research topic, conducts a telephone survey, writes a report describing the survey results and gives that report to his boss. Which step of the marketing research process has Dan omitted?
   a. Collecting data
   b. Defining and locating problems
   c. Interpreting research
   d. Designing the research project
   e. Reporting research findings

3. A study that is valid and reliable
   a. is called a marketing research study.
   b. measures what it is supposed to measure and produces almost identical results every time.
   c. is expensive to implement and complete.
   d. measures subtle differences in the population being studied.
   e. is difficult to produce without expert researchers.

4. Chelsea, Ltd., a retail clothing store chain, wants to use observation methods to gather information about shopping behavior. Which of the following should Chelsea know about observation methods of data collection?
   a. Observation uses secondary sources of data.
   b. Observation depends on mall interviews.
   c. Observation can tell Chelsea what is being done, but not why.
   d. Observation focuses on open-ended questions.
   e. Observation works best for telephone surveys.

ANSWERS TO DISCUSSION AND REVIEW QUESTIONS

1. What is a marketing information system and what should it provide? How is the value of a marketing information system measured?

    A marketing information system is a framework that provides a continuous flow of information by gathering and managing data from sources inside and outside an organization. A marketing information system provides information about prices, advertising expenditures, sales, competition, consumer behavior, and distribution expenses.

    The value of a marketing information system is measured by the improvements it makes in the marketer's ability to make decisions.

2. Where are data for a marketing information system obtained? Give examples of internal and external data.

    Data for the marketing information system can come from internal sources or external sources. Internal sources might be the company's financial and operational records, or customer contacts. External sources might be government publications, trade associations, marketing research companies, and business magazines. Examples of internal data would be advertising expenses, sales figures, and customer complaints. Examples of external data would be census information, consumer trends, or competitors' prices.

3. Define database. What is its purpose and what does it include?

    A database is a collection of information arranged for easy access and retrieval, usually stored in a computer. A database provides a marketer an expeditious way to retrieve information to be used in making marketing decisions. The database might include information from newspaper articles, company news releases, government reports, and economic data.

4. How can marketers use online services and the Internet to obtain information for decision making?

    Through online services and the Internet, marketers can access databases, send E-mail, and create and peruse World Wide Web pages. They can communicate with other marketers and customers as well.

5. Name the five steps in the marketing research process.

    - Defining and locating the problem
    - Designing the research project
    - Collecting data
    - Interpreting research findings
    - Reporting research findings

6. What is the difference between defining a research problem and developing a hypothesis?

    A research problem is the question that is to be answered. A hypothesis is an assumption or supposition about the solution.

7. Describe the different types of studies in marketing research and indicate when they should be used.

    - *Exploratory.* Used when marketers need more information about a problem or want to make a tentative hypothesis more specific.
    - *Descriptive.* Used when marketers need to understand the characteristics of certain phenomena.
    - *Causal.* Used when information is needed on causal relationships and more complex hypotheses are required. For example, does *x* cause *y*?

8. What are the major limitations of using secondary data to solve marketing problems?

    Major limitations in using secondary data concern accuracy and availability.

9. In what situation would it be best to use random sampling? quota sampling? stratified or area sampling?

    Random sampling works best when it is easy to number or identify all units in a population and give each unit a known or equal opportunity of appearing in the sample.

    Quota sampling differs from other sampling techniques because it is judgmental. It is usually limited to two or three demographic variables and to some personal or behavioral characteristics such as wearing eyeglasses or owning a cat or dog. Quota samples are often used in exploratory studies that are not projected to the total population.

    Stratified or area sampling is a form of probability sampling that is useful when units such as individuals are not available on a list but geographic areas such as blocks or census tracts can be used. Then researchers use a random selection process to pick out units or individuals to be sampled.

10. Make some suggestions for ways to encourage respondents to cooperate in mail surveys.

    An incentive such as a premium can be offered to those who participate. A well-written letter stating the importance of the survey can be helpful. Sampling from a frame or population that is interested in the topic under investigation will increase response. Using a short, easy-to-fill-out questionnaire is also helpful.

11. If a survey of all homes with listed telephone numbers is conducted, what sampling design should be used?

    A simple random sample of phone numbers would be acceptable in this case.

12. Describe some marketing problems that could be solved through information gained from observation.

    Personal observation can be used to solve problems such as shoplifting, spoilage, and breakage. Also, demographic characteristics can be observed and classified. One could observe and plot license plates on a map to obtain a geographic market profile. Other examples in which observation is important are television ratings (such as Nielsen's) and traffic flow.

COMMENTS ON THE CASES

Case 5.1   Marketing Research for V-8 Vegetable Juice, Maidenform, and AT&T 800 Service Advertising

The objective of this case is to show students how several firms have used marketing research to better tailor their marketing mixes, particularly the promotion variable, to meet the needs and wants of their specific target markets. Marketing research helped Campbell refine its advertising messages to make them simple, easy to understand, and call for action to purchase the product. Maidenform modified its promotion strategy after marketing research indicated that the firm's assumptions about its target customers' perceptions of its products were incorrect. Marketing research helped AT&T understand how its customers felt about toll-free 800 numbers, and it modified its promotion message accordingly.

Question 1 asks how marketing research helped increase the sales of V-8. Campbell used marketing research to decide how to remind consumers to purchase V-8, using in-depth consumer interviews to understand customers' perceptions and feelings about the product. Based on this research, Campbell developed a test TV commercial emphasizing the overall healthiness of V-8, the healthiness of V-8 relative to other products, the nutritional content of the product, and the vegetable goodness of the product. Subsequent testing revealed that the four-pronged approach was confusing, so Campbell simplified the promotional message to stress taste and health benefits.

The second question asks what surprising discovery research revealed to Maidenform and why the firm had overlooked this information. Marketing research revealed that there were far more lapsed purchasers of Maidenform than current users, that many women had heard of Maidenform but had never purchased a Maidenform product, and that many women did not associate the name with contemporary lifestyles. Marketing managers had made incorrect assumptions about their target market; lack of research led them to misunderstand their changing market.

The final question asks students to assess the value of AT&T's personal interviews with business executives in formulating its new advertising message. The personal interviews helped AT&T gain a better understanding of its customers' motives and buying behavior. When research indicated that reliability was a major factor in customers' choice of an 800 service, AT&T created promotional messages emphasizing the reliability of its 800 services. Testing of the advertisements confirmed the marketer's belief that reliability was the key factor. The result of the changes AT&T made to its marketing strategy was that it retained most of its 800 users even in the face of intensifying competition and changes in the law.

Video Information

Video Title: Goodbye Guesswork
Location: Tape 1, Segment 5
Length: 27:02
Video Overview: This video illustrates the use of marketing research to learn about target markets in order to develop an effective advertising campaign. Three minicases are presented to provide examples of how marketing research improved advertising for these products. Case 1 is Campbell's V-8 vegetable juice. Research indicated that advertising needed to focus more on the product as healthy while conveying a simpler, clearer message about V-8. Research on Maidenform (case 2) found that many women had heard of the product but had never purchased the brand and had little perception of it. The company developed a new creative strategy to

promote its products. AT&T (case 3) developed a strategic understanding of the 800 number concept from personal interviews with business customers. The research was used to gain insights into how AT&T should respond to expected tactics from competition. Research determined that reliability was the most important message to convey to customers.

Multiple-Choice Questions About the Video

c 1. When Campbell initially conducted marketing research to develop a strategy to counter declining sales of its V-8 product, marketing managers discovered that
    a. consumers prefer soft drinks.
    b. consumers don't like V-8.
    c. consumers needed to be reminded to purchase V-8 because of competition.
    d. the marketing strategy for V-8 was acceptable.

b 2. A major error by Maidenform marketing managers was their assumption that
    a. mall-intercept interviews are useless.
    b. Maidenform was a highly regarded brand name with fabulous, obvious attributes.
    c. women perceived the Maidenform name negatively.
    d. women associated the Maidenform name with a contemporary lifestyle.

d 3. When AT&T conducted marketing research about customers' perceptions of 800 services and their needs, marketing researchers learned that _____ was most important.
    a. transferability
    b. price
    c. validity
    d. reliability

Case 5.2   Chrysler Reinvents Itself Through Primary Research

The overall objective of this case is to illustrate how the turnaround at the Chrysler Corporation was achieved through reliance on marketing research practices, most notably the collection and analysis of primary data. The highly successful reorganization and reorientation effort, which culminated in 1992 with the introduction of the widely acclaimed Dodge Intrepid, Chrysler Concorde, and Eagle Vision, can be attributed to the company's shift to a focus on the needs of its customers. These needs—that is, what customers wanted in a new vehicle—were determined via the collection of actual customer data by a variety of means. To complement these research-driven, customer-oriented efforts, Chrysler also revamped its dealership sales incentive programs around customer satisfaction rather than merely sales volume.

    Question 1 asks the student to list the methods of primary research employed by Chrysler in the case. These include (1) customer focus group interview sessions (which led to the creation of innovative worker "platform teams" around customer-defined product category groups), (2) trade show participation in which the company actively solicited information from consumers, (3) careful analysis of customer letters, (4) the purchase, dissection, and analysis of competitive products, (5) the solicitation of information from parts and equipment suppliers, and, after actual product introduction, (6) the loaning of six thousand vehicles to local business leaders in twenty-five cities to get user opinions regarding vehicle performance.

    The second question asks the reader to discuss the survey methods successfully used by Chrysler. Here, given the company's heavy reliance on focus group interviews, the most obvious response is "personal interviews." In Chrysler's case, these methods worked well because, despite their relatively high cost, they allowed the company to explore in depth customer attitudes, product-usage behaviors, lifestyles, needs, and desires. With such information, the company was able to better develop products that satisfied actual customer needs.

Question 3 asks the student to discuss how primary research methods have been integrated into the new corporate atmosphere at Chrysler. The most obvious example involves the creation of marketing/new-product development groups as "platform teams" structured around actual customer needs as determined through focus group interviews. Also, in more general terms, the "new" Chrysler realizes that the best way to get close to customers is to actually get their input in regard to product design and performance.

6 CONSUMER BUYING BEHAVIOR

TEACHING RESOURCES QUICK REFERENCE GUIDE

Resource	Location
Purpose and Perspective	IRM, p. 111
Guide for Using Color Transparencies	IRM, p. 111
Lecture Outline	IRM, p. 111
Class Exercises, Debate Issue, and Chapter Quiz	IRM, p. 122
Class Exercise 1	IRM, p. 124
Class Exercise 2	IRM, p. 125
Debate Issue: Is it appropriate for marketers to specifically target children in their advertisements?	IRM, p. 126
Chapter Quiz	IRM, p. 127
Answers to Discussion and Review Questions	IRM, p. 128
Comments on the Cases	IRM, p. 131
Case 6.1	IRM, p. 131
Video	Tape 1, Segment 6
Video Information	IRM, p. 131
Multiple-Choice Questions About the Video	IRM, p. 132
Case 6.2	IRM, p. 132
Transparency Acetates	Transparency package
Examination Questions: Essay	TB, p. 99
Examination Questions: Multiple-Choice	TB, p. 100
Examination Questions: True-False	TB, p. 117
Author-Selected Multiple-Choice Test Items	TB, p. 446

PURPOSE AND PERSPECTIVE

We begin this chapter by defining *consumer market* and *consumer buying behavior*. We examine how the customer's level of involvement affects the type of problem solving employed and then discuss the types of consumer problem-solving processes, including routinized response behavior, limited problem solving, extended problem solving, and impulse buying. We then analyze the major stages of the consumer buying decision process: problem recognition, information search, evaluation of alternatives, purchase, and postpurchase evaluation. Next, we discuss in detail the personal, psychological, and social influences on the consumer decision-making process. Personal factors include demographic, lifestyle, and situational factors. The primary psychological influences on consumer behavior are perception, motives, learning, attitudes, and personality and self-concept. Forces that other people exert on buying behavior are called social factors. Social factors include the influence of roles and families, reference groups and opinion leaders, social class, and culture and subculture.

GUIDE FOR USING COLOR TRANSPARENCIES

There are two groups of color transparencies. The transparencies identified by a double number are the same as the figures in the text. The transparencies labeled with a number and a letter are illustrations that do not appear in the text, but they can be used as additional examples of concepts discussed.

Figure 6.2	Consumer buying decision process and possible influences on the process
Figure 6.5	Escher drawing: Are the horsemen riding to the left or to the right?
Figure 6A	Chapter 6 outline
Figure 6B	Types of consumer problem solving
Figure 6C	Levels of involvement and consumer problem-solving types
Figure 6D	How do reference groups affect purchase decisions?
Figure 6E	Cultural changes bring changes in milk consumption.
Figure 6F	Advertisement aimed at stimulating problem recognition
Figure 6G	Age, a demographics factor, affects customers' buying behavior.
Figure 6H	Expression of a lifestyle dimension
Figure 6I	Communication aimed at changing parents' attitudes about measuring children's temperatures.

LECTURE OUTLINE

I.   Consumer markets and consumer buying behavior

    A.   A **market** is an aggregate of individuals and/or organizations that have needs for products in a product class and have the ability, willingness, and authority to purchase these products.

    B.   A **consumer market** consists of purchasers and household members who intend to benefit from or consume the purchased product and who do not buy products for the main purpose of making profits.

    C.   **Consumer buying behavior** is the decision processes and acts of ultimate consumers involved in buying and using products.

II.   Types of consumer problem-solving processes

    A.   **Level of involvement** is an individual's intensity of interest in a product and the importance he or she places on a product .

        1.   Levels of involvement are classified as low, high, enduring, and situational.

        2.   A consumer's level of involvement is a major determinant of the type of problem-solving process employed.

    B.   **Routinized response behavior** is the type of consumer problem-solving process that requires very little search-and-decision effort; it is used for products that are low priced and bought frequently.

    C.   **Limited problem solving** is a type of consumer problem-solving process that buyers engage in when they purchase products occasionally and need to acquire information about unfamiliar brands in a familiar product category; it requires a moderate amount of time for information gathering and deliberation.

    D.   **Extended problem solving** is the consumer problem-solving process employed when unfamiliar, expensive, or infrequently bought products (such as homes, automobiles, and furniture) are purchased; buyers use many criteria for evaluation brands and spend more time searching for information and deciding on the purchase.

    E.   **Impulse buying,** in contrast, is an unplanned buying behavior involving a powerful urge to buy something immediately.

III.   Consumer buying decision process

    A.   The **consumer buying decision** process is a five-stage purchase decision process that includes problem recognition, information search, evaluation of alternative, purchase, and postpurchase evaluation.

        1.   The actual act of purchase is only one stage in the process and is a later stage.

        2.   Not all decision processes, once initiated, lead to an ultimate purchase; the individual may terminate the process at any stage.

3.   Not all consumer buying decisions include all five stages.

B.   Problem recognition

1.   This stage occurs when a buyer becomes aware of a difference between a desired state and an actual condition.

2.   The individual may be unaware of the problem or need.

3.   Marketers may use sales personnel, advertising, and packaging to trigger recognition of needs or problems.

4.   Recognition speed can be slow or fast.

C.   Information search

1.   This stage begins after the consumer becomes aware of the problem or need.

2.   The search for information about products will help resolve the problem or satisfy the need.

3.   There are two aspects to an information search: internal search and external search.

   a.   In the **internal search,** buyers first search their memories for information about products that might solve the problem.

   b.   In the **external search,** buyers seek information from outside sources.

      (1)   An external search occurs if buyers cannot retrieve enough information from their memories for a decision.

      (2)   Buyers seek information from friends, relatives, or public sources such as government reports or publications.

4.   Wearout results when consumers begin to pay less attention to repetitious commercials, for example, that supply external information.

5. When successful, an information search yields an **evoked set** of products or a group of brands that the buyer views as possible alternatives.

D. Evaluation of alternatives

1. In this stage, the consumer establishes a set of **evaluative criteria** against which to compare the characteristics of the products in the evoked set.

2. The consumer rates and eventually ranks the brands in the evoked set by using the criteria and their relative importance.

3. Marketers can influence consumers' evaluation by **framing** the alternatives—that is, by the manner in which they describe the alternative and attributes.

E. Purchase

1. The consumer selects the product or brand to be purchased.

2. Product availability, seller choice, and terms of sale may influence the final product selection.

3. The actual purchase is made unless the process has been terminated earlier.

F. Postpurchase evaluation

1. The buyer begins to evaluate the product after purchase, based on many of the criteria used in the evaluation of alternatives stage.

2. **Cognitive dissonance** is a buyer's doubts shortly after a purchase about whether it was the right decision.

IV. Personal factors influencing the buying decision process

A **personal factor** is one that is unique to a particular individual.

A. **Demographic factors** are individual characteristics such as age, sex, race, ethnicity, income, family life cycle, and occupation; demographic factors

1. Can influence who is involved in family decision making.

2. Can influence one's behavior.

3. Can influence the extent to which a person uses products in a specific product category.

4. Can lead to variations in buying behavior.

B. **Lifestyles** are individual patterns of living.

1. Lifestyles are expressed through activities, interests, and opinions.

2. Lifestyles affect product needs, brand preferences, media behavior, and how and where shopping occurs.

C. **Situational factors** are influences resulting from circumstances, time and location that affect the consumer buying decision process.

1. Can influence a consumer's actions in any stage of the buying process.

2. Can be divided into five categories: physical surroundings, social surroundings, time perspective, task definition, and antecedent states.

3. Include store atmosphere, product scarcity, weather, and momentary moods.

V. Psychological factors influencing the buying decision process

Psychological factors are those that operate within individuals and in part determine their general behavior, thus influencing their behavior as consumers.

A. Perception

Perception is the process of selecting, organizing, and interpreting information inputs to produce meaning.

1. An individual selects some pieces of information and ignores others.

a. **Information inputs** are the sensations received through the sense organs.

b. **Selective exposure** is the process of selecting some inputs to be exposed to our awareness while ignoring others.

    (1) An input is more likely to reach a person's awareness if it relates to an anticipated event.

    (2) A person is likely to let an input reach consciousness if the information helps satisfy current needs.

c. The selective nature of perception also results in selective distortion and selective retention.

    (1) **Selective distortion** is an individual's changing or twisting of received information when it is inconsistent with personal feelings or beliefs.

    (2) **Selective retention** is remembering information inputs that support personal feelings and beliefs and forgetting inputs that do not.

2. The second step in the perceptual process is to organize the information that does reach awareness, integrating the new information with what is already known.

3. Third, an individual's interpretation of information inputs, necessary to reduce mental confusion, is the assignment of meaning to what has been organized; interpretation is usually based on what is expected or familiar.

4. Marketers try to influence consumers' perceptions but sometimes fail.

a. A consumer's perceptual process may operate such that a seller's information never reaches the consumer's awareness.

b. A buyer may receive a seller's information and perceive it differently from the way the marketer intended.

    c.   When buyers perceive information inputs that are inconsistent with prior beliefs, they are likely to forget the information quickly.

B.   Motives

A **motive** is an internal energizing force that directs a person's behavior toward satisfying needs or achieving goals.

   1.   A buyer's actions at any time are affected not by just one motive but by a set of motives, some stronger than others.

   2.   Motives affect the direction and intensity of behavior.

   3.   **Patronage motives** are motives that influence where a person purchases products on a regular basis.

   4.   Marketers can analyze the major motives that influence whether consumers buy products.

       a.   Researchers can study motives through interviews.

          (1)   **Depth interviews** are lengthy personal interviews in which the interviewer poses nondirected questions and then probes the responses.

          (2)   In **group interviews,** the interviewer generates discussion on one or more topics among the six to twelve people in the group.

       b.   Researchers can study motives through projective techniques.

          (1)   **Projective techniques** are research methods in which subjects are asked to perform specific tasks for particular purposes while in fact they are being evaluated for other purposes.

          (2)   Examples include word-association tests and sentence-completion tests.

C.   Learning

Learning refers to changes in an individual's behavior that is caused by information and experience.

1. The learning process is strongly influenced by the consequences of an individual's behavior; behaviors with satisfying results tend to be repeated.

2. Inexperienced buyers may use different types of information than experienced shoppers familiar with the product and purchase situation.

3. Consumers learn about products directly by experiencing them or indirectly through information from salespersons, friends, relatives, and advertisements.

D. Attitudes

An **attitude** is an individual's enduring evaluation, feelings, and behavioral tendencies toward an object or idea.

1. Attitudes are learned through experience and interaction with other people.

2. Attitudes remain generally stable, but they can be changed.

3. An attitude consists of three major components: cognitive, affective, and behavioral.

4. Consumers' attitudes toward a firm and its products strongly influence the success or failure of the organization's marketing strategy.

5. Marketers use several approaches to measure consumer attitudes toward dimensions such as prices, package designs, brand names, advertisements, salespeople, repair services, store locations, features of existing or proposed products, and social responsibility activities.

    a. Direct questioning of consumers

    b. Projective techniques

    c. **Attitude scales,** which are means of measuring consumers' attitudes by gauging the intensity of individuals' reactions to adjectives, phrases, or sentences about an object.

6. Changing people's negative attitudes is a long, expensive, and difficult task and may require extensive promotional efforts.

E. Personality and self-concept

   1. **Personality** is a set of internal traits and distinct behavioral tendencies that result in consistent patterns of behavior.

      a. The uniqueness of one's personality arises from hereditary background and personal experiences.

      b. When advertisements focus on certain types of personalities, the advertiser uses personality characteristics that are valued positively.

   2. **Self-concept** is a person's own view or perception of himself or herself.

      a. Buyers purchase products that reflect and enhance their self-concept.

      b. A person's self-concept may influence whether he or she buys a product in a specific product category and may have an impact on brand selection.

VI. Social factors influencing the buying decision process

Social factors are the forces that other people exert on buying behavior.

A. Roles and family influences

   1. A **role** is a set of actions and activities that an individual in a particular position is supposed to perform, based on the expectations of the individual and surrounding persons.

   2. Each individual has many roles.

   3. An individual's roles, particularly family roles, influence to some extent that person's behavior as a buyer.

4. **Consumer socialization** is the process through which a person acquires the knowledge and skills to function as a consumer.

B. Reference groups and opinion leaders

1. A **reference group** is a group—large or small—that positively or negatively affects a person's values, attitudes, or behaviors.

2. Families, friends, church groups, and professional groups are examples of reference groups.

3. There are three major types of reference group: membership, aspirational, and dissociative.

4. A reference group is an individual's point of comparison and a source of information.

5. How much a reference group influences a purchasing decision depends on the individual's susceptibility to reference-group influence and strength of involvement with the group.

6. Reference-group influence may affect the product decision, the brand decision, or both.

7. A marketer sometimes uses reference-group influence in advertisements to promote the message that people in a specific group buy the product and are highly satisfied with it.

8. In most reference groups, one or more members stand out as opinion leaders; an **opinion leader** is a reference group member who provides information about a specific sphere that interests reference group participants.

C. Social classes

A **social class** is an open group of individuals with similar social rank.

1. The criteria used to group people into classes vary from one society to another.

2. In our society we group according to many factors, including occupation, education, income, wealth, race, ethnic group, and possessions; analyses of social class in the United States divide people into three to seven categories.

3. To some degree, individuals within social classes develop common patterns of behavior.

4. Because social class influences so many aspects of a person's life, it also affects

   a. Buying decisions

   b. Spending, saving, and credit practices

   c. Type, quality, and quantity of products

   d. Shopping patterns and stores patronized

D. Culture and subcultures

1. **Culture** is the accumulation of values, knowledge, beliefs, customs, objects, and concepts that a society uses to cope with its environments; culture includes

   a. Tangible items such as food, clothing, furniture, buildings, and tools

   b. Intangible concepts such as education, welfare, and laws

   c. The values and a broad range of behaviors accepted by a specific society

2. The concepts, values, and behavior that make up a culture are learned and passed from one generation to the next.

3. Because cultural influences affect the ways people buy and use products, culture affects the development, promotion, distribution, and pricing of products.

4. International marketers must take into account tremendous global cultural differences.

   a. People in other regions of the world have different attitudes, values, and needs.

   b. International marketers must adapt to different methods of doing business and must develop different types of marketing mixes.

5. **Subcultures** are groups of individuals who have similar values and behavior patterns but differ from people in other groups of the same culture.

   a. Subcultural boundaries are usually based on geographic designations and demographic factors.

   b. Marketers recognize that the growth in the number of U.S. subcultures has resulted in considerable variation in consumer buying behavior.

CLASS EXERCISES, DEBATE ISSUE, AND CHAPTER QUIZ

On the following pages, you will find two class exercises, a debate issue, and a chapter quiz. These are formatted in large-size type so that you can use them as class handouts or for making transparencies. Below are the authors' comments on the class exercises, the debate topic for this chapter, and the answers to the chapter quiz.

Class Exercise 1: The objective of this class exercise is to help students understand how social factors influence their consumption behaviors.

Question 1. As fraternity or sorority members, students may be influenced to stay out late for social reasons, which may conflict with their roles as student, employee, or church member. The demands of a person's many roles may be inconsistent and confusing. Some married students may describe joint decision-making situations and the influence of children. Other likely responses will relate to clothing, restaurant choice, and food or beverage consumption.

Question 2. You may also want to ask "When ordering at a restaurant, do you find that people often order the same thing?" After one person (opinion leader) has decided to order something, others may order the same thing ("I'll take what he/she ordered"). Reference groups clearly affect the choice of clothing and patronage at retail outlets. Some students may indicate that there are places they will not go because of the presence of negative reference groups.

Question 3. The cars that students drive may reflect either their present social status or their desired social status. Social class may also affect what beer, wine, or other beverages students drink. You may also want to ask "How does social class affect where you shop?"

Question 4. Ask students the following: "Have any of you been in other cultures where you saw people doing things that would never be accepted in America?" If you have international students in class, ask them what they find peculiar about the American culture. Discussion may be geared toward views of time and women.

Question 5. Students may be able to identify certain types of food (catfish in the South), clothing (surf wear in the West), vehicles (pickups in the Midwest and Southwest), or accessories (handguns in the East) that are associated with subcultures.

Question 6. Some possible examples include the following:

- *Promotion:* Show upper-class individuals in luxury car ads.
- *Product:* Design products (cars) that meet joint needs of family.
- *Price:* Offer price discounts to students with limited income.
- *Distribution:* Allocate more pickups to Midwest and Southwest.

Class Exercise 2: For this exercise, each of the stages of the consumer buying decision process should be thoroughly discussed and made available to the students before they answer these questions. There are many possible answers for each question. For example, in question 1, the recent college graduate reading *Consumer Reports* to compare automobile ratings could be in any of four stages:

- *Problem Recognition:* The consumer suddenly sees his or her present car as inferior compared to the ratings of other cars in the magazine.
- *Information Search:* The consumer has decided to buy a new car and is seeking all possible information to make an intelligent choice.
- *Evaluation of Alternatives:* The consumer has narrowed choices to a few car brands and is comparing them by using the ratings in the magazine.
- *Postpurchase Evaluation:* The consumer has just purchased a new car and is comparing its ratings to those of some other cars.

Some possible answers to the remaining questions include the following:

2. Problem recognition
3. Postpurchase evaluation
4. Purchase
5. Evaluation of alternatives
6. Problem recognition
7. Problem recognition/postpurchase evaluation
8. It depends. If using the sample leads the person to question the quality of his or her current brand of laundry detergent, then the person is most likely in the problem recognition stage. If the person is looking for another brand, it could be information search. Finally, if a person is trying to decide on a new brand of detergent, the stage is most likely evaluation of alternatives.

Debate Issue: Is it appropriate for marketers to specifically target children in their advertisements?

Chapter Quiz: Answers to multiple-choice questions are

1.	b	3.	b
2.	a	4.	a

CLASS EXERCISE 1

IMAGINE THAT YOU ARE GOING OUT TONIGHT. WHICH OF THE FOLLOWING SOCIAL FACTORS WILL INFLUENCE WHAT YOU WEAR, WHERE YOU GO, WHAT YOU DO, AND WHAT YOU WILL BUY OR CONSUME?

1. Your role as a student, family member, employee, church member, or fraternity or sorority member?

2. Identification with a positive reference group? Disassociation from a negative reference group?

3. Membership within a particular social class? Aspirations to be in a different social class?

4. Cultural values that accept or reject certain types of behavior? Gender roles: expectations of how men and women should act?

5. Membership in a subculture based on geography, age, or ethnic background?

6. Knowing how these factors affect your consumption behavior, how can marketers adjust their marketing mixes to meet your needs?

CLASS EXERCISE 2

IN WHICH STAGE OF THE CONSUMER BUYING DECISION PROCESS ARE EACH OF THE FOLLOWING PEOPLE?

1. A recent college graduate reads *Consumer Reports* to compare automobile ratings.

2. On the first day of class, a student finds out that a scientific calculator is needed for the course, but she doesn't own one.

3. After purchasing an evening gown, a woman decides that it is not quite appropriate for her special occasion.

4. A car buyer gets a loan to purchase a new car.

5. A teenager compares numerous compact disc players and narrows the choice down to two players.

6. While on the way to work, a person's automobile stalls and will not start again.

7. At an open-house party, a guest realizes that the host already owns the gift he plans to give.

8. A person receives a sample package of laundry detergent in the mail and uses it to wash a load of clothes.

DEBATE ISSUE

IS IT APPROPRIATE FOR MARKETERS TO SPECIFICALLY TARGET CHILDREN IN THEIR ADVERTISEMENTS?

YES

- Children possess billions of dollars in discretionary income and they spend almost all of it

- Children buy regularly, are responsive to peer pressure, and are heavily influenced by the hours of television advertising they watch each week

- Researchers estimate that children directly influence billions of dollars in adult purchases each year

- An astute marketer recognizes the importance of children and acts accordingly by targeting them in their advertisements

NO

- Recent research has suggested that advertising can have detrimental effects on children

- By portraying an altered sense of reality, advertising can make children more prone to need gratification

- Advertising makes children more susceptible to the effects of peer pressure

- Although children do influence adult purchases, purchase decisions are made by adults

- Marketers should target advertising toward parents, not young, impressionable children

CHAPTER QUIZ

1. Which consumer problem-solving process will probably be used in purchasing toothpaste?
   a. Extended problem solving
   b. Routinized response behavior
   c. Intensive problem solving
   d. Limited problem solving
   e. Perceptual scanning

2. As Stanley is shopping for groceries, he notices a product on the shelf and remembers that he is about to run out of it at home. In terms of the consumer buying decision process, Stanley just experienced
   a. problem recognition.
   b. purchase.
   c. postpurchase evaluation.
   d. information search.
   e. evaluation of alternatives.

3. Word-association tests and sentence-completion tests are examples of
   a. motivational specification techniques.
   b. projective techniques.
   c. group interviews.
   d. depth interviews.
   e. patronage clarification techniques.

4. Marketers who attempt to use reference-group influence in advertisements are most likely to succeed when the message indicates that
   a. people in a specific group buy the product and are highly satisfied by it.
   b. reference groups should be of little concern to the consumer.
   c. reference groups are "in" and everyone should belong to at least one.
   d. all products and brands are influenced by reference groups.
   e. people in a specific group have tried the product and dislike it.

ANSWERS TO DISCUSSION AND REVIEW QUESTIONS

1. How does a consumer's level of involvement affect his or her choice of a problem-solving process?

   The level of involvement determines the importance and intensity of interest in a product in a particular situation. A buyer's level of involvement determines why he or she is motivated to seek information about certain products and brands but virtually ignore others. The extensiveness of the buying decision process varies greatly with the consumer's level of involvement. Routinized response behavior is likely to be used for low involvement products. High involvement products frequently require limited or extended decision making.

2. Name the types of consumer problem-solving processes. List some products that you have bought using each type. Have you ever bought a product on impulse? Describe the circumstances.

   The types of consumer problem-solving processes include routinized response behavior, limited problem solving, and extended problem solving.

   Routinized response behavior occurs when people buy frequently purchased, low-cost items that need very little search-and-decision effort. Examples of routinely purchased products include milk, bread, packaged food products, and laundry services.

   Limited problem solving occurs when consumers buy products only occasionally and when they need to obtain information about an unfamiliar brand in a familiar product category. This type of decision making requires a moderate amount of time for information gathering and deliberation. Purchase decisions might include a new pest control company, a mechanic to install a muffler, or a new "healthy" cereal.

   Extended problem solving comes into play when a purchase involves unfamiliar, expensive, or infrequently bought products, such as cars, homes, or stereo systems.

   Most students probably will indicate that they have bought a product on impulse. Typical impulse products include candy, a compact disc, or a pair of jeans.

3. What are the major stages in the consumer buying decision process? Are all these stages used in all consumer purchase decisions? Why or why not?

   The major stages in the consumer buying decision process are problem recognition, information search, evaluation of alternatives, purchase, and postpurchase evaluation.

   Not all consumer decisions include all five stages. The individual may terminate the process at any stage, and not all decisions lead to a purchase. Sometimes individuals engaged in routine behavior eliminate some stages, while those engaged in extended problem solving usually go through all five stages.

4. What personal factors affect the consumer buying decision process? How do they affect the process?

   A personal factor is one that is unique to a particular person. Personal factors include demographic factors, lifestyles, and situational factors. Because of such characteristics as age, sex, or unique external circumstances, personal factors directly affect the purchase.

5. What are the five categories of situational factors that influence consumer buying behavior? Explain how each of these factors influences buyers' decisions.

Situational factors can be classified into five categories: physical surroundings, social surroundings, time perspective, task definition, and antecedent states. Physical surroundings, such as location, store atmosphere, aromas, sounds, and lighting can influence buying behavior by creating a setting that is more or less conducive to making purchases. Social surroundings influence buying behavior when a customer feels pressured to behave in a particular way depending on who is in the location where the decision is being made. The amount of time required to become knowledgeable about a product, to search for it, and to buy it all influence the buying decision process. The time of day, week, or year, such as seasons or holidays, also affect the buying decision process. Task definition requires the consumer to decide what is to be accomplished by purchasing a particular product. What the product's task is will directly influence which product to choose. Antecedent states, such as momentary moods or conditions, can influence a person's ability and desire to seek information, evaluate alternatives, or make purchases.

6. What is selective exposure? Why do people engage in it?

Selective exposure relates to receiving information and then screening it internally with only partial awareness of all of the cues received. We select some inputs and ignore many others because we cannot be conscious of all inputs at one time. An input is more likely to reach awareness if it relates to an antecedent event or to an unmet need. Thus you are more likely to notice a TV advertisement for McDonald's when you are hungry and wondering where to go for lunch.

7. How do marketers attempt to shape consumers' learning?

Marketers attempt to influence consumers' learning by getting them to experience products, such as through the use of free samples. Indirect experiences of products through product information from salespeople and advertisements are other avenues by which marketers attempt to influence purchases through the learning process.

8. Why are marketers concerned about consumer attitudes?

Consumer attitudes toward a firm and its products strongly influence the success or failure of the organization's marketing program. Negative attitudes among consumers may result in loss of sales, whereas strong positive attitudes may increase sales. Because attitudes play such an important role in determining consumer behavior, marketers seek to measure consumer attitudes toward prices, packaging, branding, advertising, salespeople, services, images, and features of new products. If a significant number of consumers hold negative attitudes toward a firm or its products, the marketing program should be changed to make attitudes more favorable.

9. How do roles and family influences affect a person's buying behavior?

A role consists of a set of actions and activities expected of a person holding a certain position within a group, organization, or institution. All individuals assume several roles depending on the number of positions they occupy. These roles might affect whether, what, where, when, or why a person buys. The roles of other persons also influence purchasing behavior. Marketers want to know not only who does the actual buying but also who influences the purchase decisions.

10. Describe reference groups. How do they influence buying behavior? Name some of your own reference groups.

A reference group is a group an individual identifies so strongly with that he or she takes on many of the values, attitudes, or behaviors of group members. The group can be large or small, and usually an individual will have several reference groups. The effect of reference groups on purchasing behavior depends on the type of product, the person's susceptibility to the group's influence, and the strength of the person's involvement with the group.

11. How does an opinion leader influence the buying decision process of reference group members?

An opinion leader is viewed as being well informed about a sphere of interest and as willing and able to share information with followers. An opinion leader is viewed as having values and attitudes that are similar to followers and thus can be trusted by the followers.

12. In what ways does social class affect a person's purchase decisions?

Individuals within social classes often exhibit common consumer behavior patterns; they share similar attitudes, values, and possessions. Social class influences a person's attitudes, perceptions, motives, personality, and learning process, all of which affect purchasing decisions. Marketers thus need to be aware of the impact of social class on consumer behavior.

13. What is culture? How does it affect a person's buying behavior?

Culture is everything in our surroundings that is made by human beings, including tangible and intangible items. Culture influences what we wear and eat, where we live, and how we live. It affects the ways we buy and use products and influences the satisfaction we receive from products. Because culture determines the ways products are purchased and used, it affects the entire marketing mix.

14. Describe the subcultures to which you belong. Identify buying behavior that is unique to one of your subcultures.

This question lets students probe the unique subculture to which they belong. Students should be encouraged to relate the particular features of their subculture to their purchasing behavior.

COMMENTS ON THE CASES

Case 6.1   In Japan, an End to All Work and No Play

This case focuses on Japanese consumers. The overall objective of this case is to demonstrate to students how major lifestyle and cultural changes lead to changes in buying behavior. The instructor may want to ask students to find additional examples of changes in the Japanese culture and resulting effects on consumption behavior prior to analyzing this case.

The initial question asks students to consider the ways in which the changing worlds of Japanese women have influenced their buying behavior. Because a significant proportion of Japanese women have entered the work force, they are more affluent and have higher status in their culture. Due to increased affluence and changes in values, Japanese women show a strong interest in high-quality brands. The Japanese have increased their expenditures for concerts, plays, travel, sports, fashion, entertainment, audiovisual equipment, and leisure products in general.

Question 2 asks which buyer behavior would be of greatest concern to marketers that wanted to increase the use of leisure facilities in Japan. In the broad sense marketers of leisure products should be concerned about culture and subcultural changes as well as changes in roles of both men and women. Marketers also would be interested in lifestyle changes, that is, changes in people's activities, interests, and beliefs. At the individual levels marketers should be concerned about how to change Japanese consumers' attitudes to make them more favorable toward leisure activities.

The third question asks students to compare high involvement and low involvement products for U.S. and Japanese consumers. Because the attitudes, values, and lifestyles of Japanese and American consumers are not the same, it is unlikely that the involvement levels with products are similar. While there is variation among individuals as to what is a high or low involvement product within a culture, there are even greater differences among people between cultures regarding this issue. Thus, all types of decision-making processes used for a particular product in Japan are likely to vary considerably from those used for that product in the United States.

Video Information

Video Title: The Newest Wave of Japanese Consumers
Location: Tape 1, Segment 6
Length: 25:12
Video Overview: Japanese consumers are changing. In Japan, production and work have traditionally taken precedence over spending and leisure time. Today, increasingly affluent Japanese with more free time than ever before are becoming active and experienced consumers. Women, young people, and urban senior citizens are three of the fastest growing consumer groups in Japan today. To accommodate the changing tastes and habits of customers, retailing, both upscale and value-oriented, is expanding. In addition, the number and variety of leisure activities and services are also growing.

Multiple-Choice Questions About the Video

d   1. According to the video, the three leading groups of Japanese consumers are
    a. senior citizens, young men, and upper middle class professionals.
    b. upper middle class professionals, women, and teenagers.
    c. single women, college students, and upper middle class professionals.
    d. women, urban senior citizens, and young people.
    e. middle-aged professionals, urban senior citizens, and young women.

a   2. "Second wave babyboomers" spend most of their money on
    a. audiovisual equipment, fashion, sports, and entertainment.
    b. movies, rock concerts, sports, and exercise equipment.
    c. fashion, music tapes and compact discs, and books.
    d. audiovisual equipment, fashion, and movies.
    e. books, music tapes and compact discs, and sports.

b   3. Changes in consumer trends are reflected in Japan's retailing environment. Some of these changes include an increase in the number of specialty shops in areas frequented by young people, an increase in the number of large shopping centers, and
    a. an increase in the number of women's specialty boutiques.
    b. efforts to make department stores more pleasant places in which to shop.
    c. an increase in the number of catalog and other nonstore sales.
    d. an extension of store hours to better serve customer needs.
    e. an increase in the number of retail outlets targeting senior citizens.

e   4. According to the video, the rise in the status of Japanese women can be attributed primarily to
    a. growing Western influence.
    b. rising salaries in traditionally female occupations.
    c. the growing number of women willing to enter traditionally male dominated professions.
    d. the growing number of single-parent households.
    e. passage of the Equal Employment Law of 1986.

b   5. In Japan, women make up _____ percent of the work force.
    a. 15
    b. 40
    c. 10
    d. 25
    e. over 50

Case 6.2   Watercress and Duck Gizzard Soup: Mmm, Mmm, Good

This case deals with the behavioral dimensions of introducing a traditional well-known domestic brand into global markets. The purpose of this case is to demonstrate to students how a successful U.S. company must consider buyer behavior issues in introducing products in international markets. It should make students aware that cultural differences can become major marketing considerations.

The first question asks students what fundamental behavioral issue is of greatest importance to marketers at Campbell's Soup when introducing canned soup to mainland

Chinese. Soup has been a major component of the Chinese diet for centuries. However, packaged soup is new to the mainland Chinese. The most fundamental behavioral question is whether or not mainland Chinese will buy packaged soup given that they have prepared their own soup for years.

The second question asks which type of behavioral variables most likely influence preference for soup flavors. Certainly, culture and subculture play a major role in food flavor preferences. Perceptions and attitudes associated with major components of soup influence how customers react to flavors. For example, most U.S. consumers would not favor soup containing snake meat.

Question 3 asks, with respect to the purchase of soup, if the type of consumer problem-solving process varies from one culture to another. In cultures where the concept of buying packaged soup is new, as in mainland China, consumers might engage in limited problem solving for the purchase of soup. However, in most countries where packaged soup is a well-accepted concept, routinized response behavior is likely to be the most common method across cultures for the purchase of soup.

7 ORGANIZATIONAL MARKETS AND BUYING BEHAVIOR

TEACHING RESOURCES QUICK REFERENCE GUIDE

Resource	Location
Purpose and Perspective	IRM, p. 135
Guide for Using Color Transparencies	IRM, p. 135
Lecture Outline	IRM, p. 135
Class Exercises, Debate Issue, and Chapter Quiz	IRM, p. 146
Class Exercise 1	IRM, p. 148
Class Exercise 2	IRM, p. 149
Debate Issue: Because reciprocity can promote favoritism and sometimes threaten competitive activity, should it be completely banned?	IRM, p. 150
Chapter Quiz	IRM, p. 151
Answers to Discussion and Review Questions	IRM, p. 152
Comments on the Cases	IRM, p. 154
Case 7.1	IRM, p. 154
Video	Tape 2, Segment 7
Video Information	IRM, p. 154
Multiple-Choice Questions About the Video	IRM, p. 155
Case 7.2	IRM, p. 156
Transparency Acetates	Transparency package
Examination Questions: Essay	TB, p. 123
Examination Questions: Multiple-Choice	TB, p. 124
Examination Questions: True-False	TB, p. 138
Author-Selected Multiple-Choice Test Items	TB, p. 446

PURPOSE AND PERSPECTIVE

In this chapter, we first describe the major types of organizational markets, including producer, reseller, government, and institutional markets. Next, we look at several dimensions of organizational buying, such as the characteristics of organizational transactions, the attributes of organizational buyers and some of their primary concerns in making purchase decisions, organizational buying methods, and the major types of organizational purchases. Then we discuss characteristics of demand for industrial products. We also cover the organizational buying decision process. In this section, we analyze the major participants in organizational buying decision processes through an examination of the buying center. Then we examine the stages of the organizational buying decision process and the factors that affect that process. Finally, we discuss the Standard Industrial Classification (SIC) system and its usefulness to organizational marketers in planning marketing strategies.

GUIDE FOR USING COLOR TRANSPARENCIES

There are two groups of color transparencies. The transparencies identified by a double number are the same as the figures in the text. The transparencies labeled with a number and a letter are illustrations that do not appear in the text, but they can be used as additional examples of concepts discussed.

Figure 7.5	Organizational buying decision process and factors that may influence it
Figure 7A	Chapter 7 outline
Figure 7B	Types of organizational markets
Figure 7C	Types of organizational purchases
Figure 7D	Hoeschst Celanese is a marketer that focuses its efforts on producer markets.
Figure 7E	Using speed as a major competitive product attribute, Minolta aims at multiple organizational markets.
Figure 7F	This Panasonic advertisement is aimed at stimulating organizational buyers to recognize that a problem exists, the first stage of the organizational buying decision process.

LECTURE OUTLINE

I.　Organizational markets

An **organizational,** or **industrial, market** consists of individuals or groups that purchase a specific kind of product for resale, direct use in producing other products, or use in general daily operations.

A.　Producer markets

1. **Producer markets** are individuals and organizations that purchase products for the purpose of making a profit by using them to produce other products or by using them in their operations.

2. A wide range of industries make up the producer markets, including agriculture, forestry, fisheries, mining, construction, transportation, communication, and utilities.

B. Reseller markets

1. **Reseller markets** consist of intermediaries that buy finished goods and resell them to make profits.

2. Resellers do not change the physical characteristics of the product except for occasional minor alterations.

3. Wholesalers purchase products for resale to retailers, to other wholesalers, and to producers, the government, and institutions.

4. Retailers purchase products for resale to final consumers.

5. When making purchase decisions, resellers consider several factors.

   a. Level of demand to determine quantity and price levels

   b. Amount of space required for the product

   c. Suppliers' ability to provide adequate quantities when and where wanted

   d. Ease of placing orders

   e. Availability of technical assistance and training programs

   f. Whether the product complements or competes with products the firm currently handles

C. Government markets

    1. **Government markets** include federal, state, county, and local governments that buy goods and services to support their internal operations and to provide products to their constituencies.

    2. The government spends billions of dollars on a wide range of goods and services.

    3. The types and quantities of products that government markets purchase reflect societal demands on government agencies.

    4. Many firms do not try to sell to the government because of the complex buying procedures necessitated by the government's public accountability.

    5. Government purchases are made through bids or negotiated contracts.

    6. Government markets, although complex, can be very lucrative.

D. Institutional markets

    1. **Institutional markets** are organizations with charitable, educational, community, or other nonbusiness goals; examples include churches, colleges, hospitals, and civic clubs.

    2. Because institutions have different goals and fewer resources than other markets, marketers may use special marketing activities to serve this segment.

II. Dimensions of organizational buying

A. Characteristics of organizational transactions

    1. Organizational transactions tend to be much larger than consumer transactions.

      a.   Suppliers often must sell their products in large quantities to make profits.

      b.   Cultivating customers who place orders may be an unprofitable use of resources.

  2.   Organizational sales generally are negotiated less frequently than consumer sales.

      a.   Some items, such as capital equipment, are used for a number of years.

      b.   Other industrial products, such as raw materials, are used continuously in production, and may need frequent replacing.

      c.   Some products are on contract for a given number of years.

  3.   Long negotiating periods requiring considerable marketing time and selling effort may be necessary to finalize purchase decisions.

      a.   Orders are frequently large and expensive.

      b.   Purchased items may be custom-built.

      c.   Several people or departments within the purchasing organization may be involved in the transaction.

  4.   **Reciprocity,** whereby two organizations agree to buy from each other, is used to a limited extent in cases where it is not prohibited by the Federal Trade Commission.

B.   Attributes of organizational buyers

  1.   Organizational buyers differ from consumer buyers because they are better informed about the products they purchase.

  2.   They seek additional information before buying to be sure products meet the organization's needs.

3. They seek psychological satisfaction from organizational advancement and financial rewards.

4. Agents who consistently exhibit rational organizational buying behavior are likely to attain personal goals because they are performing their jobs in ways that help their firms achieve organizational objectives.

C. Primary concerns of organizational buyers

1. Price is very important to organizational customers.

a. Price influences operating cost and costs of goods sold, which in turn affect the selling price and profit margin, and ultimately the organization's ability to compete.

b. A buyer of capital equipment views price as the amount of investment necessary to obtain a certain level of return or savings.

2. Level of product quality is also of concern.

a. A product must meet specifications so that its use will not result in malfunction for the ultimate consumer.

b. Obtaining a product that meets but does not exceed *specifications* is important to avoid excess costs.

2. Organization buyers value service.

a. The services that suppliers provide may be the primary element that differentiates one product offering from another.

b. Often the mix of services is likely to be the major avenue through which an organizational market can gain a competitive advantage.

c. Typical services desired by consumers:

(1) Market information

(2) Inventory maintenance

(3) On-time delivery

(4) Repair services

d. Communication channels that allow customers to ask questions, complain, submit orders, and trace shipments are an indispensable service component.

e. **Reverse marketing** is a process through which an organizational buyer develops a relationship with a supplier that shapes the products, services, operations, and capabilities of the supplier to better satisfy the buyer's needs.

D. Methods of organizational buying

1. Description is commonly used when the products are standardized according to certain characteristics and are normally graded using such standards.

2. Inspection is necessary when items have unique characteristics and vary in condition.

3. Sampling occurs when one item is taken from the lot, evaluated, and assumed to represent the characteristics of the entire lot.

4. Negotiation of contracts may be executed through several means.

a. Sellers submit bids, and the buyer negotiates terms with those holding the most attractive bids.

b. Buyers may be able to provide only a general description of the desired item.

c. Contracts may specify a base price and provisions for payment of additional costs and fees.

E. Types of organizational purchases

1. In a **new-task purchase,** the organization makes an initial purchase of an item to be used to perform a new job or to solve a new problem.

2. In a **modified rebuy,** a new-task purchase is changed on subsequent orders or when the requirements of a straight-rebuy purchase are modified.

3. A **straight rebuy purchase** is a routine purchase of the same products under approximately the same terms by an organizational buyer.

F. Demand for industrial products

Several characteristics distinguish industrial demand from consumer demand. The demand for different types of industrial products also varies.

1. Derived demand

    a. **Derived demand** is the demand for industrial products derived from the demand for consumer products.

    b. Organizational customers purchase products to be used directly or indirectly in the production of goods and services to satisfy consumers' needs.

    c. When consumer demand for a product changes, a wave is set in motion that affects demand for all firms involved in the production of that product.

2. Inelastic demand

    a. For many industrial products, **inelastic demand** is a demand that is not significantly altered by a price increase or decrease.

    b. When a sizable price increase for a component part represents a large proportion of the product's cost, demand may become more elastic; the price increase of the component part causes the price at the consumer level to rise sharply.

       c.   The inelasticity characteristic applies to market or industry demand for the industrial product but not to the demand for an individual supplier.

  3.   Joint demand

       a.   **Joint demand** involves two or more items used in combination to produce a product.

       b.   With joint demand, shortages of one item may jeopardize sales of all the jointly demanded products.

  4.   Fluctuating demand

       a.   The demand for industrial products may fluctuate enormously because it is derived from consumer demand.

       b.   When an organizational marketer's customers change their inventory policies, the firm may notice substantial changes in demand.

       c.   Significant price increases or decreases can lead to surprising changes in demand in the short run.

III.   Organizational buying decisions

Organizational buying behavior refers to the purchase behavior of producers, government units, institutions, and resellers.

A.   The buying center

  1.   The **buying center** is a group of people within an organization (including users, influencers, buyers, deciders, and gatekeepers) who are involved in making organizational purchase decisions.

       a.   Users are organizational participants who actually use the product being acquired.

b.   Influencers often are technical personnel who help develop the specifications and evaluate alternative products for possible use.

c.   Buyers select the suppliers and negotiate the terms of the purchases.

d.   Deciders actually choose the products and vendors.

e.   Gatekeepers control the flow of information to and among persons who
occupy the other roles in the buying center.

2.   The number and structure of an organization's buying centers are affected by
the organization's size, its market position, the volume and types of products
purchased, and the firm's managerial philosophy.

B.   Stages of the organizational buying decision process

1.   First stage: One or more individuals in the organization recognize that a
problem or need exists.

2.   Second stage: The development of product specifications requires that
organizational participants assess the problem or need and determine what
will be necessary to resolve or satisfy it.

3.   Third stage: This stage involves searching for possible products to solve the
problem and locating suppliers of such products.

a.   Some organizations engage in **value analysis,** an evaluation of each
component of a potential purchase: quality, design, materials, and so on.

b.   Some vendors can be eliminated because they cannot supply needed
quantities or because they have poor delivery or service records.

4.   Fourth stage: The products on the list generated in the search stage are
evaluated to determine which ones (if any) meet the product specifications;
firms evaluate suppliers as well, using **vendor analysis.**

a.   **Sole sourcing** is a situation in which an organization decides to use
only one supplier.

b.   Multiple sourcing is the selection and use of several vendors.

5.   Fifth stage: The product and the supplier are chosen, and the product is ordered.

6.   Sixth stage: The product's and supplier's performances are evaluated.

C.   Influences on organizational buying

1.   Environmental factors are forces such as competitive and economic factors, legal and regulatory factors, technological changes, and sociocultural factors.

2.   Organizational factors include the buying organization's objectives, purchasing policies, and resources as well as the size and composition of the buying center.

3.   Interpersonal factors refer to the relationships among the people in the buying center.

4.   Individual factors are the personal characteristics of individuals in the buying center, such as age, personality, educational level, income, and position in the organization.

IV.   Using Standard Industrial Classification (SIC) codes

A.   Identifying potential organizational customers

1.   Much information about organizational customers is based on the federal government's Standard Industrial Classification (SIC) system.

a.   The **Standard Industrial Classification (SIC)** is the federal government system for classifying selected economic characteristics of industrial, commercial, financial, and service organizations.

b.   The **Census of Manufacturers** further subdivides manufacturers and provides more detailed information about product classes and product items.

c. The SIC system is a ready-made tool that allows organizational marketers to divide business-to-business firms into market segments based mainly on the types of products manufactured or handled.

2. In conjunction with the SIC system, organizational marketers can use **input-output data,** which tells what types of industries purchase the products of a particular industry.

    a. A major source of input-output data is the *Survey of Current Business,* published by the Office of Business Economics, U.S. Department of Commerce.

    b. After finding out which industries purchase the major portion of an industry's output, a marketer must determine the SIC numbers for those industries.

    c. Next, the industrial marketers can ascertain the number of firms that are potential buyers nationally, by state, and by county.

3. Locating organizational customers

    a. A firm may identify and locate potential customers by using state or commercial industrial directories, such as *Standard and Poor's Register.*

        (1) These publications contain information such as name, SIC number, address, telephone number, and annual sales.

        (2) Marketers develop lists of potential customers by city, county, and state.

    b. A firm may also employ the services of a commercial data company, such as Dun & Bradstreet.

        (1) This type of service is more expedient, but more expensive as well.

        (2) A commercial data company can provide, for each company on an SIC list, name, location, sales volume, number of employees, types of products handled, names of executive officers, and other pertinent information.

B. Estimating purchase potential

In addition to deriving a list of potential customers, marketers must determine which ones to pursue, a decision usually based on estimated purchase potential.

1. An organizational marketer must first find a relationship between the size of potential customers' purchases and a variable available in SIC data, such as number of employees.

2. Establishing a relationship will probably involve a survey of a random sample of potential customers.

3. After estimating purchase sizes of potential customer segments, the marketer selects the customers to include in the target market.

4. There are several limitations to the use of SIC data to estimate purchase potential.

   a. A few industries do not have SIC designations.

   b. Double counting may occur when products are shipped between two establishments within the same firm.

   c. Some business data may be understated as a result of Census Bureau limitations.

   d. Lag time between collection of data and availability of information is usually significant.

CLASS EXERCISES, DEBATE ISSUE, AND CHAPTER QUIZ

On the following pages, you will find two class exercises, a debate issue, and a chapter quiz. These are formatted in large-size type so that you can use them as class handouts or for making transparencies. Below are the authors' comments on the class exercises, the debate topic for this chapter, and the answers to the chapter quiz.

Class Exercise 1: The objective of this class exercise is to show students that organizational buying behavior has many similarities to consumer buying behavior.

Question 1. If you ask enough students, you will eventually have all these criteria listed. Although organizations are more likely to develop formal written specifications about these concerns, final consumers also find these to be important concerns for nearly any high-involvement product category.

Question 2. Examples might include the following:

- Description: mail-order products (clothing, personal computers)
- Inspection: car, furniture, house, or any used item
- Sampling: grocery food items, mail samples, ice cream
- Negotiation: car, house, or any used item

Question 3. The situations roughly match as follows:

- New-task purchase: Extended decision making
- Modified rebuy: Limited decision making
- Straight rebuy: Routine decision making

Question 4. You might want to ask "Who plays what roles in the family when a Super Nintendo video game machine is purchased?" Children (and perhaps their parents) are the users and influencers. The mother may be the decider and the father the buyer. Older children may be the gatekeepers who control the flow of information to the parents. Grandparents might also be the buyers, while the parents may play the roles of deciders and gatekeepers. The point is that, to be successful, marketers must target the entire buying center (or family). Focusing an entire sales presentation on the user may not be effective if the decider is not persuaded.

Class Exercise 2: The purpose of this exercise is to allow students to demonstrate their understanding of different purchasing methods. Each product is typically purchased by the following methods:

1. Grain — **sampling**
2. Used vehicles — **inspection**
3. Office space — **inspection, negotiation**
4. Oranges — **description, sampling**
5. Bulldozer — **negotiation**
6. Computer and printer — **inspection**
7. Office furniture — **inspection**
8. Pens and pencils — **description**
9. Eggs — **description**
10. Assembly line equipment — **inspection, negotiation**

Debate Issue: Because reciprocity can promote favoritism and sometimes threaten competitive activity, should it be completely banned?

Chapter Quiz: Answers to multiple-choice questions are

1.	a	3.	a
2.	c	4.	b

CLASS EXERCISE 1

ALTHOUGH ORGANIZATIONAL BUYING BEHAVIOR MAY SEEM QUITE DIFFERENT FROM YOUR BUYING BEHAVIOR, THE TWO ARE MORE SIMILAR THAN YOU THINK. AS YOU ANSWER THE FOLLOWING QUESTIONS, THINK ABOUT HOW SIMILAR OR DISSIMILAR THE ORGANIZATIONAL BUYING PROCESS IS TO YOUR OWN.

1. When you buy a new shirt, compact disc, stereo, television, or car, which of the following are the most important to you?
   - Quality
   - Product information
   - Product availability
   - On-time delivery
   - Service
   - Repair services
   - Credit
   - Price

2. Give examples of products that you buy (or may buy) based on
   - Description
   - Sampling
   - Inspection
   - Negotiation

3. Match the organizational purchase situation with the consumer goods buying situation. How or why are they related?
   - New-task purchase
   - Modified rebuy
   - Straight rebuy
   - Limited decision making
   - Routine decision making
   - Extended decision making

4. How is the buying center of an organization similar to the following purchasing roles that family members play?
   - Users
   - Buyers
   - Gatekeepers
   - Influencers
   - Deciders

CLASS EXERCISE 2

ORGANIZATIONAL PURCHASES CAN BE MADE BY SEVERAL METHODS, INCLUDING DESCRIPTION, INSPECTION, SAMPLING, AND NEGOTIATION. WHICH METHOD IS MOST OFTEN USED FOR EACH OF THE FOLLOWING PRODUCTS?

1. Grain
2. Used vehicles
3. Office space
4. Oranges
5. Bulldozer
6. Computer and printer
7. Office furniture
8. Pens and pencils
9. Eggs
10. Assembly line equipment

DEBATE ISSUE

BECAUSE RECIPROCITY CAN PROMOTE FAVORITISM AND SOMETIMES THREATEN COMPETITIVE ACTIVITY, SHOULD IT BE COMPLETELY BANNED?

YES

- The Federal Trade Commission and the Justice Department monitor reciprocal agreements and stop those that are anticompetitive

- Reciprocal agreements influence purchasing agents to deal only with certain suppliers

- Reciprocal agreements can lower the morale of purchasing agents and lead to less than optimal purchases

NO

- Reciprocal agreements help lower the purchasing costs of both parties

- Reciprocity occurs most often among small businesses and is thus less likely to threaten competition

- Reciprocal agreements are good means of ensuring high-quality service and an adequate supply of needed materials

- Reciprocity is a means of establishing long-term relationships built on trust and cooperation

CHAPTER QUIZ

1. Tools, Inc., buys hammers, bolts, and other hardware items and
    sells them to hardware stores at a price that includes a profit for
    Tools, Inc. The company would be part of what type of
    organizational market?
    a. Reseller   b. Producer
    c. Consumer   d. Government
    e. Supply

2. Which method of organizational buying is most likely to be used
    when the products being purchased are standardized on certain
    characteristics and usually are graded by such standards?
    a. Homogeneous selection   b. Inspection
    c. Description   d. Sampling
    e. Negotiation

3. Barry Gluckman of WP International, a major marketer of word-
    processing systems, calls the secretary of Renee Doucette,
    director of purchasing for MMK, Inc., to set up an appointment to
    discuss an upcoming purchase of word-processing equipment.
    The secretary plays a key role as a(n) _____ in this
    purchase decision.
    a. gatekeeper   b. buyer
    c. decider   d. buying center captain
    e. order giver

4. To estimate the purchase potential of organizational customers, a
    marketer must find a relationship between the
    a. number of business establishments and the potential amount
        of customers' purchases.
    b. size of potential customers' purchases and a variable
        available in SIC data.
    c. value of industry shipments with the number of potential
        customers.
    d. number of potential customers available and a variable
        available in SIC data.
    e. size of potential customers' purchases and the value of
        industrial products.

ANSWERS TO DISCUSSION AND REVIEW QUESTIONS

1. Identify, describe, and give examples of the four major types of organizational markets.

   The four major types of organizational markets are producer markets, reseller markets, government markets, and institutional markets.

   The producer market consists of individuals and business organizations that purchase products to make a profit by using them to produce other products or by using them in their operations. Farmers are a producer market because they purchase farm machinery, fertilizer, seed, and livestock to carry out their tasks.

   The reseller market consists of intermediaries, such as wholesalers and retailers, that buy finished goods and resell them to make a profit. Sears, Roebuck is such a reseller.

   Government markets consist of federal, state, county, and local governments that, taken together, spend billions of dollars annually for goods and services to support their internal operations and their constituencies.

   Institutional markets are organizations that seek to achieve goals other than normal business goals such as profit, market share, or return on investment.

2. Regarding purchasing behavior, why are organizational buyers generally considered more rational than ultimate consumers?

   Organizational buyers usually seek and obtain more information about the product before purchasing than do ultimate consumers. They may give special attention to information about the product's functional features, specifications, and technical attributes. Most organizational purchasers seek advancement within the organization and greater financial and psychological rewards. By performing the purchasing function in a way that helps their firms achieve organizational objectives, organizational buyers can further the attainment of their personal goals.

3. What are the primary concerns of organizational buyers?

   Many of the primary considerations of organizational buyers when making purchasing decisions fall into the category of quality level, service, or price. Quality level is maintained by purchasing a product that meets a set of delineated characteristics called specifications. Products that exceed specifications may cost more without providing offsetting benefits.

   Suppliers' service to organizational customers influences these customers' costs, sales, and profits. Some of the most commonly desired services include market information, maintaining an inventory, on-time delivery, repair services and replacement parts. Open communication channels are also important.

   Price influences operating costs and costs of goods sold and thus affects the selling price and profit margin.

4. List several characteristics that differentiate organizational transactions from consumer ones.

   Organizational transactions differ from consumer ones in several ways. Orders tend to be larger, there are long negotiation periods, reciprocity sometimes plays a role in the process, and organizational buyers tend to be more informed about the products they purchase.

5. What are the commonly used methods of organizational buying?

   Most organizational buyers use one or more of the following methods: description, inspection, sampling, and negotiation. Products that are commonly standardized and normally graded using such standards may be purchased on the basis of a description of their desired characteristics. Certain products, especially those that are large, expensive, and have unique characteristics, will probably have to be inspected by the purchasers before a decision is reached. When buying decisions are based on sampling, the purchaser assumes that the sample product taken from the lot is representative of the entire lot. Negotiated contracts occur when sellers submit bids and the buyer discusses terms with those who submit the most attractive bids.

6. Why do buyers involved in a straight rebuy purchase require less information than those making a new-task purchase?

   The straight rebuy purchase is a routine procedure. The specifications and terms have been worked out, and all the major problems should have been resolved. Conversely, in a new-task purchase an organization makes an initial purchase of an item that requires the development of product specifications, vendor specifications, and procedures for future purchases.

7. How does industrial demand differ from consumer demand?

   Industrial demand differs from consumer demand in that industrial demand is (a) derived, (b) inelastic, (c) joint, or (d) fluctuating.

8. What are the major components of an organization's buying center?

   The major components or roles of a buying center are users, influencers, buyers, deciders, and gatekeepers. One person may perform several of these roles.

9. Identify the stages of the organizational buying decision process. How is this decision process used when making straight rebuys?

   The stages of the organizational buying decision process are (1) recognizing the problem, (2) establishing product specifications to solve the problem, (3) searching for products and suppliers, (4) evaluating products with respect to specifications, (5) selecting and ordering the most appropriate product, and (6) evaluating product and supplier performance.
   This decision process is not used for routine, straight rebuy purchases.

10. How do environmental, organizational, interpersonal, and individual factors affect organizational purchases?

    The level of influence of these factors varies with the buying situation, the type of product being purchased, and whether the purchase is new-task, modified rebuy, or straight rebuy.

11. What function does the SIC system help marketers perform?

    The SIC system is a ready-made tool that lets an organizational marketer divide firms into market segments based mainly on the types of product produced and/or handled. Major groups are then divided into subgroups, and each subgroup is separated into detailed industry categories. Large amounts of data for each SIC category are available through various government and nongovernment publications.

12. List some sources that an organizational marketer can use to locate the names and addresses of potential organizational customers.

One approach to identifying and locating potential customers is to use state organizational directories or commercial organizational directories such as *Standard and Poor's Register* and Dun & Bradstreet's *Market Identifiers* or *Million Dollar Directory*. Lists of potential customers can be developed for cities, counties, and states by using these sources.

Use of the services of a commercial data company, such as Dun & Bradstreet, is more expedient but also more expensive. This service can provide the organizational marketer with a list of firms and pertinent information about the resources of each firm.

COMMENTS ON THE CASES

Case 7.1   Intel Builds Brand Awareness from the Inside Out

This case illustrates a firm that serves organizational buyers of high-tech component parts. Some students may not be familiar with Intel. If that is so, you may wish to have them gather background information on the company prior to discussing this case.

The first question asks what types of organizational markets Intel serves. Intel serves producer markets because its electronic components are used in production of computers and other products. This organization also serves government markets in that some governments make direct purchases of microprocessors.

Question 2 asks about the characteristics of demand for Intel computer chips. Like demand for other industrial products, the demand for computer chips is derived demand. Sales of computers to consumers and to organizations drives the demand for Intel computer chips. At the industry level demand for computer chips is likely to be inelastic. However, the demand for Intel's chips would be elastic. Intel experiences demand fluctuations as the demand for computers rises and falls.

Question 3 asks to what extent it is possible for Intel to create customer loyalty toward its computer chips. Some students may argue that it is not likely that Intel can be successful in creating brand loyalty toward its computer chips because customers are not capable of understanding the technical differences among several computer chip brands. Other students may argue that while consumers do not fully understand the differences among various brands of computer chips, consumers are still likely to buy computers with chips that have familiar brand names. Brand familiarity can sometimes translate into some degree of brand loyalty.

The final question invites students to identify and evaluate other producers' attempts to stimulate customer preferences for ingredients or component parts. When discussing this question, students could identify and evaluate NutraSweet as well as several Du Pont products.

Video Information

Video Title: Intel Inside Market Development Program
Location: Tape 2, Segment 7
Length: 8:00

Video Overview: To boost brand awareness and preference for its products, Intel launched the "Intel Inside" program. In partnership with original equipment manufacturers (OEMs), the company is working to make its logo, the words *Intel Inside* surrounded by an oval that doesn't quite close, a symbol of quality and proven performance. The program was initiated in two phases. First came the Logo Usage Program, which outlines ways of using the logo in advertising and merchandising. The second phase, the Market Development Program, reimburses participants up to 50 percent of their media placement costs for advertising Intel 386 and 486 products that include the *Intel Inside* logo. Intel's president and CEO strongly believes that use of the Intel logo provides the company with an opportunity to focus customers on the Intel brand.

Multiple-Choice Questions About the Video

c   1. The Intel Inside program was initiated in two parts, the Logo Usage Program and the
       a. Business Development Campaign.
       b. Mutual Investment Program.
       c. Market Development Program.
       d. Intel Benefits Campaign.
       e. Quality Focus Program.

b   2. The Intel Inside program is a partnership between
       a. Intel Corporation and Apple Computer.
       b. Intel Corporation and original equipment manufacturers (OEMs).
       c. Intel Corporation and independent computer retailers.
       d. Intel Corporation and IBM.
       e. Intel Corporation and Digital Equipment Corporation.

c   3. Intel's first product-specific advertising campaign was designed to promote
       a. the 486 Business Workstation.
       b. the power and reliability of Intel microprocessors.
       c. the 386 SX microchip.
       d. the Pentium microprocessor.
       e. the compatibility of 486 microprocessors.

d   4. Intel reimburses manufacturers up to _____ percent of their media placement costs when they advertise 386 and 486 products and include the *Intel Inside* logo.
       a. 10
       b. 75
       c. 15
       d. 50
       e. 20

e   5. According to the video, the most important goal of the Intel Inside campaign is to
       a. provide an opportunity for Intel and OEMs to become partners.
       b. encourage computer retailers to sell Intel products.
       c. promote end user benefits.
       d. increase Intel's share of the microprocessor market.
       e. build brand awareness.

Case 7.2   WMX Technologies, Inc.: Turning Trash into Cash

The objective of this case is to provide students with the opportunity to analyze the problems faced by a large environmental services company. A number of students are likely to find this case of interest because it deals with environmental protection issues. Since the company may be unfamiliar to students, you may wish to ask students to research the company prior to the analysis of this case.

The initial question asks students to identify the types of organizational markets served by WMX. While Waste Management Incorporated serves all types of organizational markets, the types of customers mentioned in this case are primarily producer markets. Companies such as Alcoa, Boeing, Du Pont, General Electric, and General Motors make up producer markets.

Question 2 asks what types of issues or concerns are of greatest importance to WMX's customers. WMX customers are like to be concerned about reliability, dependability, and overall service quality. They are also concerned about the cost of the services provided by this organization.

The third question asks what recommendations students have for resolving WMX's problems. The recycler's problems are primarily being created by marketing environment factors such as competitive, legal, regulatory, and technological forces. Students' recommendations should focus primarily on resolving problems associated with these marketing environment forces.

8 TARGET MARKETS: SEGMENTATION AND EVALUATION

TEACHING RESOURCES QUICK REFERENCE GUIDE

Resource	Location
Purpose and Perspective	IRM, p. 158
Guide for Using Color Transparencies	IRM, p. 158
Lecture Outline	IRM, p. 158
Class Exercises, Debate Issue, and Chapter Quiz	IRM, p. 170
Class Exercise 1	IRM, p. 172
Class Exercise 2	IRM, p. 173
Debate Issue: Is lifestyle segmentation truly a viable means of segmenting a market?	IRM, p. 174
Chapter Quiz	IRM, p. 175
Answers to Discussion and Review Questions	IRM, p. 176
Comments on the Cases	IRM, p. 180
Case 8.1	IRM, p. 180
Video	Tape 2, Segment 8
Video Information	IRM, p. 181
Multiple-Choice Questions About the Video	IRM, p. 181
Case 8.2	IRM, p. 182
Transparency Acetates	Transparency package
Examination Questions: Essay	TB, p. 143
Examination Questions: Multiple-Choice	TB, p. 144
Examination Questions: True-False	TB, p. 160
Author-Selected Multiple-Choice Test Items	TB, p. 446

PURPOSE AND PERSPECTIVE

This chapter covers (1) the definition of a market, (2) how organizations identify target markets, and (3) how to estimate market potential and forecast sales. First we define a market and discuss various characteristics groups must possess to be considered a market. Then we describe in detail the five steps in the target market selection process. In discussing the process, we describe three targeting strategies: undifferentiated, concentrated, and differentiated. We examine in some detail the process of choosing segmentation variables and the types of variables that marketers use. Finally, we consider how to evaluate market potential and how to forecast sales.

GUIDE FOR USING COLOR TRANSPARENCIES

There are two groups of color transparencies. The transparencies identified by a double number are the same as the figures and tables in the text. The transparencies labeled with a number and a letter are illustrations that do not appear in the text, but they can be used as additional examples of concepts discussed.

Figure 8.1	Target market selection process
Figure 8.2a	Targeting strategies: Undifferentiated
Figure 8.2b	Targeting strategies: Concentrated
Figure 8.2c	Targeting strategies: Differentiated
Figure 8.5	Segmentation variables for consumer markets
Figure 8.8	The nine family life cycle stages as a percentage of all households for 1970 and 1990
Table 8.1	Lifestyle dimensions
Figure 8A	Chapter 8 outline
Figure 8B	The three types of targeting strategies
Figure 8C	Variables for segmenting organizational markets
Figure 8D	Distribution of age in the U.S. in 1995 and percent change 1990–1995
Figure 8E	Percent change in state populations 1990–1995
Figure 8F	Distribution of household income
Figure 8G	Types of sales forecasts
Figure 8H	The fundamental concept behind Lifetime television is segmentation based on gender. Lifetime is television for women.

LECTURE OUTLINE

I.   What are markets?

A **market** is an aggregate of people who have needs for products in a product class and who have the ability, willingness, and authority to purchase such products.

II.   Target market selection process

Marketers generally employ a five-step process for target market selection.

III. Step 1: Identify the appropriate targeting strategy

The targeting strategy used is affected by target market characteristics, product attributes, and the organization's objectives and resources.

    A. Undifferentiated targeting strategy

        1. The **undifferentiated targeting strategy** is one in which an organization defines an entire market for a particular product as its target market, designs a single marketing mix, and directs it at the entire market .

        2. The underlying assumption is that the needs of the target market for specific kinds of product are very similar; thus the business can satisfy most customers with a single marketing mix.

        3. There are two requirements for effective use of this approach.

            a. A **homogeneous market** is one in which a large proportion of customers have similar needs for a product.

            b. The organization must be able to develop and maintain a single marketing mix that satisfies customers' needs.

    B. Concentrated targeting strategy through market segmentation

        1. **Heterogeneous markets** are markets made up of individuals or organizations with diverse product needs.

        2. **Market segmentation** is the process of dividing the total market into market groups that have relatively similar product needs for the purpose of designing a marketing mix that will more precisely match the needs of individuals in a selected segment.

        3. A **market segment** consists of individuals, groups, or organizations with one or more similar characteristics that cause them to have relatively similar product needs.

4. There are five conditions for effective segmentation.

   a. Consumers' needs for the product must be heterogeneous.

   b. The segments must be identifiable and divisible.

   c. The total market should be divided so that segments can be compared with respect to estimated sales potential, costs, and profits.

   d. At least one segment must have enough profit potential to justify the development and maintenance of a special marketing mix for that segment.

   e. The organization must be able to reach the chosen segment with a particular marketing mix.

5. Two strategies for segmenting markets are the concentrated targeting strategy and the differentiating targeting strategy.

C. **Concentrated targeting strategy** is a strategy in which an organization targets a single market segment using one marketing mix.

   a. Advantages

      (1) Specialization gives the firm an opportunity to analyze the characteristics and needs of a distinct customer group carefully and then focus all marketing efforts into satisfying that group's needs.

      (2) A firm can generate large sales volume by reaching a single segment.

      (3) A firm with rather restricted resources is able to compete with much larger organizations.

   b. Disadvantages

      (1) If the segment's demand for the product declines, the company's financial strength also declines.

(2) Success in one segment may preclude entry into another segment.

D. **Differentiated targeting strategy** is a strategy in which an organization targets two or more segments by developing a marketing mix for each segment.

    a. Advantages

        (1) A business can increase its sales in a total market by focusing on more than one segment.

        (2) Sales to additional market segments may absorb excess production capacity.

    b. Disadvantages

        (1) A greater number of production processes, materials, and skills means higher production costs.

        (2) Several distinct promotion plans and distribution methods are required, resulting in higher marketing costs.

IV. Step 2: Determine which segmentation variables to use

A. **Segmentation variables** are characteristics of individuals, groups, or organizations that are used for dividing a total market into segments. Marketers consider the following factors when choosing segmentation variables.

    1. The segmentation variable should be related to customers' needs for, uses of, or behavior toward the product.

    2. The variable must be measurable.

    3. The company's resources and capabilities determine the number and size of segment variables.

    4. Choice of segmentation variables is a critical step because an inappropriate variable limits the chances of developing a successful marketing strategy.

C.   Variables for segmenting consumer markets

   1.   Demographic variables

       a.   Those commonly used by marketers include age, gender, race, ethnicity, income, education, occupation, family size, family life cycle, religion, and social class.

       b.   They are often closely related to consumers' product needs and purchasing behavior.

       c.   They can be readily measured through observation or survey methods.

   2.   Geographic variables

       a.   Geographic variables include climate, terrain, natural resources, population density, and subcultural values.

       b.   **Market density** is the number of potential customers per unit of land area, such as a square mile.

       c.   **Geodemographic segmentation** divides people into zip code areas and smaller neighborhoods based on lifestyle and demographic information.

       d.   **Micromarketing** is an approach to market segmentation in which organizations focus precise marketing efforts on very small geographic markets.

   3.   Psychographic variables

A psychographic variable can be used by itself to segment a market or combined with other segmentation variables. The following are the types most commonly used to segment markets.

       a.   Personality characteristics

(1) These are useful when products are similar to competing products and consumers' needs are not greatly affected by other segmentation variables.

(2) Marketers almost always emphasize personality characteristics that are valued positively in our culture.

b. Motives

(1) Markets are divided according to consumers' reasons for making a purchase.

(2) Appearance, affiliation, safety, convenience, and status all relate to motives.

c. Lifestyle segmentation

(1) Lifestyle segmentation groups individuals according to how they spend their time, the importance of their surroundings, their values and beliefs, and some socioeconomic characteristics.

(2) This variable encompasses numerous characteristics related to people's activities, interests, and opinions.

(3) A popular study of lifestyle is the Value and Lifestyle Program (VALS); its research has identified

(a) Three broad consumer groups: Outer-Directed, Inner-Directed, and Need Driven

(b) Five basic lifestyle groups: Strugglers, Action-Oriented, Status-Oriented, People-Oriented, and Actualizers

b. Limitations of psychographic segmentation

(1) They are difficult to measure accurately.

(2)   Their links to consumers' needs are sometimes obscure and unproven.

(3)   The firm may be unable to reach segments resulting from psychographic segmentation.

4.   Behavioristic variables

    a.   These variables commonly involve consumers' product usage.

        (1)   Users and nonusers

        (2)   Heavy, moderate, and light users

    b.   How consumers use or apply the product may be used as a basis for segmentation.

    c.   **Benefit segmentation** is the division of a market according to the various benefits that consumers want from the product.

D.   Variables for segmenting organizational markets

1.   Geographic location: Variations in organizations' demands result from differences in climate, terrain, consumer preferences, or similar factors.

2.   Type of organization: Required product features, distribution systems, price structures, and selling strategies may vary among different types of organizations.

3.   Customer size: An organization's size may affect the purchasing procedures and types and quantities of products desired.

4.   Product use: How a firm uses products affects the types and amounts of the products purchased and the manner in which they are purchased.

V.   Step 3: Develop market segment profiles

A. Market segment profiles describe the similarities among potential customers within a segment and explain the differences among people and organizations in different market segments.

B. A profile can deal with demographic characteristics, geographic factors, product benefits sought, lifestyles, brand preferences, or usage rates.

C. Market segment profiles provide marketers with an understanding of how an organization can use its capabilities to serve potential customer groups.

VI. Step 4: Evaluate relevant market segments

A. Sales estimates

1. Potential sales for a segment can be measured along several dimensions, including product, geographic area, time, and level of competition.

2. **Market potential** is the total amount of a product that customers will purchase within a specified period at a specific level of industrywide marketing activity from all firms in an industry.

   a. It can be stated in terms of dollars or units and can refer to a total market or to a market segment.

   b. When analyzing market potential, it is important to indicate the time frame and the level of industry marketing activities.

3. **Company sales potential** is the maximum percentage of a market potential that an individual firm within an industry can expect to obtain for a specific product.

   a. Factors that influence a company's sales potential are the size of the market sales potential, the magnitude of industrywide marketing activities, and the intensity and effectiveness of the firm's marketing activities relative to those of its competitors.

   b. There are two general approaches to measuring sales potential: breakdown and buildup.

(1)   The **breakdown approach** measures company sales potential based on a general economic forecast for a specific time period and the market potential derived from it; the marketing manager starts with broad comprehensive forecasts of general economic activity, estimates market potential, and then estimates the company's sales potential.

(2)   The **buildup approach** measures company sales potential by estimating how much of a product a potential buyer in a specific geographic area will purchase in a given time period, multiplying the estimate by the number of potential buyers, and adding the totals of all geographic areas considered.

B.   Competitive assessment

1.   Sales estimates may be misleading unless they are tempered with competitive information.

2.   Several questions should be raised regarding competitors in the segments being considered.

a.   How many competitors are there?

b.   What are their strengths and weaknesses?

c.   Do several competitors have major market shares and together dominate the segment?

d.   Can the company create a marketing mix to compete effectively against competitors' marketing mixes?

e.   Is it likely that new competitors will enter a segment?

f.   If so, how will these competitors affect the firm's ability to compete successfully in the segment under consideration?

C.   Cost estimates

1. Meeting the needs of a target segment can be expensive.

2. If costs are too high, marketers may decide the segment is inaccessible.

VII. Step 5: Select specific target markets

A. Marketers first decide whether there are enough differences in customers' needs to warrant the use of market segmentation at all.

1. If customer needs are homogeneous, the undifferentiated approach may be the best choice.

2. If customer needs are heterogeneous, then one or more target markets must be selected.

B. The firm's management must consider whether the organization has the financial resources, managerial skills, labor expertise, and facilities that will allow it to enter and effectively compete in selected segments.

VIII. Developing sales forecasts

A. A **sales forecast** is the amount of a product that the firm actually expects to sell during a specific period at a specified level of marketing activities.

1. Businesses use sales forecasting for planning, organizing, implementing, and controlling activities.

2. Lack of realistic sales forecasts is a common reason why businesses fail.

B. Sales forecasting techniques

1. **Executive judgment;** this type of forecast

a. Is based on the intuition of one or more executives

b. Is inexpensive and expedient

   c.   Works fairly well when product demand is relatively stable

   d.   Is based solely on past experience

   e.   Is highly unscientific

2.   Surveys

   a.   **A customer forecasting survey** is a survey of customers regarding the quantities of products that they intend to buy during a specific period.

      (1)   Customers must be willing and able to make accurate estimates of future product requirements.

      (2)   Surveys reflect buying intentions, not actual purchases.

      (3)   Surveys usually require large amounts of time and money.

   b.   **A sales-force forecasting survey** consists of estimates by members of a firm's sales force of the anticipated sales in their territory for a specified period.

      (1)   Salespeople are closer than other company personnel to customers and should know more about customers' future product needs.

      (2)   Forecasts can be prepared for single territories, divisions, regions, or the total market.

      (3)   For the survey to be effective, salespeople must be accurate and consistent estimators.

      (4)   The survey should be administered so that salespeople will believe they are making a definite contribution by helping to develop sales goals.

      (5)   Salespeople should be assured that their forecasts are not used to set their sales quotas.

c.   The **expert forecasting survey** is a sales forecast prepared by experts such as economists, management consultants, advertising executives, college professors or other persons outside the firm.

d.   The **Delphi technique** is a procedure in which experts create initial forecasts, submit them to the company for averaging, and then refine the forecasts; the ultimate goal is to develop a highly accurate sales forecast.

3.   Time series analysis

a.   With **time series analysis** a forecaster uses historical data to discover patterns in the firm's sales over time and generally involves trend, cycle, seasonal, and random factor analyses.

b.   **Trend analysis** focuses on aggregate sales data from a period of several years, to determine general trends in annual sales.

c.   **Cycle analysis** is examination of sales figures over a period of three to five years to ascertain whether sales fluctuate in a consistent, periodic manner.

d.   **Seasonal analysis** is an analysis of daily, weekly, or monthly sales figures to evaluate the degree to which seasonal factors influence sales.

e.   **Random factor analysis** attempts to attribute erratic sales variations to random, nonrecurrent events.

4.   **Regression analysis**

a.   This method of predicting sales is based on finding a relationship between past sales and one or more variables such as population or income.

b.   Simple regression analysis uses one independent variable, whereas multiple regression analysis includes two or more independent variables.

c.   These methods are used only when a precise relationship can be established and are therefore futile when no historical data exists, as with a new product.

5.   **Market tests**

    a.   A **market test** involves making a product available to buyers in one or more test areas and measuring purchases and consumer responses.

    b.   Market tests provide information about consumers' actual purchases

    c.   They are effective in estimating sales of new products or of existing products in new geographic areas

    d.   The chief disadvantages of market tests are that they are time-consuming and expensive.

6.   Using multiple forecasting methods

    a.   Although some businesses rely on a single sales forecasting method, most use several to attempt to validate the results from one technique.

    b.   Methods used for short-range forecasts are often inappropriate for long-range forecasting.

CLASS EXERCISES, DEBATE ISSUE, AND CHAPTER QUIZ

On the following pages, you will find two class exercises, a debate issue, and a chapter quiz. These are formatted in large-size type so that you can use them as class handouts or for making transparencies. Below are the authors' comments on the class exercises, the debate topic for this chapter, and the answers to the chapter quiz.

Class Exercise 1: The objective of this class exercise is to gain a thorough understanding of segmentation variables by designing a target market for a new retail operation.

Question 1. Other ways of asking this question are "What kinds of retail stores do you wish were available here?" and "What kind of restaurant or retail outlets have you seen in other places that might work here?" Students can usually think of successful operations in their home towns that are not available locally. It is important to stress the necessity of the market being large enough or the segment being profitable enough to support their choice of retail operation.

Question 2. Students could spend the entire class period on this question, so encourage them to remain brief. An example might be this: Open an upscale restaurant and bar that serves dinners ($7–$12) and drinks, located on the corner of University Avenue and First Street.

Question 3. The answer to this question will depend on the type of product or service being offered, but students often assume a concentrated strategy is best when a differentiated targeting strategy is more appropriate. For instance, most restaurants have breakfast, lunch, dinner, and perhaps late night segments, each having different needs.

Question 4. This question should take up the majority of the exercise time. Ask students to look carefully at *each* variable to determine if it will help develop a better marketing mix to meet customer needs. Most students will define their target markets by demographic or geographic variables because psychographic and behavioristic variables are harder to understand. Push them by asking, "Why would people go to your store?" (motives) and "What are they really buying at your store besides the product?" (benefits).

Class Exercise 2: This exercise is designed to get students to think in terms of segmentation variables discussed in the chapter. For example, what demographic, geographic, psychographic, or lifestyle variables could have been used to segment the market for baby food (variable 2)? Lifestyle segmentation variables could include:

1. Consumers who want nothing but all-natural ingredients
2. Upscale consumers who want gourmet baby food
3. Time-conscious consumers who need instant or quick meals for their babies

Many other combinations are possible. Encourage students to be creative and imaginative. Like most exercises, there are no right or wrong answers. The following list includes variables or characteristics that could be used to segment markets for specific products.

1.	Recreational vehicles (RVs)	**age, income**
2.	Baby food	**family life cycle, age**
3.	Rolls Royce automobiles	**income, social class**
4.	Snow tires	**climate**
5.	Hotel rooms	**income, business vs. tourism**
6.	Magazines	**age, job, education, ethnicity**
7.	Soft drinks	**age, sex**
8.	Movies	**age, family life cycle**
9.	Shoes	**age, income, lifestyle**
10.	Bicycles	**income, age, lifestyle**
11.	Air passenger service	**income, business vs. tourism**
12.	Cameras	**lifestyle, occupation, income**
13.	Swimsuits	**age, climate, sex**
14.	Restaurants	**income, age, city size, lifestyle**

Debate Issue: Is lifestyle segmentation truly a viable means of segmenting a market?

Chapter Quiz: Answers to multiple-choice questions are

1.	a	3.	b
2.	b	4.	e

CLASS EXERCISE 1

YOU HAVE JUST WON THE LOTTERY, AND AFTER GIVING HALF TO CHARITY YOU NOW HAVE $500,000 TO BEGIN A NEW RETAIL OPERATION IN YOUR LOCAL AREA. WHAT KIND OF OPERATION WILL YOU OPEN?

1. **What market or segment of a market exists in your area with unfulfilled needs or wants?**

2. **Briefly describe the nature of the operation you would open to meet the needs of a specific market segment(s).**
   a. Product or service?
   b. Price range?
   c. Location?

3. **Will you use a concentrated or a differentiated targeting strategy? Why.**

4. **What segmentation variables will be useful in describing your target market(s)? Why?**

CLASS EXERCISE 2

IDENTIFY ONE OR SEVERAL
CHARACTERISTICS OR VARIABLES THAT
COULD BE USED TO SEGMENT THE MARKETS
FOR EACH OF THE FOLLOWING PRODUCTS.

1. Recreational vehicles (RVs)
2. Baby food
3. Rolls Royce automobiles
4. Snow tires
5. Hotel rooms
6. Magazines
7. Soft drinks
8. Movies
9. Shoes
10. Bicycles
11. Air passenger service
12. Cameras
13. Swimsuits
14. Restaurants

DEBATE ISSUE

IS LIFESTYLE SEGMENTATION TRULY A VIABLE MEANS OF SEGMENTING A MARKET?

YES

- Lifestyle segmentation allows marketers to demonstrate how their products fit in with consumers' activities, interests, and opinions

- Lifestyle segmentation has been used very effectively to segment newspaper readers into such groups as Vanguards (upscale professional women), New Breed Workers (young men who read sports and entertainment), and Senior Solid Conservatives (long-time corporate employees active in community affairs)

- Marketers who are aware of consumers' lifestyles can plan their activities with greater insight and effectiveness

NO

- Human beings are far too complex for lifestyle segmentation to be of any practical use to marketers

- Lifestyle variables such as personality, interest, and activities are too difficult to measure accurately

- Research has provided little evidence to support the notion that lifestyle variables actually affect consumer behavior

- Because human values and lifestyles are constantly changing and evolving, lifestyle segmentation can provide nothing more than stereotypes of human behavior

CHAPTER QUIZ

1. The type of targeting strategy in which an organization directs its marketing efforts at several segments is called a(n) _____ targeting strategy.
   a. differentiated
   b. total market
   c. concentrated
   d. undifferentiated
   e. integrated

2. Curtis Mathis television sets, with their reputations for extremely high quality and dependability, are largely marketed to and purchased by families who cannot afford other entertainment options. Curtis Mathis uses _____ as a key segmentation variable.
   a. gender
   b. income
   c. age
   d. ethnicity
   e. education

3. Variables such as geographic location, type of organization, customer size, and type of product usage are used to segment _____ markets.
   a. consumer
   b. organizational
   c. government
   d. international
   e. most target

4. Using the breakdown approach to sales potential, estimates are made
   a. initially by referring to specific geographic factors.
   b. by establishing levels of marketing effort that will be required to achieve specific levels of sales.
   c. without reference to industry marketing efforts.
   d. without reference to general economic conditions.
   e. by starting with general economic conditions.

ANSWERS TO DISCUSSION AND REVIEW QUESTIONS

1. What is a market? What are the requirements for a market?

   A market is an aggregate of people who, as individuals and/or organizations, have needs for products in a product class and have the ability, willingness, and authority to purchase such products. For an aggregate of people to be a market, they must need the product, have the ability to purchase it, be willing to purchase it, and have the authority to purchase it.

2. In your local area, can you identify a group of people with unsatisfied product needs who represent a market? Could this market be reached by a business organization? Why or why not?

   In answering this question, students should demonstrate that their suggested markets meet the requirements of a market as discussed in question 1.

3. Outline the five major steps in the target market selection process.

   Although marketers may use various methods for selecting a target market, they commonly use a five step process. Step 1 is to identify the appropriate targeting strategy. The three basic strategies are undifferentiated strategy, concentrated strategy, and differentiated strategy. After determining which targeting strategy to use, marketers move to Step 2, determining which segmentation variables to use. There are specific variables for both consumer and organizational markets. Step 3 is to develop market segment profiles so that marketers better understand how their organization can use its capabilities to serve potential customer groups. In Step 4, marketers evaluate relevant market segments, analyzing sales estimates, competition, and estimated costs for each segment. The fifth and final step is to select specific target markets. Marketers must decide whether there are enough differences in customers' needs to recommend segmentation and, if so, in which of these segments to participate.

4. What is an undifferentiated strategy? Under what conditions is it most useful? Describe a present marketing situation in which a company is using an undifferentiated strategy. Is the business successful? Why or why not?

   When an organization designs a single marketing mix and directs it at the entire market for a particular product, it is employing an undifferentiated targeting strategy. This strategy is effective under two conditions. First, the market must be homogeneous. A large proportion of customers in a total market must have similar needs for the product. If customers have a variety of needs, the company will not be able to satisfy them with one product. Second, the company must be able to develop and maintain a single marketing mix that satisfies customers' needs. It must identify common needs among most customers in the total market and possess the means to reach a sizable portion of that market.

5. What is market segmentation? Describe the basic conditions required for effective segmentation. Identify several firms that use segmentation.

   In market segmentation, (a) the total market is divided into groups consisting of people with relatively similar product needs and (b) a marketing mix (or mixes) is (are) designed to fit precisely the needs of the people in a segment (or segments).

For this process to be effective, consumers' needs must be heterogeneous; the segments must be identifiable and divisible; the segments must be comparable in terms of sales potential, costs, and profit; and one segment must have enough profit potential to justify the development and maintenance of a marketing mix for that segment. In addition, the firm must be able to reach the chosen segment with a particular marketing mix.

6. List the differences between the concentrated and the differentiated strategies. Describe the advantages and disadvantages of each strategy.

The main difference between the concentrated strategy and the differentiated strategy of market segmentation is that the concentrated strategy directs marketing efforts toward a single market segment using one marketing mix, whereas the differentiated strategy directs marketing efforts at two or more market segments using a different marketing mix for each segment.

The concentrated strategy enables a firm to specialize in one market segment and penetrate it effectively, thereby creating larger sales volume. Also, it allows a firm with limited resources to compete with larger firms. The concentrated strategy can be risky, however, because the firm relies solely on one segment; if the strategy fails, the firm has nothing to offset the decline. Also, if the firm becomes well entrenched in one segment, it may have difficulty expanding into other segments because of its image.

The differentiated strategy enables a firm to increase total sales by focusing on more than one segment. This is especially useful if a firm has excess production capacity, because it allows the firm to use this capacity. However, the cost of production usually increases with increased production runs; the firm typically must increase its marketing activities to implement several distinct distribution and promotion plans for different segments.

7. Identify and describe four major categories of variables that can be used to segment consumer markets. Give examples of product markets that are segmented by variables in each category.

The four major categories of market segmentation variables are demographic, geographic, psychographic, and behavioristic.

Demographic variables include such items as sex, age, income, marital status, and the like. These types of variables are used frequently because they are measurable and closely related to customers' product needs.

Geographic variables include climate, terrain, natural resources, population density, and subcultural values.

Psychographic variables include personality, motives, and lifestyles. Psychographic variables can be used alone to segment markets or be combined with other segmentation variables. However, psychographic variables are difficult to measure accurately.

Behavioristic variables are customer characteristics directly related to consumers' relationships to the product, such as product usage rate.

When discussing examples, students should be encouraged to use local and regional as well as national examples.

8. What dimensions are used to segment organizational markets?

Organizational markets are segmented according to geography, type of organization, customer size, and product use.

9. Define geodemographic segmentation. Name several types of firms that might employ this type of market segmentation, and explain why.

   A type of demographic segmentation, geodemographic segmentation groups people in ZIP codes or smaller neighborhood units based on income, education, occupation, type of housing, ethnicity, family life cycle, and level of urbanization. In this way, marketers are able to isolate precise demographic units where demand for a specific product is concentrated and design special advertising campaigns, promotions, pricing, and other features of micromarketing.

   Students' answers to this part of the question will vary. Example: Financial and health care service providers might want to use geodemographic segmentation. A neighborhood composed mostly of senior citizens on fixed incomes, for example, would require particular health care services. Another composed of upper-income professionals might be an appropriate target for certain financial services.

10. What is a market segment profile? Why is it an important step in the target market selection process?

    A market segment profile describes similarities among potential customers within a segment and explains the differences among people and organizations in different market segments. Profiles are composed of a variety of elements such as geographic or demographic factors, lifestyles, product benefits sought, brand preferences, and usage rates. Developing profiles is necessary in order to more accurately assess the degree to which the organization's products fit potential product needs and to better understand how its capabilities will serve potential customer segments.

11. Describe the important factors that marketers should analyze in order to evaluate market segments.

    After identifying several appropriate potential market segments, marketers evaluate them further to eliminate some from continued attention. Three factors that marketers analyze for each segment are sales estimates, competition, and estimated costs. Potential sales can be estimated with respect to product level, geographic area, time, and level of competition. Market potential, expressed as dollars or units, is the total amount of a product that customers will purchase within a specified period from all firms in an industry. Company sales potential is the maximum percentage of market potential that an individual company within an industry can expect to gain for a specific product. In addition to obtaining sales estimates, firms must consider their competitors. Unless firms evaluate other organizations that operate in segments under consideration, sales estimates can be deceptive. For example, if a number of competitors already operate within a potential segment, marketers may decide that despite excellent sales estimates, that segment doesn't provide adequate marketing opportunities. Finally, marketers must estimate the costs of developing unique product features, appealing package design, ample warranties, extensive advertising, and other marketing mix requirements. The costs of reaching particular segments may simply be too high.

12. Why is a marketer concerned about sales potential when trying to find a target market?

    Sales potential is important to a marketer because the firm incurs a certain cost in developing and maintaining a marketing mix. To achieve long-term survival, the firm must be able to recover these costs and make at least a reasonable profit. By estimating the sales potential of possible target markets, a marketer is in a better position to achieve long-term survival. Estimates of sales potential are necessary to determine which market segments are substantial enough to justify the development of marketing mixes.

13. Why is selecting appropriate target markets important to an organization that wants to adopt the marketing concept philosophy?

According to the marketing concept philosophy, an organization should attempt to provide products that satisfy customers' needs through a coordinated set of activities that also allows the organization to achieve its goals. Customer satisfaction is the major aim of the marketing concept. To successfully adopt the marketing concept, therefore, identifying the right target market is critical. For example, if an organization chooses a market that doesn't need or want a product or can't afford it, customers will not be satisfied and sales will be poor. However, companies that analyze target markets carefully and choose appropriately have more likelihood of serving customers' needs and achieving their own objectives.

14. What is a sales forecast? Why is it important?

The sales forecast is the amount of a product that a company expects to sell over a period at a specified level of marketing activity. The development of a sales forecast is important because many operating units within the company use the forecast in planning, organizing, implementing, and controlling their activities, and their success depends on its accuracy.

15. What are the two primary types of surveys a company might use to forecast sales? Why would a company use an outside expert forecasting study instead?

The two primary types of surveys a company might use to forecast sales are the customer forecasting survey and the sales-force forecasting survey. In the first type, marketers ask customers what types and quantities of products they plan to purchase during a specific period. In the second type, the sales force estimates anticipated sales in their territories for a specified period of time.

Sometimes companies decide to use an outside expert forecasting survey instead of conducting their own. Economists, management consultants, college professors, and other experts have knowledge about specific markets, and because they are outsiders can remain more objective. In addition, outside expert surveys avoid some of the potential drawbacks of sales-force surveys such as biases based on recent sales experience, intentional underestimation of sales potential because of the belief that sales goals will be determined by the forecast, or dislike of paperwork. Therefore, an outside survey is apt to be more objective than those conducted by inside personnel, and possibly more accurate.

16. Under what conditions are market tests useful for sales forecasting? Discuss the advantages and disadvantages of market tests.

Market tests are especially useful for testing new products because no previous sales history is available for those products. In addition, market tests are useful if the test areas represent the entire market because testing the product in a few cities is considerably cheaper than introducing it to the entire market.

The primary advantages of market tests are that they measure actual purchasing behavior rather than buying intentions and the volume of purchases can be measured against various levels of marketing activities. However, market tests are time-consuming and expensive. Also, consumers' responses may vary after the test, making the test a poor indicator of market response.

17. Discuss the benefits of using multiple forecasting methods.

Most firms use multiple sales forecasting methods. While all forecasting methods have value, none are without drawbacks. Executive judgment is not necessarily objective. Customer surveys are time-consuming and expensive. Sales force surveys and market tests each have several drawbacks. Time series analysis is not always dependable. Regression analysis is not useful for predicting new product sales. A benefit of using multiple forecasting methods is that one method can make up for the shortcomings of another. In addition, marketers can use one or more methods to validate the results of another.

Multiple forecasting methods are also useful when a company markets a variety of product lines or when a single product is sold in different segments. Because different forecasting methods are more accurate for different length forecasts, organizations may find it effective to use one forecast method to predict short-range sales and another to predict long-range sales.

COMMENTS ON THE CASES

Case 8.1   Ryka Athletic Shoes: By Women, For Women, Helping Women

The objective of this case is to present students with a situation that allows them to discuss several issues associated with target market selection and analysis. You may wish to ask students the types of problems that exist for athletic shoe marketers when the brand name is not especially well known. Also, ask female students specifically if they believe that most so-called women's athletic shoes are not necessarily designed for women but in fact are men's shoes slightly modified into smaller sizes. Because most students are quite familiar with athletic shoe brands, this case should be interesting and the discussion lively.

The first question asks students what type of general targeting strategy Ryka uses. Ryka uses a concentrated targeting strategy. Ryka focuses specifically on manufacturing and marketing only high-performance athletic shoes that fit women's feet.

The second question asks students to identify which segmentation variables Ryka uses. Ryka uses gender as a segmentation variable in that it produces shoes only for women. In addition, Ryka is using benefit segmentation because its shoes are designed to provide comfort and a great fit and are intended for a specific use.

The last question asks students to evaluate the sales and marketing vice president's decision to shift the company's marketing focus from its cause (preventing violence against women) to its shoes. Students' answers will vary considerably. Some are likely to argue that the cause is important enough that people will take an interest in purchasing the shoes or at least will give more than a fair chance to considering the Ryka brand. Others will argue that when people shop for shoes, they are looking for specific characteristics such as fit and end use of the product more than seeking to support or endorse a particular cause, even though the cause is very important.

Video Information

Video Title: Ryka Sales Training
Location: Tape 2, Segment 8
Length: 10:40
Video Overview: Sheri Poe is the founder and president of Ryka, Inc., manufacturer of athletic shoes designed specifically for women. Poe believes that other shoe designers focus on men and children, but none have made shoes that really fit women's feet. Ryka shoes are anatomically designed to be correct for women's feet, are lighter weight, and use a patented system that provides cushioning and shock absorption for the heel and ball of the foot.

Poe was raped while in college, and when she started her company, one of her goals was to help women. When women purchase Ryka athletic shoes, a portion of the purchase price goes toward the prevention of violence against women. Poe established "Ryka Rose," a nonprofit foundation that supports treatment centers, community education, and violence prevention programs. The core of Ryka's marketing message, both to retailers and customers, is that they can make a difference.

Multiple-Choice Questions About the Video

b 1. As part of its commitment to being a socially responsible firm, Ryka donates a portion of its pre-tax profits to what organization?
    a. Olympic Fund
    b. The Ryka Rose Foundation
    c. The Fellowship of Christian Athletes
    d. The United Negro College Fund
    e. The National Organization of Women

d 2. Design features that make Ryka athletic shoes fit women's feet include
    a. more flexible construction, wider base of support, and wider instep.
    b. lower arch support and narrower base of support.
    c. wider heels and more flexible construction.
    d. lower heels, higher arch, and wider base of support.
    e. wider instep, lower arch, and lower base of support.

c 3. When she founded Ryka, Sheri Poe's primary goals were to make athletic shoes specifically designed to fit women and to
    a. create a complete line of athletic and fashion footwear for women.
    b. expand into women's exercise and athletic clothing.
    c. help women who have been victims of violence.
    d. design athletic shoes specifically designed to fit children.
    e. open her own retail outlets carrying exclusively Ryka products.

a 4. To provide maximum shock absorption and cushioning on impact, Ryka created its patented
    a. Nitrogen Energy Sphere system.
    b. Air Lift system.
    c. Sure-Foot Wrap system.
    d. Cushion Uplift system.
    e. Sure Energy system.

Case 8.2   *Sports Illustrated* **Scores Through Segmentation**

This case focuses on *Sports Illustrated*'s uses of market segmentation. Students should find this case of interest due to the popularity of this product among students.

The first question asks what type of targeting strategy *Sports Illustrated* is using. *Sports Illustrated* is pursuing several market segments, with specifically designed marketing mixes for each segment. Thus, this organization is using a differentiated targeting strategy.

Question 2 asks which kinds of segmentation variables are being employed by *Sports Illustrated*. *Sports Illustrated* is using geographic segmentation based on regions. It is also using age as a basis for segmentation.

The third question asks if there are other types of segmentation that *Sports Illustrated* marketers should consider. Marketers at *Sports Illustrated* could consider segmentation based on gender, which would provide a *Sports Illustrated* for men and a *Sports Illustrated* for women. The two products could vary, especially with regard to articles and advertisements about men's and women's fitness and health.

Last, students are asked to evaluate the decision to not offer *Sports Illustrated Classic* as a regular magazine. *Sports Illustrated Classic* is a version of the standard magazine aimed primarily at older readers. Students' answers to this question will vary considerably. Some will argue that there is a growing segment of mature readers and that a special version could be designed to meet the needs of older Americans. Other students may argue that older readers tend to be less interested in sports and thus will question the feasibility of targeting this segment.

9 PRODUCT CONCEPTS

TEACHING RESOURCES QUICK REFERENCE GUIDE

Resource	Location
Purpose and Perspective	IRM, p. 184
Guide for Using Color Transparencies	IRM, p. 184
Lecture Outline	IRM, p. 184
Class Exercises, Debate Issue, and Chapter Quiz	IRM, p. 194
Class Exercise 1	IRM, p. 196
Class Exercise 2	IRM, p. 197
Debate Issue: In terms of product management, can following the product life cycle (PLC) philosophy be detrimental?	IRM, p. 198
Chapter Quiz	IRM, p. 199
Answers to Discussion and Review Questions	IRM, p. 200
Comments on the Cases	IRM, p. 202
Case 9.1	IRM, p. 202
Video	Tape 2, Segment 9
Video Information	IRM, p. 203
Multiple-Choice Questions About the Video	IRM, p. 203
Case 9.2	IRM, p. 203
Transparency Acetates	Transparency package
Examination Questions: Essay	TB, p. 165
Examination Questions: Multiple-Choice	TB, p. 166
Examination Questions: True-False	TB, p. 179
Author-Selected Multiple-Choice Test Items	TB, p. 447

PURPOSE AND PERSPECTIVE

This chapter covers fundamental concepts relating to (1) definition of a product, (2) consumer and organizational product classification schemes, (3) product mix and product line concepts, (4) product life cycles, (5) product positioning, (6) organizing to manage products, and (7) other product-related characteristics. It provides definitions and examines the basic relationships necessary for understanding the role of product in the marketing mix. Students often believe that products are related more to production than to marketing. We point out that products can be goods, services, ideas, or all three. The chapter examines organizational alternatives in managing products, including the product manager, market manager, and venture team approaches. Many real-world examples are presented to illustrate product concepts.

GUIDE FOR USING COLOR TRANSPARENCIES

There are two groups of color transparencies. The transparencies identified by a double number are the same as the figures in the text. The transparencies labeled with a number and a letter are illustrations that do not appear in the text, but they can be used as additional examples of concepts discussed.

Part 3 Opener	Product decisions
Figure 9.4	The concepts of product mix width and depth applied to selected Procter & Gamble products
Figure 9.5	The four stages of the product life cycle
Figure 9.9	Hypothetical perceptual map for pain relievers
Figure 9A	Chapter 9 outline
Figure 9B	Classification of products
Figure 9C	Three approaches to differentiating products
Figure 9D	Organizational forms for managing products
Figure 9E	Huggies uses product design and features to differentiate its Pull-Ups from competitor's products.
Figure 9F	DIRECTV uses head-to-head product positioning to compete against cable-based competitors.

LECTURE OUTLINE

I.   What is a product?

    A.   A **product** is everything, both tangible and intangible, that a buyer receives in an exchange.

    B.   A product is a network of attributes, including functional, social, and psychological utilities or benefits.

C. A product can be an idea, a service, a good, or any combination of the three, including supporting services such as installation, guarantees, product information, and promises of repair or maintenance.

    1. A **good** is a tangible physical entity.

    2. A **service** is an intangible result of the application of human and mechanical efforts to people or objects.

    3. An **idea** is a concept, philosophy, image, or issue.

D. When buyers purchase a product, they actually buy the benefits and satisfactions that they think the product will provide.

II. Classifying products

A. **Consumer products** are products purchased to satisfy personal and family needs; they are categorized according to how buyers *generally* behave when purchasing a specific item.

    1. **Convenience products** are relatively inexpensive, frequently purchased items for which buyers exert only minimal purchasing effort.

        a. The buyer spends little time planning the purchase of a convenience item or comparing available brands.

        b. A convenience product normally is marketed through many retail outlets.

        c. Because sellers experience high inventory turnover, per-unit gross margins can be relatively low.

        d. Producers of convenience products can expect little promotional effort at the retail level.

    2. **Shopping products** are items for which buyers are willing to expend considerable effort in planning and making the purchase.

a. Buyers allocate considerable time to comparing stores and brands in prices, product features, qualities, services, and perhaps warranties.

b. Although shopping products are purchased less frequently and are more expensive than convenience products, buyers of shopping products are not extremely loyal to their brands.

c. Shopping products require fewer retail outlets than convenience products.

d. Because shopping products are purchased less frequently, causing lower inventory turnover, intermediaries expect to receive higher gross margins.

e. Usually, the producer and the intermediary expect some cooperation from each other in providing parts and repair services and performing promotional activities.

3. **Specialty products** have one or more unique characteristics, and buyers are willing to expend considerable effort to obtain them.

a. Buyers actually plan the purchase of a specialty product; they know exactly what they want and will not accept a substitute.

b. Specialty items often are distributed through a limited number of retail outlets.

c. Like shopping goods, specialty products are purchased infrequently, causing lower inventory turnover; thus gross margins must be relatively high.

4. **Unsought products** are products purchased to solve a sudden problem, products of which customers are unaware, and products that people do not necessarily think about buying.

a. The consumer generally does not think of buying these products on a regular basis.

b. These products require aggressive personal selling to make consumers aware of their potential benefits.

c. Examples include emergency automobile repairs, cemetery plots, life insurance, and encyclopedias.

B. **Organizational products** are purchased to use in a firm's operations, to resell, or to use in the manufacture of other products; the are classified according to their characteristics and intended uses in an organization.

1. **Raw materials** are basic materials that become part of a physical product.

   a. Other than the processing required to transport and physically handle the product, raw materials have not been processed when a firm buys them.

   b. Raw materials often are bought in large quantities according to grades and specifications.

2. **Major equipment** includes large tools and machines used for production purposes.

   a. This equipment is usually expensive and intended to be used in a production process for a considerable period of time.

   b. Marketers of major equipment frequently must provide a variety of services, including installation, training, and repair and maintenance assistance and may even help finance the purchase.

3. **Accessory equipment** does not become a part of the final physical product but is used in production or office activities.

   a. Compared with major equipment, accessory items usually are much cheaper, purchased routinely with less negotiation, and treated as expense items rather than as capital items because they are not expected to last as long.

   b. Sellers do not have to provide the multitude of services expected of major equipment marketers.

4. **Component parts** become a part of the physical product and are either finished items ready for assembly or products that need little processing before assembly.

   a. Buyers purchase component parts according to their own specifications or industry standards.

   b. Component parts suppliers must provide consistent quality and on-time deliveries.

5. **Process materials** are used directly in the production of other products.

   a. Unlike component parts, process materials are not readily identifiable.

   b. Process materials are purchased according to industry standards or the purchaser's specifications.

6. **Consumable supplies** are items that facilitate an organization's production and operations but do not become part of the finished product.

   a. Supplies are standardized items used in a variety of situations and are purchased by many different organizations.

   b. Because supplies can be divided into three categories—maintenance, repair, and operating supplies—they sometimes are called **MRO items.**

7. **Organizational services** are the intangible products or industrial services that many organizations use in their operations and include financial products, legal services, marketing research services, and janitorial services.

   a. Purchasers must decide whether to provide their own services internally or to obtain them outside the organization.

   b. This decision depends largely on the costs associated with each alternative and how frequently the services are needed.

III.   Product line and product mix

A.   A **product item** is a specific version of a product that can be designated as a distinct offering among an organization's products.

B.   A **product line** is a group of closely related product items that are considered a unit because of marketing, technical, or end-use considerations.

   1.   Marketers must understand buyers' goals if they hope to come up with the optimal product line.

   2.   Specific items in a product line usually reflect the desires of different target markets or different consumer needs.

C.   A **product mix** is the composite, or total, group of products that an organization makes available to customers.

   1.   The **depth of product mix** is the number of different products offered in each product line.

   2.   The **width of product mix** is the number of product lines a company offers.

IV.   Product life cycles

Product life cycle is the progression of a product through four stages: introduction, growth, maturity, and decline.

A.   The **introduction stage** of the life cycle begins with the product's first appearance in the marketplace, when sales are zero and profits are negative.

   1.   During this stage, it is important to communicate product features, uses, and advantages to buyers.

   2.   There may be only a few sellers with enough resources, technological knowledge, and marketing know-how to launch the product successfully.

   3.   Initially, a higher price may be required to recoup expensive marketing research or development costs.

B.   During the **growth stage,** sales rise rapidly and profits reach a peak, then start to decline.

   1.   This stage is critical to a product's survival because competitive reactions to the product's success during this period will affect its life expectancy.

   2.   Profits decline late in this stage because increased competition drives down prices and creates the need for heavy promotional expenses.

   3.   At this point, a typical marketing strategy encourages strong brand loyalty and competes with aggressive emulators of the product.

   4.   An enterprise tries to strengthen its market share and develop a competitive niche by identifying and emphasizing the product's benefits.

C.   During the **maturity stage,** the sales curve peaks and starts to decline as profits continue to decline.

   1.   This stage is characterized by severe competition, since many brands are in the market.

   2.   Weaker competitors are squeezed out or lose interest in the product.

   3.   Fresh promotional and distribution efforts, such as mass media advertising and dealer-oriented promotion, are typical.

   4.   Buyers' knowledge of the product reaches a high level.

D.   During the **decline stage,** sales fall rapidly.

   1.   Declining sales may be caused by new technology or social trends.

   2.   The marketer considers weeding items from the product line to eliminate those not returning a profit.

   3.   The marketer may cut promotion efforts, eliminate marginal distributors, and, ultimately, plan to phase out the product.

V. Product differentiation

> **Product differentiation** is the process of creating and designing products so that customers perceive them as different from competing vendors. The three physical aspects of product differentiation that companies must consider are product quality, product design and features, and product support services.

A. **Product quality** refers to the overall characteristics of a product that allow it to perform as expected in satisfying customer needs.

   1. Expectations and perceptions of quality vary by customer.

   2. **Level of quality** is the amount of quality possessed by a product.

   3. **Consistency of quality** is the degree to which a product is the same level of quality over time.

B. Product design and features

   1. **Product design** refers to how a product is conceived, planned, and produced; it involves the total sum of all the product's physical characteristics.

      (a) One component of design is **styling,** the physical appearance of a product.

      (b) Most consumers seek out products with good looks and functionality.

   2. **Product features** are specific design characteristics that allow a product to perform certain tasks.

C. Product support services

   1. **Customer services** are human or mechanical efforts or activities a company provides that add value to a product.

   2. Customer services can include delivery, installation, customer training, and warranties.

VI.   Product positioning and repositioning

A.   **Product positioning** refers to the decisions and activities intended to create and maintain a certain concept of the firm's product in the customer's minds.

B.   Marketers try to position a product so that it seems to possess the characteristics that the target market most desires.

C.   Positioning can be designed to result in head-to-head confrontation or to avoid it.

1.   Head-to-head confrontation may be better if the product's characteristics are at least equal to those of competitive brands, if the product is lower priced, or if the product is higher priced but its performance is superior to its competitors' offerings.

2.   Positioning to avoid competition may be better when the product is not significantly better, when the brand has unique characteristics, or when marketers want to keep a new brand from cannibalizing sales of their existing brands.

D.   A good marketing program lets buyers easily identify the product's distinguishing attributes, which increases the chance that they will purchase the product.

E.   Repositioning can be accomplished by physically changing the product, its price, its distribution, or its image through promotional efforts.

VII.   Organizing to manage products

There are several alternatives to the traditional functional form of business organization.

A.   The product manager approach

1.   A **product manager** is the person within an organization responsible for a product, product line, or several distinct products that make up a group.

2. The **product manager** holds a staff position in a multiproduct company in which the large number of products makes it more difficult to use other organizational forms.

3. A **brand manager** is a type of product manager who is responsible for a single brand.

4. Product managers operate cross-functionally to coordinate the activities, information, and strategies involved in marketing an assigned product.

5. This form of organization is used by many large, multiple-product companies in the consumer packaged-goods business.

B. The market manager approach

1. A **market manager** is the person responsible for managing the marketing activities that serve a particular group of customers.

2. This approach is especially useful when a firm uses different types of activities to market products to several diverse customer groups.

C. The venture team approach

1. The **venture team** is a cross-functional team that creates entirely new products that may be aimed at new markets.

2. Venture teams, unlike product managers or market managers, are responsible for all aspects of a product's development.

3. Venture teams work outside established organizational divisions to create innovative approaches to new products and markets, which lets the company take advantage of opportunities in highly segmented markets.

4. Venture teams and other innovative organizational forms are especially necessary in well-established firms that must manage mature products and also encourage the development of new products.

    a. A venture department is a separate department or division formed to find, develop, and commercialize promising new-product or new-business areas; members are drawn from different functional areas of the company.

b.   When the commercial potential of a new product has been demonstrated, the members may return to their functional areas or join a new or existing division to manage the product.

c.   The new product may be turned over to an existing division, a market manager, or a product manager.

CLASS EXERCISES, DEBATE ISSUE, AND CHAPTER QUIZ

On the following pages, you will find two class exercises, a debate issue, and a chapter quiz. These are formatted in large-size type so that you can use them as class handouts or for making transparencies. Below are the authors' comments on the class exercises, the debate topic for this chapter, and the answers to the chapter quiz.

Class Exercise 1: This exercise is designed to help students understand how properly classifying consumer products affects marketing efforts.

1.   Answers will vary. The idea is to have students determine the degree of brand loyalty they exhibit for each product category so that they can answer the next question.

2.   Responses to these questions will vary, but similarities should emerge. The differences should help make the point that the classification is dependent on the target market and individual consumer perceptions. For instance, some might see shampoo as a specialty good for which only one brand will do; life insurance should seem like an obvious unsought good, but some may see suits and dresses as unsought goods.

3.   Product classifications relate to marketing mix as follows:

	Convenience	Shopping	Specialty	Unsought
Profit margin	Low	Medium	High	High
Manufacturer or retail promotion	Manufacturer	Both	Both	Both
Distribution intensity (no. of retail outlets)	High	Medium	Low	Low
More self-service or personal selling	Self-service	Personal selling	Personal selling	Personal selling

Class Exercise 2: The goal of this exercise is to help students understand product positioning—that is, customers' perceptions of a product's attributes—by considering the position of several products. Possible answers:

1. Volvo automobiles   safe
2. Keds athletic shoes   **inexpensive, simple comfort**
3. Montblanc writing instruments   **more expensive**
4. Diet Coke   **superior taste**
5. Hampton Inn   **for business travel**
6. Dom Perignon champagne   **premium taste**
7. Curtis Mathes television sets   **better quality**
8. Avis Rent-A-Car   **more responsive**
9. Just for Men hair color   **for men only**
10. Subway sandwiches   **alternative fast food**

Debate Issue: In terms of product management, can following the product life cycle (PLC) philosophy be detrimental?

Chapter Quiz: Answers to multiple-choice questions are

1.	b	3.	c
2.	d	4.	a

CLASS EXERCISE 1

1. List the brand name of the product you usually prefer for each of the following product categories:

Car/truck   Soft drink   Shampoo
Compact disc player   Bicycle   Toothpaste
Suit or dress   Life insurance

2. Which of these brands are you
   a. likely to buy frequently?
   b. willing to spend considerable effort to obtain?
   c. willing to accept substitutes for?

Based on this information, group the eight products into the following product classifications: convenience, shopping, specialty, or unsought.

3. How does the classification influence the marketing mix factors?

	Convenience	Shopping	Specialty	Unsought
Profit margin				
Manufacturer or retail promotion				
Distribution intensity (number of retail outlets)				
More self-service or personal selling				

CLASS EXERCISE 2

DESCRIBE THE FOLLOWING BRANDS' RELATIVE POSITIONING IN THEIR PRODUCT CATEGORIES:

1. Volvo automobiles
2. Keds athletic shoes
3. Mont Blanc writing instruments
4. Diet Coke
5. Hampton Inn
6. Dom Perignon champagne
7. Curtis Mathes television sets
8. Avis Rent-A-Car
9. Just For Men hair color
10. Subway sandwiches

DEBATE ISSUE

IN TERMS OF PRODUCT MANAGEMENT, CAN FOLLOWING THE PRODUCT LINE CYCLE (PLC) PHILOSOPHY BE DETRIMENTAL?

YES

- Difficult to determine specific stage of PLC
- "Self-fulfilling prophecy"
- Self-fulfilling prophecy can cause the PLC to be shortened and thus curtail profit potential
- Self-fulfilling prophecy can have significant effects on product mix

NO

- Must be accompanied by other analytical techniques
- Can properly plan for new product development or improvement
- Better able to determine when a product should be harvested or receive reinvestment
- Proper marketing strategies will facilitate optimal resource allocation

CHAPTER QUIZ

1. Products are classified as being organizational (industrial) or consumer products depending on the
   a. goals of the organization.
   b. buyer's intended use of the product.
   c. seller's intended use of the product.
   d. location of use.
   e. types of outlets from which they are purchased.

2. Which stage of the product life cycle is characterized by severe competition?
   a. Decline
   b. Plateau
   c. Introduction
   d. Maturity
   e. Stabilization

3. The process of creating and designing products so that consumers perceive them as different from competing products is called
   a. product creation.
   b. process design.
   c. product differentiation.
   d. product designation.
   e. product incubation.

4. A product manager in a large multiproduct company
   a. oversees a product, a product line, or several distinct products that make up an interrelated group.
   b. is responsible for a single brand.
   c. is seldom involved in the planning function.
   d. is involved mainly with product financing.
   e. is responsible for different markets.

ANSWERS TO DISCUSSION AND REVIEW QUESTIONS

1. List the tangible and intangible attributes of a pair of Nike athletic shoes. Compare the benefits of the Nike shoes with those of an intangible product, such as a hairstyling in a salon.

    This question is intended to get students to recognize that product benefits are more than the visible, tangible attributes. Tangible attributes of a pair of Nike shoes include the quality of the leather and other materials, inside supports, cushioned heels, and long-lasting soles. Intangible attributes include product image, the fact that these shoes are a prized possession for a special group of consumers, and identification with athletic, fitness-oriented individuals.

    The attributes of a pair of shoes are more visible than are the attributes of hairstyle. One who markets a hairstyling service must deal with intangible characteristics such as image, fashion, and confidence.

2. A product has been referred to as a "psychological bundle of satisfaction." Is this a good definition of a product? Why or why not?

    Products do provide psychological benefits as well as satisfaction, but they are more than this simple definition implies. The tangible and intangible attributes include functional, social, and psychological utilities of all parts of the product. Stating that a product is a "psychological bundle of satisfaction" does not make it explicit that some products provide mechanical and functional features that help accomplish a task but do not necessarily provide a great deal of psychological stimulation. For example, a car's fan belt is desired for the functional benefits it provides; these benefits are probably more important than psychological aspects.

3. Is a personal computer sold at a retail a store a consumer product or an organizational product? Defend your answer.

    The classification of products into the organizational or consumer class depends on the buyer's purpose and intent. If a personal computer is purchased for a consumer's home use, it is a consumer product. If it is purchased for a business office, it is an industrial or organizational product.

4. How do convenience products and shopping products differ? What are the distinguishing characteristics of each type of product?

    Convenience products (milk, pay telephones, and gasoline) are purchased at the closest retail facility. Shopping products (clothing and furniture) are purchased after comparisons and alternatives have been evaluated. Distinguishing characteristics include frequency of purchase, time of consumption, searching time, margins, and product adjustment. Convenience products rank lower than shopping products in terms of searching time, margins, adjustment, and time of consumption. Convenience products also are replaced more often than shopping products.

5. In the category of organizational products, how do component parts differ from process materials?

Component parts become a part of the physical product and are either finished items ready for assembly or products that need little processing before assembly. Although they become part of a larger product, component parts often can be identified and distinguished easily.

Process materials are used directly in the production of products; unlike component parts, they are not readily identifiable.

6. How does an organization's product mix relate to its development of a product line? When should an enterprise add depth to its product lines rather than width to its product mix?

Product mix is the composite of products that a firm sells. The product line includes a group of products closely related in terms of marketing, technical, or end-use considerations. For example, toothpaste is a product Procter & Gamble sells: Gleem II and Crest are the two brands in the product line. A firm should add depth to the product line when there is greater opportunity to profit by building on current marketing expertise and consumers' acceptance in a particular market. Launching new products to add to the marketing mix may require new marketing channels, promotion, pricing techniques, and production facilities. Many firms have expanded by increasing the width of their product mixes and depth of their product lines.

7. How do industry profits change as a product moves through the four stages of its life cycle?

During the introduction stage, profits are negative. The firm should break even as the growth stage is reached, and profits should increase rapidly and show the highest profit-to-sales ratio during late growth. Profits decline during maturity and usually drop further during the decline stage.

8. What is the relationship between the concepts of product mix and product life cycle?

Most firms are not tied to a single product. They often have a number of products in the product mix, and different products are usually at different stages of the product life cycle. This means that new products must be introduced and the life of existing products prolonged to meet organizational sales goals.

9. What type of organization might use a venture team to develop new products? What are the advantages and disadvantages of such a team?

The venture team approach is appropriate for new products, especially those designed for markets with which the company is unfamiliar. A venture team offers several advantages. The responsibility for all product development remains with a group that develops the product from inception to commercialization. Usually, the organizational chart is horizontal rather than vertical; this cuts across all formal organizational lines. Finally, all functional areas are involved. Disadvantages of the venture team are that it disrupts the formal organizational system and does not offer complete continuity. Often, after the product is developed, it is turned over to a product manager.

10. Describe the various ways in which a camcorder can be differentiated from its competitors. Are these characteristics real or perceived?

A camcorder can be differentiated by its size, shape, and color, which is its style. It can also be differentiated by its specific features, such as the location of the buttons, or switches, the ease in programming for recording and playback, and its warranty and repair locations. The brand name can also be used for differentiation. The characteristics of its style, location of switches or buttons, and ease of use are all real attributes. The warranty and repair locations, while not visible or tangible at the time of purchase, are also real attributes. However, the image created by the brand name may be only a perception. For instance, one company making camcorder models that are sold under several different brand names.

11. Explain how the term *quality* has been used to differentiate products in the automobile industry in recent years. What are some of the makes and models of automobiles that come to mind when you hear the term *high quality* and *poor quality*?

We have heard the phrase "Quality is Job 1" on commercials for Ford automobiles and references to "commitment to quality" on Chrysler commercials. While the term "quality" has varied definitions, we usually associate high quality with a Mercedes-Benz, Infiniti, Lexus, Cadillac, or Lincoln Continental, and low quality with the ill-fated Yugo.

COMMENTS ON THE CASES

Case 9.1   The Positioning of the New *American Heritage Dictionary*

The primary objective of this case is to illustrate how the Houghton Mifflin Company successfully positioned its new *American Heritage Dictionary* (AHD). The case further depicts the power of positioning as a marketing tool in that the dictionary industry—prior to the company's aggressive action—was hardly characterized by marketing maneuvers. It shows that positioning can be a very important part of overall marketing strategy.

The initial question asks the student to decide whether the AHD was positioned to avoid or facilitate direct competition with other dictionary products, and to give a rationale for this decision. Here, a case can be made for either the avoidance or facilitation of direct competition. In regard to avoidance, since the new AHD has unique characteristics that may be important to a specific segment of buyers—like the distinctive black jacket—it may be considered as "positioned away from" competing—that is, red-covered—products. However, a strong case may also be made for the direct competition scenario, since the new AHD may be justifiably considered "positioned at" the competition due to its possessing superior performance characteristics and being offered at a lower price, attributes that were then heavily promoted.

Question 2 asks the reader to identify and discuss those product characteristics on which the new AHD was differentially positioned. The salient characteristics include not only the product's size, cover color, improved readability, and lower relative price, but, possibly more important, the general fact that the product was aggressively marketed at all—in an industry not accustomed to such activity. This suggests that Houghton Mifflin is the first company in the industry to establish a distinct position in the minds of customers. The benefits of this aggressive positioning strategy are clearly reflected in the remarkable success of the product.

The final question asks the student to identify the type of consumer product represented by the new AHD. Although it does not fit exactly into any of the standard consumer product categories, given that the product is one likely to invoke some degree of consumer planning as regards its purchase, it is probably best viewed as a *shopping product*. It is too expensive to be a convenience product and probably not unique enough to be considered a specialty product, although a case could be made for the latter in light of the highly successful and innovative positioning of the product.

Video Information

Video Title: The New American Heritage Dictionary
Location: Tape 2, Segment 9
Length: 11:00
Video Overview: The Houghton Mifflin Company's remarkably successful positioning of the new AHD exemplifies the importance of establishing for a new product a unique and distinctive position in the customer's mind in regard to unique and meaningful product benefits. By virtue of the AHD being the first aggressively marketed and clearly positioned product in the dictionary industry, the company reaped huge benefits.

Multiple-Choice Questions About the Video

a   1. Houghton Mifflin's successful marketing of the new AHD may be attributed to
     a. the positioning of the product on the basis of unique and meaningful benefits.
     b. being the first company to actively market its product in the industry.
     c. offering a lower-priced dictionary with better features.
     d. effective advertising campaigns.
     e. the positioning of the product to avoid direct competition with existing products.

c   2. As exemplified in this case, positioning is important because
     a. it allows the marketer to charge a higher price.
     b. it establishes for the product a distinct difference to build advertising campaigns around.
     c. it establishes for the product a distinct difference relative to the competition in the mind of consumers.
     d. in any particular industry there are only a limited number of available positions.
     e. it allows the marketer to experiment with the variables of the marketing mix in a more creative fashion.

Case 9.2   Schwinn: Reviving a Classic American Brand

The goal of this case is to give students an opportunity to discuss some basic concepts of product decision making by examining a well-known company's attempts to stage a comeback and regain competitive strength. The Schwinn organization has been around for over a hundred years; the Schwinn name is a widely recognized, familiar, and respected bicycle brand. In recent times, however, the Schwinn organization has been struggling.

The first question asks students to discuss how Schwinn mountain bicycles would be classified. Schwinn mountain bicycles could be classified as either a shopping product or a specialty product, depending on the customer's decision processes and behavior during the purchase process. The fact that Schwinn mountain bicycles are in the $1,500 price range is likely to mean that they are distributed through exclusive distribution, which would contribute to the product being classified as a specialty product.

Question 2 asks about the bicycle industry's stage in the product life cycle. The bicycle industry is in the mature stage of the product life cycle. There is strong competition among a significant number of competitors. Competitors use relatively small differences to distinguish their brands. Some competitors are being driven from the marketplace.

The third question asks students to evaluate the Schwinn management decision to launch the Cruiser. Students' assessments of the move will vary. On the one hand, students may argue that the Cruiser represents a return to the past, yielding products that are not "cutting-edge" machines. The Cruiser sounds like a very traditional bicycle produced by Schwinn for a number of years. Introduction of this product will reinforce Schwinn's image as an old-fashioned, nonprogressive, noninnovative organization. On the other hand, students may argue that the introduction of the Cruiser is a good idea because there are enough customers out there who will want this kind of bike. These customers are older individuals who are seeking a simple, well-constructed, relatively inexpensive bicycle.

10 DEVELOPING AND MANAGING PRODUCTS

TEACHING RESOURCES QUICK REFERENCE GUIDE

Resource	Location
Purpose and Perspective	IRM, p. 206
Guide for Using Color Transparencies	IRM, p. 206
Lecture Outline	IRM, p. 206
Class Exercises, Debate Issue, and Chapter Quiz	IRM, p. 215
Class Exercise 1	IRM, p. 217
Class Exercise 2	IRM, p. 218
Debate Issue: Is test marketing always necessary when launching a new product?	IRM, p. 219
Chapter Quiz	IRM, p. 220
Answers to Discussion and Review Questions	IRM, p. 221
Comments on the Cases	IRM, p. 225
Case 10.1	IRM, p. 225
Video	Tape 2, Segment 10
Video Information	IRM, p. 225
Multiple-Choice Questions About the Video	IRM, p. 226
Case 10.2	IRM, p. 227
Transparency Acetates	Transparency package
Examination Questions: Essay	TB, p. 185
Examination Questions: Multiple-Choice	TB, p. 186
Examination Questions: True-False	TB, p. 199
Author-Selected Multiple-Choice Test Items	TB, p. 447

PURPOSE AND PERSPECTIVE

This chapter examines several ways to improve an organization's product mix, including managing existing products through line extensions and product modifications. Next we discuss how firms develop new products, from idea generation to commercialization, and how people accept these new products through the product adoption process. We address issues and decisions associated with managing products during all life cycle stages, including the elimination of weak products from the product mix.

GUIDE FOR USING COLOR TRANSPARENCIES

There are two groups of color transparencies. The transparencies identified by a double number are the same as the figures in the text. The transparencies labeled with a number and a letter are illustrations that do not appear in the text, but they can be used as additional examples of concepts discussed.

Figure 10.3   Phases of new-product development
Figure 10.4   Concept test for a tick and flea control product
Figure 10.6   Stages of expansion into a national market during commercialization
Figure 10.8   Distribution of product adopter categories
Figure 10.11   Product elimination process
Figure 10A   Chapter 10 outline
Figure 10B   Product adoption process
Figure 10C   Neutrogena HeatSafe is a line extension.
Figure 10D   Folger's uses advertisements to create awareness and interest to facilitate customer's movement through the product adoption process.
Figure 10E   Example of a new product

LECTURE OUTLINE

I.   Managing existing products

An organization can overcome weaknesses and gaps in its existing product mix through line extension or product modification.

A.   A **line extension** is the development of a product that is closely related to one or more products in an existing product line.

1.   A line extension is specifically designed to meet somewhat different needs of customers.

2.   Line extensions are more common than new products because they are a less expensive, lower risk alternative for increasing sales.

B. **Product modification** means changing one or more characteristics of a firm's product and removing the original product from the line.

1. Product modification is less risky than new-product development.

2. Three conditions must exist for product modification to improve the firm's product mix.

    a. The product must be modifiable.

    b. The customer must be able to perceive that a modification has been made.

    c. The modification should make the product more consistent with customers' desires.

3. There are three major ways to modify products.

    a. **Quality modifications** are changes to a product's dependability and durability, usually executed by altering the materials or the production process.

        (1) Increased quality may allow the firm to charge a higher price by creating customer loyalty and decreasing price sensitivity.

        (2) Reduced quality may allow the firm to lower its price and direct the item at a more price-sensitive market.

        (3) Some companies have been able to both increase quality and reduce cost of a product.

    b. **Functional modifications** are changes that affect a product's versatility, effectiveness, convenience, or safety.

        (1) These modifications make a product useful to more people and thus enlarge its market.

(2)   These changes can place the product in a favorable competitive position by providing benefits that other brands do not offer and helping the firm achieve a progressive image.

c.   **Aesthetic modifications** change the sensory appeal of a product by altering its taste, texture, sound, smell, or appearance.

(1)   Aesthetics of a product can differentiate it from competing brands to gain market share.

(2)   The major drawback in using aesthetic modifications is that their value is subjective.

II.   Developing new products

A genuinely new product offers innovative benefits and is frequently expensive and risky to develop and introduce. The **new-product development process** is a seven-phase process for introducing products.

A.   **Idea generation,** the first step in the development process, occurs when firms seek product ideas to achieve organizational objectives.

1.   Firms trying to maximize product effectiveness usually develop systematic approaches to new-product development.

2.   At the heart of innovation is a purposeful, focused effort to identify new ways to serve a market.

3.   New ideas may be generated internally or externally.

4.   Brainstorming and incentives or rewards for a good idea are typical intrafirm devices to encourage the development of ideas.

B.   In phase two, **screening,** the most promising ideas are selected for further review.

1.   Ideas are analyzed to determine whether they match the organization's objectives, resources, and abilities.

2. The potential market, the needs and wants of buyers, possible environmental changes, and possible cannibalizations of current products are also analyzed and weighed.

3. Using a checklist of new-product requirements to ensure a systematic approach, more ideas are rejected during screening than in any other stage.

C. Stage three is **concept testing**, seeking potential buyers' responses to a product idea. A sample of potential buyers is presented with a product idea to determine their attitudes and initial buying intentions regarding the product.

1. Low cost enables a firm to test more than one concept for the same product before it invests considerable resources in research and development.

2. Product development personnel use the results of concept testing to find out which aspects of the product are most important to potential customers.

3. Concept tests consist of a brief written or oral description of the concept followed by a series of questions on the product's advantages, disadvantages, and price.

D. During stage four, **business analysis,** the product idea is evaluated to determine its potential contribution to the firm's sales, costs, and profits.

1. The product's fit with the organization's existing product mix is analyzed.

2. Present and future market demands for the product are studied.

3. The product's effect on the firm's sales, costs, and profits is projected.

   a. Future sales and profits are difficult to estimate and not particularly precise.

   b. Breakeven payback analysis may be used.

4. Expected environmental and competitive changes and their effects on future sales, costs, and profits are examined.

5. The capabilities of the organization's research, development, engineering, and production are considered.

6. New facilities are planned, and use of present facilities is reviewed.

7. The relative ease of obtaining financing is measured against overall organizational goals.

E. In stage five, **product development,** the firm finds out if it is technically feasible to produce the product and if it can be produced at costs low enough to make the final price reasonable.

1. The idea or concept is converted into a prototype or working model that should reveal the tangible and intangible attributes associated with the product in consumers' minds.

2. The functionality of the prototype must be tested, including performance, safety, and convenience.

3. The specific level of product quality is determined based on what price the target market views as acceptable and on the quality level of the firm's own and competing products.

4. Branding, packaging, labeling, pricing, and promotion are determined during the latter part of development.

F. Stage six, **test marketing,** is the limited introduction of the product to gauge the extent to which potential customers will actually buy it.

1. Test marketing is not an extension of screening and development stages, but a sample launching of the entire marketing mix.

2. Test marketing provides several important benefits.

a. It minimizes the risk of product failure.

b. It lets marketers expose a product in a natural marketing environment to obtain a measure of its sales performance.

    c.   It allows marketers to identify any weaknesses in the product itself or in other aspects of the marketing mix.

    d.   Marketers can experiment in different test areas with advertising, price, and packaging variations.

    3.   Test marketing is also expensive and involves risks.

        a.   Competitors may try to jam the testing program by increasing promotion of their own products.

        b.   Competitors may copy the product in the testing stage and rush to introduce a similar product.

        c.   Some alternative methods, such as simulated test marketing, are less expensive and less risky.

    G.   Stage seven, **commercialization,** is the phase of deciding on full-scale manufacturing and marketing plans and preparing budgets.

        1.   Marketing management analyzes the results of test marketing to find out what changes in the marketing mix are needed before the product is introduced.

        2.   The organization refines plans for production, quality control, distribution, and promotion.

        3.   Enormous amounts of money spent during this stage on marketing and manufacturing may not be recovered for several years.

        4.   Products are usually introduced in stages, starting in a set of geographic areas and gradually expanding into adjacent areas.

III.   The product adoption process

    A.   The **product adoption process** are the stages that buyers go through in accepting a product.

1. *Awareness:* Buyers become aware of the product.

2. *Interest:* Buyers seek information and are receptive to learning about the product.

3. *Evaluation:* Buyers consider the product's benefits and determine whether to try it.

4. *Trial:* Buyers examine, test, or try the product to determine its usefulness.

5. *Adoption:* Buyers purchase the product and can be expected to use it to solve problems.

B. When an organization introduces a new product, people do not all begin the adoption process at the same time, nor do they move through it at the same speed.

1. **Innovators** are the first to adopt a new product; they enjoy trying new products and tend to be venturesome.

2. **Early adopters** choose new products carefully and are viewed as "the people to check with" by buyers in remaining categories.

3. **Early majority** people adopt just prior to the average person; they are deliberate and cautious in trying new products.

4. **Late majority** people are skeptical and adopt new products only when they feel it is necessary.

5. **Laggards** are the last to adopt and are oriented toward the past and suspicious of new products.

IV. Product life cycle management

A. Marketing strategy in the growth stage

1. The goal in this stage is to establish the product's position and fortify it by encouraging brand loyalty.

2. Sales momentum must be supported by adjustments in the marketing mix.

   a. The marketer might expand product offerings to appeal to more specialized markets.

   b. The marketer should analyze the product position in relation to competing products and correct weak or omitted attributes.

   c. The marketer should see that gaps in the marketing channel are filled and that the physical distribution system is running efficiently.

   d. Advertising expenditures may be slightly lower than in the introductory stage but are still substantial; as sales increase, promotion costs as a percentage of total sales should drop.

   e. Price cuts can facilitate price competition and discourage new competitors from entering the market.

B. Marketing strategy for mature products

   1. Because many products are in the maturity stage, marketers must know how to deal with these products and be prepared to adjust their marketing strategy.

   2. Slower market growth, increased competitive action, and a greater emphasis on changing a product's price, promotion, and distribution characterize the maturity stage.

   3. Finding new product uses and users can play a major role in increasing sales and remaining competitive in the maturity stage.

C. Marketing strategy for declining products

   1. At this stage, sales curves turn downward and marketers must determine whether to eliminate a product or reposition it in an attempt to extend its life.

   2. Usually a declining product has lost its distinctiveness because similar competing products have been introduced.

3. During a product's decline, marketers usually employ the following strategies:

    a. Outlets with strong sales volume are maintained, and unprofitable outlets are weeded out.

    b. Advertising expenditures are at a minimum.

    c. Current pricing can be maintained, increased, or decreased.

        (1) Maintaining the price may squeeze out all possible profits despite decline in sales.

        (2) Prices may be increased as costs rise if a loyal core market still wants the product.

        (3) Prices may be cut to reduce existing inventory so that the product can be deleted.

V. Product elimination

Product elimination is the process of deleting a product from the product mix when it no longer satisfies a sufficient number of customers.

A. A weak product is a drain on potential profitability and the marketer's time and resources.

B. It is often difficult to drop a product over the protests of management, salespeople, and loyal customers.

C. Instead of letting a weak product become a financial burden, a firm should periodically and systematically review and analyze its contribution to the firm's sales for a given time frame.

D. There are three ways to eliminate products.

    1. A *phase out* lets the product decline without changing the marketing strategy.

2. A *runout* policy calls for increased marketing efforts in core markets, elimination of some marketing expenditures, or price reductions to exploit any strengths left in the product.

3. *Dropping* the product immediately is the best strategy when losses are too great to prolong its life.

CLASS EXERCISES, DEBATE ISSUE, AND CHAPTER QUIZ

On the following pages, you will find two class exercises, a debate issue, and a chapter quiz. These are formatted in large-size type so that you can use them as class handouts or for making transparencies. Below are the authors' comments on the class exercises, the debate topic for this chapter, and the answers to the chapter quiz.

Class Exercise 1: This exercise asks students to create new-product ideas using the first four phases of the new-product development process.

Your class or group is a venture team, designed to create entirely new products. Students work for the _____ company (you or students decide).

1. *Idea generation.* Ask students to think of something they wish were available that isn't. Reviewing recent advances in areas such as telecommunications or thinking about things they've seen in science fiction or futuristic movies may help stimulate discussion. You can classify ideas in terms of product modifications (quality, function, or aesthetics). Caution the class not to criticize any ideas at this stage.

2. *Screening.* Product development moves from the general to the specific. This phase gets more detail-oriented and requires that students' creative ideas now show some practicality. (You may want to allow some leeway on technical feasibility because you may not know if it can be done or not.) Some may develop ideas that are workable but are not needed or wanted by consumers. Remind students that more ideas are rejected in this stage than in any other.

3. *Concept testing*
    a. Concept testing is most likely to occur through focus groups but can be done in other ways.
    b. Not all new product ideas have to be concept tested.

4. *Business analysis*
    a. Some products may generate initial interest but produce no long-term profits. An example is no-run pantyhose, which can be made but would produce diminishing demand.
    b. Another firm may produce a similar product and capitalize on its superior market position. Regulatory and social forces may not allow continued sales of some questionable products.
    c. Secondary data for product categories may help estimate sales potential and typical industry costs. An experiment or survey could measure consumer buying intentions.

Class Exercise 2: The objective of this exercise is for students to apply the product life cycle to existing products. Answers:

1.	Videocassette recorders (VCRs)	**maturity**
2.	Digital display watches	**decline**
3.	Blue jeans	**maturity**
4.	Laptop computers	**growth**
5.	CB radios	**decline**
6.	Wine coolers	**maturity**
7.	Fax machines	**growth**
8.	Minivans	**growth**
9.	Compact discs	**growth**
10.	Rubic's cube	**decline**
11.	Skateboards	**maturity**
12.	Tourism in Eastern Europe	**growth**
13.	Typewriters	**decline**
14.	Black-and-white television sets	**decline**
15.	Peanut butter	**maturity**

Debate Issue: Is test marketing always necessary when launching a new product?

Chapter Quiz: Answers to multiple-choice questions are

1.	a	3.	b
2.	e	4.	e

CLASS EXERCISE 1

YOUR CLASS OR GROUP IS A VENTURE TEAM DESIGNED TO CREATE ENTIRELY NEW PRODUCTS. YOU WORK FOR THE _____ COMPANY.

1. *Idea generation.* You can get ideas for new products for the company from personnel, customers, competitors, ad agencies, consultants, and private research firms. One method you can use now is brainstorming ideas. Make a list of possible product ideas.

2. *Screening.* Pick the ones you think are most feasible.
   a. Do you really think that this product can be made and marketed? What kinds of resources (financial and technological) would be required?
   b. Does the product fit with the nature and wants of buyers? Do people really care about what the product offers?

3. *Concept testing*
   a. How could you best present the product concept to consumers to get their reactions?
   b. Is it necessary to conduct concept testing on each product?

4. *Business analysis.* Determine potential for profit.
   a. Is demand strong enough to justify entering the market, and will demand endure?
   b. How might environmental and competitive changes affect future results?
   c. How could research be used to help estimate sales, costs, and profits?

CLASS EXERCISE 2

IN WHAT STAGES OF THE PRODUCT LIFE CYCLE ARE THE FOLLOWING PRODUCTS?

1. Videocassette recorders
2. Digital display watches
3. Blue jeans
4. Laptop computers
5. CB radios
6. Wine coolers
7. Facsimile (fax) machines
8. Minivans
9. Compact discs
10. Rubic's cube
11. Skateboards
12. Travel to Eastern Europe
13. Typewriters
14. Black and white television sets
15. Peanut butter

DEBATE ISSUE

IS TEST MARKETING ALWAYS NECESSARY WHEN LAUNCHING A NEW PRODUCT?

YES

- Reduces risk of product failure

- Provides opportunity to refine various marketing mix components (variations in promotion, price, packaging, distribution)

- Allows a firm to "preview" the product's performance in the marketplace relative to competitors

- Based on test marketing results, some products are not commercialized

NO

- Unnecessary if previous stages of introduction process were performed accurately

- Invalid possibly because of competitive interference

- Tips off competitors about firm's new products

- Competitors can monitor test marketing

- In some cases the costs of a product failure may be less than the cost of test marketing

CHAPTER QUIZ

1. Changes that affect the sensory appeal of a product by altering its taste, texture, sound, smell, or visual characteristics are called _____ modifications.
   a. aesthetic
   b. functional
   c. operational
   d. quality
   e. feature

2. The group of managers has been assigned the task of developing a new product, has gotten several good ideas, and is now in the process of using a checklist to assess each idea. The managers are at what stage of the new-product development process?
   a. Business analysis
   b. Product testing
   c. Idea generation
   d. Commercialization
   e. Screening

3. If an individual is aware of a product and is self-motivated to find information regarding a product, in what stage of the product adoption process is that person?
   a. Information stage
   b. Interest stage
   c. Evaluation stage
   d. Trial stage
   e. Awareness stage

4. The product elimination process is similar to the _____ step of the new-product development process because both involve deciding whether the product should be in the product mix.
   a. idea generation
   b. screening
   c. product development
   d. test marketing
   e. business analysis

ANSWERS TO DISCUSSION AND REVIEW QUESTIONS

1. Compare and contrast the three major ways of modifying a product.

   Any product modification changes one or more of a product's characteristics. The three major ways to modify a product are to alter its quality, function, or aesthetics. Changes affecting a product's dependability and durability are quality modifications. Functional modifications are those that affect a product's versatility, effectiveness, convenience, or safety. Quality modifications usually can be made by altering materials or the production process. Functional modifications usually require that the product be redesigned. Aesthetic modifications are less tangible than either quality or functional ones because they change the way a product tastes, sounds, smells, or looks rather than how it actually works. Although consumers usually perceive quality and functional changes as improvements, aesthetic modifications are more subjective and therefore more risky.

2. Identify and briefly explain the seven major phases of the new-product development process.

   The seven major phases of new-product development are market generation, screening, concept testing, business analysis, product development, test marketing, and commercialization. Idea generation is the activity in which business and other organizations look for product ideas that will help them accomplish their objectives. New-product ideas can come from internal sources such as marketing managers, researchers, sales personnel, engineers, or other organizational personnel. They can also be generated outside the company from customers, competitors, advertising agencies, management consultants, and private research organizations. In the screening phase, products with the greatest potential are selected for further consideration. Product ideas are analyzed to determine whether they fit the organization's objectives and resources and whether or not the organization can produce and market the product.

   Concept testing is a low-cost procedure to determine consumers' initial reaction to a product idea. During concept testing, a small sample of potential buyers is presented with a product idea through a written or oral description to discover their attitudes and initial buying intentions regarding the product. Concept testing is followed by the business analysis phase, in which the product idea is evaluated to determine its potential contribution to the firm's sales, costs, and profits. Marketers evaluate how well the product fits with the existing product mix, the strength of market demand for the product, the types of environmental and competitive changes to be expected, and how these changes might affect the product's future sales, costs, and profits.

   Product development is the phase in which the organization discovers the technical feasibility of producing the product and whether or not it can be produced at costs that will result in a reasonable final price. The company creates a prototype and then performs laboratory tests on performance, safety, convenience, and other functional qualities. If the tests indicate that the product merits test marketing, marketers begin to make decisions regarding branding, packaging, labeling, pricing, and promotion.

   Test marketing involves a limited introduction of a product in geographic areas chosen to represent the intended market. The goal is to determine the reactions of probable buyers. The last phase of product development is commercialization, the stage in which plans for full-scale manufacturing and marketing are refined and settled, and budgets for the product are prepared. During this phase the organization has expenditures for plant, equipment, and personnel, advertising, personal selling, and other types of promotion.

3. Do small companies that manufacture one or two products need to be concerned about developing and managing products? Why or why not?

Any manufacturing firm, regardless of size or number of products, must be concerned about developing and managing products. This may be especially critical to a firm with one or a few products, because the firm's profits (and sales) are derived entirely from this product. To maintain its current position, the firm must continuously seek ways to improve its product and thus remain competitive; otherwise, customers will turn to substitute products that provide similar benefits. Managing the product involves more than product modification; it also includes designing appropriate promotion, pricing, and distribution strategies that are based on an appraisal of environmental factors such as economic, technological, social, consumer, and legal/political forces.

4. Why is product development a cross-functional activity within an organization? That is, why must finance, engineering, manufacturing, and other functional areas be involved?

Long-range strategic planning strengthens the firm's commitment to product development. Such commitment involves various functional areas in the process of commercializing a product idea. To develop the product successfully, a firm typically needs several years and considerable resources (which is a capital budgeting problem). The legal function is essential in obtaining patents and copyrights, clearing brand names, and so on. Engineering needs to develop the product idea into a product that customers want (based on marketing information) and that the firm is capable of producing (production). The financial commitment for developing product prototypes, acquiring appropriate production equipment, testing the product in the market, and launching the product may be substantial; thus, the financial function is necessary to obtain needed capital and maintain the proper cash flows.

5. What is the major purpose of concept testing, and how is it accomplished?

Concept testing allows an organization to determine consumers' initial reactions to a product idea before investing considerable resources in research and development. To determine initial attitudes and buying intentions about a product, marketers present a small sample of potential buyers with the product idea, either in written or oral form. Concept tests consist of a brief description of the concept followed by a series of questions on the product's attractiveness, benefits, advantages over competitors, price, and possible improvements. Product development personnel use the test results to identify those product characteristics that potential customers find most valuable.

6. What are the benefits and disadvantages of test marketing?

Benefits:
- Marketers can expose a product in a natural environment to gauge its sales performance.
- Marketers can identify perceived weaknesses in the product or other parts of the marketing mix.
- Marketers can experiment with variations in the advertising, price, and packaging in different test markets.
- Marketers can measure the extent of brand awareness, brand switching, and repeat purchases that result in variations in the marketing mix.

Disadvantages:
- Test marketing can be expensive.
- Test marketing can delay new product introduction.
- Competitors may emerge with their own similar product as a result of the new product in a test market.
- Competitors may skew the results of the marketing measurements by offering sales and promotions or increasing the advertising on their own current product line.
- Test markets may yield erroneous results and cause full-fledged introductions of new products that will not be successful.

7. Why does the process of commercialization sometimes take a considerable amount of time?

Organizations usually launch a product in stages, beginning in a limited geographic area and gradually expanding to include other areas. Using this process, known as a rollout, means taking years to market a product on a national scale. For example, a product may first be marketed in only one city, then in the state in which the city is located, then in adjacent states, and eventually in remaining states. At any time during this process, the company may decide to make changes that slow the operation even more, such as packaging, advertising, or price changes. Gradual product introduction is often necessary because it takes time to establish a system of wholesalers and retailers, develop a distribution network, and manufacture the product in required quantities.

8. What are some of the ways in which a company can improve new-product implementation success?

- Talk with consumers; know what they want.
- Set realistic sales goals.
- Ensure cooperation from all areas of the company (research, manufacturing, marketing, and distribution) before launching the product.
- Look for consumer acceptance, costs, and sales support at each stage of product development.
- Test the market long enough to get an accurate reading.
- Evaluate all product failures before proceeding.

9. What are the stages in the product adoption process, and how do they affect the commercialization phase?

a. *Awareness.* The buyer becomes aware of the product.
b. *Interest.* The buyer seeks information and is receptive to learning about the product.
c. *Evaluation.* The buyer considers the product's benefits and determines whether to try it.
d. *Trial.* The buyer examines, tests, or tries the product to determine its usefulness relative to his or her needs.
e. *Adoption.* The buyer purchases the product and can be expected to use it when the need for this general type of product arises again.

The adoption model has several implications for the commercialization phase. The company must promote the product in order to create widespread *awareness* of its existence and its benefits. Samples or simulated trials help buyers make initial purchase decisions. Buyer opinions are reinforced through the marketer's emphasis of quality control during the *evaluation* stage. Production and distribution must be linked to patterns of *adoption* and repeated purchases.

10. What are the five major adopter categories that describe the length of time required for a customer to adopt a new product, and what are the characteristics of each?

- Innovators, the first to adopt a new product, enjoy trying new products and are venturesome.
- Early adopters chose new products next and are viewed as the "people to watch" by the remaining adopter categories.
- Early majority buyers adopt just prior to the average consumer and are usually deliberate and cautious when trying new products.
- Late majority adopters are skeptical and usually adopt new products because of economic reasons or social pressure.
- Laggards are the last to adopt a new product and are considered to be oriented toward the past and suspicious in nature.

11. In what ways does the marketing strategy for a mature product differ from the marketing strategy for a growth product?

During the growth stage of a product's life cycle, product sales are increasing. At the same time, competitors are entering the market with products that appeal to specific market segments. At this stage, the goal of the marketing strategy is to establish the product's position and encourage brand loyalty by attracting those market segments that are most interested in the product. To achieve market penetration, marketers focus on increasing the number of dealers and keeping the distribution system running smoothly. To compete effectively with challengers, marketers may have to increase the use of segmentation.

By the time a product reaches the maturity stage, its position has been firmly established, and because weaker competitors have dropped out, competition is not as intense. However, the benefits or qualities that customers want from the product may change over time, requiring changes in marketing strategy to keep the product competitive. Strategy changes from a focus on expanding the dealer network to a focus on intensifying service to dealers and providing them with incentives to sell the brand. To maintain sales and market share, marketers develop and promote new uses for the product as well as employ a greater mixture of pricing strategies, including markdowns and price incentives. The critical difference between the marketing strategy for a growth product and a mature product is that the goal of the former is to increase sales by making the product widely available and firmly establishing its position, and the goal of the latter is to keep from losing ground as the product ages.

12. What types of problems are caused by a weak product in a product mix?

Weak products reduce an organization's profitability in several ways. First, they drain resources that could be used to modify stronger products or develop new ones. Second, because fewer marginal products are manufactured, per-unit production costs increase. Third, the negative feelings customers may develop toward a weak product may be transferred to other company products, thereby reducing sales.

13. Describe the most effective approach for eliminating weak products from a product mix.

The most effective method for eliminating products is to employ a periodic systematic review in which each product is evaluated to determine its value to the organization's product mix. The review analyzes not only a product's contribution to current sales, but includes projections of future sales, costs, and profits. It considers the merits of changing the marketing strategy to improve the product's performance and provides an organization with the information it requires to determine when to eliminate a product. Once a decision is made to eliminate a product, a firm can use a phase out approach, a runout approach or can drop the product immediately.

COMMENTS ON THE CASES

Case 10.1 Product Management at Outboard Marine Corporation

The goal of this case is to provide an example of an organization involved in strategic product management.

The first question asks whether OMC's new 175-horsepower engine constitutes a modified product, a line extension, or a new product. The 175-HP engine is not new product because OMC has produced marine engines for years, nor is this a new-to-the-world type of product. OMC's new 175-HP engine is a line extension because this product is marketed *in addition to* the older 150-HP engine, which is still in the organization's product line.

Question 2 asks students to assess the strengths and weaknesses of the process that OMC used to develop the new 175-HP engine. One strength of the process is that the company incorporated a large amount of new technology in the engine that provides benefits sought by customers. Another strength of the process is that OMC assessed the weaknesses of its 150-HP engine so that these weaknesses and customer objections could be overcome with the development of the new engine. A major weakness of the process that OMC used is that OMC did not seek as much input from retailers or customers regarding the desired characteristics and benefits of the new engine prior to developing it.

The last question asks students to evaluate OMC's approach of selling its older models at competitive prices and making the new 175-HP engine available at a significantly higher price. This approach allowed OMC to use the older model as a competitive tool by pricing it below competitive models. Also this approach allowed OMC to market its new 175-HP engine at a price that would help the organization recover its costs of research and development and initial marketing efforts more quickly. Through this approach OMC was also able to use the lower-priced 150-HP engine as a stepping stone to marketing its new engine in that it could more easily justify the higher price of the new engine by comparing the characteristics and benefits of the new engine with those of its predecessor.

Video Information

Video Title: Managing the Product
Location: Tape 2, Segment 10
Length: 8:57
Video Overview: Outboard Marine Corporation, manufacturer and marketer of marine engines, boats, and boat accessories, has adopted an aggressive strategy of product management. When the company's executives recognized that their 150-horsepower marine engine had lost its appeal with customers, Outboard Marine did not take the typical approach of boosting sales

through product modification or repositioning. Instead, the company introduced a new product, its superior 175-horsepower engine, and offered customers two choices, the old model at reduced prices or the upgraded model at a higher price.

Multiple-Choice Questions About the Video

c   1. According to the video, Outboard Marine manages its products in order to
    a. prolong product life, compete head-to-head with competitors, and maximize profits.
    b. increase sales, prolong product life, and increase product offerings.
    c. prolong product life, increase sales, and maximize profits.
    d. compete head-to-head with competitors, increase product offerings, and increase sales.
    e. increase sales, maximize profits, and increase product offerings.

c   2. Instead of modifying its existing 150-horsepower marine engine to regain market dominance, Outboard Marine
    a. offered sales incentives to its retail dealers.
    b. began advertising in more media that reached its target market.
    c. introduced a new, more powerful engine and offered customers a choice between the two products.
    d. increased the number of potential customers by increasing the number of channels through which it distributes its engines.
    e. launched several sales promotions aimed at increasing sales.

a   3. When a product enters the maturity stage of its life cycle, Outboard Marine asks two questions relating to product management; they are: "Is the segment large enough to justify investing in an entirely new product?" and
    a. "Has the market changed?"
    b. "Will the new product cannibalize sales of mature products?"
    c. "Can the mature product be repositioned?"
    d. "Would a new product be price competitive?"
    e. "Have new competitors entered the market?"

b   4. What is the primary target market for Outboard Marine's new 175-horsepower Evinrude motor?
    a. Manufacturers of recreational marine craft
    b. Bass fishermen
    c. Powerboat racing competitors
    d. Upscale consumers with annual incomes of over $100,000
    e. Powerboat retailers

d   5. According to the video, three common techniques for managing products when their sales decline are to
    a. reposition the product, modify the target market, and increase advertising.
    b. modify the product, modify the target market, and increase sales promotion.
    c. reposition the product, decrease advertising, and increase sales promotion.
    d. modify the product, reposition the product, and modify the target market.
    e. modify the target market, generate more publicity, and increase sales promotion.

Case 10.2 Pepsi Cola Struggles with Product Introductions

The purpose of this case is to examine how Pepsi-Cola uses product development aggressively to compete with Coca-Cola. Students will be familiar with some of the new products offered by Pepsi and are likely to hold strong opinions regarding soft drink brands.

The first question asks students to identify the stage of the product life cycle for cola-flavored soft drinks. Cola-flavored soft drinks are in the maturity stage of the product life cycle.

The second question asks whether Crystal Pepsi was a new product or a modified product, from the perspective of Pepsi employees. From their perspective, Crystal Pepsi was a modified product rather than a new product, since Pepsi has been producing soft drinks for many, many years. The type of modification represented by Crystal Pepsi is aesthetic modification.

Question 3 asks students to evaluate Pepsi's use of new-product development as a means of competing with Coca-Cola. Introducing new products makes an organization like Pepsi appear to be aggressive and innovative. Although Pepsi's new-product development efforts have not always worked, the company has successfully launched several new products, including Diet Pepsi.

11 BRANDING AND PACKAGING

TEACHING RESOURCES QUICK REFERENCE GUIDE

Resource	Location
Purpose and Perspective	IRM, p. 229
Guide for Using Color Transparencies	IRM, p. 229
Lecture Outline	IRM, p. 229
Class Exercises, Debate Issue, and Chapter Quiz	IRM, p. 243
Class Exercise 1	IRM, p. 245
Class Exercise 2	IRM, p. 246
Debate Issue: Should fast food restaurants use environmentally responsible packaging even when such packaging is less effective in preserving product quality?	IRM, p. 247
Chapter Quiz	IRM, p. 248
Answers to Discussion and Review Questions	IRM, p. 249
Comments on the Cases	IRM, p. 253
Case 11.1	IRM, p. 253
Video	Tape 2, Segment 11
Video Information	IRM, p. 253
Multiple-Choice Questions About the Video	IRM, p. 254
Case 11.2	IRM, p. 254
Transparency Acetates	Transparency package
Examination Questions: Essay	TB, p. 203
Examination Questions: Multiple-Choice	TB, p. 204
Examination Questions: True-False	TB, p. 213
Author-Selected Multiple-Choice Test Items	TB, p. 447

PURPOSE AND PERSPECTIVE

This chapter defines and discusses branding, packaging, and labeling. It begins with a discussion of the value of branding and then discusses brand loyalty, which includes three levels: brand recognition, brand preference, and brand insistence. Brand equity, types of brands (manufacturer, private distributor, and generic), and brand name selection are discussed. We also deal with methods of protecting brands, covering such issues as trademarks and protecting a brand from becoming generic. The section also examines branding policies—individual branding, family branding, and brand extension. Brand licensing is also discussed.

Next, we examine major packaging issues, in particular, the functions of packaging, packaging strategies, and various types of packaging. The chapter ends with a discussion of labeling, including legal labeling requirements.

GUIDE FOR USING COLOR TRANSPARENCIES

There are two groups of color transparencies. The transparencies identified by a double number are the same as the figures and tables in the text. The transparencies labeled with a number and a letter are illustrations that do not appear in the text, but they can be used as additional examples of concepts discussed.

Table 11.1	Top ten names in brand quality
Figure 11.3	Percentage of users of selected products who are loyal to one brand
Figure 11.5	The changing dynamics of brand selection
Figure 11.6	Major elements of brand equity
Table 11.3	The world's most valuable brands
Figures 11.7	Top ten private branded product groups
Table 11.4	Companies that spend the most on packaging
Figure 11A	Chapter 11 outline
Figure 11B	Requirements of an effective brand name
Figure 11C	Preference for private brands of food by age and sex
Figure 11D	Top-ranked licensed properties having sold over $1 billion in products since 1978
Figure 11E	Brand symbols are sometimes used to aid in creating favorable brand associations which, in turn, help to build brand equity.
Figure 11F	Category-consistent packaging facilitates product recognition by customers.

LECTURE OUTLINE

I. Branding

    A. Definitions of branding terms

        1. A **brand** is a name, term, symbol, design, or other feature that identifies one seller's good or service as distinct from those of other sellers.

2. A **brand name** is that part of a brand that can be spoken, including letters, words, and numbers; a brand name is often a product's only distinguishing characteristic.

3. A **brand mark** is an element of a brand that cannot be spoken, often a symbol or design.

4. A **trademark** is a legal designation indicating that the owner has exclusive use of the brand or part of that brand and that others are prohibited by law from using it.

5. A **trade name** is the legal name of an organization rather than the name of a specific product.

B. Value of branding

1. To buyers

    a. Brands help buyers identify specific products that they like and do not like, which facilitates the purchase of those items that satisfy individual needs.

    b. A brand helps a buyer evaluate the quality of products, especially when the person lacks the ability to judge a product's characteristics; that is, a brand may symbolize a certain quality level to a purchaser, and the person in turn lets that perception of quality represent the quality of the item.

    c. A brand helps reduce a buyer's perceived risk of purchase.

    d. A brand can give buyers the psychological reward that comes from owning a brand that symbolizes status.

2. To sellers

    a. Sellers' brands identify each firm's products, which makes repeat purchasing easier for consumers.

b. To the extent that buyers become loyal to a specific brand, the firm's market share for that product achieves a certain level of stability, which allows the firm to use its resources more efficiently.

c. When a firm develops some degree of customer loyalty to a brand, it can maintain a fairly consistent price for the product instead of having to cut the price repeatedly to attract customers.

C. Brand loyalty

1. **Brand loyalty** is a customer's favorable attitude toward a specific brand, which affects the likelihood of consistent purchase of this brand when the need arises for a product in this product category; brand loyalty can be categorized into three levels.

    a. **Brand recognition** exists when a customer is aware that a brand exists and views it as an alternative to purchase if his or her brand is unavailable or if the other available brands are unfamiliar to the customer.

    b. **Brand preference** is a stronger degree of brand loyalty, in which a customer definitely prefers one brand over competitive offerings and will purchase the brand if available, but will not go out of his or her way to find it.

    c. **Brand insistence** is the strongest degree of brand loyalty, in which a customer strongly prefers a specific brand, will accept no substitute, and will go to great lengths to acquire it.

2. Although brand loyalty is a challenge to build, it makes a significant contribution to a sustainable competitive advantage.

3. Brand loyalty seems to be on the decline.

    a. This is due in part to marketers' increased reliance on sales, coupons, and other promotions, and in part to the array of similar products from which customers can choose.

    b. According to a 1993 Roper poll, past experience with a brand, price, quality, and personal recommendations of others are more important than how well a brand is known.

D.   Brand equity

1.   **Brand equity** is the marketing and financial value associated with a brand's market strength.

2.   The elements of brand equity include proprietary brand assets, such as patents and trade marks, as well as brand name awareness, brand loyalty, perceived brand quality, and brand association.

   a.   Awareness of a brand name leads to familiarity, and familiar brands are more likely to be viewed as reliable and of acceptable quality than unfamiliar ones.

   b.   Customers with brand loyalty are less vulnerable to competitors' actions and provide brand visibility and reassurance to potential new customers.

   c.   Perceived brand quality helps to support a premium price, allowing a marketer to avoid severe price competition because a brand name can actually stand for and be used to judge actual quality.

   d.   Marketers associate a type of lifestyle or certain personality with a particular brand to appeal to consumers who can relate to the image.

3.   Although brand equity is difficult to measure, one company will pay a premium to purchase a brand from another company because it is less risky than developing its own.

E.   Types of brands

1.   **Manufacturer brands** are initiated by producers and ensure that producers are identified with their products at the point of purchase.

   a.   A manufacturer brand usually requires that a producer get involved with distribution, promotion, and (to some extent) pricing decisions.

   b.   The producer tries to stimulate demand for the product, which tends to encourage intermediaries to make the product available.

2. **Private distributor brands** (or private brands, store brands, or dealer brands) are initiated and owned by resellers; manufacturers are not identified on the products.

    a.   Retailers and wholesalers use private distributor brands to develop more efficient promotion, generate higher gross margins, and improve store images.

    b.   Private distributor brands give retailers or wholesalers freedom to purchase products of a specified quality at the lowest cost without disclosing the identity of the manufacturer.

3. **Generic brands** indicate only a product category and do not include the company name or other identifying terms.

    a.   Generic brands are usually sold at lower prices than are comparable branded items.

    b.   Sales of generic brands account for less than 1 percent of all grocery sales.

4. Competition between manufacturer brands and private distributor brands is intensifying in several major product categories.

    a.   The development of multiple manufacturer brands and distribution systems has helped combat the increased competition from private brands.

    b.   By developing new brand names, manufacturers can adjust various elements of the marketing mix to appeal to different target markets.

    c.   Production of private distributor brands lets the manufacturer use excess capacity during periods when its own brands are at nonpeak production.

F.   Selecting a brand name

1.   Marketers should consider a number of factors when selecting a brand name.

    a.   The name should be easy for customers to say, spell, and recall.

b.   If possible, the brand name should suggest the product's uses and special characteristics in a positive way and avoid negative or offensive references.

c.   If a marketer intends to use a brand for a product line, the brand must be designed to be compatible with all products in the line.

d.   A brand should be designed so that it can be used and recognized in all types of media.

e.   Brand names can be created from single or multiple words, initials, numbers, or combinations of these.

f.   To avoid terms that have negative connotations, marketers sometimes use fabricated words that have no meaning when they are created.

2.   Brand names can be created internally by the organization, by outside consultants, or by hiring a company specializing in brand name development.

3.   Even though branding considerations apply to both goods and services, there are some special dimensions of service branding.

a.   The brand name of a service is usually the same as the company name.

b.   Service brands must be flexible enough to encompass a variety of current services as well as new ones that a company might offer in the future.

c.   Service marketers often use a symbol along with a brand name to make the brand distinctive and to convey an image.

G.   Protecting a brand

1.   Marketers should take steps to protect their exclusive rights to a brand.

a.   Marketers should design a brand name that they can protect easily through registration; this protects trademarks for twenty years and allows them to be renewed indefinitely.

b.   The company should be certain that the selected brand is unlikely to be considered as infringement on any brand already registered with the U.S. Patent and Trademark office.

2.   The marketer must guard against letting a brand name become a generic term used to refer to a general product category because generic terms cannot be protected as exclusive brand names.

a.   Brand names can be protected from becoming generic terms in several ways.

(1)   Firms can spell the name with a capital letter.

(2)   They can use the name as an adjective to modify the name of the general product class.

(3)   Including the word *brand* just after the name is helpful.

(4)   Firms can indicate that the brand is trademarked with the symbol ®.

3.   In many foreign countries brand registration is not possible. The first firm to use a brand in such a country has the rights to it.

4.   Brand counterfeiting is harmful because the usually inferior counterfeit product undermines consumers' confidence in their loyalty to the brand and reduces the brand owners' revenues from marketing their legitimate products.

5.   In 1988, the Trademark Law Revision Act was enacted to increase the value of the federal registration system relative to foreign competitors and to protect consumers from counterfeiting, confusion, and deception.

H.   Branding policies

1.   In establishing branding policies, the firm must first decide whether to brand its products at all.

a.   When an organization's product is homogeneous and similar to competitors' products, it may be difficult to brand.

b. Some marketers of products that traditionally have been branded have adopted a policy of not branding; this practice is often called **generic branding,** in which only the product category is indicated.

2. If a firm chooses to brand its products, it may opt for one or more branding policies.

a. **Individual branding** is a policy of naming each product differently.

   (1) A major advantage of individual branding is that when an organization introduces a poor product, the negative images associated with it do not contaminate the company's other products.

   (2) Individual branding policies may facilitate the use of market segmentation when a firm wishes to enter many segments of the same market; separate, unrelated names can be used with each brand aimed at a specific segment.

b. In **family branding,** all of the firm's products are branded with the same name or at least part of the name; family branding is beneficial because the promotion of one item with the family brand promotes the firm's other products.

c. In **brand-extension branding,** a firm uses one of its existing brand names as part of a brand for an improved or new product that is usually in the same product category as the existing brand.

3. Branding policy is influenced by the number of the firm's products, the characteristics of its target markets, the competing products available, and the firm's resources.

I. Brand licensing

1. A growing number of companies are letting approved manufacturers use their trademarks on other products for a licensing fee.

2. Advantage of licensing include extra revenue, low cost, free publicity, new images, and trademark protection.

3. Disadvantages of licensing include lack of manufacturing control and too many unrelated products bearing the same name.

II. Packaging

Packaging involves the development of a container and a graphic design for a product.

A. Packaging functions

1. Packaging protects the product or maintains its functional form by reducing damage that could affect its usefulness and increase costs.

2. The size or shape of a package may relate to the product's storage, convenience of use, or replacement rate.

3. Packaging promotes a product by communicating its features, uses, benefits, and image.

B. Major packaging considerations

1. Marketers should try to determine through research how much customers are willing to pay for packages.

2. Developing tamper-resistant packaging is very important.

3. Marketers should consider how much continuity among their package designs is desirable.

a. If a firm's products are unrelated or aimed at vastly different target markets, no continuity may be the best policy.

b. With **family packaging**, a firm designs similar packaging for all its products or includes one major design element in every package; sometimes this approach is used only for lines of products.

4. Marketers must consider the package's promotional role.

a.   The package can be used to attract customers' attention and encourage them to examine the product.

b.   Through verbal and nonverbal symbols, the package can inform potential buyers about the product's content, features, uses, advantages, and hazards.

c.   A firm can create desirable images and associations by using certain colors, designs, shapes, and textures in packages.

d.   A package may perform a promotional function when it is designed to be safer or more convenient to use if such characteristics stimulate demand.

e.   To develop a package that has definite promotional value, a designer must consider size, shape, texture, color, and graphics.

(1)   Beyond the obvious minimal limitation that the package must be large enough to hold the product, a package can be designed to appear taller or shorter.

(2)   The shape of the package can help communicate a particular message.

(3)   Color in packages is often used to attract attention; people associate certain feelings and connotations with specific colors.

5.   Marketers must consider whether to develop packages that are environmentally responsible. Marketers must carefully balance society's desires to preserve the environment against consumers' desires for convenience.

C.   Packaging and marketing strategy

1.   Packaging can be a major component of a marketing strategy.

a.   A unique cap or closure, a better box or wrapper, or a more convenient container size may give a firm a competitive advantage.

b.   The right type of package for a new product can help it gain market recognition very quickly.

c.   Marketers should view packaging as a major strategic tool for convenience products.

2.   Marketers alter packaging for a number of reasons.

a.   A package may be redesigned because new product features need to be highlighted.

b.   Package changes may be necessary to compete in foreign markets.

c.   Packages may be altered to make the product more convenient or safer to use.

d.   Marketers may change a package because new packaging materials become available.

e.   Marketers may alter a package to reposition an existing product.

3.   A secondary-use package is one that can be reused for purposes other than its initial use.

a.   Secondary-use packages can be viewed by customers as adding value to products.

b.   Secondary-use packaging can be used to stimulate unit sales.

4.   Category-consistent packaging is used to package products in line with the packaging practices associated with a particular product category.

5.   Innovative packaging such as a unique cap, design, applicator, or other feature will sometimes be used by marketers to make the product completely distinctive.

      a.   Using innovative packaging can be effective if the innovation makes the product safer or easier to use.

      b.   Unique packages sometimes make a brand stand out next to its competitors.

      c.   Using innovative packaging usually requires a considerable amount of resources.

6.   Marketers sometimes package products in twin packs, tri-packs, six-packs, or other forms of multiple packaging.

      a.   Multiple packaging is likely to increase demand because it increases the amount of the product available at the point of consumption.

      b.   Multiple packaging is not appropriate for infrequently used products.

      c.   Multiple packaging can make products easier to handle and store, and facilitate special price offers.

      d.   Multiple packaging may increase consumer acceptance of a product by encouraging buyers to try it several times.

7.   Packaging may be changed to make it easier to handle in the distribution channel.

      a.   Changes made might involve the outer carton, special bundling, shrink-wrapping, or palletizing.

      b.   Sometimes the shape of a package may be changed to facilitate handling.

      c.   Outer containers are sometimes changed so that they will more easily proceed through automated warehousing systems.

8.   Criticisms of packaging

1. Some packages suffer from functional problems; they do not work well or are inconvenient.

2. Certain types of packages have a questionable impact on the environment.

3. Much packaging criticism focuses on safety problems such as packages with sharp edges or those using aerosol propellants.

4. Sometimes packages are perceived as deceptive.

    a. Shapes, colors, or designs sometimes make a product appear larger than it actually is.

    b. Inconsistent use of size designations can lead to customer confusion.

    c. Sometimes the cost of the package is higher than the cost of the product itself.

III. Labeling

A. **Labeling** involves providing identifying, promotional, or other information on package labels.

1. Labeling can be used to facilitate the identification of a product by presenting the brand and a unique graphic design.

2. The label can indicate the grade of the product.

3. Labels can provide information about the product.

    a. The source of the product

    b. The contents and major features of the product

      c.   How to use and care for the product

      d.   Nutritional information as well as type, style, and number of servings

    4.   Labels can provide a promotional function by using attention-attracting graphics.

B.   Several federal laws address packaging and labeling.

    1.   Some federal laws require disclosure of such information as textile identification, potential hazards, and nutritional information.

    2.   Although consumers respond favorably to the inclusion of such information on labels, research on consumers' actual use of such information yields mixed results.

    3.   The 1966 Fair Packaging and Labeling Act focuses on mandatory requirements, voluntary adoption of packaging standards, and the provision of power to the Federal Trade Commission and the Food and Drug Administration to establish and enforce packaging regulations.

    4.   The 1990 Nutrition Labeling and Education Act required the FDA to review labeling practices.

      a.   As a result, the FDA issued new labeling guidelines.

      b.   Food processors must now indicate the number of calories and the amount of protein, fat, carbohydrates, and vitamins contained in a product.

C.   The **universal product code (UPC)** is a series of lines identifying a product and containing inventory and pricing information that is read by an electronic scanner.

D.   Because many similar products are available, the label becomes an attention-getting device, or "silent salesperson," and an important element in the marketing mix.

CLASS EXERCISES, DEBATE ISSUE, AND CHAPTER QUIZ

On the following pages, you will find two class exercises, a debate issue, and a chapter quiz. These are formatted in large-size type so that you can use them as class handouts or for making transparencies. Below are the authors' comments on the class exercises, the debate topic for this chapter, and the answers to the chapter quiz.

Class Exercise 1: The purpose of this exercise is to reinforce an understanding of brand components and policies and the functions of packaging.

1. Students often get these components mixed up, particularly the first two. Coke cans offer a good chance to explain the difference between the brand name Coca-Cola and the script design that makes up the brand mark. The students will usually note the trademark registration ®. The trade name—the official name of the company—is marked on the back of the can. The fact that "Coke" is referred to generically may also bring up the point that firms spend a great deal of resources to retain brand name rights.

2. Replaceable caps (on 16-oz. drinks) help preserve taste; airtight containers and expiration dates help ensure freshness. Package sizes are generally produced in amounts that meet individual consumer needs (e.g., 2-oz. candy bars; 12-oz. drinks, five sticks of gum) for appropriate prices. A production orientation might only produce one size, for instance. Most students are so accustomed to the packages of these items that they rarely recognize the role of communication. Effective packaging reinforces successful promotional campaigns by reminding consumers of the benefits and image produced by advertisements at the point of purchase.

3. Coca-Cola products are good examples of individual and brand-extension branding, although students may be unaware that besides Coke, many bottlers also produce other soft drinks that do not carry the Coke brand name. Examples are Fresca and Barq's Root Beer. Some candy bars may provide examples of family branding (Nestlé or Hershey's).

4. Usually, students will violate one of these guidelines, which points to why some consulting firms now specialize in developing new company or brand names.

Class Exercise 2: The purpose of this exercise is to have students consider the importance of the major requirements of an effective brand name.

1. *Easy to say, spell, and recall*

   Surf detergent
   Biz detergent
   Zee paper towels
   Tone soap
   Jif peanut butter
   Pert shampoo

2. *Communicates major product benefits*

   No-Yolks pasta
   Clean & Clear (skin care products)
   Dustbuster (hand-held vacuum)
   Quick-Lash mascara
   Reach toothbrush
   Carpet-Fresh (rug and room deodorizer)

3. *Suggests product uses or special features*

    Glass Works (glass cleaner)
    Mop & Glo (floor cleaner)
    Soft Scrub (cleanser)

4. *Distinctive to set it apart from competitors*

    Orville Redenbacher (popcorn)
    Reebok (athletic shoes)
    Häagen-Dazs (ice cream)
    Molly McButter (butter substitute)
    Yoplait (yogurt)

Debate Issue: Should fast-food restaurants use environmentally responsible packaging even when such packaging is less effective in preserving product quality?

Chapter Quiz: Answers to multiple-choice questions are

1.	c	3.	d
2.	c	4.	d

CLASS EXERCISE 1

1. Observe your nearest candy wrapper or soft drink container and identify the
   a. brand name,
   b. brand mark,
   c. trademark, and
   d. trade name.

2. Using the wrapper or container, explain how packaging performs three functions: protection, convenience, and communication.

3. Is the manufacturer of the product using individual, family, or brand-extension branding?

4. You work for a firm that is introducing a new chocolate candy bar that contains an extra amount of caffeine. Develop a brand name that
   a. is easy for customers to say, spell, and recall.
   b. positively suggests uses and special characteristics.
   c. indicates major product benefits.
   d. can be protected easily through registration.

CLASS EXERCISE 2

IN DEVELOPING A BRAND NAME, IT IS IMPORTANT TO CONSIDER THE REQUIREMENTS OF AN EFFECTIVE CHOICE, AS LISTED HERE. FOR EACH OF THE FOLLOWING REQUIREMENTS, GIVE SEVERAL EXAMPLES OF BRAND NAMES THAT SATISFY THAT REQUIREMENT.

1. Easy to say, spell, and recall
2. Communicates major product benefits
3. Suggests product uses or special features
4. Distinctive to set the product apart from competing brands

DEBATE ISSUE

SHOULD FAST-FOOD RESTAURANTS USE ENVIRONMENTALLY RESPONSIBLE PACKAGING EVEN WHEN SUCH PACKAGING IS LESS EFFECTIVE IN PRESERVING PRODUCT QUALITY?

YES

- Traditionally, fast-food marketers have used too much packaging, which creates unnecessary amounts of garbage going into landfills

- Traditionally, the type of materials used were not biodegradable

- Fast-food marketers must focus on the long-term impact on the environment rather than on product packaging that provides the greatest amount of customer satisfaction when the product is consumed

NO

- A fast-food marketer should use a package that allows the customer to receive the highest-quality food product at the point of purchase

- Proper disposal of a package, after the customer no longer needs it, is not the responsibility of the fast-food restaurant organization

- Most fast-food customers prefer to have the highest-quality food product, even if the package is not environmentally responsible

CHAPTER QUIZ

1. Private distributor brands are initiated and owned by resellers or retailers and do not identify the manufacturer of the product. Which of the following is an example of a private distributor brand?
    a. Green Giant corn
    b. IBM computers
    c. Sears' Kenmore washers
    d. Little Debbie snack cakes
    e. Nike Air Jordan basketball shoes

1. A _____ brand type is considered the *least* protectable under existing trademark regulations.
    a. descriptive
    b. fanciful
    c. generic
    d. symbolic
    e. suggestive

3. To promote an overall company image, packages of Pillsbury cake and cookie mixes have similar designs and colors. This approach is known as
    a. family branding.
    b. brand managing.
    c. line consistency.
    d. family packaging.
    e. product grouping.

4. Federal laws require the disclosure of such information as nutritional information, potential hazards, and
    a. product colors.
    b. address of the producer.
    c. date of manufacture.
    d. textile identification.
    e. brand mark.

ANSWERS TO DISCUSSION AND REVIEW QUESTIONS

1. What is the difference between a brand and a brand name? Compare and contrast the terms "brand mark" and "trademark."

    A brand is a name, term, symbol, design, or a combination of these that identifies a seller's products and differentiates them from competitors' products. A brand name is that part of a brand that can be spoken, including letters, words, and numbers.
    A brand mark is the element of a brand that cannot be spoken, such as a symbol or design. A trademark is a legal designation indicating that the owner has exclusive use of a brand or part of a brand and that others are prohibited by law from using it.

2. How does branding benefit consumers? marketers?

    Brands aid buyers by helping them identify specific products that they like and do not like, which in turn facilitates the purchase of items that satisfy individual needs. A brand also helps a buyer evaluate the quality of products, especially when the person lacks the ability to judge a product's characteristics. Brands identify a seller's products, which facilitates repeat purchases by consumers. To the extent that buyers become loyal to a specific brand, the firm's market share for that product achieves a certain level of stability. A stable market share places a firm in a position to use its resources more efficiently. When a firm develops some degree of customer loyalty for a brand, it can charge a premium price for the product. Branding helps an organization introduce a new product that carries the name of one or more of its existing products. Branding facilitates promotional efforts because each branded product indirectly promotes all the firm's other products that are similarly branded.

3. What are the three major degrees or levels of brand loyalty?

    Brand loyalty is the customer's favorable attitude toward a specific brand. The three levels of brand loyalty are brand recognition, brand preference, and brand insistence. Brand recognition, the mildest form of brand loyalty, exists when a customer is aware that the brand exists and views it as an alternative to purchase. Brand preference, a stronger degree of brand loyalty, exists when a customer definitely prefers one brand over competitive offerings; however, if the brand is not available, the customer will accept a substitute. Brand insistence, the strongest degree of brand loyalty, exists when a customer not only strongly prefers a specific brand, but will not accept a substitute.

4. What is brand equity? Identify and explain the major elements that underlie brand equity.

    Brand equity is the marketing and financial value associated with a brand's strength in the market. Four major elements underlie brand equity: brand name awareness; brand loyalty; perceived brand quality; and brand associations. Being aware of a brand leads to brand familiarity, resulting in increased levels of comfortableness with the brand. Customers are more likely to choose familiar brands over unfamiliar ones. Brand loyalty allows an organization to keep its existing customers, and loyal customers reassure potential new ones. Customers associate a certain level of perceived overall quality with a brand. A brand name can even substitute for actual judgment of quality when customers are themselves unable to make quality judgments about products and rely on the brand as an indicator of quality. The final component of brand equity is the set of associations linked to a brand. Positive associations contribute significantly to a brand's equity.

5. Compare and contrast manufacturer brands, private distributor brands, and generic brands.

    Manufacturer brands are initiated by producers and ensure that producers are identified with their products at the point of sale. These brands usually require a producer to become involved in distribution, promotion, and, to some extent, pricing decisions. Manufacturer brands include Green Giant, Apple Computer, and Levi's jeans.

    Private distributor brands are initiated and owned by resellers or retailers and do not identify the manufacturer or producer. Private brands are used to develop more efficient promotion, generate higher gross margins, and improve store images. These brands include IGA (Independent Grocers' Alliance), Sears' Craftsman, and Walmart's "Sam's Choice" beverages and snacks.

    A generic brand indicates only the category of the product (such as aluminum foil, saltines, or peanut butter) and does not include the company name or manufacturer. Generic brands are usually sold at lower prices than are comparable brand names.

6. Identify the factors that a marketer should consider in selecting a brand name.

    When selecting a brand, marketers must consider a number of factors. A brand name should be easy to say, spell, and remember. To avoid consumer confusion, brands should be compatible with those of other products in the product line. Choosing a name that suggests the product's uses and special characteristics as well as indicating the product's major benefits is important. Marketers try to select a brand that is distinctive enough to set it apart from competitors but avoids negative or offensive implications. Finally, marketers strive to choose a brand that can be used and recognized in all types of media. Because service brands are usually the same as the company name, service marketers do not always have the flexibility to choose a brand that meets all of the above criteria.

7. The brand name Xerox is sometimes used generically to refer to photocopying and Kleenex is used to refer to tissues. How can these corporations protect their brand names, and why should they want to?

    A generic term is used to refer to a general product category. Generic terms cannot be protected as exclusive brand names. To keep a brand name from becoming a generic term, the firm should spell it with a capital letter and use it as an adjective to modify the name of the general product class. An organization can deal with this problem directly by advertising that its brand is a trademark and should not be used generically. The firm can also indicate that the brand is trademarked by placing the symbol ® next to the brand name.

    If these brand names are not protected by their owners, then companies will lose their rights to be the sole users of these names. The terms can then be used generically, as was the case for aspirin and elevator.

8. What are the major advantages and disadvantages of licensing?

    Brand licensing involves an agreement whereby a company allows approved manufacturers to use its trademark on other products for a licensing fee. The advantages of licensing include

a. Extra revenue earned from the licensing fee
b. Low-cost or free publicity
c. New images that potentially give new life to a brand
d. Trademark protection

Disadvantages of licensing may be

a. Lack of manufacturing control that could hurt the company's reputation; that is, if inferior products bear a company's brand, consumers may extend negative opinions to the firm's own products as well.
b. Consumers may be confused by too many unrelated products carrying the same name.
c. Agreements may fail because of poor timing, inappropriate distribution channels, or mismatching product and name.

9. Describe the functions that a package can perform. Which function is most important? Why?

A package can perform several functions, including protection, economy, convenience, and promotion. First, packaging materials are needed to protect the product or to maintain it in functional form. The package should effectively reduce damage that could affect the product's usefulness and increase costs (economy). Second, consumers may be concerned with convenience. Third, packaging can promote a product by communicating its features, uses, benefits, and image.

10. When developing a package, what are the main factors that a marketer should consider?

When making packaging decisions, marketers must take into account a variety of issues. Cost is a critical consideration when developing a package. Some available processes and designs are very expensive, so before making packaging decisions, marketers engage in research to determine how much customers are willing to pay for packages. Because packaging must comply with the Food and Drug Administration's packaging regulations, marketers make sure that packages are tamper resistant. When new technology is developed or new legislation is passed, marketers modify packages to protect consumers and comply with the law. Another consideration is how much consistency of packaging there should be among the various products an organization markets. If products are aimed at different target markets, marketers may opt for no consistency, but if the desire is to promote an overall company image, a firm may package all its products in a similar way, an approach known as family packaging. A package's promotional role is an important consideration because packages inform potential buyers about the product's content, features, uses, advantages, and hazards along with creating a product image. Marketers try to choose features that enhance a package's promotional value. The size and shape of a package must lend itself to easy handling by wholesalers and retailers, or they may refuse to carry the product. Finally, marketers must consider the issue of environmentally responsible packaging, attempting to balance concern for the environment with consumers' preference for convenience.

11. In what ways can packaging be used as a strategic tool?

Because a package has the potential for giving a product a competitive edge, marketers often regard packaging as an important strategic tool. Altering a package can make a product more convenient or safer, promote a new feature, or assist product repositioning.

A secondary-use package, one that can be reused for purposes other than its initial use, can stimulate sales. Because certain product categories are characterized by recognizable types of packaging, an organization often uses these traditional shapes and colors when introducing a brand in one of those categories to facilitate easy recognition by potential buyers. Sometimes an innovative package design attracts consumers by distinguishing a brand from its competitors, resulting in increased sales. For certain types of products, multiple packaging is used to increase demand. This strategy is based on the belief that if consumers have more of a product at home, they will use more and want more. In addition, multiple packs can make products easier to handle and simplify special price offers. Handling-improved packaging facilitates distribution and shelving, making a product more attractive to those who handle and sell it.

12. What are the major criticisms of packaging?

Several aspects of packaging evoke criticism. The simplest criticism is that some packages just don't work well. Environmental irresponsibility, such as lack of biodegradability, is a growing packaging criticism. Some critics focus on safety issues, such as containers with sharp edges or aerosol containers that contain health hazards. Finally, packaging is sometimes criticized as being deceptive. For example, certain shapes or colors may make a product appear larger than it actually is.

13. What are the major functions of labeling?

Marketers use labeling in a variety of ways. By highlighting the brand with an eye-catching graphic design, the label can facilitate product identification. Labels serve a descriptive function, specifying the product's source, contents, major features, use, and care. For certain products, labels can be strictly informative, furnishing specific product grade, nutritional content, and number of servings. Through the use of attention-getting graphics, labels also serve a valuable promotional function.

14. In what ways can labeling requirements impact an industry?

New labeling requirements, either for the food industry in nutritional labeling, or for other products to warn of hazardous use, may require a company to redesign its packaging. This could mean additional costs, which must be considered in establishing the price to the consumer. An entire industry (such as the meat industry) may be impacted by new governmental regulations requiring labeling where it has never occurred before. The new labeling may provide opportunities for different producers and different products to engage in competitive marketing. Whereas before, meat was usually considered a "commodity" and not thought of in terms of specific brands, new labeling may provide opportunities for "brands" of meats, poultry, or fish, and therefore product differentiation. An example of brands in the poultry industry is the Frank Perdue chicken selections.

COMMENTS ON THE CASES

Case 11.1 Labeling Requirements in the Red Meat Industry

The primary objective of this case is to illustrate the importance of product packaging and labeling as an element of product marketing strategy. This is done, in a most general sense, by explaining how the potentially problematic effects of changes in consumer tastes towards red meat and increased governmental regulations on packaging and labeling content were dealt with by the red meat industry in a manner proving beneficial to its marketing efforts. Specifically, faced with these obstacles, the industry set out to strategically alter package design and label content to meet new federal regulations, while at the same time providing consumers with information that helped clear up deleterious misconceptions about its products, thus better positioning red meat against competitive products in the marketplace.

The initial question asks how the functional and promotional aspects of packaging interact in this case. Here, the red meat industry set out to integrate the two qualities by providing packaging and labeling that did more than merely serve to transport the product from the store shelf to the home, as had been the case in the past. Faced with the more informative and utilitarian labeling and packaging designs of competitive products, the industry realized that it must add more value to the product by improving packaging design, while at the same time providing consumers with the type of information they had come to demand for purposes of making meat purchase decisions.

Question 2 asks the reader to (a) assess the costs and benefits associated with meeting new federal meat labeling regulations and (b) discuss whether or not red meat marketers should wait for the regulations to be formally passed into law before taking corrective action. Here, led by the National Live Stock and Meat Board (NLSMB), the industry reasoned that the new regulations were merely requiring meat marketers to supply consumers with information that they needed to make purchase decisions. At that time, consumers were receiving such information from competitors, but not from marketers of red meat. Therefore, despite the fact that the changes represented added expense at a time when the marketers were not legally required to make these changes, from a competitive perspective, the sooner they were implemented, the better.

The third question asks the reader to discuss, in specific fashion, how labeling and packaging might be used by the red meat industry to make its products more competitive. As discussed in the case, these elements of product strategy can and should be used to clear up common misconceptions of red meat being perceived as unhealthy relative to competitive products. Also, as previously stated, they should be used to provide consumers with information that they require to make meat purchase decisions.

Video Information

Video Title: The Meat Consumer 1992
Location: Tape 2, Segment 11
Length: 16:11
Video Overview: The red meat industry has proactively responded to proposed federal labeling requirements in a manner facilitating better positioning of its products in the marketplace. Because the industry is looking at these regulations as a long-term opportunity rather than merely as a threat (i.e., by increasing short-term costs), labeling and packaging can be modified to better meet the needs of customers.

Multiple-Choice Questions About the Video

c   1. According to red meat industry officials, how will the proposed federal meat labeling regulations affect the industry?
      a. They will hurt it by boosting sales of poultry and fish products.
      b. They will hurt the industry by adding production costs likely to be recouped only by drastically raising the price of red meat products.
      c. They will benefit the industry by providing customers with information that they need to make meat purchase decisions.
      d. They will benefit red meat marketers by lowering their short-term costs.
      e. Meeting the new regulations is not likely to impact the red meat industry, since information contained in product labeling is not important to consumers.

d   2. How does the NLSMB propose that red meat marketers respond to the proposed federal labeling regulations?
      a. Proactively, calling for red meat producers to improve product quality immediately
      b. Reactively, suggesting that the regulations represent nothing but added costs to industry members
      c. Reactively, telling industry producers and retailers to wait and see how competitors react to the new regulations once they are formally passed into law
      d. Proactively, suggesting that the requirements represent an opportunity to better promote red meat products
      e. Proactively, calling for an immediate recall of all poorly labeled meat products

b   3. The NLSMB views product packaging and labeling as
      a. important elements of promotional strategy due to their ability to catch the attention of passing shoppers.
      b. important elements in product strategy from both a functional and promotional perspective.
      c. unimportant, due to the fact that consumers care only about the product itself.
      d. important in the sense that consumers are able to read the price and get the product home safely.
      e. factors that are important only insofar as efficient production of packaging and labeling materials can lower product prices.

Case 11.2   Evian's New Bottle Promises Marketing and Environmental Benefits

The objective of this case is to present a situation that allows students to analyze the strategic opportunities offered by a new package. Some students will have strong feelings regarding the consumption of bottled water as well as the use of environmentally sensitive packaging. To launch into a discussion of this case, you may wish to ask students how frequently they drink bottled water.

The first question asks students to indicate what major packaging functions the new package performs especially well compared to the old Evian package. Due to its collapsibility, the new package is more environmentally sensitive. Also the promotional role that it plays is stronger because of the package's uniqueness. The previous package was imitated by many competitors. Having a unique package such as the new Evian package allows this brand to be distinctive and to stand out among competitors.

The second question asks which packaging strategies discussed in this chapter are most likely to be consistent with what Evian hopes to achieve with its new package. The development of the new package provides the company with an opportunity to promote the benefits of the new package, which in turn helps to promote the product in general. The fact that the package is innovative also makes the brand as well as the company appear to be progressive and innovative. Being able to promote the package as being more environmentally sensitive is likely to be consistent with the values of those persons who consume upscale bottled water.

The third question asks "In what ways is Evian's new package environmentally sensitive?" Students must also evaluate Evian marketers' view that bottled water drinkers are likely to be concerned about environmental issues and therefore may be influenced to buy Evian because of its package. The package is easily crushed to a small size, making it more environmentally sensitive. By breaking down to a smaller piece of material, it will occupy less space in landfills. With regard to the second part of this question, student answers will vary based on individual opinions. It is reasonable to accept the assumption of Evian marketers that people who drink bottled water care about the environment and that an environmentally sensitive package would be important to them.

12 SERVICES

TEACHING RESOURCES QUICK REFERENCE GUIDE

Resource	Location
Purpose and Perspective	IRM, p. 257
Guide for Using Color Transparencies	IRM, p. 257
Lecture Outline	IRM, p. 257
Class Exercises, Debate Issue, and Chapter Quiz	IRM, p. 266
Class Exercise 1	IRM, p. 268
Class Exercise 2	IRM, p. 269
Debate Issue: Does Domino's sell a product rather than a service?	IRM, p. 270
Chapter Quiz	IRM, p. 271
Answers to Discussion and Review Questions	IRM, p. 272
Comments on the Cases	IRM, p. 274
Case 12.1	IRM, p. 274
Video	Tape 2, Segment 12
Video Information	IRM, p. 275
Multiple-Choice Questions About the Video	IRM, p. 276
Case 12.2	IRM, p. 276
Transparency Acetates	Transparency package
Examination Questions: Essay	TB, p. 219
Examination Questions: Multiple-Choice	TB, p. 220
Examination Questions: True-False	TB, p. 233
Author-Selected Multiple-Choice Test Items	TB, p. 447

PURPOSE AND PERSPECTIVE

We begin with a discussion of the nature of services, focusing on the growing importance of service industries in our economy. We address the unique characteristics of services—intangibility, perishability, heterogeneity, client-based relationships, and customer contact—and analyze the problems these characteristics present to marketers. We next present various classification schemes that can help service marketers develop marketing strategies. Then we focus on service quality, addressing customer evaluation of service quality and the four factors affecting service quality specifications, employee performance, and management of service expectations. Finally, we define nonprofit marketing and examine the development and control of nonprofit marketing strategies.

GUIDE FOR USING COLOR TRANSPARENCIES

There are two groups of color transparencies. The transparencies identified by a double number are the same as the figures in the text. The transparencies labeled with a number and a letter are illustrations that do not appear in the text, but they can be used as additional examples of concepts discussed.

Figure 12.2   The service continuum
Figure 12.5   Service quality model
Figure 12A   Chapter 12 outline
Figure 12B   Growth in services
Figure 12C   Unique service characteristics
Figure 12D   Categories of service
Figure 12E   Dimensions of service quality
Figure 12F   British Airways attempts to tangibilize the comfort of its unique new business-class cradle seat.
Figure 12G   The U.S. government promotes the benefits of joining one of the armed forces after graduation.
Figure 12H   MovieFone is an example of a high contact, equipment-based service.
Figure 12I   Child care, such as that provided by Kindercare, is an example of a high-contact labor intensive service.

LECTURE OUTLINE

I.   The nature and importance of services

    A.   A **service** is an intangible product involving a deed, a performance, or an effort that cannot be physically possessed.

    B.   Services as products should not be confused with customer service, which involves any service activity that adds value to the product.

C. Service industries account for 74 percent of the U.S. gross domestic product (GNP) and 76 percent of U.S. nonfarm jobs.

D. Economic growth and lifestyle changes have led to the expansion of the service sector, including consumer and business services.

II. Characteristics of services

There are six distinguishing characteristics of services that differentiate them from goods.

A. **Intangibility** means a service is unperceivable by the senses.

1. A services cannot be seen, touched, tasted, or smelled.

2. A service cannot be physically possessed by a consumer.

3. Customers cannot sense a service to evaluate it prior to purchase.

4. Effective advertising is difficult and must include tangible use that symbolize the service.

5. Price of producing and delivering a service is difficult to determine.

B. **Inseparability** of production and consumption means that a service is produced and consumed at the same time.

1. Service providers must be carefully trained because of their importance in the delivery process.

2. Customers can affect the outcome of the service purchased by themselves or another customer.

C. **Perishability** means that storing unused service capacity for future use is impossible.

1. **Peak demand** is the point in time when customers want to use a particular service.

2. **Off-peak demand** is the time when consumers do not want to use the service.

3. Marketers must work to eliminate unused capacity, which occurs during off-peak demand.

D. **Heterogeneity** is variation in quality.

    1. Services that are people-based are susceptible to variation in quality.

    2. Variations can occur with services provided by different organizations, the same organization, different people, or the same person and are therefore very difficult to control.

    3. One advantage of heterogeneity is that a service can be customized to meet the needs of individual consumers.

E. **Client-based relationships** results in satisfied customers who use a service repeatedly over time.

    1. The success of many services depends on creating and maintaining interaction with customers that result in client-based relationships.

    2. A concentrated effort to provide quality services builds a relationship in which customers become very loyal and are unlikely to switch to a competitor; this process is called relationship marketing.

F. **Customer contact** comprises the necessary interaction between the provider and the customer needed to deliver the service.

    1. Customer contact varies depending on the service.

    2. Satisfied employees lead to satisfied customers.

3. Service organizations must train employees to perform customer-oriented behavior and reward them for success.

4. Organizations may restructure some services from high-contact to low-contact to gain control over quality and minimize problems.

III. Classification of service products

Services are a diverse group of products and can be meaningfully analyzed in two ways: As a continuum of pure goods to pure services or by service categories.

A. The service continuum

1. Services fall on a continuum from pure goods (tangible) to pure services (intangible).

2. Pure goods typically do not exist in today's business environment since practically all goods marketers also provide customer services.

3. The further a product is on the intangible side of the continuum, the more an organization must understand the important characteristics of services.

B. Categories of services

1. Services can be categorized according to different dimensions.

   a. The market or type of customer they serve—consumer or business

   b. The degree of labor-intensiveness—people-based or equipment-based

   c. The degree of customer contact—high or low

   d. The skill of the service provider—professional or nonprofessional

   e. The goal of the service provider—profit or nonprofit

2. People-based services are prone to fluctuations in quality.

3. High-contact services typically require the customer to go to the service production facility and be present to receive the service.

4. Professional services tend to be more complex and more highly regulated than nonprofessional services.

IV. Service quality

Service quality is defined as customers' perception of how well a service meets or exceeds their expectations; marketers are thus forced to examine their quality from the customer's point of view.

A. Customer evaluation of service quality

1. Service quality is difficult to evaluate because services do not possess **search qualities**—that is, tangible attributes that can be judged before the purchase of a product (such as color, style, size, feel or fit).

2. Service quality must be judged on

a. **experience qualities,** or attributes that can be judged only during purchase or consumption of a service.

b. **credence qualities,** or attributes that consumers are unable to evaluate even after purchasing and consuming a service because of lack of knowledge or skill.

3. Marketers must learn how customers evaluate service quality on tangibles, reliability, responsiveness, assurance, and empathy, all of which have links to employee performance.

B. Delivering exceptional service quality

1. Providing high-quality service on a consistent basis is very difficult.

2. Organizations can take steps to increase the likelihood of providing exceptional service with an understanding of the following four factors that affect service quality: understanding customer expectations, meeting service quality specifications, employee performance, and management of service expectations.

3. By understanding customer expectations, a service can be designed to meet or exceed those expectations.

   a. The difference between a desired level of service and an acceptable level of service is a customer's zone of tolerance.

   b. Customer needs and expectations are determined through comment cards and daily interaction.

4. Service quality specifications are goals set in terms of employee or machine performance to help ensure good service delivery.

   a. The specifications must be tied to needs expressed by customers.

   b. To provide high quality service successfully, managers must become role models with a commitment to quality.

5. Employee performance is critical to customer perceptions of service quality.

   a. Customer-contact employees in most service industries are often the least-trained and lowest-paid members of the organization.

   b. Evaluations and compensation systems help ensure that customer-contact employees perform their jobs well.

6. Service companies must manage service expectations to ensure that customers have realistic expectations of what the company can provide.

   a. Service expectations are very significant in customer evaluations of service quality.

   b. Expectations can be set through promises in advertising and external communication.

c. To deliver on promises made, a company needs to have good internal communication among its departments.

d. Customers tell four times as many people about bad service as they do about good service.

V. Nonprofit marketing of services

Nonprofit marketing includes marketing activities conducted by individuals and organizations to achieve some goal other than ordinary business goals of profit, market share, or return on investment; nonprofit marketing is divided into two categories: nonprofit-organization marketing and social marketing.

A. Why is nonprofit marketing different?

1. Although the chief beneficiary of the business enterprise is the owner, the beneficiaries of the nonprofit enterprise include clients, members, and the public at large.

2. Nonprofit marketing offers a greater opportunity for creativity than most business organizations enjoy.

3. Nonprofit marketing may be controversial.

a. The controversial nature of a nonprofit organization may require the marketing manager to make more value judgments about participation.

b. Marketing does not attempt to state what an organization's goals should be or to debate the issue of nonprofit versus business goals; marketing attempts only to provide a body of knowledge and concepts to help further the organization's goals.

B. Nonprofit marketing objectives

1. The basic aim of nonprofit organizations is to obtain a desired response from a target market.

2. Nonprofit marketing objectives should be stated in terms of serving perceived needs and wants of a target public rather than in terms of a product because the product may become obsolete, leaving the organization without an objective or purpose.

C. Developing nonprofit marketing strategies

1. The marketer first must pinpoint the target market.

    a. The **target public** is a collective of individuals who have an interest in or concern for an organization, a product, or a social cause.

    b. Once an organization is concerned about exchanging values or obtaining a response from the public, it is viewing the public as a market.

    c. The nonprofit organization target market includes client publics and general publics.

        (1) The **client public** is the direct consumer of the product; most of the attention in developing a marketing strategy is directed toward the client public.

        (2) The **general public** is the indirect consumer of the product.

        (3) Techniques and approaches to segmenting and defining target markets in the business organization also apply to nonprofit target markets.

2. Developing a marketing mix

    a. The product in a nonprofit organization typically deals with ideas and services more often than with goods.

        (1) Problems in developing a product configuration evolve when an organization fails to define what is being provided.

        (2) The marketing of ideas and concepts is more abstract and requires much effort to present benefits.

b. Distribution, or the availability of nonprofit products, is necessary for exchange to take place.

    (1) If the product is an idea, selecting the right media (the promotional strategy) to communicate the idea will facilitate distribution.

    (2) By nature, services consist of assistance, convenience, and availability. Availability is part of the total service (product).

    (3) The traditional concept of the marketing channel may need to be revised for nonprofit marketing.

c. Promotion is used widely in nonprofit organizations to communicate with clients and the public.

    (1) Direct mail is the primary means of fundraising for social services.

    (2) Personal selling is used widely, although it may be called something else, such as recruiting or fundraising.

    (3) Sales promotion is used widely when nonprofit organizations undertake special events to obtain funds, communicate ideas, or provide services.

d. The broadest definition of price (valuation) must be used to develop the nonprofit marketing strategy. Price should be viewed as the exchange of something of value for something else of value.

    (1) **Opportunity cost** is the value of the benefit that is given up by selecting one alternative over another.

    (2) Financial price may or may not be charged for a nonprofit product.

    (3) Pricing strategies of nonprofit organizations often place the public's and clients' welfare before matching costs with revenue.

CLASS EXERCISES, DEBATE ISSUE, AND CHAPTER QUIZ

On the following pages, you will find two class exercises, a debate issue, and a chapter quiz. These are formatted in large-size type so that you can use them as class handouts or for making transparencies. Below are the authors' comments on the class exercises, the debate topic, and the answers to the chapter quiz.

Class Exercise 1: This exercise focuses on how recognizing the characteristics of services can enhance services marketing strategies.

> *Question 1.* You pay for a ticket that gets you a seat to watch a game, which otherwise is not tangible (possessible). In effect, you buy a memory of the ball game. Thus, to gain customer loyalty, it is important that everything influencing that memory be positive. Setting tickets prices, then, is highly related to how consumers perceive the value of the ballgame experience. More tangible products, such as food and souvenirs, are bought and should contribute positively to the experience. Sports teams make great efforts to increase tangibility by arranging events where fans meet the players (shake hands, obtain autographs). Promotional campaigns with memorable slogans are also efforts to increase tangibility.

> *Question 2.* Busch Stadium management spends extensive time training personnel to deal with unruly fans and to stop problems before they happen. Food selection includes a wide variety of quality food (pizza, Mexican, varieties of ice creams). Bad food makes bad memories, and lack of vending availability or slow food service means missed innings. Narrow rows, dirty or crowded restrooms, and limited food offerings do little to make fans want to go to a game when the team is losing. Some students may argue that having a winning team is most important, but the point should be emphasized that because team performance varies, the rest of the experience should be standardized at a high quality level.

> *Question 3.* Ticket sales cannot be inventoried and sold at a later time. Sales promotions may be used to fill the park to capacity on slow nights or at games against weaker teams.

> *Question 4.* Any part of the service that involves people (players, attendants, vendors, food service providers) will be subject to varying levels of performance. Clearly, this means that attention should be paid to personnel selection, training, and compensation. Good service comes from meeting or exceeding customers' expectations of consistent quality.

Class Exercise 2: By focusing on consumer outcomes, this exercise is designed to have students think about the types of businesses these companies are actually in and the markets they are truly serving.

There are no right or wrong answers for this exercise; outcomes sought will vary depending on the customer. Possible answers:

1. Banks—investment opportunities, convenience, peace of mind
2. Plumbing repairs—24-hour service, trouble-free plumbing
3. Education—opportunities, social development, learning
4. Hospitals—surgery, emergency care, wellness
5. Police protection—peace of mind, crime reduction, emergency service
6. Legal counseling—legal advice, estate planning, legal representation
7. L. A. Lakers basketball—entertainment, excitement

8. State Farm Auto Insurance—fast claim handling, peace of mind, protection from loss
9. Dry cleaning—clean clothing, convenience, image enhancement
10. Utilities—efficient repairs, uninterrupted service

Debate Issue: Does Domino's sell a product rather than a service?

Chapter Quiz: Answers to multiple-choice questions are

1.	c	3.	c
2.	d	4.	e

CLASS EXERCISE 1

THE ST. LOUIS CARDINALS BASEBALL ORGANIZATION IS OWNED BY ANHEUSER-BUSCH, WHICH ALSO OPERATES BUSCH STADIUM, HOME OF THE CARDINALS. DESPITE BEING LOCATED IN A RELATIVELY SMALL MARKET, THE CARDINALS HAVE SET ATTENDANCE RECORDS. MUCH OF THIS SUCCESS IS THE RESULT OF EFFECTIVE SERVICES MARKETING AT THE BALLPARK, WHICH MAKES ATTENDING GAMES AN ENJOYABLE EXPERIENCE FOR FANS, WHETHER THE CARDINALS WIN OR LOSE.

1. What part of your experience at a baseball game is primarily intangible? What are you paying for when you go to a ballgame?

2. Consumers have difficulty separating the producer (the Cardinals and Busch Stadium) from the consumption experience (which includes fan behavior, food vending, seats or bleachers). Why would this be important for the management at Busch Stadium to understand? In other words, can you go see a winning team play but not enjoy the game, or vice-versa?

3. Busch Stadium holds around 55,000 fans. What difference does it make that services are highly perishable? How would this influence sales promotion activity?

4. What aspects of the baseball game experience are susceptible to heterogeneity? What does this say about the importance of employing high-quality personnel?

CLASS EXERCISE 2

FOR EACH OF THE FOLLOWING SERVICES, WHAT IS THE OUTCOME SOUGHT BY THE BUYER?

1. Banks
2. Plumbing repairs
3. Education
4. Hospitals
5. Police protection
6. Legal counseling
7. L.A. Lakers basketball
8. State Farm Auto Insurance
9. Dry cleaning
10. Utilities

DEBATE ISSUE

DOES DOMINO'S SELL A PRODUCT RATHER THAN A SERVICE?

<u>YES</u>

- Advertising campaign stresses quality and freshness

- Consumers are buying a hot, fresh pizza with their choice of toppings, tangible things implying that Domino's is selling a product

<u>NO</u>

- Consumers are buying guaranteed speedy delivery, which is a service

- Domino's has redefined the pizza industry as a service because it delivers a hot, recently prepared pizza to the customer's doorstep

CHAPTER QUIZ

1. Marketers in the airline industry sometimes find it difficult to promote their product because unused airplane seats cannot be stored. This problem illustrates which one of the following unique features of services?
   a. Intangibility
   b. Inseparability
   c. Perishability
   d. Heterogeneity
   e. Marketability

2. Which of the following services is the least labor-intensive?
   a. Education
   b. Hair care
   c. Auto repairs
   d. Exercise and fitness club
   e. Legal counsel

3. As Stan and Anna Walicki meet with the account representative at Landmark Bank, they are shown a sample of what their monthly statement will look like. Providing such sample documents allows Landmark to add tangibility to which of the following qualities?
   a. Experience
   b. Credence
   c. Search
   d. Perishability
   e. Inseparability

4. Distribution for nonprofit organizations is
   a. unimportant because physical movement does not take place.
   b. not an important decision variable.
   c. coordinated by middlemen.
   d. inefficient rather than efficient.
   e. typically characterized by short channels.

ANSWERS TO DISCUSSION AND REVIEW QUESTIONS

1. Identify the major unique service characteristics, and discuss the marketing problems that arise from these unique characteristics?

    Services are intangible, inseparable, heterogeneous, perishable, involve customer contact, and have client-based relationships. Intangibility causes problems such as impossibility to store, inability to protect through patents, inability to display or readily communicate, and pricing difficulty. Inseparability means that the consumer is involved in production, and centralized mass production is difficult. Heterogeneity makes it difficult to standardize or control the quality of the service produced. Perishability means that the service cannot be stockpiled or inventoried.

2. Choose a service product, then explain how major unique characteristics of services in general relate to this particular service.

    Students' answers will vary according to the examples they suggest.

3. Discuss the major ways by which service products can be classified.

    Services can be classified by (a) type of market (consumer or industrial); (b) degree of labor intensiveness (people-based or equipment-based); (c) degree of customer contact (high or low); (d) skill of service provider (professional or nonprofessional); and (e) the goal of the service provider (profit or nonprofit).

4. Analyze a house cleaning service in terms of the five classification schemes, and discuss the implications for marketing mix development.

    House cleaning (in the home) is a consumer service, people-based, low contact, nonprofessional, and profit-oriented. Students should generate various marketing mix schemes.

5. What is service quality?

    Service quality can be defined as customers' perceptions of how well a service meets or exceeds their expectations. Customers, not organizations, judge service quality; therefore, service marketers must judge quality from their customers' viewpoint. Service organizations first discover what customers expect and then produce service products that meet or exceeds those expectations.

6. Why do customers experience difficulty in judging service quality?

    Because services are intangible, customers cannot see, feel, taste, or hear them, and judging their quality is thus extremely difficult. Although goods have tangible attributes that can be judged before purchase, services must be judged only during purchase and consumption.

7. Identify and discuss the five components of service quality. How do consumers evaluate these components?

a. The *tangibles* component includes the physical evidence of the service. Consumers evaluate these through the appearance of the facilities, the appearance of service personnel, and the tools or equipment used to provide the service.

b. The *reliability* component includes the consistency and dependability in performing the service. Consumers evaluate this through criteria such as accurate billing or recordkeeping and on-time performance of services.

c. The *responsiveness* component includes the willingness or readiness of employees to provide the service. Evaluation of this component depends on the returning of customer phone calls, providing prompt service, or handling of urgent requests.

d. The *assurance* component includes the knowledge/competence of employees and their ability to convey trust and confidence. This component is evaluated through the perceived knowledge and skills of the employees, the company's name and reputation, and the personal characteristics of the employees.

e. The *empathy* component includes the caring and individual attention provided by employees. Evaluation criteria include the listening skills of the employee, the sincere caring about the customer's interests, and personalized attention.

8. What is the significance of tangibles in services marketing?

Tangibles include the facilities, employees, or communications associated with a service. They help to form a part of the product and are often the only aspects of a service that can be viewed prior to purchase. For example, the tangibles associated with a rock concert might be its communications (radio advertisements), facilities (stadium or convention center where the concert will be held), and the employees (ticket sales representatives). Since these elements are experienced prior to the actual service itself (concert), marketers must pay close attention to them and make sure they are consistent with the image of the service product.

9. How do search, experience, and credence qualities affect the way consumers view and evaluate services?

Search qualities can be viewed prior to purchase. Experience qualities (satisfaction, courtesy, and so forth) can be assessed only after purchase. Credence qualities cannot be assessed even after purchase and consumption. Because services are mainly intangible, there are few search qualities to evaluate. Because the product cannot be seen or touched prior to purchase, experience qualities are often the key means of assessing satisfaction. To illustrate, an airline's performance is best evaluated after passengers arrive at their final destinations. Credence qualities are usually based on reputation and image. For example, it is hoped that the image of a doctor or lawyer is related to past performance and that the product (performance) has consistency. In the long run, experience qualities are probably the most important in evaluating services.

10. What steps should a service company take to provide exceptional service quality?

To deliver exceptional service quality, an organization should first understand the needs and expectations of its customers. Methods of determining these needs and expectations can include marketing research, such as surveys and focus groups, comment cards, or asking employees who have close contact with customers. Next, the organization should establish goals or standards to help ensure that these customer needs and expectations are satisfied.

After service quality standards are set, organizations should take steps to ensure that customer-contact employees perform their jobs well; this involves training, providing them with information about customers, informing them about service expectations, and basing compensation on customer-oriented measures of performance such as friendliness and customer satisfaction. Finally, service organizations must manage service expectations. Through advertising and internal communication, services set realistic service expectations and make sure they deliver what they promise.

11. How does nonprofit marketing differ from marketing in for-profit organizations?

Nonprofit marketing is conducted by individuals and organizations devoted to some goal other than the ordinary goals of business, which are profit, market share, or return on investment. Business marketing is usually conducted for the benefit of an owner, shareholder, or manager. Examples of nonprofit marketing would be marketing aimed at increasing contributions to a particular charity or at encouraging people to recycle. These nonprofit enterprises benefit clients, members, or the public at large. In addition, nonprofit marketing often allows more opportunity for creativity than most business organizations.

12. What are the differences among clients, publics, and customers? What is the difference between a target public and a target market?

Clients are often considered as those individuals directly involved in an exchange transaction with a nonbusiness organization. Publics involve members of society who may have an interest in the exchange transaction between private parties. The term *customer* is used synonymously with *client*. If a nonbusiness organization views the entire society as the group to which it directs its message and with which to exchange, then the general public becomes the same as the target market.

13. Discuss the development of a marketing strategy for a university. What marketing decisions must be made as the strategy is developed?

The development of a marketing strategy for a university would consist of pinpointing a target market (defined in terms of the types of students the university would serve) and developing a marketing mix. The marketing mix would relate to the product (the types of educational programs offered), promotion (including the advertising and personal selling activities of the university), availability or distribution (where the university is located and its various branches), and the price (tuition and other expenses of attending a university).

COMMENTS ON THE CASES

Case 12.1   Fireworks by Grucci Entertains America

This case focuses on an entertainment company as a service provider. The objective of this case is to allow students to consider some of the distinctive characteristics associated with the marketing of services. You may want to ask your students about their experiences associated with professionally produced fireworks exhibitions.

The first question asks students to discuss the characteristics of services shown in Table 12.1 (text, p. 275) as they relate to the services provided by Fireworks by Grucci. With respect to the intangibility characteristic, Grucci is fortunate in that there are a number of tangible aspects associated with their services. Some of these aspects are very visually stimulating. The issue of inseparability of production and consumption clearly does exist for the services provided by Grucci. Citizens and clients must be present when the service is produced in order to consume it. Certainly the services provided by Grucci are highly perishable. Persons who do not attend a fireworks production cannot take advantage of that service at a later time. Because much of a fireworks production relies heavily on planning and implementation done by human beings rather than equipment, it is likely that this service is affected by heterogeneity. With respect to client-based relationships, marketers at Grucci clearly are concerned about developing and maintaining long-term relationships with customers, whether they be government units or business organizations. Regarding customer contact, the customer must be present at the fireworks production in order to receive the benefit of the service. Thus, these services are viewed as high-contact services.

The second question asks how customers evaluate the quality of Grucci's services. Grucci's customers include governmental officials and business decision makers. Both sets of customers will evaluate quality to some degree based on how easy it is to deal with employees at the Grucci organization. Business organizations use Fireworks by Grucci productions to entertain and to motivate employees. Thus, businesspeople are concerned about the extent to which fireworks productions lead to happy and motivated employees. Government officials will evaluate the quality of Grucci's services based on the size of crowds that are attracted to fireworks productions and on the response of citizens who attend.

Question 3 asks students to evaluate the methods that Fireworks by Grucci uses to promote its services. Fireworks by Grucci employs personal selling and public relations and, to some degree, relies on word-of-mouth communications. This organization uses no advertising. Students' evaluations of Grucci's promotional efforts will vary considerably. Some students are likely to express concern that Grucci does not advertise.

Video Information

Video Title: Grucci: The First Family of Fireworks
Location: Tape 2, Segment 12
Length: 9:08
Video Overview: Started in Italy during the 1800s, Fireworks by Grucci moved to the United States in 1870. The company struggled to survive during the Depression and again during the 1960s, when interest in extravagant displays waned, but the firm has gone on to become the world's premier pyrotechnic company with a reputation for excellence. Fireworks by Grucci was the first American fireworks company to win the Gold Medal at the Monte Carlo International Fireworks Championship.

Although Grucci employs the latest technology in production of its displays, every firework is handmade to ensure quality and safety. Grucci custom-designs every production, from small displays to major exhibitions such as presidential inaugurations, to meet each customer's specific needs. Grucci's customers include communities, businesses, and political organizations.

Multiple-Choice Questions About the Video

e 1. Fireworks by Grucci was the first American fireworks company to win
   a. the gold medal at the International Fireworks Festival in Rome.
   b. the international Pyrotechnic Medal of Excellence.
   c. acceptance into the International Pyrotechnic Institute.
   d. the medal for most innovative display at the World Championship of Fireworks.
   e. the Gold Medal at the International Fireworks Championship at Monte Carlo.

c 2. According to the video, Grucci maintains safety and quality by
   a. requiring employees to undergo several months of training before setting up displays.
   b. employing the latest technology to build its fireworks.
   c. insisting on hand building its fireworks.
   d. employing only experienced Grucci family members at the management level.
   e. adhering strictly to established industry safety and quality standards.

a 3. To meet the specific needs of its clients, Grucci
   a. custom-designs each firework display.
   b. offers a variety of firework packages priced to fit the budgets of individual clients.
   c. includes clients in the planning stages of the firework display.
   d. provides precise synchronization between music and aerial and ground displays.
   e. creates new and unique special effects for each event.

d 4. According to the video, setting up a large Grucci display requires
   a. as much as two weeks to complete.
   b. installing state-of-the-art sound equipment to enhance the visual display.
   c. a minimum of forty workers.
   d. 7 miles of cable and 25 tons of sand.
   e. both state and local permits.

Case 12.2   Harrah's Casinos Gambles on its Strategy

The purpose of this case is to provide students with an opportunity to discuss issues regarding services marketing as they apply to a specific service provider. Some of the students may find the discussion of gaming to be interesting because of the growth of this industry over the last decade.

Question 1 asks students to use the categories discussed in Table 12.2 and classify the gaming services provided by Harrah's. Table 12.2 (text, p. 281) classifies services based on five categories: type of market, degree of labor-intensiveness, degree of customer contact, skill of the service provider, and goal of the service provider. With respect to type of market, Harrah's aims primarily at consumer markets. With regard to the degree of labor intensiveness, Harrah's tends to be an equipment-based service provider. While dealers interact directly with some gaming customers, many gaming customers rely on equipment based gaming. The degree of customer contact is high because the customer needs to be in the casino to enjoy gaming. With respect to the skill of the service provider, the skill would be classified as nonprofessional rather than professional because most Harrah's employees do not require extensive professional training and certification. The goal of the service provider is to make a profit; casinos are not established to be nonprofit organizations.

Question 2 asks students to describe Harrah's attitude toward the service quality issue. Harrah's extends to its customers an unconditional guarantee of service excellence. The organization has a rating system that tracks customers' opinions. Harrah's surveys its customers regarding their experiences at their gaming facilities.

The third question asks how Harrah's differentiates its product mix from those of its competitors. Students are also asked to evaluate this strategy. While many of Harrah's competitors are trying to attract families by providing activities and events for children, Harrah's is aiming at adults and is not marketing to families. Harrah's believes that adults with children are too distracted or too tired to spend enough time in their casinos gambling. Thus, they prefer to attract adults who leave the kids at home, want to interact with other adults, and come to enjoy themselves gambling.

13 MARKETING CHANNELS

TEACHING RESOURCES QUICK REFERENCE GUIDE

Resource	Location
Purpose and Perspective	IRM, p. 279
Guide for Using Color Transparencies	IRM, p. 279
Lecture Outline	IRM, p. 279
Class Exercises, Debate Issue, and Chapter Quiz	IRM, p. 286
Class Exercise 1	IRM, p. 288
Class Exercise 2	IRM, p. 289
Debate Issue: Does cutting out the intermediary cut costs?	IRM, p. 290
Chapter Quiz	IRM, p. 291
Answers to Discussion and Review Questions	IRM, p. 292
Comments on the Cases	IRM, p. 295
Case 13.1	IRM, p. 295
Video	Tape 2, Segment 13
Video Information	IRM, p. 295
Multiple-Choice Questions About the Video	IRM, p. 296
Case 13.2	IRM, p. 296
Transparency Acetates	Transparency package
Examination Questions: Essay	TB, p. 237
Examination Questions: Multiple-Choice	TB, p. 237
Examination Questions: True-False	TB, p. 250
Author-Selected Multiple-Choice Test Items	TB, p. 447

PURPOSE AND PERSPECTIVE

This chapter analyzes marketing channels and intermediaries. We begin by examining the functions of marketing channels, including creating utility and facilitating exchange efficiencies. We also examine the justification for intermediaries. We divide types of marketing channels into those for consumer products and those for industrial products. We introduce the fundamentals of supply chain management, channel integration (including vertical and horizontal dimensions), vertical marketing systems, and the intensity of market coverage. Next, we discuss factors that influence the selection of distribution channels. We cover the behavioral aspects of marketing channels, including the concepts of channel cooperation, conflict and leadership. The chapter concludes by examining the legal ramifications of selected channel management practices.

GUIDE FOR USING COLOR TRANSPARENCIES

There are two groups of color transparencies. The transparencies identified by a double number are the same as the figures in the text. The transparencies labeled with a number and a letter are illustrations that do not appear in the text, but they can be used as additional examples of concepts discussed.

Part 4 Opener	Distribution decisions
Figure 13.1	Efficiency in exchange provided by an intermediary
Figure 13.3	Typical marketing channels for consumer products
Figure 13.4	Typical marketing channels for industrial products
Figure 13A	Chapter 13 outline
Figure 13B	Speeding supply chain cycle times
Figure 13C	Godiva uses dual distribution.
Figure 13D	The Dooney & Bourke All Weather Leather collection is marketed through exclusive distribution.
Figure 13E	Marketing activities performed by intermediaries
Figure 13G	Legal issues in channel management
Figure 13H	New marketing channels for grocery items

LECTURE OUTLINE

The **distribution** component of the marketing mix focuses on the decisions and actions involved in making products available to consumers when and where they want to purchase them.

I.   The nature of marketing channels

A.   A **marketing channel** (or channel of distribution) is a group of individuals and organizations that directs the flow of products from producers to customers. Providing customer benefits should be the driving force behind all marketing channel activities.

B. A **marketing intermediary** (middleman) links producers to other middlemen or to ultimate product users through contractual arrangements or through the purchase and resale of products.

   1. Wholesalers buy and resell products to other wholesalers, to retailers, and to industrial customers.

   2. Retailers purchase products and resell them to ultimate consumers.

C. Channel decisions are critical because they determine a product's market presence and buyers' accessibility to the product.

D. Marketing channels create utility.

   1. Time utility is having products available when customers want them.

   2. Place utility is having products available where customers want to purchase them.

   3. Possession utility provides the customer with access to the product to use or to store for future use.

E. Marketing channels facilitate exchange efficiencies.

   1. Marketing intermediaries can reduce the cost of exchanges by performing certain services or functions.

   2. Eliminating wholesalers would not do away with the need for the services they provide.

II. Types of marketing channels

A.   Channels for consumer products

    1.   Producer to consumer is a direct channel that includes customers who harvest their own fruit from commercial growers or buy goods directly from factories.

    2.   The producer-to-retailer-to-consumer channel is used by large retailers, such as Sears, that buy in large quantities from manufacturers.

    3.   The producer-to-wholesaler-to-retailer-to-consumer channel is a practical option for a producer that sells to hundreds of thousands of consumers through thousands of retailers, such as producers of convenience goods.

    4.   The producer-to-agent-to-wholesaler-to-retailer-to-consumer channel is used for products intended for mass distribution, such as processed foods.

B.   Channels for industrial products

    1.   The producer-to-industrial-buyer channel is necessary for many manufacturers of industrial goods because industrial buyers often prefer to communicate directly with the producer, especially for expensive or technically complex products.

    2.   Producers and industrial buyers may be linked by an **industrial distributor,** an independent business organization that takes title to products and carries inventories for resale to industrial buyers.

    3.   Producers and industrial buyers may be linked by a manufacturers' agent or representative, an independent businessperson who sells complementary products of several producers in assigned territories and is compensated through commissions.

    4.   The fourth channel includes both a manufacturers' agent and an industrial distributor between the producer and industrial customer.

C.   Multiple marketing channels and channel alliances

    1.   Manufacturers may use several marketing channels simultaneously to reach diverse target markets.

2.   **Dual distribution** is the use of two or more marketing channels for distributing the same products to the same target market.

3.   A **strategic channel alliance** exists when the products of one organization are distributed through the marketing channels of another organization.

III.   Intensity of market coverage

Intensity of market coverage refers to the number and kinds of outlets in which a product is sold. The choice depends on the characteristics of the product and the target market.

A.   **Intensive distribution,** using all available outlets to distribute a product, is appropriate for convenience products.

B.   **Selective distribution,** using only some available outlets in an area to distribute a product, is appropriate for shopping products, such as stereos.

C.   **Exclusive distribution,** using only one outlet in a large area to distribute a product, is suitable for products purchased infrequently, consumed over a long period of time, or requiring service or information to fit buyers' needs, such as expensive imported sports cars.

IV.   Supply chain management

Supply chain management refers to long-term partnerships among channel members working together to reduce inefficiencies, costs, and redundancies in the entire marketing channel in order to satisfy customers. It starts with the customer and involves everyone in the channel cooperating to achieve the optimal level of efficiency and service to reduce marketing channel costs, improve all members' profits, and satisfy customer requirements.

A.   Channel integration

1.   **Vertical channel integration** combines two or more stages of the channel under one management.

a. Total vertical channel integration encompasses all functions, from producer to ultimate buyer.

b. Members coordinate efforts to reach a desired target market.

2. A **vertical marketing system (VMS)** is a marketing channel in which channel activities are coordinated or managed by a single marketing channel member to achieve efficient, low-cost distribution aimed at satisfying target market customers.

   a. *Corporate VMSs* combine all channel stages from producer to consumer under a single ownership.

   b. *Administered VMSs* are composed of independent channel members with a high degree of interorganizational management achieved by informal coordination.

   c. *Contractual VMSs* involve interorganizational relationships formalized through contracts.

      (1) Franchise organizations provide wholesalers or retailers with products, ideas, and managerial skills.

      (2) Wholesaler-sponsored groups are independent retailers that band together under the contractual leadership of a wholesaler.

      (3) Retailer-sponsored cooperatives own and operate their wholesalers.

3. **Horizontal channel integration** combines institutions at the same level of operation under one management.

   a. Advantages include economies of scale and efficiencies in purchasing, marketing research, advertising, and specialized personnel.

   b. Disadvantages include decreased flexibility, coordination difficulties, and the need for more marketing research and large-scale planning.

B.   Channel cooperation, conflict, and leadership

Each channel member performs a different role and has expectations for every other member. Channel partnerships facilitate effective supply chain management.

1.   Channel cooperation is vital if each member expects to gain something from other members.

   a.   If a marketing channel is a unified supply chain, individual members will be less likely to create disadvantages for other members.

   b.   If channel members agree to direct their efforts toward common objectives, roles can be structured for maximum marketing effectiveness.

2.   Channel conflict stems from disagreements about how to attain goals and unmet goal expectations.

   a.   If self-interest creates misunderstandings about role expectations, frustration and conflict may result.

   b.   If dealers overemphasize competing products or diversify into other product lines, conflicts may develop.

   c.   If producers attempt to circumvent intermediaries, conflict may develop.

   d.   Partnerships can be reestablished by specifying the role of each intermediary and instituting measures of channel coordination.

3.   Channel leadership is assumed when a channel member influences and directs overall channel performance.

   a.   Leaders must possess **channel power**—the ability to influence the goal achievement of other members.

   b.   Leadership may be assumed by producers, retailers, or wholesalers.

V. Legal issues in channel management

    A. Dual distribution, the practice of distributing the same product through two or more different channel structures or selling similar products through different channels under different brand names, is legal when it promotes competition.

    B. Restricted sales territories exist when manufacturers prohibit intermediaries from selling its products outside designated sales areas. Their legality depends on the manufacturer's intent and on the effect on the market of restriction.

    C. **Tying agreements** exist when a supplier furnishing a product to a channel member stipulates that the member must purchase other products as well.

        1. *Full-line forcing* occurs when a supplier requires that channel members purchase the supplier's entire line to obtain any of the products.

        2. Tying agreements are considered legal when the supplier alone can provide a particular quality of product, when the intermediary is free to carry competing products as well, and when the company has just entered the market.

    D. **Exclusive dealing** occurs when a manufacturer forbids an intermediary to carry products of competing manufacturers. It is illegal under the following circumstances.

        1. It blocks competitors from as much as 10 percent of the market.

        2. The sales revenue involved is sizable.

        3. The manufacturer is much larger than the dealer.

    E. Refusal to deal

        1. Producers have the right to choose the channel member with which they will do business (and to reject others).

        2. However, suppliers may not refuse to deal with wholesalers for resisting anticompetitive policies or practices.

CLASS EXERCISES, DEBATE ISSUE, AND CHAPTER QUIZ

On the following pages, you will find two class exercises, a debate issue, and a chapter quiz. These are formatted in large-size type so that you can use them as class handouts or for making transparencies. Below are the authors' comments on the class exercises, the debate topic, and the answers to the chapter quiz.

Class Exercise 1: The objective of this class exercise is to aid student understanding of the dimensions of channel selection and their possible relationships with channel conflict.

Question 1. These manufacturers have the resources to control their own channels and apparently have altered objectives to include increased coverage in new segments. Many manufacturers suggest that since outlet stores are located outside metro areas, they are not competing directly with retailers. The buyer behavior of outlet store shoppers is different from that of upscale department store shoppers: for outlet store shoppers, price is the deciding factor and customer service is unimportant. Because most items in an outlet store are past season, retailers are usually unwilling to carry them (product attributes are different). The economy and social forces (environmental forces) may encourage people to shop for value rather than for status.

Question 2. If market coverage is seen as a continuum, then these manufacturers have moved from a selective or exclusive intensity to a more intensive coverage. As coverage intensifies, customer service is decreased (particularly at outlet stores). Additionally, consumers' perceptions of brand quality typically decrease as coverage intensity increases.

Question 3. Retailers expect manufacturers to supply relatively exclusive rights to distribute their branded goods. In the case of outlet stores, manufacturers have deviated from their role as producer to the role of retailer. (This might be a good time to define *wholesaling* and *retailing*.) Additionally, it appears that some manufacturers are selling some new items through outlet stores. It is also likely that manufacturers did not effectively or honestly communicate their distribution intentions to retailers.

Question 4. If retailers try to use coercive power, they will most likely hurt themselves by eliminating some of their best-selling brands. The conflict might be resolved by specifying the roles of each channel member (i.e., who sells what season merchandise).

Class Exercise 2: The purpose of this exercise is to improve students' understanding of the intensities of market coverage. Answers:

1.	Potato chips	intensive
2.	Gucci handbags	exclusive
3.	Large-screen televisions	selective
4.	Rolex watches	exclusive
5.	Clinique beauty aid packages	selective
6.	Carbonated beverages	intensive
7.	Range Rover vehicles	exclusive
8.	Stereo systems	selective
9.	Guess? jeans	selective
10.	IBM personal computers	selective
11.	Gasoline	intensive
12.	Massage chairs	selective
13.	Jaguar automobiles	exclusive

14. Nintendo video games   **selective**
15. Reebok shoes   **selective**

Debate Issue: Does cutting out the intermediary cut costs?

Chapter Quiz: Answers to multiple-choice questions are

1.	a	3.	b
2.	a	4.	c

CLASS EXERCISE 1

MANY MANUFACTURERS SELL PRODUCTS IN OUTLET STORES AT 25 TO 70 PERCENT OFF RETAIL PRICES. RETAILERS DO NOT LIKE THE ADDED COMPETITION FROM THEIR OWN SUPPLIERS DESPITE MANUFACTURERS' CLAIMS THAT THEY ARE ONLY SELLING LAST SEASON'S MERCHANDISE.

1. How could organizational objectives, buyer behavior, product attributes, or environmental forces affect a manufacturer's decision to distribute through outlet stores?

2. By selling in outlet stores, how have these manufacturers changed their intensity of market coverage? How is customer service different at an outlet store?

3. Which of the following may be responsible for the conflict between manufacturers and retailers?
   • Lack of clear communication
   • Deviation from role expectations
   • Diversification into product lines traditionally handled by other intermediaries.

4. Should the retailers develop store brands, refuse to stock certain items, or focus their buying power on one supplier or group of suppliers? How should the conflict be resolved?

CLASS EXERCISE 2

IDENTIFY THE INTENSITY OF MARKET COVERAGE FOR EACH OF THE FOLLOWING PRODUCTS:

1. Potato chips
2. Gucci handbags
3. Large-screen televisions
4. Rolex watches
5. Clinique beauty aid products
6. Carbonated beverages
7. Range Rover vehicles
8. Stereo systems
9. Guess? jeans
10. IBM personal computers
11. Gasoline
12. Massage chairs
13. Jaguar automobiles
14. Nintendo video games
15. Reebok shoes

DEBATE ISSUE

DOES CUTTING OUT THE INTERMEDIARY CUT COSTS?

YES

- Intermediaries make a significant profit on the products they carry

- Some wholesalers are inefficient and tend to be parasitic

- Eliminating intermediaries can cut these costs and decrease the time it takes for products to reach consumers

- Companies that are truly concerned about customer service will eliminate intermediaries and take responsibility for performing their tasks

NO

- Intermediaries make significantly less profit than retailers

- Wholesalers survive by providing certain functions more efficiently than other channel members

- Producers would have to provide additional functions, often at greater expense and time than using wholesalers

- To survive, wholesalers must be more efficient and more customer-focused than alternative marketing institutions

CHAPTER QUIZ

1. **If IBM decides to make changes in its marketing channels, the strategic significance is that channel decisions**
   a. are long-term commitments.
   b. are short-term commitments.
   c. are easier to change than prices.
   d. are easier to change than promotion.
   e. are impossible to change.

2. **In an administered vertical marketing system (VMS), interorganizational relationships are**
   a. achieved by informal coordination.
   b. formalized through contracts.
   c. combined under the ownership of a single organization.
   d. guided by legal agreements.
   e. achieved by clearly defining the obligations and rights of all channel members.

3. **Highly perishable consumer products**
   a. have long shelf lives.
   b. are marketed through short channels.
   c. are much less expensive to distribute.
   d. are always distributed through middlemen.
   e. provide the highest profit margins.

4. **If Ralston Purina forced Kroger's grocery chain to place all of its products in the stores' most favorable locations, it would be**
   a. demonstrating sound channel leadership.
   b. insisting on exclusive exposure.
   c. exercising channel power.
   d. minimizing channel conflict.
   e. creating a coordinate system.

ANSWERS TO DISCUSSION AND REVIEW QUESTIONS

1. Describe the major functions of marketing channels. Why are most functions better accomplished through combined efforts of channel members?

   The major functions of marketing channels include creating utility and facilitating exchange efficiencies. Marketing channels create time utility by making products available when customers want them, place utility by having them where customers can purchase them, and possession utility by providing customers the opportunity to use or store products. Because intermediaries are specialists at the services they provide, they can make exchanges more efficient. All of the services that intermediaries provide are necessary. By dividing responsibilities, each channel member becomes expert at what each does, making the marketing channel more efficient and therefore providing more reliable service to ultimate consumers.

2. Can one channel member perform all channel functions?

   One channel member cannot always perform all channel functions most efficiently. The member often lacks the capacity or facilities needed to perform each function, so it may be more efficient for other channel members to perform some or even all of the channel functions.

3. "Shorter channels are usually a more direct means of distribution and therefore are more efficient." Comment on this statement.

   Shorter marketing channels are not always the most efficient method of distribution. If this statement were true, there would be no need for wholesalers and all products would flow directly from producers to consumers. Durable household goods and convenience goods such as candy and gum are by their nature usually sold in convenient locations. Without longer channels, it would cost the producers more to get their products directly to the many outlets that sell the products.

4. Why do consumers often blame intermediaries for distribution inefficiencies? List several of the reasons.

   To consumers, intermediaries are not always visible in the distribution system and therefore are not worth what they cost. Throughout history, form utility has been perceived as having more value for consumers than time and place utility. However, many consumers do not realize that if the intermediaries are eliminated, either the producer or the consumer must perform the intermediaries' functions, leading to higher prices if the producer must perform those functions. Many people believe that intermediaries are parasitic and therefore contribute to inefficiency. In other words, consumers do not understand the role and function of intermediaries.

5. Compare and contrast the four major types of marketing channels for consumer products. Through which type of channel is each of the following products most likely to be distributed: (a) new automobiles, (b) saltine crackers, (c) cut-your-own Christmas trees, (d) new textbooks, (e) sofas, and (f) soft drinks?

The first type of consumer product channel is from producer directly to consumer. Although this type of channel is the simplest, it is not always the cheapest or most efficient. The second type of channel is producer to retailer to consumer and is efficient when large retailers can buy in large quantities from producers. The third channel, producer to wholesaler to retailer to consumer, is one of the most traditional types and is practical for producers of goods that sell to hundreds of thousands of consumers. The last type of consumer products distribution channel is from producer to agent to wholesaler to retailer to consumer. This method is most often used by producers of mass-marketed products.

The specified products are most likely to be distributed as follows:

(a) New automobiles—producer to retailer to consumer

(b) Saltine crackers—producer to food broker to wholesaler to retailer to consumer. In some cases, the producer may sell to a wholesaler, without using a broker.

(c) Cut-your-own Christmas trees—producer to consumer

(d) New textbooks—producer to retailer to consumer

(e) Sofa—producer to wholesaler to retailer to consumer, or possibly producer to retailer to consumer

(f) Soft drinks—because soft drinks are bottled locally, producer to retailer to consumer

6. Outline the four most common channels for industrial products. Describe the products and/or situations that lead marketers to choose each channel.

The first type of channel for industrial products is the direct channel from producers to industrial buyers. Expensive and technically complex products such as computers and aircraft are often sold through direct channels. A second industrial distribution channel is from producer to industrial distributor to industrial buyer. This channel is used when a product has broad market appeal, is easily stocked and serviced, is sold in small quantities, and is needed rapidly. The third industrial channel is from producer to manufacturer's agent to industrial buyer. This channel is effective for highly seasonal products. The last common channel for industrial products is from producer to agent to industrial distributor to industrial buyer. This type of channel is practical when the industrial marketer wants to cover a large geographic area but does not maintain a sales force or when a marketer wants to enter a new geographical region without expanding its existing sales force.

7. Describe an industrial distributor. What types of products are marketed through industrial distributors?

An industrial distributor is an intermediary that markets industrial products. Although it is an independent business organization, the industrial distributor takes title to products and carries inventories. An industrial product is one that is used in production or in everyday business activities, as opposed to ultimate consumption. The industrial distributor usually carries standardized industrial products, such as maintenance supplies and tools. The functions of industrial distributors vary with the number of links in the channel.

8. Under what conditions is a producer most likely to use more than one marketing channel?

A producer uses more than one marketing channel to reach diverse target markets, such as when the same product is directed to both consumers and industrial buyers. In other cases, companies may sell similar products under different brand names through multiple channels, a practice called *dual distribution.*

9. Explain the differences between intensive, selective, and exclusive methods of distribution.

   In intensive distribution, the product is distributed through many outlets for the convenience of customers; products include candy, gum, and soft drinks. Selective distribution is used for typewriters, stereos, and other products that buyers want to compare in terms of price, design, and style. Exclusive distribution is used for specialty products that are purchased infrequently or require a high degree of adjustment to buyers' needs, such as Rolex watches and Jaguar automobiles.

10. Name and describe firms that use (a) vertical integration and (b) horizontal integration in their marketing channels.

    Firms that use vertical integration in their marketing channels include Kentucky Fried Chicken, Exxon, and Safeway. All these firms combine two or more stages of their distribution channels under one management. For example, Kentucky Fried Chicken delivers food products and supplies to its own franchise operators.
        Firms that use horizontal integration include Wal-Mart, IGA, and Sears. These firms combine institutions at the same level in the channel. For instance, Wal-Mart integrates horizontally by adding more retail outlets, and IGA integrates horizontally by taking over or adding more wholesale outlets.

11. Explain the major characteristics of each of the three types of vertical marketing systems (VMSs)—corporate, administered, and contractual.

    A VMS is a centrally controlled marketing channel. A *corporate VMS* combines successive channel stages from producers to consumers under a single ownership. An *administered VMS* is a centrally coordinated system with a channel leader to establish strategy. In a *contractual VMS,* channel members are linked by legal agreements that spell out each member's rights and obligations.

12. "Channel cooperation requires that members support the overall channel goals to achieve individual goals." Comment on this statement.

    Cooperation is required of all channel members to provide an integrated system that will deliver the products customers desire. Failure of one link in the channel could cause customer dissatisfaction and therefore channel failure.

13. Under what conditions are tying contracts, exclusive dealing, and dual distribution judged illegal?

    Tying contracts exist when a supplier furnishes a product to a channel member with the stipulation that the channel member purchase other products as well. Most tying contracts are illegal unless the supplier alone can provide a particular quality of products, the intermediary is free to carry competing products, or the company has just entered the market. Exclusive dealing occurs when a manufacturer forbids an intermediary to carry products of competing manufacturers. It is considered illegal if (a) it blocks competitors from as much as 10 percent of the market, (b) the sales revenue involved is sizable, or (c) the manufacturer is much larger than the dealer. Dual distribution occurs when a producer distributes the same product through two or more different channel structures. It is not usually considered illegal unless it inhibits competition. For example, a manufacturer might use a company-owned outlet to drive independent firms out of business.

COMMENTS ON THE CASES

Case 13.1   CUTCO Cutlery: Differentiation via Direct Sales

The objective of this case is to let students explore the marketing channels for one company's products. Class discussion could be initiated by asking students if they have seen advertisements recruiting salespersons for CUTCO products, or whether any students have experience selling CUTCO products.

The first question asks students to discuss the strengths and weaknesses of Alcas's direct selling approach to the sales and distribution of CUTCO cutlery. Alcas's direct selling approach has been very successful, with sales approaching $85 million. This approach allows the firm to target its products to customers' needs through one-on-one, in-home demonstrations. Weaknesses of this approach include increasing competition, particularly firms making better use of technology, and relying solely on direct sales, especially when more and more consumers are working outside the home and are unavailable for in-home demonstrations.

The second question asks whether the marketing channel traditionally employed for CUTCO products is vertically or horizontally integrated. Alcas appears to be vertically integrated in that it owns both the manufacturer and the direct seller of CUTCO cutlery.

The final question asks students to discuss the level and nature of channel power now held by Alcas and the impact on the firm's power of diversifying to include online marketing. As owner of both the manufacturing and sales arms of its marketing system, Alcas wields great control over its marketing channel. However, the firm's reliance on direct sales may limit its opportunities. If the firm were to diversify into online marketing or other marketing channels, it may increase sales and gain market share.

Video Information

Video Title: Direct Selling on the Global Frontier
Location: Tape 2, Segment 13
Length: 12:53
Video Overview: CUTCO has successfully differentiated its products from those of its competitors through its use of a unique distribution channel. By utilizing direct sales composed primarily of college students, CUTCO has a niche quite different from traditional quality knife manufacturers. In-home demonstrations allow potential customers to see the effectiveness of the knives and to test them personally. CUTCO is expanding internationally and using a "Tupperware" approach to marketing its knives, having housewives hold parties to show their products.

Multiple-Choice Questions About the Video

d   1. Which of the following best describes the current marketing channel for CUTCO cutlery?
   a. Producer to consumer
   b. Producer to retailer to consumer
   c. Producer to wholesaler to consumer
   d. Producer to agent to consumer

a   2. If CUTCO begins selling its cutlery online, it will be utilizing what type of marketing channel?
   a. Producer to consumer
   b. Producer to retailer to consumer
   c. Producer to wholesaler to consumer
   d. Producer to agent to consumer

b   3. CUTCO's primary sales force consists of
   a. company-employed sales representatives.
   b. college students recruited as independent sales agents.
   c. housewives recruited as independent sales agents.
   d. retailers.

Case 13.2   New Distribution Channels for Automobiles

The purpose of this case is to show students that marketing channels for specific products change over time to meet the needs of consumers and marketing channel members.

The first question asks why CarMax is using a "new" marketing channel for automobiles. Circuit City launched CarMax, a chain of used car superstores, after recognizing an opportunity to capitalize on its strengths in customer service, logistics, sales of high-dollar merchandise, and financing to develop a "new" marketing channel in response to increasing sales of used vehicles and increasing consumer dissatisfaction with traditional channels.

The second question asks how a new-car franchise dealer's marketing channel differs from the "new" marketing channels. A new-car franchise dealer is a marketing intermediary, a retailer, that sells new vehicles through a contractual arrangement with the manufacturer. As such it must honor all rules specified by the manufacturer for the sale of its vehicles. Used car marketing channels, including that utilized by CarMax, have no relationship with manufacturers; they simply sell and buy used cars and are not limited to just one or a few brands.

Question 3 asks what would happen if auto manufacturers bypassed their traditional dealer system and used multiple channels to distribute cars. If auto manufacturers began using multiple marketing channels, one result would be channel conflict as traditional franchise dealers suddenly faced competition from more retailers. If manufacturers bypassed franchise dealers altogether in favor of auto superstores such as CarMax, mass retailers such as Wal-Mart, and online retailing, consumers would have greater choices when buying vehicles. However, some of the functions of the traditional retailers, such as inventory, service, and information about vehicle features, would have to be passed on to other members of the channel—the manufacturer, the retailer, or even the consumer. While many consumers would appreciate the new marketing channels and be willing to assume some marketing channel roles (such as educating themselves about car features before buying), many others may prefer the more traditional channels. Manufacturers observing the success of CarMax may well be motivated to experiment with new and multiple channels, but they must take care to continue to satisfy their target market and meet their obligations as supply chain members.

14 WHOLESALING

TEACHING RESOURCES QUICK REFERENCE GUIDE

Resource	Location
Purpose and Perspective	IRM, p. 298
Guide for Using Color Transparencies	IRM, p. 298
Lecture Outline	IRM, p. 298
Class Exercises, Debate Issue, and Chapter Quiz	IRM, p. 304
Class Exercise 1	IRM, p. 306
Class Exercise 2	IRM, p. 307
Debate Issue: Are manufacturer's agents and representatives losing their position in the marketing channel?	IRM, p. 308
Chapter Quiz	IRM, p. 309
Answers to Discussion and Review Questions	IRM, p. 310
Comments on the Cases	IRM, p. 312
Case 14.1	IRM, p. 312
Video	Tape 2, Segment 14
Video Information	IRM, p. 312
Multiple-Choice Questions About the Video	IRM, p. 313
Case 14.2	IRM, p. 314
Transparency Acetates	Transparency package
Examination Questions: Essay	TB, p. 255
Examination Questions: Multiple-Choice	TB, p. 256
Examination Questions: True-False	TB, p. 269
Author-Selected Multiple-Choice Test Items	TB, p. 447

PURPOSE AND PERSPECTIVE

This chapter defines *wholesaling* and *wholesaler*. We begin with a discussion of the nature and importance of wholesaling. We examine the services wholesalers offer producers and retailers, pointing out that wholesaling functions must be performed during distribution of all goods, whether or not a wholesaling institution is involved. Next, we classify wholesalers based on the activities they perform in the marketing channel. We describe three general categories of wholesale establishments: (1) merchant wholesalers, (2) agents and brokers, and (3) manufacturers' sales branches and offices. We also cover five types of facilitating organizations that assist in performing wholesaling activities: public and bonded warehouses, finance companies, transportation companies, trade shows, and trade marts. The chapter closes with a discussion of changing trends in wholesaling.

GUIDE FOR USING COLOR TRANSPARENCIES

There are two groups of color transparencies. The transparencies identified by a double number are the same as the figures and tables in the text. The transparencies labeled with a number and a letter are illustrations that do not appear in the text, but they can be used as additional examples of concepts discussed.

LECTURE OUTLINE

I. The nature and importance of wholesaling

   A. **Wholesaling** refers to all transactions in which products are bought for resale, for making other products, or for general business operations.

   B. A **wholesaler** is an individual or organization engaged in facilitating and expediting exchanges that are primarily wholesale transactions.

   C. Distribution of all goods requires wholesaling activities, whether or not a wholesaling firm is involved.

   D. Services for producers

Wholesalers provide many services to producers and manufacturers.

1. Wholesalers serve as extensions of a producer's sales force because they sell a manufacturer's products to retailers and initiate sales contracts.

2. Wholesalers provide several forms of financial assistance, such as paying transportation costs and holding inventories, which in turn reduce producer inventories and capital required.

3. Wholesalers serve as information conduits within the marketing channels.

E. Services for retailers

1. Most wholesalers are selling specialists that help their retailer customers coordinate supply sources and select inventory.

2. Wholesalers perform physical distribution activities more efficiently than producers or retailers because they buy in large quantities and deliver in small lots.

3. Wholesalers maintain wide product lines at relatively low cost, relieving retailers of storage and warehousing costs.

II. Classifying wholesalers

A. Classification criteria

1. Whether a wholesaler is owned by the producer

2. Whether a wholesaler takes title to products

3. The breadth and depth of a wholesaler's product lines

B. **Merchant wholesalers** are independent organizations that take title to goods and assume risks associated with ownership; they generally buy and sell products to industrial or retail customers.

1. **Full-service wholesalers** offer the widest possible range of wholesaling activities, including wide product availability, bulk-breaking functions, financial assistance, and technical service and advice.

   a. **General merchandise wholesalers** carry a very wide product mix but offer limited depth within product lines. They deal in such products as drugs, hardware, detergents, and cosmetics.

   b. **Limited-line wholesalers** carry only a few product lines but offer an extensive assortment within those lines; examples are groceries, lighting fixtures, and computers.

   c. **Specialty-line wholesalers,** such as a shellfish wholesaler, carry the narrowest range of products and offer detailed product knowledge and depth of choice. **Rack jobbers** are specialty-line wholesalers that own and maintain their own display racks in drugstores and supermarkets. Examples are wholesalers of cosmetics and magazines.

2. **Limited-service wholesalers** provide some marketing services and specialize in a few functions. They are important in distributing specialty foods and perishable items; Table 14.2 (text, p. 329) compares the services offered by limited-service wholesalers.

   a. **Cash-and-carry wholesalers** are intermediaries whose customers pay cash and furnish their own transportation.

   b. **Truck wholesalers** (also called truck or wagon jobbers) transport a limited line of products directly to customers for on-the-spot inspection and selection. They are often small operators who own and drive their own trucks.

   c. **Drop shippers,** or desk jobbers, take title to goods and negotiate sales but never take actual possession of products. They forward orders and arrange carload shipments for direct delivery.

   d. **Mail-order wholesalers** use catalogs instead of sales forces to sell products.

C. Agents and brokers negotiate purchases and expedite sales but do not take title to products. They are **functional middlemen** that perform a limited number of services in exchange for a commission. **Agents** represent buyers or sellers on a permanent basis. **Brokers** are usually employed temporarily.

1. **Manufacturer's agents** are independent intermediaries who represent two or more sellers and usually offer customers complete product lines.

   a. They sell and take orders much as a manufacturer's sales office does.

   b. They are restricted to particular territories and handle noncompeting and complementary products.

   c. The advantages they offer include their wide range of contacts and stronger customer relationships.

   d. The chief disadvantage is the higher commission rate charged for new-product sales.

2. **Selling agents** market either all of a specified product line or a manufacturer's entire output.

   a. They perform every wholesaling activity except taking title to products, and they usually assume the sales functions for several producers at a time.

   b. They have no territorial limits and have complete authority over price, promotion, and distribution.

   c. They are used most often by small producers or manufacturers that find it difficult to maintain a marketing department because of seasonal production or other factors.

   d. They represent noncompeting product lines and are commonly used in distribution of textiles and coal.

3. **Commission merchants,** or factor merchants, receive goods on consignment from local sellers and negotiate sales in large central markets.

   a. They have broad powers in setting prices and terms of sale, and they specialize in obtaining the best price possible under market conditions.

   b. They offer planning assistance and sometimes extend credit but usually do not provide promotional support.

4.   Brokers seek out buyers or sellers and assist in negotiating exchanges; a broker's primary purpose is to bring buyers and sellers together.

    a.   They are not involved in financing, possession, or price setting but offer specialized knowledge of a product and a network of established contacts.

    b.   They are useful to sellers of products that are marketed only occasionally, such as insurance or real estate.

    c.   **Food brokers** sell food and general merchandise items to wholesalers, grocery chains, and other buyers.

D.   Manufacturers' sales branches and offices

1.   **Sales branches** are manufacturer-owned operations that sell products and provide support services for manufacturers' sales forces.

2.   **Sales offices** are manufacturer-owned operations that provide services normally associated with agents.

III.   Facilitating agencies

Facilitating agencies engage in activities that support marketing channel functions, such as shipping, insurance, or advertising. They often perform distribution tasks more efficiently than regular intermediaries in the marketing channel.

A.   Public warehouses are storage facilities available for a fee.

1.   Many warehouses process orders, deliver, collect accounts, and maintain display rooms for products.

2.   To use goods as collateral, a channel member may place products in a bonded warehouse.

B.   Finance companies provide financing to wholesalers and retailers by taking title to products while allowing the wholesalers and retailers to retain physical possession of the goods.

1. Floor planning enables wholesalers and retailers to offer a greater selection of products.

2. Factors are organizations that provide clients with working capital by buying their accounts receivable or by loaning money using accounts receivable as collateral.

C. Transportation companies help manufacturers transport products and sometimes take over functions of other intermediaries.

1. Forms of transportation include rail, truck, air, pipeline, and water carriers. Each form offers unique advantages.

2. Transportation companies can sometimes eliminate the need for large inventories and branch warehouses and can also perform accumulation functions.

D. **Trade shows** are industry exhibitions that enable manufacturers and wholesalers to exhibit products to potential buyers and assist in selling and buying functions.

E. **Trade marts** are relatively permanent facilities that firms can rent to exhibit products year round.

IV. Changing patterns in wholesaling

A. The distinction between the wholesaling activities that any business can perform and the traditional wholesale establishment is becoming blurred as manufacturers, retailers, and facilitating agencies perform wholesaling functions.

B. Wholesaler consolidation

1. Like most major industries, the wholesale industry is experiencing a great number of mergers.

2. Merging allows wholesaling firms to achieve more efficiency in the face of declining profit margins.

3. Consolidation gives larger wholesalers more pricing power over producers.

4. One result of consolidation is that more wholesalers are specializing.

C. Productivity and quality

1. A major trend is improving quality and productivity.

2. Companies are streamlining the way products move through the marketing channel to reduce costs, increase service, and improve profits.

3. Wholesalers are forging new relationships with manufacturers and retailers.

4. Wholesalers are benefiting from computer networks that allow various supply chain members to share information and coordinate distribution.

D. Global expansion

1. Wholesalers are very important in reaching global markets.

2. In the future, more wholesalers will probably penetrate global markets by operating without considering borders between countries.

CLASS EXERCISES, DEBATE ISSUE, AND CHAPTER QUIZ

On the following pages, you will find two class exercises, a debate issue, and a chapter quiz. These are formatted in large-size type so that you can use them as class handouts or for making transparencies. Below are the authors' comments on the class exercises, the debate topic, and the answers to the chapter quiz.

Class Exercise 1: The objective of this class exercise is to help students understand the path that goods normally must take to get from producer to retailer.

Question 1. This question is designed to help students understand why many companies need merchant wholesalers. Even if a small firm has sufficient capital to branch out into new markets, its managers are unlikely to have the expertise offered by a merchant wholesaler.

Question 2. Dependent on the breadth of market coverage required for the new product line, the marketing channel may be shorter or longer. Traditionally, household furniture can take almost any route from manufacturer to retailer.

Question 3. The choice between options A and B will depend on the type of services desired by the new company. After that decision, the most plausible choice within option

A is either a limited-line or specialty-line wholesaler. These wholesalers carry narrow and deep product lines and sell mainly to retailers that require specialized market knowledge and service. Within option B, the most plausible choices are a manufacturer's agent, selling agent, or commission merchant. Using a manufacturer's agent may be the best alternative if the new company can support its own marketing activities. However, if the new company has a limited marketing department, then a selling agent may be a better choice. Using a commission merchant may be useful if the new company wishes to sell locally or regionally.

Class Exercise 2: The objective of this exercise is to improve students' recognition of various types of wholesalers. Answers:

1. Broker
2. Drop shipper
3. Selling agent
4. Mail order
5. Cash and carry
6. Truck
7. Commission
8. Manufacturer's agent

Debate Issue: Are manufacturer's agents and representatives losing their position in the marketing channel?

Chapter Quiz: Answers to multiple-choice questions are

1. b	3. b
2. b	4. a

CLASS EXERCISE 1

ASSUME THAT YOU HAVE FORMED YOUR OWN COMPANY TO PRODUCE HOUSEHOLD FURNITURE. HOW ARE YOU GOING TO GET YOUR PRODUCTS TO THE FINAL CONSUMER?

1. Which of the following services or functions would you need from a wholesaler?
   - Provide market coverage
   - Make sales contacts
   - Inventory storage
   - Handle orders
   - Collect market information
   - Furnish customer support

2. What would be the typical marketing channel for your product?

3. Assuming that you will not sell directly to retailers, you have two options to distribute your product:

   Option A. You personally sell the product to wholesalers, who in turn will sell to retailers. With this option, you must determine what kind of wholesaler you will use.

   Option B. You let someone else sell the product to wholesalers, retailers, or both. With this option, you must select a broker, manufacturer's agent, selling agent, or commission merchant to locate and sell to wholesalers or retailers (or both), most likely on a commission basis. This means that you will make 10 to 15 percent less than with option A.

Explain why you chose option A or B.

CLASS EXERCISE 2

Types of Wholesaler	Takes Possession of Products	Delivers Merchandise to Customers	Provides Credit	Takes Title to Products	Common Products Carried
1. _____	No	No	No	No	Used in industrial equipment
2. _____	No	No	Yes	Yes	Building materials
3. _____	No	Yes	Yes	No	Textiles
4. _____	Yes	No	Sometimes	Yes	Office supplies
5. _____	Yes	No	No	Yes	Groceries and office supplies
6. _____	Yes	Yes	Sometimes	Yes	Perishables
7. _____	Yes	Yes	Sometimes	No	Agricultural commodities
8. _____	Sometimes	Sometimes	No	No	Apparel and accessories

DEBATE ISSUE

ARE MANUFACTURER'S AGENTS AND REPRESENTATIVES LOSING THEIR POSITION IN THE MARKETING CHANNEL?

YES

- Large retailers are bypassing agents and buying directly from manufacturers

- Well-known retailers such as Wal-Mart, Lowe's, and Builder's Square have started demanding direct purchase agreements with manufacturers

- Manufacturers are able to provide products to retailers at lower cost than a retailer receives from an agent or representative

- As price competitiveness increases among retailers, more and more retailers are likely to bypass manufacturer's agents and representatives

NO

- Manufacturer's agents and representatives still play a vital role for small- and medium-sized retailers

- Agents and representatives can provide purchasing and storage capabilities to those retailers that cannot handle the responsibility alone

- Agents and representatives can help lower the purchasing and personnel costs of smaller retailers

- Agents and representatives must reconsider their strategic objectives and begin concentrating on small- and medium-sized retailers that may be more profitable than are the large firms

CHAPTER QUIZ

1. Which of the following services would a wholesaler *least* likely provide to a manufacturer?
   a. Assume the risks of selling to poor credit customers
   b. Look for and coordinate supply sources
   c. Pay the costs of transporting goods
   d. Provide up-to-date information on market developments
   e. Serve as an extension of the manufacturer's sales force

2. Lynn Taylor sells Revlon cosmetics on consignment to grocery stores, maintains the display racks, and restocks when necessary. Lynn's job is best described as a
   a. drop shipper.
   b. rack jobber.
   c. general merchandise wholesaler
   d. cash-and-carry wholesaler.
   e. truck jobber.

3. The growth of strong retailers such as Circuit City and Best Buy in consumer electronics are changing supply chain relationships by
   a. dealing directly with wholesalers because wholesalers have lower costs.
   b. dealing directly with producers, performing the wholesaler's job at a lower cost.
   c. dealing directly with agents to lower costs.
   d. dealing directly with consumers to avoid transportation and materials handling costs.
   e. maintaining traditional relationships with wholesalers and expanding rapidly.

4. The three predominant changes occurring in wholesaling today are
   a. wholesaler consolidation, improved quality and productivity, and globalization of wholesale markets.
   b. wholesaler consolidation, the development of new types of wholesalers, and global expansion.
   c. wholesaler specialization, the increased use of consultants, and global expansion.
   d. the increased use of computer technology, the development of new types of retailers, and global expansion.

ANSWERS TO DISCUSSION AND REVIEW QUESTIONS

1. Is there a distinction between wholesalers and wholesaling? If so, what is it?

   A wholesaler is an individual, business, or establishment that functions as an intermediary, selling to industrial, reseller, and institutional users. Wholesaling activities can be performed by any channel member, including retailers and producers. Wholesaling includes all market transactions in which purchases are intended for resale or for use in making other products.

2. Would it be appropriate for a wholesaler to stock both interior wall paint and office supplies? Under what circumstances would this product mix be logical?

   In some situations, a small business or office might want to buy these two products together, but in general this product mix would not have great demand. By selling paint and office supplies, a wholesaler would limit the number of people who wanted paint for reasons other than painting an office. Therefore, at the retail level, these products are not usually stocked in the same store.

3. What services do wholesalers provide to producers and retailers?

   For producers, wholesalers perform specialized accumulation and allocation functions, thereby letting producers concentrate on developing products that match consumers' wants. Wholesalers also provide services such as financial assistance, storage, and transportation, and they are excellent sources of information and working capital.

   Wholesalers help retailers select inventory and negotiate final purchases. Wholesalers also provide transportation, storage, information, materials handling, and warehousing. Because they provide the fastest delivery at the lowest cost, they create time and place utilities.

4. Drop shippers take title to products but do not accept physical possession. Commission merchants take physical possession of products but do not accept title. Defend the logic of classifying drop shippers as wholesale merchants and commission merchants as agents.

   Drop shippers are classified as wholesale merchants because they take title and assume risk of product ownership, although they do not take physical possession. Commission merchants take physical possession but do not assume the risk associated with product ownership; they return unsold merchandise to the owner. Product ownership therefore differentiates agents from merchants and determines the classifications of drop shipper and commission merchant.

5. What are the advantages of using agents to replace merchant wholesalers? What are the disadvantages?

   The advantage of using agents to replace merchant wholesalers is that selling expenses can sometimes be lowered because agents receive a commission only when they sell a product for the producer. Also, agents may work harder for a company if they are compensated through commissions. The disadvantages of using agents are that (a) agents generally do not perform as many functions for the producer as do merchant wholesalers; (b) agents cannot be controlled to the extent that merchant wholesalers can; (c) agents do not assume risk and do not help the producer own stocks of inventory; and (d) agents usually will not perform any transportation or storage functions.

6. What, if any, are the differences in the marketing services that manufacturer's agents and selling agents perform?

Manufacturer's agents represent several sellers and sell products to customers as a product line. They are limited to selling in specific territories. Selling agents market all of a specified product line or the entire output of a manufacturer. They have considerable control over marketing efforts and do not have geographical restrictions.

7. Why are manufacturers' sales offices and branches classified as wholesalers? Which independent wholesalers are replaced by manufacturers' sales branches? Which independent wholesalers are replaced by manufacturers' sales offices?

Manufacturers' sales offices and branches are classified as wholesalers by the U.S. Census of Business because their main function is to perform wholesaling activities. Manufacturers' sales branches serve the same functions as merchant wholesalers, and manufacturers' sales offices serve essentially the same function as agents.

8. "Public warehouses are really wholesale establishments." Please comment.

Public warehouses are not wholesaling establishments, but often they perform many of the wholesaling activities merchant wholesalers usually perform. Public warehouses often store merchandise and assist with transactions between the owner of the merchandise and the buyer. Unlike wholesaling establishments, however, public warehouses do not take title to merchandise or assume risk, nor do they serve as agents. Their major purpose is storage and communications, not selling.

9. Explain the role of facilitating organizations. Identify three facilitating organizations and explain how each type performs this role.

Facilitating organizations are highly specialized firms that perform some wholesaling functions.

   a. Transportation companies help manufacturers and retailers transport products without the aid of middlemen. These companies often combine small shipments into full loads to decrease costs to customers.

   b. Trade shows and trade marts assist in buying and selling functions by allowing manufacturers or retailers to exhibit products to potential buyers.

   c. Public warehouses provide storage facilities, alleviating producers of the need to build their own or use a merchant wholesaler's. They also often provide services such as placing orders, delivering goods, and maintaining display rooms.

   d. Finance companies make loans to wholesalers and retailers by assuming ownership of products while allowing the wholesalers and retailers to retain physical possession of the goods. Factors also provide working capital by buying accounts receivable and may provide management expertise as well.

10. Discuss the major trends in wholesaling today. How do these changes provide opportunities for growth of wholesaling?

The wholesaling industry is changing in response to changes in the marketing environment. Major changes include increasing consolidation within the wholesaling industry, the increasing importance of quality and productivity, and the increasing importance of wholesalers in reaching global markets. Wholesalers that grow through geographic expansion, merger or acquisition, or improved productivity will control most of the wholesale business by the year 2000. The future of independent wholesalers, agents, and brokers depends on their abilities to delineate markets and furnish desired services. Wholesalers, agents, and brokers able to meet market needs will likely grow. The greatest growth potential for wholesalers involves global markets. Encouraged by developments such as the North American Free Trade Agreement, increasing numbers of wholesalers are seeking opportunities in other countries. Some analysts predict that wholesalers that avoid international markets may find growth difficult.

COMMENTS ON THE CASES

Case 14.1   Fleming: Success Through Service

This case familiarizes students with the operations of a large wholesaler and raises some issues regarding how wholesalers compete with one another. Fleming is *the* largest U.S. food wholesaler.

Question 1 asks students to classify Fleming as to type of wholesaler. Because of the large number of services provided to both manufacturers and retailers, Fleming is classified as a full-service wholesaler. Fleming carries a broad assortment of products. The large number of product lines would place Fleming in the category of a general merchandise wholesaler.

Question 2 asks how Fleming is trying to gain an edge over its competitors. One way Fleming is trying to gain a competitive edge is through purchasing some of its competitors, which allows it to increase its size. If the growth is properly managed, the larger size can make Fleming more competitive. Fleming is also trying to gain a competitive edge by providing an extremely large number of services, especially to retailers. The wholesale giant wants to make sure that it gives retailers no reason to do business with competitors. Fleming is especially interested in providing retailers with services that will make them more cost efficient and so improve their performance.

Question 3 asks what services Fleming is providing to its customers. Through the use of technology, Fleming provides its customers with high-speed delivery and products at reasonable prices. Fleming provides its customers with numerous private labeled product lines that offer them higher profits. The wholesaler also provides retailers with merchandising, management, and operations advice and counseling. Fleming furnishes its customers with electronic services, including order entry, scanning equipment, and computer software, that improve the efficiency of store management. Fleming offers retailers employee training programs, site selection services, and store design. Retailers can also obtain financial services from Fleming, such as loans for equipment, inventory, and store leasing.

Video Information

Video Title: Fleming Companies Incorporated Overview
Location: Tape 2, Segment 14
Length: 7:00

Video Overview: Fleming Companies is the largest wholesale food distributor in the United States. The company's competitive edge derives from its ability to provide its customers with excellent service. Using electronic order entry and mechanized order selection and loading systems, Fleming can make deliveries twelve hours after orders are placed. In addition to supplying food, household items, and health and beauty products to retail supermarkets, Fleming also provides its customers with assistance in store planning and development, retail counseling, training programs, electronic services (order entry, scanning equipment, computer programming), and financial services.

Multiple-Choice Questions About the Video

c 1. In addition to supplying food and other items to retail supermarkets, Fleming Companies serves its customers by
   a. stocking shelves, designing end-aisle displays, and creating point-of-purchases promotions.
   b. offering special discounts on items that are regularly purchased in large quantities.
   c. providing store planning, retail counseling, training programs, and electronic and financial services.
   d. operating in-store services such as pharmacies, photo development, and video rental.
   e. providing advertising and promotional material created specifically for individual retail chains or sir 'c outlets.

b 2. Use of technology such as computer scanning and mechanized order selection and loading makes it possible for Fleming to deliver products to stores _____ hours after order entry.
   a. 24
   b. 12
   c. 18
   d. 6
   e. 36

b 3. Because Fleming Companies purchases food products in very large quantities,
   a. the distributor can operate warehouses and distribution centers throughout the United States, Mexico, and the Caribbean.
   b. the distributor can offer its customers substantial savings.
   c. the company focuses primarily on food distribution rather than on other products such as household items and health and beauty aids.
   d. the company can avoid stock-outs.
   e. the company is able to obtain a higher profit margin than other wholesalers.

a 4. To lower its customers' costs, Fleming offers them _____ products as well as products with national brand names.
   a. private label
   b. generic
   c. regional
   d. restricted label
   e. unbranded

Case 14.2   McKesson Drug Company Prepares for Health Care in the Twenty-First Century

Students are often less familiar with wholesalers and wholesaling operations than other types of marketing institutions. The goal of this case therefore is to provide students with an opportunity to become more familiar with a wholesaling establishment. Due to the possible changes in health care delivery, McKesson is in a position to face a number of marketing opportunities and challenges over the next decade.

Question 1 asks students to identify what type of wholesaler McKesson Drug Company is. McKesson is a limited-line wholesaler because it carries relatively few product lines but offers an extensive assortment of products within those lines.

Question 2 asks what services McKesson provides to producers and to retailers. For producers, McKesson provides vital linkages to retailers, maintains inventories of products to reduce the inventory levels carried by producers, reduces market risk for producers, and provides considerable amounts of information regarding retailers and ultimate consumers. For retailers, McKesson maintains inventories and provides very quick order processing and fulfillment, provides credit, provides equipment and other computer technology, and designs programs to help them succeed.

The third question asks why McKesson is so focused on helping drug retailers remain successful. One way to keep customers is to help them prosper. If retail druggists decline, then McKesson's wholesaling opportunities decline as well. Helping its customers be successful in turn helps McKesson be successful.

15 RETAILING

TEACHING RESOURCES QUICK REFERENCE GUIDE

Resource	Location
Purpose and Perspective	IRM, p. 316
Guide for Using Color Transparencies	IRM, p. 316
Lecture Outline	IRM, p. 316
Class Exercises, Debate Issue, and Chapter Quiz	IRM, p. 326
Class Exercise 1	IRM, p. 328
Class Exercise 2	IRM, p. 329
Debate Issue: Is franchising the best way to own a business?	IRM, p. 330
Chapter Quiz	IRM, p. 331
Answers to Discussion and Review Questions	IRM, p. 332
Comments on the Cases	IRM, p. 336
Case 15.1	IRM, p. 336
Video	Tape 2, Segment 15
Video Information	IRM, p. 336
Multiple-Choice Questions About the Video	IRM, p. 336
Case 15.2	IRM, p. 337
Transparency Acetates	Transparency package
Examination Questions: Essay	TB, p. 273
Examination Questions: Multiple-Choice	TB, p. 274
Examination Questions: True-False	TB, p. 285
Author-Selected Multiple-Choice Test Items	TB, p. 447

PURPOSE AND PERSPECTIVE

This chapter is devoted exclusively to retailing because retailers are intermediaries with which students are familiar and retailing offers many career opportunities. As we point out in the chapter, retail institutions make final exchanges with ultimate consumers; thus retailing is a visible and important link in the marketing channel. Here we focus on retailing fundamentals and the broad strategic decisions that retail institutions must make. First, we overview the nature of retailing. Then we classify the major types of retailers. We also examine several forms of nonstore retailing and analyze the concept of franchising. We describe various types of planned shopping centers. We cover several strategic issues in retailing, including location, positioning, store image, and scrambled merchandising. We close with a discussion of the wheel of retailing hypothesis.

GUIDE FOR USING COLOR TRANSPARENCIES

There are two groups of color transparencies. The transparencies identified by a double number are the same as the figures in the text. The transparencies labeled with a number and a letter are illustrations that do not appear in the text, but they can be used as additional examples of concepts discussed.

Figure 15.8	The wheel of retailing
Figure 15A	Chapter 15 outline
Figure 15B	Retailing giants in the theme park industry
Figure 15C	What do catalogs cost?
Figure 15D	How to succeed in retailing as a small business
Figure 15E	Types of stores that sell crayons
Figure 15F	San Marcos factory shops are outlets that provide name brands at lower prices.
Figure 15G	Lady Foot Locker promotes a highly athletic image to its customers.
Figure 15H	Dunlop Tire provides a Web site so that its customers can shop via their home computers.
Figure 15I	General merchandise retailers
Figure 15J	Managing retail success
Figure 15K	High volume items sold at Wal-Mart
Figure 15L	Talbots is a specialty retailer and a catalog direct marketer.

LECTURE OUTLINE

I. The nature of retailing

A. **Retailing** includes all transactions in which the buyer intends to consume the product through personal, family, or household use. A **retailer** is an organization that purchases products for the purpose of reselling them to ultimate consumers.

B. Retailing is important to the national economy.

C. Retailers add value, provide service, and assist in making product selections.

    1. Retailer image can enhance the value of the product.

    2. Retailers facilitate comparison shopping.

    3. The value of the product is increased through delivery, credit, and repair services.

    4. Retail personnel can demonstrate to consumers how a product can address a need or solve a problem.

D. Retailers are the critical link between producers and ultimate consumers because they provide the environment in which exchanges with ultimate consumers occur.

E. Traditional retailing is being challenged by direct marketing channels that provide home shopping through catalogs, television, and even the Internet.

F. New store formats and advances in information technology are making the retail environment highly dynamic and competitive.

G. The key to success in retailing is to have a strong customer focus and a retail strategy that provides the appropriate level of service, product quality, and innovativeness that consumers desire.

H. Retailers are also finding global opportunities.

II. Major types of retail stores

A. One way to classify retailers is by ownership.

    1. An **independent store** is a single retail outlet owned by an individual, partnership, or corporation.

    2. A **chain store** is a retail outlet that is part of a multiple-outlet organization, often owned by a corporation. A company can own multiple chains, which is referred to as **portfolio retailing.**

3. **A franchise store** is owned by a franchisee who has contracted with the parent company (franchiser) to market specific products under conditions specified by the franchiser.

B. A second way to classify retailers is by breadth of products offered, such as general merchandise retailers and specialty retailers.

1. **General merchandise retailers** offer a variety of product lines, stocked in considerable depth.

   a. **Department stores** are large retail organizations employing at least twenty-five people and characterized by wide product mixes.

      (1) Department stores are distinctively service-oriented.

      (2) They obtain a large proportion of their sales from apparel, accessories, and cosmetics.

      (3) They have encountered problems in recent years, such as high overhead and expenses, which they have responded to by bankruptcy, streamlining, major remodeling, expansion, and/or new locations.

   b. **Discount stores** are self-service, general merchandise outlets regularly offering brand-name and private brand products at low prices.

      (1) They accept lower margins in exchange for higher sales volume

      (2) They carry a wide, carefully selected assortment of products, including appliances, housewares, clothes, and toys.

   c. **Supermarkets** are large, self-service stores that carry a complete line of food products as well as some nonfood products.

      (1) Consumers make more than three-quarters of all grocery purchases in supermarkets.

    (2)   To remain competitive, supermarkets are cutting (or sometimes expanding) services, emphasizing low prices, and using sales promotion.

    (3)   They are also implementing technological changes such as electronic scanners to increase efficiency and competitiveness.

d.   **Superstores** are giant retail outlets that carry all food and nonfood products found in supermarkets as well as other routinely purchased consumer products.

    (1)   They may offer services such as laundry, automotive repair, check cashing, bill paying, and snack bars.

    (2)   They combine features of both discount stores and supermarkets.

    (3)   Consumers are attracted to superstores by lower prices and the convenience of one-stop shopping.

    (4)   Other food retailers are adding merchandise or supersize outlets to compete with the superstores.

e.   **Hypermarkets** combine supermarket and discount store shopping in one location.

f.   **Warehouse clubs** are large-scale, members-only selling operations combining cash-and-carry wholesaling and discount retailing.

    (1)   They offer a broad range of merchandise with shallow product lines and high sales volume.

    (2)   To keep prices down, they provide very few services.

g.   Warehouse and catalog showrooms

    (1)   **Warehouse showrooms** are retail facilities characterized by large, low-cost buildings; warehouse materials handling technology; vertical merchandise display; large, on-premises inventory; and minimum services.

(2)   **Catalog showrooms** are a form of warehouse showroom where consumers shop from catalogs and where products are stored out of buyers' reach.

2.   Specialty retailers carry a narrow product mix with deep product lines; they do not sell specialty items unless they complement the overall product mix.

a.   **Traditional specialty retailers** are limited-line stores that carry a narrow mix with deep product lines.

(1)   Single-line stores carry unusual depth in one main product category.

(2)   Specialty retailers usually sell shopping goods such as jewelry, clothes, sporting goods, or computers.

(3)   Most are independently owned, although chain specialty stores are increasing in number.

(4)   Specialty retailers attempt to provide a unique store image and to attract specific market segments; they succeed by knowing their customers and providing what they want.

b.   **Off-price retailers** buy manufacturers' seconds, overruns, returns, and off-season production runs at below-wholesale prices for resale to consumers at deep discounts.

(1)   They offer limited lines of national brand and designer merchandise, usually clothing, shoes, or housewares.

(2)   They charge 20 to 50 percent less than department stores for comparable merchandise, but offer few customer services.

c.   **Category killers** are very large specialty stores that concentrate on a single product line and compete on the basis of low prices and enormous product availability.

III.   Nonstore retailing

Nonstore retailing is the selling of goods and services outside the confines of a retail facility. This form of retailing accounts for an increasing percentage of retail sales.

A. **Direct selling** is the marketing of product to ultimate consumers through face-to-face sales presentations at home or in the workplace.

    1. Benefits of direct selling

        a. Customers get personal attention.

        b. Products are presented at convenient times and locations for customers.

    2. Limitations of direct selling

        a. Direct selling is the most expensive form of retailing.

        b. Some customers believe that practices of direct sellers are unscrupulous and fraudulent.

        c. Some communities strictly control or prohibit direct selling.

B. **Direct marketing** is the use of the telephone and nonpersonal media to communicate product and organizational information to customers who can then purchase products by mail, E-mail, or telephone.

    1. **Catalog marketing** occurs when an organization provides a catalog from which customers make selections and place orders.

    2. **Direct-response marketing** occurs when a retailer advertises a product and makes it available through mail or telephone orders.

    3. **Telemarketing** is the performance of marketing-related activities by telephone.

    4. **Television home shopping** presents products to television viewers who can purchase products through toll-free numbers by using credit cards.

5.   **Online retailing** makes products available through computer connections.

C.   **Automatic vending** is the use of machines to dispense products selected by customers when money is inserted.

1.   It is one of the most impersonal forms of retailing.

2.   Machines provide continuous, efficient utility but require frequent servicing and repair.

IV.   Franchising

Franchising is an arrangement whereby a supplier (franchiser) grants a dealer (franchisee) the right to sell products in exchange for some type of consideration, such as a percentage of sales. Franchising is rapidly increasing.

A.   Major types of retail franchises

1.   A producer may franchise stores to sell a certain brand-name item (e.g., automobiles).

2.   A producer may license distributors to sell a given product to retailers (e.g., soft drinks).

3.   A franchiser may simply provide a carefully developed and controlled marketing strategy (e.g., fast-food restaurant).

B.   Advantages and disadvantages of franchising

1.   Franchising enables a franchisee to start a business with limited capital and to make use of the business experience of others.

2.   Franchised outlets are generally more successful than independent outlets.

3.   However, the franchiser can dictate many aspects of the business, and the franchisee must pay to use the franchiser's name, products, and assistance.

V.   Strategic issues in retailing

Consumer purchases are often the result of social influences and psychological factors. A retailer's objective must be to make products available, create a stimulating shopping environment, and develop marketing strategies that will increase store patronage.

A.   Location

1.   Location is the least flexible and one of the most important issues because it dictates the limited geographic trading area from which a store draws its customers.

2.   Ease of movement to and from the site is important.

3.   Important characteristics of a site include types of surrounding stores, size and shape of building, and terms of rent, lease, or ownership.

4.   Retailers can choose from among several types of locations.

   a.   Free-standing structures

   (1)   Allow retailers to position themselves physically away from or close to their competitors

   (2)   Are used frequently by automobile dealers and fast-food restaurants

   b.   Traditional business districts consist of structures usually attached to one another and located in a central part of a town or city. Although some of these districts are old and decaying, a number of communities are preserving and revitalizing them.

   c.   **Neighborhood shopping centers** usually consist of several small convenience and specialty stores.

   (1)   They serve customers who live less than a ten-minute drive away (2- to 3-mile radius).

(2)   They usually hold product mixes to essential products with limited lines.

d.   **Community shopping centers** include one or two department stores and some specialty and convenience stores.

(1)   They serve a larger geographic area and draw customers who want specialty products not found in neighborhood shopping centers.

(2)   They include a wide range of product mixes and deep product lines.

e.   **Regional shopping centers** usually have the largest department stores, widest product mixes, and deepest product lines of all centers.

(1)   They have 150,000 or more consumers in their target markets, including consumers traveling from extended distances to find products and prices not available in their hometown.

(2)   Shopping center tenants are more likely to be national chains.

f.   Nontraditional shopping centers

(1)   Factory outlet malls feature discount and factory outlet stores owned by manufacturers of major brand-name products. They attract customers by offering lower prices for quality products.

(2)   Miniwarehouse malls sell space to retailers, wholesalers, or light manufacturers, which then operate retail facilities out of warehouse bays.

(3)   A third type is emerging, one that does not include a traditional anchor department store.

(4)   Some shopping center developers are combining off-price stores with category killers in "power center" formats.

B.   Retail positioning

1. **Retail positioning** involves identifying an unserved or underserved market niche, or segment, and serving the segment through a strategy that distinguishes the retailer from others in the minds of persons in that segment.

2. Retailers position themselves in several ways.

    a. As sellers of high-quality, premium-priced products

    b. As marketers of reasonable-quality products at everyday low prices

C. Store image

1. A store image is a functional and psychological picture in the consumer's mind that is acceptable to the store's target market.

2. **Atmospherics,** the physical elements in a store's design that appeal to consumers' emotions and encourage consumers to buy, helps to create an image and position a retailer.

    a. Exterior elements include the appearance of the storefront, display windows, and store entrances, and degree of traffic congestion.

    b. Interior elements include aesthetic considerations, such as lighting, wall and floor coverings, and store fixtures, and sensory elements, such as color and sound.

    c. Retailers must determine the atmosphere the target market wants and adjust atmospheric variables accordingly.

3. Store image also depends heavily on the store's reputation for integrity, service, location, product assortment, pricing, promotional activities, and community development.

4. Other influencing factors are target market characteristics such as social class, lifestyle, income, and purchase behavior.

D. Scrambled merchandising

1. **Scrambled merchandising** involves adding unrelated products lines to an existing mix.

2. Retailers that adopt this strategy hope to convert stores into one-stop shopping centers, generate customer traffic, realize higher profit margins, and/or increase impulse purchases.

3. Scrambled merchandising can reduce merchants' own expertise in buying, selling, and servicing because merchants must deal with diverse marketing channels.

4. It can blur a store's image in consumers' minds.

5. It intensifies competition among traditionally distinct types of stores.

E. The wheel of retailing

1. This hypothesis attempts to account for the evolution and development of new types of retail stores.

2. The **wheel of retailing** hypothesis holds that new businesses enter the market with low prices, margins, and status and become more elaborate and expensive as they attempt to broaden their customer bases. Finally, they emerge at the high end of the scale, competing with newer discount retailers following the same process.

3. The wheel of retailing, along with other changes in the marketing environment and buying behavior itself, requires that retailers adjust in order to survive and compete.

CLASS EXERCISES, DEBATE ISSUE, AND CHAPTER QUIZ

On the following pages, you will find two class exercises, a debate issue, and a chapter quiz. These are formatted in large-size type so that you can use them as class handouts or for making transparencies. Below are the authors' comments on the class exercises, the debate topic, and the answers to the chapter quiz.

Class Exercise 1: The objective of this class exercise is to help students understand strategic issues in retailing by developing an original retail store concept.

Question 1. Students will typically develop specialty store ideas, since they recognize the difficulty of going head to head with larger chain stores. You may also want your students to think in terms of atypical approaches like vending ("Venda-Bait" sells buckets of fishing bait for $1.50 in the Ozarks; videocassette vending machines in large metro areas) or scrambled merchandising (7-Eleven stores with a Hardee's restaurant or Kmart stores with a Little Caesar's restaurant inside; McDonald's located in nontraditional outlets like campuses or zoos).

Question 2. As students respond to this question, press them to define each location in terms of types of stores and market reached. Offering local examples of each may also help students better understand the concepts. A common oversight by students is a decision to locate in a regional shopping center without considering the likely high lease costs. You might also want to talk about why local stores are vacant; most towns have a retail location that changes owners about once a year. Possible reasons could be poor parking and difficult entry, deteriorating or limited facilities, image of surrounding stores, and the like.

Question 3. Although it is difficult for students to think of an entire product assortment, they should go beyond naming only one type of product to be sold. You can carry this discussion further by asking about retail positioning, atmospherics, and store image.

Class Exercise 2: The goal of this exercise is to help students understand the importance of having store names that help customers easily identify the type of store. Some of these are effective, others are not. Answers:

1. The Shape of Things — **hairstyling salon**
2. The Chicken Oil Company — **restaurant**
3. Wings 'n' Things — **restaurant**
4. The Paper Bear — **gift/novelty item shop**
5. Prioriteas — **upscale foods/beverages**
6. Specially For You — **florist/gift shop**
7. The Waist Basket — **fitness center**
8. Bless Your Heart — **health food restaurant**
9. Clean And Lean — **laundromat/fitness center**
10. Bombay Bicycle Club — **restaurant**
11. The Lollipop — **children's clothing store**
12. Feather Your Nest — **linens store**
13. Rolling Thunder — **skating rink**
14. Creations — **silk-screened T-shirts**
15. Me Too Wee Two — **adult women and children's clothing**

Debate Issue: Is franchising the best way to own a business?

Chapter Quiz: Answers to multiple-choice questions are

1. d		3. c	
2. d		4. c	

CLASS EXERCISE 1

ASSUME THAT YOU HAVE BEEN GIVEN AMPLE FUNDS TO INVEST IN A NEW RETAIL VENTURE. BE AS CREATIVE AS POSSIBLE.

1. Determine the type of retail store you want to open. Be specific about the characteristics of the store type. Include product assortment, target market(s), service level, and price level.

2. Where will you locate?
   a. Be sure to consider
      - Ease of movement in, around, and out of the location
      - Size and shape of the building
      - Likely terms of rent or lease
      - Surrounding stores
   b. Would you want to locate in a free-standing store or in a
      - Traditional business district
      - Neighborhood shopping center
      - Community shopping center
      - Regional shopping center
      - Nontraditional shopping center

3. Describe your product assortment in terms of depth, width, and quality.
   a. Which products will be the most important to consumers?
   b. Will consumers want other complementary products when they shop?

CLASS EXERCISE 2

FOLLOWING IS A LIST OF RETAIL BUSINESSES. WHAT TYPES OF PRODUCTS ARE SOLD BY EACH ONE?

1. The Shape of Things
2. The Chicken Oil Company
3. Wings 'n Things
4. The Paper Bear
5. Prioriteas
6. Specially For You
7. The Waist Basket
8. Bless Your Heart
9. Clean And Lean
10. Bombay Bicycle Club
11. The Lollipop
12. Feather Your Nest
13. Rolling Thunder
14. Creations
15. Me Too Wee Too

DEBATE ISSUE

IS FRANCHISING THE BEST WAY TO OWN A BUSINESS?

YES

- Franchisees can start a business with limited capital

- Franchisees can take advantage of the business experience of others

- A franchisee usually receives operations and management training

- Franchised names are usually widely recognized

- Franchised outlets are generally more successful than independently owned businesses

NO

- Franchising does not give entrepreneurs the independence they desire—they are still working for someone else

- In some cases, franchisees are not allowed to make crucial decisions

- The more successful the franchisee, the greater the royalties and fees paid to the franchiser

- Franchisees are never justly compensated for their hard work and success

CHAPTER QUIZ

1. A narrow product mix with a deep product line would most likely be carried by
    a. mass merchandisers.
    b. supermarkets.
    c. discount stores.
    d. specialty retailers.
    e. warehouse showrooms.

2. Kevin Willis is talking with Pete Anderson about purchasing a Wendy's franchise. Pete tells Kevin that one of the major advantages of franchising for him to consider is the
    a. higher start-up costs.
    b. greater freedom it provides.
    c. individuality it offers.
    d. higher success rate for franchises.
    e. gross margin it provides.

3. The wheel of retailing is a hypothesis that holds that new types of retailers often enter the market as
    a. low-status, high-margin, high-priced operators.
    b. low-status, low-margin, high-priced operators.
    c. low-status, low-margin, low-priced operators.
    d. high-status, low-margin, low-priced operators.
    e. high-status, low-margin, high-priced operators.

4. A direct-response retailer would probably select television home shopping over online retailing to sell a new kitchen device because of
    a. lower costs of selling.
    b. easier financial transactions.
    c. superior ability to demonstrate the product.
    d. superior ability to offer the product at a lower price.
    e. decreased cycle time.

ANSWERS TO DISCUSSION AND REVIEW QUESTIONS

1. What is the value added to the product by retailers? What value is added by retailers for producers and ultimate consumers?

   Retailers add value to products in several ways. Image enhances the value of the product. Through its location, a retailer facilitates comparison shopping. A product's value is increased when the retailer offers services such as delivery, credit, and repair. Retail sales personnel can also demonstrate how products help solve customers' problems. Retailers link producers and ultimate consumers by providing the environment in which exchanges with ultimate consumers take place. Producers have a place to sell their products. Ultimate consumers benefit from the resulting availability of a broad array of products.

2. Differentiate between the two general categories of retail stores based on breadth of product offering.

   The two categories of retailing stores based on breadth of product offering are general merchandise retailers and specialty retailers. General merchandise retailers offer a broad variety of product lines. In contrast, specialty retailers emphasize narrow product lines.

3. What are the major differences between discount stores and department stores?

   Discount stores are self-service, general merchandise outlets that regularly offer brand-name merchandise at low prices. Department stores are large retail organizations characterized by wide product mixes. These two types of retail outlets differ in several respects. First, discount stores are mass merchandisers; that is, they generally offer fewer customer services than department stores and emphasize low prices, high turnover, and large sales volume. Rather than having structured departments, the discount store uses a central check-out procedure. These stores are often in less convenient locations than department stores.

   Department stores are distinctly service-oriented, offering services such as credit, delivery, personal assistance, returns, and a pleasant atmosphere. They are structured by departments, and different atmospheres can be created in each department. They are located more conveniently than discount stores, usually in a major shopping area.

4. How does a superstore differ from a supermarket?

   Supermarkets are large, self-service stores that carry a complete line of food products plus some nonfood products. Superstores are giant retail outlets that combine features of supermarkets and discount houses. They carry all food and nonfood products usually found in supermarkets as well as most consumer products purchased on a routine basis, such as housewares, appliances, and clothing. Superstores also offer services ranging from snack bars and check cashing to dry cleaning and automotive repair.

5. How can department stores continue to compete effectively against discount stores, superstores, and warehouse clubs?

   Because department stores traditionally offer a variety of services, and because their operating expenses are higher than those of most other retailers, department stores have lost customers to discount stores, superstores, and warehouse clubs. To compete directly with these lower-priced retailers, many department stores are expanding their budget-priced lines. To maintain convenience for their customers, many department stores have opened stores in suburban shopping centers and malls. In addition, their service orientation may help them compete against lower-priced retailers that provide little if any customer service.

6. In what ways are traditional specialty stores and off-price retailers similar? How do they differ?

Traditional specialty retailers and off-price retailers are similar in that both are specialty retailers. They often carry similar lines of merchandise and generally offer narrower product mixes than department stores and mass merchandisers.

Traditional specialty retailers and off-price retailers differ in several respects. Traditional specialty retailers offer more depth in their product lines than off-price retailers because the latter often buy "leftover" merchandise from manufacturers. Traditional specialty retailers offer more services than off-price retailers and usually have an exclusive store image. In addition, off-price stores charge 20 to 50 percent less than traditional retailers for comparable merchandise.

7. Describe the three major types of nonstore retailing. List some products you have purchased through nonstore retailing in the last six months. Why did you choose this method for making your purchases instead of going to a retail outlet?

The three major types of nonstore retailing are direct selling, direct marketing, and automatic vending. Direct selling is the marketing of products to ultimate consumers through face-to-face sales presentations at home or in the workplace. Direct marketing is the use of nonpersonal media (telephone, mail, E-mail) to communicate product and organizational information to customers. Automatic vending is the use of machines to dispense products.

The last parts of this question will elicit individual responses. Students will probably state convenience and availability as their reasons for choosing nonstore retailing.

8. Why is door-to-door selling a form of retailing? Some consumers feel that direct response orders skip the retailer. Is this true?

Door-to-door selling is a form of retailing because it involves an exchange with ultimate consumers. Direct response orders do not bypass the retailer. A mail-order house makes final exchanges with ultimate consumers and thus can be considered a retailer.

9. Evaluate the following statement: Telemarketing, television home shopping, and online retailing will eventually eliminate the need for traditional forms of retailing.

Student opinions will vary considerably on this question, but there are some issues that ought to surface in their answers. There is little question that telemarketing, television home shopping, and online retailing will change the way consumers acquire products by providing more alternatives. However, these alternatives will probably not altogether replace retail stores and other forms of nonstore shopping. Catalog shopping, for example, has been around for over 100 years, and retail stores have not disappeared. In addition, many consumers want personal service, especially when purchasing products with complex or new technology, or very expensive products. Traditional forms of retailing can provide these services, whereas telemarketing, television home shopping, and online retailing cannot.

10. If you were to open a retail business, would you prefer to open an independent store or to own a store under a franchise arrangement? Explain your preference.

There are advantages to both owning an independent store and owning a store under a franchise arrangement. Under a franchise arrangement, a supplier grants a dealer the right to sell products in exchange for some type of consideration. For example, the franchiser can offer equipment, buildings, management know-how, marketing assistance, and an established reputation in exchange for a percentage of sales. With an independent business, however, the owner has complete control over the elements of the retailing mix and is not bound by the franchiser's rules.

11. What major issues should be considered when determining a retail site location?

Because of its inflexible nature, the location of a retail outlet is one of the most important strategic issues a retailer must address. Location dictates the limited geographic trading area from which a store can draw its customers. Retailers must evaluate potential locations on the basis of several factors:

a. Ease of movement, including factors such as pedestrian and vehicular traffic, parking, and transportation

b. Site characteristics, such as the types of stores in the area, the lease terms, and the size, shape, and visibility of the lot or building

c. Compatibility with nearby retailers—that is, the degree to which stores complement one another, thereby generating traffic

12. Describe the three major types of shopping centers. Give examples of each type in your area.

a. Neighborhood shopping centers consist of small grocery stores, gas stations, and fast-food restaurants. They serve consumers who live less than a ten-minute drive from the center. A typical neighborhood shopping center might have a Safeway supermarket, an Eckerd drugstore, and a McDonald's fast-food restaurant.

b. Community shopping centers include one or two department stores and some specialty stores as well as convenience stores. They serve a larger geographic area than neighborhood centers. A community shopping center might be a small mall with a locally owned department store, a Baker's shoe store, a Hallmark card store, and a small drugstore that sells convenience goods.

c. Regional shopping centers usually have the largest department stores with the widest product mixes and deepest product lines. They target more than 150,000 people and often host special events. The Galleria in Dallas is an example of a regional shopping center, containing several national department stores and several hundred specialty stores and restaurants.

13. Discuss the major factors that help determine a retail store's image.

A retail store's image is a functional and psychological picture in the consumer's mind. A store must project an image that is acceptable to its target market. Seven factors contribute to a retail store's image:

a. Atmospherics, or physical elements in a store's design that appeal to consumers' emotions and encourage them to buy

b. Reputation for integrity

c. Location, including accessibility and surrounding retailers

d. Merchandise assortment offered

e. Pricing

f. Promotional activities

g. Involvement in community activities

14. How does atmosphere add value to products sold in a store? How important is atmospherics for convenience stores?

The term *atmospherics* describes the physical elements in a store's design that appeal to consumers' emotions and encourage consumers to buy. Atmospherics add value to products sold in a store in that enhances the products or the products' benefits by offering the psychological rewards of shopping in pleasant surroundings.

Although atmospherics is less important in convenience stores than in shopping and specialty stores, convenience retailers should still consider them. For example, a 7-Eleven would want its atmospherics to convey the image of quick and easy service.

15. Is it possible for a single retail store to have an overall image that appeals to sophisticated shopper, extravagant ones, and bargain hunters? Why or why not?

A retail store may have great difficulty presenting an overall image that appeals to sophisticated and extravagant shoppers and bargain hunters because these shoppers have different motives. However, a department store may successfully do so because it can tailor atmospherics, pricing, and other store image factors to specific departments, some targeted to extravagant shoppers and others aimed at bargain hunters.

16. In what ways does the use of scrambled merchandising affect a store's image?

Scrambled merchandising is the addition of unrelated products and product lines to an existing product mix. Scrambled merchandise can adversely affect a store's image unless it is done carefully. If stores add unrelated products to their product mixes, their established images can become blurred in consumers' minds. On the other hand, a store's objective may include becoming a one-stop shopping outlet, which scrambled merchandising can help accomplish.

COMMENTS ON THE CASES

Case 15.1   The Container Store: The Definitive Place to Get Organized

The objective of this case is to analyze a retail organization that has become highly successful. The founders took an innovative idea and through effective management and slow deliberate expansion have built a very solid and highly effective retail company.

The first question asks what type of retail store The Container Store is. The Container Store is a traditional specialty retailer.

Question 2 asks students to describe The Container Store's strategy, using each retailing strategic issue discussed in the chapter. Students should be encouraged to look specifically at the section titled "Strategic Issues in Retailing." Then, after their review, they should take each component of this section and discuss it relative to The Container Store.

The third question asks whether or not The Container Store founders should use franchising for developing new stores rather than relying strictly on expansion through company stores. One of The Container Store's strengths has been slow, deliberate, controlled expansion with the focus on getting the right locations. While franchising would speed the expansion process, management would be forced to give up some control. Losing this control might threaten one of The Container Store's major strengths—to provide customer satisfaction. One can argue, however, that a number of retail organizations have used franchising arrangements to expand quickly and have established management systems to control the quality of both products and customer service.

Video Information

Video Title: The Container Store—Wrap It Up
Location: Tape 2, Segment 15
Length: 13:00
Video Overview: The Container Store is a retail chain selling reasonably priced storage and organization merchandise such as desktop and closet organizers, boxes and wrapping paper, shoe racks and coat hangers, jars and bottles, and pantry organizers. The company's philosophy is that the key to success is to provide quality customer service. Employees at all levels are knowledgeable about products and are able as well as authorized to help customers. Store layouts are planned for shopping pleasure and customer convenience. Ceilings are tall, natural lighting is abundant, and big bold signs make specific types of products easy to locate. Computerized inventory control and timely delivery from the warehouse allow outlets to replenish shelves every two days, minimizing the likelihood that customers will not be able to find what they are looking for.

Multiple-Choice Questions About the Video

c   1. According to the video, The Container Store's primary marketing goal is to
         a. increase its share of the storage and organization merchandise market.
         b. attract customers with frequent additions to its product lines.
         c. offer products that can't be found anywhere else.
         d. increase sales volume.
         e. exceed customer expectations.

b 2. The Container Store operates with the philosophy that
   a. success comes from selling ideas, not products.
   b. providing quality customer service leads to success.
   c. offering the lowest prices leads to success.
   d. avoiding diversification is the key to success.
   e. all employees work in the customer service department.

d 3. According to The Container Store executives, the most important aspect of a decision to expand is
   a. pinpointing the new store's opening date.
   b. preparing the inventory.
   c. developing the distribution plan.
   d. finding the best location for a new store.
   e. hiring and training new personnel.

a 4. At The Container Store, customer orientation and _____ are essential in providing superior customer service.
   a. product knowledge
   b. knowledge of selling techniques
   c. merchandising skills
   d. extensive training
   e. a friendly atmosphere

b 5. At The Container Store distribution center, employees working in the pricing line put bar codes on products, monitor product quality, and
   a. oversee automated data entry.
   b. help manage inventory control.
   c. package products for shipment to retail outlets.
   d. sort products according to function.
   e. adjust distribution methodology.

Case 15.2   Walt Disney Co.

This case profiles various aspects of the Walt Disney Co., particularly with regard to retail strategy (location, image, retail positioning). Class discussion may be initiated by asking how many students have been to Disney World, Disneyland, or other Disney-owned parks or resorts. Students who have patronized Disney establishments may have additional comments about how Disney positions itself and creates a specific retail image.

Question 1 asks how Disney is positioning itself. Through hard work, careful attention to detail, and exceeding customer expectations, Disney is positioning its theme parks and resorts as places where people can have fun, relax, and leave their cares behind. At Vero Beach, for example, the resort is patterned after the glamorous elegance of an old Florida Inn, and guests' stays are carefully crafted to entertain families with activities for both parents and children.

The second question asks students to describe how Disney is using atmospherics to create a positive entertainment experience for its guests. (This has been partially answered with the first question, which should help students see that atmospherics and retail positioning clearly relate.) At the Disney theme parks, Disney strives for cleanliness, quality, and friendliness to ensure that guests have a good time while participating in the many activities offered. Color, lighting, music, and other physical elements are also used to entertain guests and make them feel good.

The final question asks how Disney's culture contributes to its success. Knowing that happy employees enjoy providing quality service, Disney empowers its employees and tries to provide a positive work environment to keep them happy. To ensure that employees provide guests with a satisfying experience, Disney has tried to create a positive culture that emphasizes cleanliness, quality, and friendliness. Employees are socialized into this culture through a three-day training program. The company's mission and history, as well as hard work and attention to detail, reinforce this culture and give employees guidance in ambiguous situations.

16 PHYSICAL DISTRIBUTION

TEACHING RESOURCES QUICK REFERENCE GUIDE

Resource	Location
Purpose and Perspective	IRM, p. 340
Guide for Using Color Transparencies	IRM, p. 340
Lecture Outline	IRM, p. 340
Class Exercises, Debate Issue, and Chapter Quiz	IRM, p. 351
Class Exercise 1	IRM, p. 353
Class Exercise 2	IRM, p. 354
Debate Issue: Should robots replace people in a physical distribution system?	IRM, p. 355
Chapter Quiz	IRM, p. 356
Answers to Discussion and Review Questions	IRM, p. 357
Comments on the Cases	IRM, p. 361
Case 16.1	IRM, p. 361
Video	Tape 2, Segment 16
Video Information	IRM, p. 361
Multiple-Choice Questions About the Video	IRM, p. 361
Case 16.2	IRM, p. 362
Transparency Acetates	Transparency package
Examination Questions: Essay	TB, p. 289
Examination Questions: Multiple-Choice	TB, p. 290
Examination Questions: True-False	TB, p. 303
Author-Selected Multiple-Choice Test Items	TB, p. 447

PURPOSE AND PERSPECTIVE

The primary objective of this chapter is to provide an understanding of how physical distribution activities are integrated into marketing channels and contribute to overall marketing strategies. First, we examine basic concepts of physical distribution and their importance. Next, we discuss physical distribution activities in detail, beginning with the three aspects of order processing: order entry, order handling, and order delivery. We note the importance of efficient materials handling, or the physical handling of products. In the next section, we consider the essential processing functions a warehouse performs and differentiate among private warehouse facilities, public facilities, and distribution centers. We describe the concepts of economic order quantity (EOQ) and just-in-time (JIT). Then we discuss the five major modes of transportation, analyze transportation selection criteria, and explain how two or more modes of transportation may be combined for greater efficiency. Finally, we examine the strategic relationship of physical distribution to other elements in the marketing mix: product design and packaging, pricing, and promotion.

GUIDE FOR USING COLOR TRANSPARENCIES

There are two groups of color transparencies. The transparencies identified by a double number are the same as the figures and tables in the text. The transparencies labeled with a number and a letter are illustrations that do not appear in the text, but they can be used as additional examples of concepts discussed.

Figure 16.5   Economic order quantity (EOQ) model
Figure 16.8   Proportion of intercity freight carried by various transportation modes, 1970 and 1992
Table 16.1   Typical transportation modes for various products
Table 16.2   Relative ratings of transportation modes by selection criteria
Figure 16A   Chapter 16 outline
Figure 16B   What does physical distribution cost the average company?
Figure 16C   Trends in warehousing

LECTURE OUTLINE

I.   The importance of physical distribution

     A.   **Physical distribution** refers to the activities—order processing, inventory management, materials handling, warehousing, and transportation—used to move products from producers to consumers and other end users.

         1.   Planning an efficient physical distribution system is crucial to developing an effective marketing strategy because it can decrease costs and increase customer satisfaction.

2. Physical distribution deals with physical movement and inventory holdings both within and among marketing channel members.

3. Physical distribution systems must meet the needs of the supply chain as well as customers.

4. Physical distribution managers strive for a reasonable balance among service, costs, and resources. They determine what level of customer service is acceptable and realistic, then develop a "system" outlook to minimize total distribution costs and cycle time.

B. Meeting customer service standards

1. Customer service standards are the level and quality of service that a firm's management aims to provide for its customers.

2. Customers require a variety of services.

   a. At the most basic level, they need fair prices, acceptable product quality, and dependable deliveries.

   b. At a higher level, they may also want sizable inventories, efficient order processing, availability of emergency shipments, progress reports, post-sale services, prompt replacement of defective items, and warranties.

3. Customers' inventory requirements influence the expected level of physical distribution service.

4. Because customers' needs vary, companies must analyze and adapt to customer preferences.

5. Companies must also examine the service levels competitors offer and match or exceed those standards when the costs of providing the services can be justified by the sales generated.

6. Services are provided most effectively when service standards are developed and stated in measurable terms.

C. Reducing total distribution costs

1.   Although physical distribution managers try to minimize the costs associated with physical distribution activities, decreasing costs in one area often raises them in another.

2.   Using a total cost approach to physical distribution, in which managers view physical distribution as a system rather than a collection of unrelated activities, shifts the emphasis from lowering separate costs of individual activities to minimizing overall distribution costs.

3.   A distribution system's lowest total cost is never the result of using a combination of the cheapest functions; instead it is the lowest overall cost compatible with the company's stated service objectives.

D.   Reducing cycle time

1.   Reducing **cycle time,** the time it takes to complete a process, is a major goal of physical distribution because it can reduce costs and/or increase customer service.

2.   Many companies are using cycle-time reduction to gain a competitive advantage.

II.   Order processing

A.   **Order processing** is the receipt and transmission of sales order information.

B.   Efficient order processing facilitates product flow.

C.   There are three main tasks in order processing.

1.   Order entry begins when customers or salespersons place orders by mail, telephone, or computer.

2.   Order handling involves several tasks.

a.   Transmission of orders to the warehouse

b.   Verification of product availability

    c.   Checking of prices, terms, and customers' credit ratings

    d.   Instructions to the warehouse to fill the order

  3. Order delivery

    a.   The warehouse schedules pickup with an appropriate carrier.

    b.   Premium transportation is used if the customer is willing to pay for rush service.

    c.   The customer is billed; inventory records are adjusted; and the order is delivered.

  E. Methods of order processing

    1. Manual order processing suffices for a small volume of orders and is more flexible in special situations.

    2. **Electronic data interchange (EDI)** integrates order processing with production, inventory, accounting, and transportation.

      a.   EDI is an information system for the supply chain.

      b.   Many companies are pushing their suppliers toward EDI to reduce distribution costs and cycle times.

      c.   The Internet is another opportunity for EDI systems.

III. Inventory management

  A. Inventory management involves developing and maintaining adequate assortments of products to meet customer needs.

  B. Because a firm's investment in inventory represents a significant portion of its total assets, inventory decisions have a major impact on physical distribution costs and level of customer service potential.

1. Carrying too few products results in **stockouts,** which lead to a loss of customers.

2. Carrying too many products increases carrying costs and the risks of product obsolescence, pilferage, and damage.

3. The objective is to minimize inventory costs while maintaining an adequate supply of goods.

C. Determining when to order

1. The **reorder point** is an inventory level that signals the need to place a new order.

2. Knowledge of order lead time, usage rate, and safety stock are required for determining the reorder point.

    a. **Order lead time** is the average time lapsed between placing the order and receiving it.

    b. **Usage rate** is the rate per time period that a product's inventory is used or sold.

    c. **Safety stock** is the amount of extra inventory that a firm keeps to guard against stockouts.

3. Reorder point = (order lead time × usage rate) + safety stock

4. The **fixed order-interval system** is an approach in which products are ordered at predetermined intervals.

D. Deciding how much to order

1. To decide how much to order, two sets of costs must be analyzed.

    a. Inventory-carrying costs include warehousing and interest costs, insurance expenses, and cost of obsolescence, product deterioration, and pilferage.

      b.   Order-processing costs include counting inventory, filling out purchase orders, and computer and communication expenses.

   2.   **Economic order quantity (EOQ)** is the order size that has the lowest total of both order-processing costs and inventory-carrying costs.

   3.   **Just-in-time (JIT)** inventory approach means that products arrive just as they are needed for use in production or for resale.

IV.   Materials handling

   A.   **Materials handling** is the physical handling of products, and it is important in both efficient warehouse operations and transportation.

   B.   It is often determined by characteristics of the product itself and product packaging.

   C.   It should increase a warehouse's usable capacity, reduce the number of times a product is handled, and improve customer service and satisfaction.

   D.   Handling systems

      1.   **Unit loading,** grouping one or more boxes on a skid or pallet, permits efficient movement of loads by forklifts, trucks, or conveyor systems.

      2.   **Containerization,** the consolidation of many items into a single container, increases efficiency and security in shipping.

V.   Warehousing

   A.   **Warehousing** is the design and operation of facilities for storing and moving goods.

      1.   It provides time utility by compensating for dissimilar rates of production and consumption.

      2.   It helps stabilize prices and availability of seasonal items.

B.   Warehousing functions

1.   Receiving goods

2.   Identifying goods

3.   Sorting goods

4.   Dispatching goods to storage

5.   Holding goods

6.   Recalling and picking goods

7.   Collecting the shipment

8.   Dispatching the shipment

C.   Types of warehouses

1.   **Private warehouses** are operated by companies for distributing their own products.

   a.   They are most feasible when a firm's warehouse needs in a given geographic market are stable and substantial enough to make long-term commitments to fixed facilities.

   b.   They are appropriate for firms requiring special handling and storage features.

   e.   Disadvantages include high fixed costs and little flexibility in moving inventory to more strategic locations.

2.   **Public warehouses** rent storage space and distribution facilities (and sometimes provide distribution services) to other firms.

a.   They are useful to firms with seasonal production or low-volume storage needs.

b.   They offer variable costs, which are usually lower than those at private warehouses.

c.   A **field public warehouse** is established at the site of the owner's inventory.

d.   Public warehouses often provide **bonded storage** for imported or taxable products.

3.   **Distribution centers** are large, centralized warehouses that receive goods from factories and suppliers, regroup the goods into orders, and ship the orders to customers quickly.

a.   Their focus is on active movement of goods rather than passive storage.

b.   They are designed and located for rapid flow of products.

d.   Benefits include improved customer service and product availability, minimized delivery time, lower transportation costs, and lower inventory costs.

VI.   Transportation

Transportation adds time and place utility to a product by moving it from where it is made to where it is purchased and used.

A.   **Transportation modes** are the means of moving goods: railroads, trucks, waterways, airways, and pipelines.

1.   Railroads

a.   Carry bulky freight overland for long distances

b.   Haul more intercity freight than other modes of transportation, but their share of the transportation market has declined

2. Trucks

    a. Provide the most flexible schedules and routes

    b. Are often used in conjunction with other modes of transport

    c. Are classified into common, contract, and private carriers

    d. Travel faster than trains but are more expensive, more vulnerable to bad weather, and often criticized for loss, damage to freight, and delays

3. Waterways

    a. Are the cheapest method of shipping heavy, low-value nonperishables

    b. Offer considerable capacity

    c. May not be able to access many markets without supplementary overland transportation

    d. Are slow and vulnerable to weather but extremely fuel efficient

4. Airways

    a. Are the fastest and most expensive mode

    b. Are most often used for perishable goods, high-value, low-bulk items, and emergency shipments

    c. Account for just 2 percent of total ton-miles carried, but their importance as a transportation mode is growing

5. Pipelines

    a. Are the most automated of the transportation modes

b.   Usually belong to the shipper and carry the shipper's products

c.   Move products slowly but continuously and at relatively low cost

d.   Are reliable but contents are subject to shrinkage from evaporation

B.   Criteria for selecting transportation modes

1.   Cost

a.   Marketers must determine whether benefits derived are worth the expense.

b.   When speed is less important, marketers prefer lower costs.

c.   Generally, deregulation of transportation has cut expenses and increased efficiency.

2.   Speed

a.   Is measured by the total time a carrier has possession of goods, including pickup and delivery time

b.   Affects a marketer's ability to provide service

c.   Allows shippers to take advantage of transit time to process orders for goods en route

3.   Dependability

a.   Is determined by consistency of service provided

b.   Affects inventory levels and costs

c.   Also refers to security problems, which vary considerably among transportation modes and geographic regions

4. Load flexibility

    a. Is the degree to which a transportation mode can provide appropriate equipment and conditions for moving specific kinds of goods

    b. Is important when shipments require special facilities, such as refrigerated boxcars

5. Accessibility

    a. Is a carrier's ability to move goods over a specified route or network

    b. Can provide a point of competitive differentiation for carriers that service areas their competitors do not

6. Frequency

    a. Is how often a company can send shipments by a specific transportation mode

    b. Varies considerably among modes: pipelines can be continuous, whereas waterways and railroads offer more limited schedules

C. Coordinating transportation services

1. **Intermodal transportation** is the combination and coordination of two or more transportation modes.

2. Containerization consolidates many items into a single large container sealed at the point of origin and opened at the destination.

    a. Piggyback shipping combines truck trailers and railway flat cars.

    b. Fishyback shipping combines trucks and water carriers.

    c. Birdyback shipping combines trucks and air carriers.

3. **Freight forwarders** combine shipments from several organizations into efficient lot sizes.

4. **Megacarriers** are freight transportation companies that provide several methods of shipment.

VII. Strategic issues in physical distribution

A. Physical distribution functions account for about half of all marketing costs.

B. Product design and packaging must allow for efficient stacking, storage, and transportation.

C. Competitive pricing may depend on the firm's ability to provide reliable delivery or emergency shipments of replacement parts and may encourage large purchases through quantity discounts.

D. Promotion must be coordinated with distribution functions.

E. Order processing must be able to handle additional sales resulting from promotion.

F. Distribution must consider warehousing and transportation costs, which influences organizational policies on stockouts and centralized (or decentralized) inventory.

G. Improving physical distribution starts by closing the gap with customers.

H. No single distribution system is ideal for all situations, and any system must be evaluated continually and adapted as necessary.

CLASS EXERCISES, DEBATE ISSUE, AND CHAPTER QUIZ

On the following pages, you will find two class exercises, a debate issue, and a chapter quiz. These are formatted in large-size type so that you can use them as class handouts or for making transparencies. Below are the authors' comments on the class exercises, the debate topic, and the answers to the chapter quiz.

Class Exercise 1: The objective of this class exercise is to help students understand the role of physical distribution activities in achieving superior customer service.

Question 1. It is important to prioritize customer demands to know which services customers are more willing to pay for. Additionally, tradeoffs must be considered between those things that some customers want, but whose costs might outweigh the benefits. In part (a), the most expensive services are likely to be emergency shipping, maintaining inventories, and after-sale service. However, these costs must be weighed against the consumer goodwill they will provide. In part (b), ask students, "What would happen if Domino's didn't have the 30-minute guarantee?" If no service objectives are set, it affects both employees (who don't try as hard) and customers (who receive inconsistent service). In part (c), press students to determine if their prices take into account the costs of handling particularly small or large orders or emergency orders. Likewise, are the costs of potential lost sales from lower performance levels considered?

Question 2. A related question to ask would be "What types of problems do you have when ordering at a fast-food restaurant?" Students can especially identify with this question. Problems can be overcome by properly handling complaints, offering customers progress reports, checking inventory/credit before completing an order, offering substitutes, and electronic order processing.

Question 3. Stockouts usually mean lost sales. Reorder points and EOQ using a marketing information system can reduce problems, as can heavily stocking items sold most often.

Class Exercise 2: The objective of this exercise is to help students recognize characteristics of different transportation modes. Answers:
1. waterways
2. airways
3. pipelines
4. railroads
5. trucks

Debate Issue: Should robots replace people in a physical distribution system?

Chapter Quiz: Answers to multiple-choice questions are

1.	e	3.	c
2.	b	4.	d

CLASS EXERCISE 1

YOU ARE OPERATING A NEW OFFICE SUPPLY DELIVERY SERVICE IN TOWN AND MUST SET THE PHYSICAL DISTRIBUTION POLICIES FOR THE FIRM. YOUR MAIN OBJECTIVE IS TO DECREASE COSTS WHILE INCREASING SERVICE. YOU MUST DETERMINE WHAT LEVEL OF CUSTOMER SERVICE IS ACCEPTABLE YET REALISTIC. WHILE DOING SO, YOU MUST KEEP IN MIND THE NEEDS OF YOUR PRIMARY TARGET MARKET.

1. In terms of customer service, which of the following are likely to be most important to your target market?

   - Availability
   - Quality
   - Progress reports
   - After-sale service
   - Replacement of defective items
   - Timeliness
   - Sizable inventories
   - Warranties and guarantees
   - Emergency shipments
   - Efficient order processing

   a. Which of these are going to be most costly to provide?
   b. Develop service standards that are specific, measurable, and appropriate for delivery (i.e., How long will delivery take?)
   c. How much will you charge for delivery and other services?

2. In terms of order processing, why do some firms have problems with order entry, order handling, and order delivery? How are you going to prevent and overcome such problems?

3. If your inventory is kept too low, stockouts will occur. What will consumers do when faced with a stockout situation? How might reorder points, EOQ, electronic equipment, and JIT help avoid stockouts?

CLASS EXERCISE 2

IDENTIFY THE TRANSPORTATION MODES WITH THE FOLLOWING CHARACTERISTICS:

Mode	Cost	Speed	Depend-ability	Load Flexibility	Access-ibility	Frequency
1. _____	Very low	Very slow	Average	Very high	Limited	Very low
2. _____	Very high	Very fast	High	Low	Average	Average
3. _____	Low	Slow	High	Very low	Very limited	Very high
4. _____	Moderate	Average	Average	High	High	Low
5. _____	High	Fast	High	Average	Very high	High

DEBATE ISSUE

SHOULD ROBOTS REPLACE PEOPLE IN A PHYSICAL DISTRIBUTION SYSTEM?

YES

- The use of robots in physical distribution can increase speed and efficiency and decrease costs and mistakes

- Since they increase speed and reduce costs, robots allow for greater customer service

- Robots are easier to manage than people because they are programmed to perform certain tasks repetitively

- Robots eliminate the worries of inefficiency and other managerial problems such as labor disputes, wages, and employee sickness

NO

- Although robotics play an important role in a physical distribution system, people are still the essential ingredient to any successful system

- Robots cannot think or make decisions

- Because no system is perfect, people must be available to make decisions when something goes wrong

- Replacing employees with robots means putting people out of work—an action that could cause resentment among the company's customers

CHAPTER QUIZ

1. Order handling involves all of the following activities *except:*
   a. the credit department approves the purchase.
   b. the order is transmitted to the warehouse.
   c. the availability of product is verified.
   d. the warehouse is instructed to fill the order.
   e. the customer places a purchase order.

2. Sara Wells's job is to check the computer-generated invoice against the actual items being shipped to each customer. Her job falls into which one of the following warehouse functions?
   a. Identifying goods
   b. Collecting the shipment
   c. Dispatching the shipment
   d. Recalling goods
   e. Receiving goods

3. Galvonics Aluminum has been selling 1,500 pounds of two-inch aluminum bars every month. While the amount the firm expects to sell will remain the same, it plans to cut the size of the order it places with Alcoa in half. This move will directly increase _____ costs.
   a. resellers'
   b. carrying
   c. order-processing
   d. storage
   e. inventory management

4. The degree to which a transportation mode can provide the appropriate equipment and conditions for moving specific kinds of goods is its
   a. cost.
   b. transit time.
   c. reliability.
   d. load flexibility.
   e. accessibility.

ANSWERS TO DISCUSSION AND REVIEW QUESTIONS

1. Discuss the cost and service tradeoffs in developing a physical distribution system.

    The main objective of physical distribution is to decrease costs while increasing service. Companies often give customer service high priority, and service may be as important in attracting customers as the cost of the company's product. On one hand, the large inventories and rapid transportation essential for high levels of customer service drive up costs. On the other hand, reduced inventories and slower, cheaper methods of transportation result in customer dissatisfaction and lost sales. Therefore, the overall objective of a service policy should be to improve customer service to the point where an increase in sales from the service will just offset any increase in distribution costs associated with the service.

2. What factors must physical distribution managers consider when developing a customer service mix?

    There are several factors a physical distribution manager should consider when developing a customer service mix. Because service needs vary from customer to customer, the manager must first analyze and adapt to customer preferences. The manager should also examine the service levels competitors offer. Then the manager may try to identify and correct the causes of customer complaints and billing and shipping errors.

3. Why should physical distribution managers develop customer service standards?

    Services are provided most effectively when managers develop service standards. If these standards are stated in terms that are specific, measurable, and appropriate for the product and are communicated clearly, both employees and customers will better understand what the company can offer. For example, a company should have a policy of stating a standard delivery time and rigorously enforcing this time. With such standards, the customer not only will know which services a company offers but can expect the services to be performed accordingly. A policy of setting and maintaining service standards will increase customer satisfaction.

4. What is the advantage of using a total distribution cost approach?

    Physical distribution managers strive to minimize the cost of each element in the system (order processing, materials handling, warehousing, inventory, and transportation). However, decreasing costs in one area often may increase costs in another. The total cost approach to physical distribution calls for analyzing the costs of all possible combinations of distribution alternatives, even those that might be too expensive by themselves. By using the total cost approach, physical distribution managers can view the distribution system as a whole rather than as a collection of unrelated activities. Because a distribution system's minimized cost is the lowest overall cost compatible with the company's stated service objectives rather than a function of a combination of the cheapest elements, the total cost approach is advantageous.

5. What are the main tasks involved in order processing?

There are three main order-processing tasks. Order entry begins when customers or salespersons place purchase orders by mail, telephone, or computer. Order handling involves verifying product availability, approving the credit purchase, and filling the order. Order delivery involves scheduling pickup with an appropriate carrier.

6. Discuss the advantages of using an electronic order-processing system. Which types of organizations are most likely to utilize electronic order processing?

Order processing can be performed manually or electronically. Because it lets a company integrate order processing, production, inventory control, accounting, and transportation planning into a total information system, electronic order processing has distinct advantages over manual processing. It can cut several days from the order cycle, eliminate the need for the vendor to rekey information, and reduce the amount of inventory the company must carry.

Electronic order processing is practical for companies that process a large volume of orders, both from customers and to suppliers. Wal-Mart stores and about three hundred of its suppliers use electronic order processing, which enables them to transmit purchase orders directly from a central processing center to a vendor, giving Wal-Mart the advantages discussed above.

7. Describe the costs associated with inventory management.

Inventory management involves the development and maintenance of adequate product assortments to meet customer needs. There are several forms of costs associated with inventory management. Carrying costs include expenditures for storage space, materials handling, financing, insurance, taxes, and losses due to spoilage. Replenishment costs relate to the purchase of merchandise (price, handling charges, and processing costs). Stockout costs include sales and customer goodwill lost due to the demand for goods exceeding the supply on hand as well as the processing expenses of backordering. A company must control the costs of obtaining and maintaining inventory to meet its goals and objectives.

8. Explain the tradeoffs inventory managers face when reordering products or supplies. How is the reorder point computed?

When reordering merchandise, inventory managers face tradeoffs based on the amount of safety stock being carried. Large safety stocks ensure product availability, improvements of customer service, and lower order-processing costs because orders are placed less frequently. Small safety stocks result in higher order-processing costs through frequently reordering but lower the overall cost of carrying inventory. The reorder point is computed by multiplying the lead time by the usage rate, and adding the safety stock.

9. How can managers improve inventory control? Give specific examples of techniques.

Managers can improve inventory control by planning a system so that the number of products sold and the number of products in stock are determined at certain checkpoints. For example, a tag containing information about product size, color, and model can be removed from the item at the checkout stand and used in inventory control. Computerized cash registers provide continuous inventory and sales updates (e.g., grocery stores use optical scanners to read the universal product code on each product).

10. How does a product's package affect materials handling procedures and techniques?

Packaging's protection functions have a strong impact on physical distribution. Decisions about packaging materials and methods affect the efficiency of physical handling. Materials handling techniques and procedures should maximize a warehouse's usable capacity, reduce the number of times a product is handled, and improve customer service. The design of the package should be coordinated to help meet these objectives. For example, a package's size and shape should allow the goods to be stacked and moved efficiently, and its material and design should ensure the package's ability to withstand rigorous handling.

11. What is containerization? Discuss the major benefits.

Containerization is consolidating many items into a single large container that is sealed at the point of origin and opened at the destination. Containerization broadens the capacities of the transportation system by enabling shippers to transport a wider range of cargoes with speed, reliability, and stable costs. It is energy efficient, decreases the need for expensive security measures, and reduces losses and damage.

12. Explain the major differences between private and public warehouses. What is a field public warehouse?

A private warehouse is operated by a company for the purpose of distributing its own products. Private warehouses provide benefits such as property appreciation and tax shelters but also incur fixed costs such as insurance, taxes, maintenance, and debt expenses. They provide little flexibility when a company wishes to move inventories to more strategic locations.

Public warehouses rent storage space and physical distribution facilities to other firms. Public warehouse costs are variable rather than fixed (and therefore are usually lower).

A field public warehouse is established by a public warehouse at the customer's inventory location. The warehouser then becomes the custodian of the products and issues a receipt that can be used as collateral for a loan.

13. Under what circumstances should a firm use a private warehouse instead of a public one?

A firm should use a private warehouse if it believes that its warehouse needs in a given geographic market are substantial and stable enough to warrant a long-term commitment to fixed facilities. A firm might also choose a private warehouse if its products require special handling and storage or the firm wants to maintain control over the warehouse's design and operation.

14. The focus of distribution centers is on active movement of goods. Discuss how distribution centers are designed for the rapid flow of products.

Distribution centers are designed to move goods to customers quickly and efficiently. They are one-story buildings (to eliminate the need for elevators) and have easy access to transportation networks such as major highways. The distribution center is highly automated and computerized to facilitate product flows. It serves customers in regional markets to emphasize quick product grouping and shipping.

15. Compare the five major transportation modes as to costs, speed, dependability, load flexibility, accessibility, and frequency.

Railroads are inexpensive means for shipping products overland for long distances. Transit time for railroads is high; however, improving technologies and innovations allow some trains to bypass classification yards, reducing transit time. Railways are fairly reliable, capable of providing specific equipment and conditions for particular goods (refrigeration), and accessible because of the currently improving network of rail lines. Security on railroads is fairly easy to maintain; the traceability of products transported on railways depends largely on the individual shipping organization.

Trucks provide the most flexible schedules because they can go almost anywhere. Costs of distribution through motor vehicles are higher because of the small shipments carried. The vehicles are more vulnerable to bad weather. They are less reliable and traceable because the smaller shipments result in rehandling of the products.

Waterways are the cheapest method for shipping low-value goods. This mode of transportation is slow, however, and cannot serve inland markets without supplementary transport. Damage caused by water and weather is a factor. Security and traceability are fairly stable because of the small amount of handling involved in large shipments.

Airways are the fastest and most expensive method of shipping. The capacity of air transport depends on the individual aircraft. This method can reduce theft and damage to products, helping lower total costs. Like waterways, however, air transportation must be supplemented with another transportation method.

Pipelines are the most automated transportation modes. They are characterized by limited accessibility but are reliable and ensure low product damage and theft. Pipelines move products slowly but continuously. Allowances should be made for shrinkage, usually caused by evaporation.

16. Discuss the ways marketers can combine or coordinate two or more modes of transportation. What is the advantage of doing this?

Containerization is a recent transportation innovation that allows marketers to consolidate many items into a single, large container that can then be transported efficiently by any of the transportation modes available to distribution managers.

Freight forwarders combine shipments for several organizations into efficient lots and buy transportation space from various types of carriers.

Megacarriers are freight transportation companies that provide several methods of shipment and often offer warehousing, consulting, and leasing services.

The advantage of coordinating two or more modes of transportation is that it allows physical distribution managers to take advantage of the benefits various carriers offer while compensating for their deficiencies. For example, trucking offers more flexibility but costs more than railways. Combining the two carriers is cheaper than using only trucking and provides more accessibility than railways alone.

17. Identify the types of containerized shipping available to physical distribution managers.

The three types of containerized shipping available to physical distribution managers allow greater flexibility in speed and cost:
- *Piggyback* is combining truck trailers with flatbed rail cars.
- *Fishyback* is combining truck trailers with water carriers.
- *Birdyback* is combining truck trailers with air carriers.

COMMENTS ON THE CASES

Case 16.1   Airborne's Competitive Dogfight

The purpose of this case is to provide students with an opportunity to reflect on some issues that are associated with physical distribution decisions. To add interest to this case analysis, you want to ask students to research several major companies that provide overnight express services.

The first question asks on which transportation selection criteria would Airborne be rated high and low? Relative to other transportation modes, Airborne would be rated high on cost, speed, and dependability. This type of service would be rated average on accessibility and frequency and would be rated low on load flexibility.

Question 2 asks how Airborne has managed to keep its cost low and what benefits have resulted. To keep costs low, Airborne limits its service to delivering small packages, which reduces the need for aircraft modification. In the past Airborne has also kept its costs low by focusing primarily on the corporate customer as opposed to trying to serve many different market segments. Airborne's use of a great deal of technology has helped keep its cost low and still maintain a high level of customer satisfaction. The main benefit of keeping costs low is that it allows Airborne to charge lower prices and thus be a very competitive bidder for large corporate contracts.

The third question asks whether the use of overnight express services can result in suboptimization? Suboptimization is a situation in which actions to reduce costs in one area result in increased costs in other areas. It can occur with the use of any transportation mode. Certainly, the use of overnight express services can result in suboptimization. However, suboptimization also may be avoided by using overnight express services.

Video Information

Video Title: Airborne Express Delivering Satisfaction Worldwide
Location: Tape 2, Segment 16
Length: 5:39
Video Overview: Along with Federal Express and United Parcel Service, Airborne Express is one of the major express delivery services in the United States. Airborne serves 180 countries around the world and handles over 500,000 packages a day. The company's goal is to provide business customers with reliable on-time delivery at the lowest possible price. To facilitate speed and dependability, Airborne employs state-of-the-art technology such as computerized package tracking and shipment processing, and electronic data entry. The company also prides itself on providing personalized customer service. To succeed in today's increasingly competitive market, Airborne is lowering some of its prices for large-volume customers, expanding services, and targeting more small and mid-size companies.

Multiple-Choice Questions About the Video

c   1. According to the video, Airborne Express's goal is to
     a. increase the number of packages it delivers from 500,000 a day to 750,000 a day.
     b. capture market share from Federal Express and United Parcel Service.
     c. deliver packages where they should be, on time all of the time.
     d. expand its service to include private as well as corporate customers.
     e. increase efficiency by expanding the number of distribution centers it operates.

e   2. The _____ is Airborne's computerized method for combining order entry with shipment processing.
    a. strategic conduit
    b. just-in-time inventory control system
    c. strategic distribution alliance
    d. electronic interchange system
    e. linkage system

b   3. Airborne's _____ system allows customers to weigh, route, label, invoice, and track packages from their own location.
    a. Electronic Interchange
    b. Libre
    c. Individualized Tracking
    d. Self-Tracking
    e. Omni

b   4. According to the video, Airborne employees refer to the heart of Airborne's service network as
    a. Network Central.
    b. the Sort.
    c. the Zone.
    d. Central Control.
    e. the Hub.

a   5. To keep its own costs down, Airborne
    a. owns, maintains, and rebuilds its own fleet of aircraft.
    b. operates local customer service centers only.
    c. operates only within the continental United States.
    d. requires its customers to weigh, label, and invoice their own packages.
    e. switched from overnight to second and third day delivery.

Case 16.2   The Home Depot Initiates New Cooperation in Supply Chain Management

This case explores how one retailer has assumed a marketing channel leadership role in order to reduce its supply chain physical distribution costs and improve customer service for all members of its supply chain.

The first question asks students to explain why physical distribution is so important in Home Depot's marketing strategy. The Home Depot has a marketing strategy of providing superior customer service, low prices, and a broad product assortment. With more than 350 stores, each stocking 40,000 to 50,000 items for both ultimate consumers and contractors, managing inventory efficiently and avoiding stockouts are crucial to The Home Depot's success. Failure to provide the products customers want when they want them will send those customers to competitors such as Builder's Square, Furrow's, and other retailers.

The second question asks how The Home Depot has positioned itself as a leader of supply chain management in the home improvement industry. The Hope Depot has re-engineered itself to become more efficient in terms of logistics, inventory control, security, and electronic data systems; implemented a core carrier program that requires its suppliers to switch to designated regional and national transportation carriers; formed the Inbound Logistics

Consortium to help regional trucking companies provide better service, faster delivery, and greater efficiency; and insisted that its own suppliers ship products on plastic slipsheets, which the firm believes are more efficient and less wasteful.

The third question asks why The Home Depot has formed a cooperative partnership with Wal-Mart and other competitors. The Home Depot has formed cooperatives with other firms involved in the home improvement industry in order to boost efficiency and improve customer service for all members of its own supply chain. By helping regional trucking companies become more efficient (through the Inbound Logistics Consortium), for example, all members of The Home Depot's supply chain benefit from better service, faster delivery, and lower costs, which they can pass on to their customers. In order to be effective, such changes may best be implemented on an industrywide scale, even though competitors benefit as well. The overall result is better service—as well as greater product choice and lower prices—for ultimate consumers.

17
PROMOTION: AN OVERVIEW

TEACHING RESOURCES QUICK REFERENCE GUIDE

Resource	Location
Purpose and Perspective	IRM, p. 365
Guide for Using Color Transparencies	IRM, p. 365
Lecture Outline	IRM, p. 366
Class Exercises, Debate Issue, and Chapter Quiz	IRM, p. 377
Class Exercise 1	IRM, p. 379
Class Exercise 2	IRM, p. 380
Debate Issue: Should cigarette and beer companies be allowed to sponsor sporting events?	IRM, p. 381
Chapter Quiz	IRM, p. 382
Answers to Discussion and Review Questions	IRM, p. 383
Comments on the Cases	IRM, p. 385
Case 17.1	IRM, p. 385
Video	Tape 2, Segment 17
Video Information	IRM, p. 386
Multiple-Choice Questions About the Video	IRM, p. 386
Case 17.2	IRM, p. 387
Transparency Acetates	Transparency package
Examination Questions: Essay	TB, p. 309
Examination Questions: Multiple-Choice	TB, p. 310
Examination Questions: True-False	TB, p. 322
Author-Selected Multiple-Choice Test Items	TB, p. 447

PURPOSE AND PERSPECTIVE

This chapter is the first of three dealing with promotion decisions and activities. Its primary objective is to give students an overview of promotion. First, we present a theoretical foundation on which to build an understanding of promotion. Consequently, the first part of this chapter focuses on the role of promotion in organizations, the communication process, and the objectives of promotion. Next, we introduce the concept of the promotion mix and briefly describe the major elements that constitute it (promotion mix elements are discussed in greater detail in Chapters 18 and 19). Then we analyze a number of factors that affect marketers' decisions when selecting specific ingredients to include in a promotion mix for a product. Finally, we examine some criticisms and defenses of promotion.

GUIDE FOR USING COLOR TRANSPARENCIES

There are two groups of color transparencies. The transparencies identified by a double number are the same as the figures and tables in the text. The transparencies labeled with a number and a letter are illustrations that do not appear in the text, but they can be used as additional examples of concepts discussed.

Part 5 Opener	Promotion decisions
Figure 17.2	Information flows into and out of an organization
Figure 17.3	The communication process
Table 17.1	Possible objectives of promotion
Figure 17.5	The four possible elements of a promotion mix
Figure 17.9	Comparison of push and pull promotional strategies
Figure 17A	Chapter 17 outline
Figure 17B	Importance of word-of-mouth communication varies among product categories
Figure 17C	Primary factors affecting the choice of promotion mix components
Figure 17D	Assessing the major criticisms of promotion
Figure 17E	Discussion issue: Using this advertisement as an example, explain how part of this advertisement relates to the communications process. Compare the role of the illustration to that of the verbal part of this advertisement relative to the communication process.
Figure 17F	The maker of Defend, a flea and tick control product, uses advertisements such as the one here to create awareness of this new approach to flea and tick control.
Figure 17G	While promotion is sometimes criticized for promoting products that may be harmful to the environment, promotion can also be used to promote environmentally sensitive products.

LECTURE OUTLINE

I. The role of promotion

    A. **Promotion** is communication with individuals, groups, or organizations to directly or indirectly facilitate exchanges by informing and persuading one or more of the audiences to accept an organization's products.

        1. To facilitate exchanges directly, marketers communicate with selected audiences about their companies and their goods, services, and ideas.

        2. Marketers indirectly facilitate exchanges by focusing information about company activities and products on interest groups, current and potential investors, regulatory agencies, and society in general.

        3. **Cause-related marketing** links purchase of products to philanthropic efforts for a particular cause favored by the target market.

        4. Promotion can play a comprehensive communication role. Some promotional activities can be directed toward helping a company justify its existence and maintain positive, healthy relationships between itself and various groups in the marketing environment.

    B. To develop and implement effective promotional activities, a firm must obtain and use information from the marketing environment, often from its marketing information system. The degree to which marketers can effectively use promotion to maintain positive relationships with environmental forces depends largely on the quantity and quality of information an organization takes in.

II. Promotion and the communication process

    A. **Communication** is a sharing of meaning. Both the sender and receiver of the information must share an understanding of the symbols used to transmit information—usually pictures or words.

    B. Implicit in this definition of communication is the notion of transmission of information because sharing necessitates transmission.

        1. Communication begins with a **source,** which is a person, group, or organization that has a meaning it intends and attempts to share with a receiver or an audience.

2. To transmit meaning, a source must place the meaning into a series of signs that represent ideas or concepts. This is called the coding process, or encoding.

   a. The **coding process** converts meaning into a series of signs. When coding a meaning, the source should try to use signs that the receiver or audience uses for referring to the concepts the source intends.

   b. The **receiver** is the individual, group, or organization that decodes a coded message.

3. To share a coded meaning with the receiver or audience, a source must select and use a medium of transmission. A **medium of transmission** is the means of carrying the coded message from the source to the receiver or audience.

   a. When a source chooses an inappropriate medium of transmission, a coded message may reach the wrong receivers.

   b. If an inappropriate medium is chosen, a coded message may reach the intended receivers in an incomplete form because the intensity of the transmission is weak.

4. In the **decoding process,** signs are converted by the receiver into concepts and ideas.

   a. The meaning that a receiver decodes is seldom exactly the same as the meaning the source intended.

   b. When the result of decoding differs from what was coded, noise exists. **Noise,** anything that reduces a communication's clarity and accuracy, has many sources and may affect any or all parts of the communication.

      (1) When a source selects a medium of transmission through which an audience does not expect to receive a message, noise is likely to occur.

      (2) Noise sometimes arises within the medium of transmission.

      (3) Noise will occur if the source uses a sign that is unfamiliar to the receiver or has a different meaning than the one intended.

(4)   A receiver may be unaware of a coded message because his or her perceptual processes block it out.

5.   The receiver's response to a message is **feedback** to the source.

    a.   During feedback, the receiver or audience is the source of the message that is directed toward the original source, which then becomes a receiver. Thus communication can be viewed as a circular process.

    b.   During face-to-face communication, such as in a personal selling situation, both verbal and nonverbal feedback can be immediate, enabling communicators to adjust their messages quickly to improve the effectiveness of their communication.

    c.   When mass communication such as advertising is used, feedback is often slow and difficult to recognize.

6.   Each communication channel is limited as to the volume of information it can handle effectively. This limit, called **channel capacity,** is determined by the least efficient component of the communication process.

III.   Objectives of promotion

Although there are several objectives of promotion, these differ widely from one organization to another and within organizations over time.

A.   Create awareness

1.   Considerable amount of promotion is directed at creating awareness of new products, new brands, and brand extensions.

2.   For existing products, promotional efforts increase brand awareness, product feature awareness, awareness of image-related issues, and awareness of operational characteristics.

B.   Stimulate demand

1. **Primary demand** is demand for a product category rather than for a specific brand of product.

   a. Primary demand is created through **pioneer promotion,** which informs potential customers about the product: what it is, what it does, how it can be used, and where it can be purchased.

   b. Sometimes an industry trade association uses promotional efforts to stimulate primary demand.

2. **Selective demand** is demand for a specific brand.

   a. Marketers employ promotional efforts that single out strengths and benefits of a specific brand.

   b. Advertising campaigns, free samples, and consumer contests and sweepstakes are promotional activities that stimulate selective demand.

C. Encourage product trial

   1. Activities to keep potential adopters interested after awareness stage

   2. Activities include free samples, coupons, test drives, or limited free-use offers, contests, and games

D. Identify prospects

   1. Certain types of promotional efforts are directed at identifying customers who are interested in firm's product and are most likely to buy.

   2. Advertisements may provide direct response information forms or toll-free response lines.

   3. Customers who fill out information blanks or call organizations usually have higher interest in products.

E. Retain loyal customers

1.   Costs of retaining customers are usually lower than those for acquiring new ones.

2.   Common promotional activities directed at retaining loyal customers are frequent flier programs and special offers for existing customers only.

3.   Reinforcement advertising assures current users that they have made the right choice.

F.   Facilitating reseller support

1.   Strong relationships with resellers are important to a firm's capability to maintain a competitive advantage.

2.   Use of some promotional methods helps organizations achieve this goal.

G.   Combat competitive promotional efforts

1.   May prevent sales or market share loss

2.   Common in extremely competitive consumer products markets

H.   Reduce sales fluctuations

1.   Demand for many products varies because of climate, holidays, or seasons.

2.   Promotional activities are designed to stimulate sales during sales slumps or low-demand periods.

IV.   The **promotion mix**—a combination of promotional methods used to promote a specific product.

Several types of promotional methods can be used to communicate with individuals, groups, and organizations. The four possible ingredients of a promotion mix are advertising, personal selling, publicity, and sales promotion. For some products, firms use all four ingredients; for other products, two or three suffice.

A. Advertising

1. Advertising is a paid form of nonpersonal communication about an organization and its products that is transmitted to a target audience through a mass medium such as television, radio, newspapers, magazines, direct mail, mass transit vehicles, outdoor displays, or catalogs.

2. Individuals and organizations use advertising to promote goods, services, ideas, issues, and people.

3. Because advertising is a highly flexible promotional method, it offers the options of reaching a large target audience or focusing on a small, precisely defined segment of the population.

4. Advertising offers several benefits.

   a. Advertising can be an extremely cost-efficient promotional method because it can reach a vast number of people at a low cost per person.

   b. Advertising lets the user repeat the message a number of times.

   c. The visibility an organization gains from advertising enhances the firm's public image.

5. Advertising also has several disadvantages.

   a. Although its cost per person reached may be low, its absolute dollar outlay can be extremely high, limiting and sometimes preventing the use of advertising in a promotion mix.

   b. Advertising rarely provides rapid feedback.

   c. It is difficult to measure the effects of advertising on sales.

   d. Advertising ordinarily has less persuasive impact on customers than personal selling.

B. Personal selling

    1. Personal selling involves informing customers and persuading them to purchase products through personal communication in an exchange situation.

    2. Like advertising, personal selling has both advantages and limitations.

        a. The cost of reaching one person through personal selling is considerably more than through advertising, but personal selling efforts often have greater impact on customers.

        b. Personal selling provides immediate feedback.

        c. The salesperson can take advantage of several types of communication in addition to verbal language.

            (1) **Kinesic communication,** or body language, includes movement of one's head, eyes, arms, hands, legs, or torso.

            (2) **Proxemic communication** occurs when either party varies the physical distance that separates the two parties.

            (3) **Tactile communication** is communication through touching.

C. Public relations

    1. Public relations is a broad set of communication efforts used to create and maintain favorable relationships between an organization and its publics.

    2. Publicity, which is a public relations tool, is nonpersonal communication in news story form about an organization, its products, or both, that is transmitted through a mass medium at no charge.

    3. Public relations can be used to help combat the negative effects of a crisis or unpleasant situation.

D. Sales promotion

1. Sales promotion is an activity and/or material that acts as a direct inducement, offering resellers, salespersons, or consumers added value or incentive for the product.

2. Marketers frequently rely on sales promotion to improve the effectiveness of other promotion-mix ingredients, especially advertising and personal selling.

3. Use of sales promotion appears to be growing faster than advertising.

V. Selecting promotion mix ingredients

Marketers vary the compositions of promotion mixes for many reasons. An organization's promotion mix (or mixes) is a changing part of the marketing mix. The specific promotion mix ingredients employed and the intensity with which an organization uses them depend on a variety of factors. **Integrated marketing communication** is the coordination of promotional elements and other marketing efforts to maximize total informational and promotional impact.

A. Promotional resources, objectives, and policies

The organization's promotional resources, objectives, and policies all affect the types of promotion used.

1. The quality of an organization's promotional resources affects the number and relative intensity of promotional methods included in the promotion mix.

    a. If a company's promotional budget is extremely limited, the firm is likely to rely on personal selling because it is easier to measure a salesperson's contribution to sales than to measure the effect of advertising.

    b. A business must have a sizable promotional budget to use regional or national advertising and sales promotion activities.

2. An organization's promotional objectives also influence the types of promotion used.

    a. If a company's objective is to create mass awareness of a new convenience good, its promotion mix is likely to lean heavily toward advertising, sales promotion, and possibly public relations.

b. If a company hopes to educate consumers about the features of durable goods, its promotion mix may combine a moderate amount of advertising, possibly some sales promotion, and a great deal of personal selling because this is an excellent way to inform customers about these types of products.

B. Characteristics of the target market

The size, geographic distribution, and socioeconomic characteristics of an organization's target market also help dictate the ingredients to be included in a product's promotion mix.

1. If the size of the market is limited, personal selling probably will be emphasized because it can be effective for reaching a small number of people. When markets for a product consist of millions of customers, organizations use advertising and sales promotion.

2. If a company's customers are concentrated in a small geographic area, personal selling is more feasible than if the customers are dispersed across a vast area. Advertising may be more practical when the company's customers are numerous and not concentrated.

3. Demographic characteristics such as age, income, or education level may dictate the types of promotional techniques that a marketer selects.

C. Characteristics of the product

The characteristics of the product also influence the promotion mix ingredients.

1. Generally, promotion mixes for industrial products concentrate heavily on personal selling, whereas consumer goods promotion relies heavily on advertising. However, this generalization should be treated cautiously. Industrial goods producers do use some advertising to promote goods.

2. Marketers of seasonal products may have to emphasize advertising, and possibly sales promotion, because off-season sales may be insufficient to support an extensive year-round sales force.

3. A product's price influences the composition of the promotion mix.

a.   High-price products call for more personal selling because consumers associate greater risk with the purchase of such products and usually want the advice of a salesperson.

b.   For low-price convenience items, marketers use advertising rather than personal selling at the retail level. The profit margins on many of these items are too low to justify the use of salespersons, and most customers do not need assistance from them.

4.   The stage of the product life cycle affects marketers' decisions regarding the promotion mix.

a.   In the introduction stage, a considerable amount of advertising may be necessary for both industrial and consumer products to make potential users aware of the new product.

b.   The growth and maturity stages necessitate heavy emphasis on advertising for consumer nondurables, whereas industrial products often require a concentration of personal selling and some sales promotion during these stages.

c.   In the decline stage, marketers usually decrease their promotional activities.

5.   The intensity of market coverage at which a product is distributed may influence the composition of its promotion mix.

a.   When a product is marketed through intensive distribution, the firm depends heavily on advertising and sales promotion.

b.   Promotion mixes of products distributed through selective distribution vary considerably in terms of the types and numbers of promotional methods used.

c.   Products distributed exclusively are promoted primarily through personal selling.

6.   A product's use can also affect the combination of promotional methods employed.

D.   Costs and availability of promotional methods

The costs of promotional methods and the availability of promotional techniques are major factors to analyze when developing a promotion mix.

1.   National advertising and sales promotion efforts require large expenditures; however, if they reach extremely large numbers of people, the cost per individual may be quite small.

2.   Although there are numerous media vehicles within the United States, a firm may find that no available advertising medium effectively reaches a certain market.

E.   Push and pull channel policies

One element marketers should considered is whether to use a push policy or a pull policy.

1.   With a **push policy,** the producer promotes the product to the next institution down the marketing channel.

2.   With a **pull policy,** the firm promotes directly to consumers with the intention of developing a strong consumer demand for the products.

VI.   Criticisms and defenses of promotion

A number of specific criticisms have been lodged against promotional activities.

A.   Some promotions are believed to be deceptive or unethical. The increased number of laws, the efforts of government regulatory agencies, and self-regulation have caused a decrease in deceptive promotion.

B.   Promotions are often blamed for higher prices. However, if promotion is working to stimulate demand, producing and marketing larger quantities can work to reduce prices.

C.   Critics of promotion claim that promotion manipulates consumers by persuading them to buy products they do not need. Without promotion, many needs would still exist; marketing does not create needs, but capitalizes on them.

D.   Promotions are sometimes criticized for encouraging materialism. Marketers assert that values are instilled at home and promotion does not change people into materialistic consumers.

E.   Critics question whether promotion helps consumers enough to be worth the costs. Consumers do benefit, for promotions inform them about a product's uses, features, advantages, prices, or purchase locations.

F.   Organizations are often criticized for promoting products associated with violence, sex, and unhealthy activities. Those who defend such promotion argue that as long as it is legal to sell a product, promoting it should also be allowed.

CLASS EXERCISES, DEBATE ISSUE, AND CHAPTER QUIZ

On the following pages, you will find two class exercises, a debate issue, and a chapter quiz. These are formatted in large-size type so that you can use them as class handouts or for making transparencies. Below are the authors' comments on the class exercises, the debate topic, and the answers to the chapter quiz.

Class Exercise 1: This exercise focuses on how components of the communication process influence the effectiveness of the promotion mix. Pose the exercise questions after the following activity:

Bring a necktie to class for this exercise. Select a student volunteer who knows how to tie a necktie properly. Select another volunteer who knows nothing about tying a necktie. Ask the volunteers to stand back to back in front of the class. Give the tie to the second student and ask the first student to explain how to tie the tie. Occasionally, you'll have students who can communicate the procedure, but generally the second student is left wearing something less than a perfectly tied tie.

Question 1. This is personal selling in that immediate feedback was available and the source was trying to inform and persuade the receiver through personal communication.

Question 2. As with many problems marketers have with producing meaningful ads and personal sales presentations, the source was very familiar with the uses of the product while the receiver was not. The source must consider the characteristics of the receiver.

Question 3. Invariably, the students will laugh and make other distracting noises. The source may be using signs unfamiliar to the receiver (e.g., "Take one end and wrap it around the other end," without specifying which end or how to wrap it), or the receiver's perceptual processes may block it out (being in front of peers may change willingness or ability to decode information).

Question 4. Personal selling provides *immediate* verbal and nonverbal *feedback*. This circular process allows the salesperson to adapt the presentation so that it is meaningful to the receiver. Conversely, feedback from advertising is often slow and difficult to recognize (even though the audience does often talk back to the television set). Advertisers may not recognize feedback until sales or attitudes change, which may take months during and after the campaign. The advantages of personal selling, then, are the feedback and greater individual impact, despite its high per-person cost. The absolute cost of advertising and poor feedback may preclude some from using it, but its cost efficiency, visibility, and image enhancement make it ideal for some products with mass appeal.

Question 5. Often the first student will be trying to explain something while the second student is still trying to process the last command (and while the audience is offering their advice).

Question 6. Demonstration with body language and touching would have helped.

Class Exercise 2: This exercise should teach students that promotional efforts cannot always be easily and clearly classified into advertising, publicity, sales promotion, or personal selling. In the real business world, each category often overlaps with the others. The promotional efforts described in the exercise can be classified as follows:

1. **Advertising and sales promotion**
2. **Personal selling**
3. **Publicity**
4. **Advertising and sales promotion**
5. **Personal selling and sales promotion**

This exercise raises an interesting question: Can national advertisers, like McDonald's, hope to have a successful sales promotion effort without using advertising?

Debate Issue: Should cigarette and beer companies be allowed to sponsor sporting events?

Chapter Quiz: Answers to multiple-choice questions are

1. c	3. a
2. a	4. b

CLASS EXERCISE 1

1. What promotion mix element was this communication process most like?

2. What problems did the source have with the coding process?

3. How did noise affect the decoding process?

4. How is feedback different in a personal selling situation versus using mass communications? What are the pros and cons associated with each form?

5. How does channel capacity affect the ability to properly share meaning? Did the source (and other sources of noise) exceed the receiver's ability to effectively decode all information?

6. How might it have helped if the source had been able to use kinesic and tactile communication? How might the receiver respond with proxemic communication?

CLASS EXERCISE 2

THE PROMOTION MIX INCLUDES ADVERTISING, PUBLICITY, SALES PROMOTION, AND PERSONAL SELLING. HOW WOULD YOU CLASSIFY EACH OF THE FOLLOWING PROMOTION EFFORTS?

1. McDonald's uses television to tell consumers about free french fries with the purchase of a Big Mac.

2. A Toyota salesperson tells customers about the quality of Michelin tires.

3. CNN has a story about Energizer's latest ad campaign. The story features a commercial with the Energizer bunny.

4. Quaker Oats places an ad in *Good Housekeeping* magazine with a coupon attached.

5. A pharmaceutical salesperson leaves free samples with a physician.

DEBATE ISSUE

SHOULD CIGARETTE AND BEER COMPANIES BE ALLOWED TO SPONSOR SPORTING EVENTS?

YES

- Cigarettes: banned from broadcast media, so sporting events are one of the most important advertising avenues

- Beer: one of the best ways to reach target market

- Quality of sporting events could suffer without the sponsorship of cigarette and beer companies

- Freedom of speech is a basic right in America; because the selling of cigarettes and beer is legal, these companies have a right to advertise

NO

- Cigarette smoking is dangerous

- Promotes and legitimizes consumption

- Children cannot escape exposure to advertising at sporting events short of not being present

- Associating beer and cigarette products with sporting events lowers the image of those sports

CHAPTER QUIZ

1. The Main Street Deli decides to run its advertisements for its lunch specials on a local AM radio station. Marketing research later reveals that the restaurant's target market listens primarily to FM stations. This promotion program suffered from an error in the selection of
   a. shared symbols.
   b. targeted customers.
   c. the medium of transmission.
   d. decoded meanings.
   e. noise minimizers.

2. Advertising, personal selling, sales promotion, and public relations are called
   a. promotion mix ingredients.
   b. marketing mix components.
   c. characteristics of a product.
   d. advertising tools.
   e. nonpersonal communication.

3. Which of the following target market characteristics are most important to consider before determining the promotion mix ingredients?
   a. The size, geographic distribution, and demographic characteristics
   b. The cultural diversity and population size
   c. The age, sex, religion, and race characteristics
   d. Existing product adoption categories
   e. Existing levels of price consciousness

4. Promotion tends to
   a. create needs.
   b. capitalize on existing needs.
   c. be overly focused on the self-actualization needs.
   d. overemphasize physiological and safety needs.
   e. avoid focusing on people's needs.

ANSWERS TO DISCUSSION AND REVIEW QUESTIONS

1. What is the major task of promotion? Do firms ever use promotion to accomplish this task and fail? If so, give several examples.

   Promotion's major task is to communicate with individuals, groups, or organizations directly or indirectly to facilitate exchanges by influencing one or more of them to accept the organization's products. It is possible to use promotion to accomplish this objective and fail. Inconsistent communications or the use of nonessential information directed toward the organization's audience could lead to failure. Students should be able to provide examples of these occurrences, such as promotion directed toward them for expensive or luxury items in which they have no interest or cannot afford. Items such as champagne, luxury cars, or gourmet restaurants could represent this type of failure in communication.

2. What is communication? Describe the communication process. Is it possible to communicate without using all the elements in the communication process? If so, which ones can be omitted?

   Communication is a sharing of meaning. The communication process involves several steps. First, the source places the meaning into a code, a process sometimes called *coding*. The source must use signs that are familiar to the receiver or audience and refer to the same concepts or ideas. The coded message is sent through a medium of transmission to the receiver or audience. After the receiver or audience receives the message, the message is decoded and the receiver usually supplies feedback to the source. When the decoded message differs from what was encoded, a condition called *noise* exists.
   Communication is not possible without using all the elements in the communication process.

3. Identify several causes of noise. How can a source reduce noise?

   Noise may arise from faulty printing processes, interference or static in television or radio transmissions, laryngitis, or the use of unfamiliar signs that have multiple meanings.
   A source can reduce noise by employing familiar signs that the audience or receiver uses to refer to concepts or ideas. Signs with multiple meanings are detrimental to the communication process because they result in noise. The choice of the proper medium of transmission is important to avoid noise that arises from reaching the wrong audience or from weak transmissions.

4. Describe the possible objectives of promotion and discuss the circumstances under which each of these objectives might be used.

   Promotional objectives differ widely from one organization to another and within organizations over time. A considerable amount of promotion is directed at *creating awareness* of new products, new brands, or brand extensions. Creating awareness is important for existing products when marketers want to increase brand awareness, product feature awareness, awareness of image-related issues, or awareness of operational characteristics. When an organization is the first to introduce an innovative product, it uses pioneer promotion to *stimulate primary demand*. Primary demand is demand for a product category rather than for a specific product. To build selective demand, demand for a specific product, marketers employ promotional efforts based on the strengths and benefits of a specific brand. When customers stall during the evaluation stage of the product adoption process, marketers use certain kinds of promotions to *encourage product trial.* The objective of some promotional activities is to *identify prospective customers* who are interested in the firm's products and are most likely to buy. Because the costs of retaining customers are usually much lower than those of acquiring new ones, one objective of promotion is to *retain loyal customers.* Using some promotional methods helps organizations *maintain strong relationships with resellers,* which is critical to maintaining a competitive advantage. Sometimes marketers use promotions to offset or *lessen the effects of a competitor's promotional program.* These types of programs are most commonly used by firms in extremely competitive consumer products markets. Finally, promotional techniques are used to *increase sales during slow periods,* thereby reducing sales fluctuations.

5. Identify and briefly describe the four major promotional methods that can be included in an organization's promotion mix.

Advertising is a paid form of nonpersonal communication about an organization and/or its products that is transmitted to a target audience through a mass medium. *Personal selling* is informing customers and persuading them to purchase products through personal communication in an exchange situation. *Sales promotion* is an activity and/or material that acts as a direct inducement, offering resellers, salespersons, or consumers added value or incentive for the product. *Public relations* is a broad set of communication efforts used to create and maintain favorable relationships between an organization and its publics. Public relations tools can include reports, brochures, and event sponsorship. Publicity, which is part of public relations, is nonpersonal communication in news story form about an organization, its products, or both that is transmitted through a mass medium at no charge.

6. What forms of interpersonal communication besides language can be used in personal selling?

Communication may be accomplished through the use of kinesic, proxemic, or tactile communication. Kinesic communication is body language. Proxemic communication involves varying the physical space between the parties involved in communication. Tactile communication involves touching, such as handshaking.

7. How do market characteristics determine which promotional methods to include in a promotion mix? Assume that a company is planning to promote a cereal to both adults and children. Along what major dimensions would these two promotional efforts have to be different?

Market characteristics that influence the composition of the promotion mix include the size, geographic distribution, and socioeconomic characteristics of the market. If a company was promoting a cereal to both adults and children, it would use different advertising and sales promotion efforts for each market. Advertising appeals to children might include cartoon characterizations of the cereal, and the sales promotion might include a small toy. In the adult market, such methods would not be suitable; nutritional information, recipes, or a contest might be appropriate.

8. How can a product's characteristics affect the composition of its promotion mix?

   Both the type of product being promoted and the characteristics of that product affect the composition of the promotion mix. Whether the product is an industrial or consumer good will affect the composition of the promotion mix. Whether a consumer good is a durable or nondurable good is another factor. Product characteristics such as seasonality, price, stage of the product's life cycle, intensity of distribution of the product, and uses of the product are also determinants of the promotion mix.

9. Evaluate the following statement: "Appropriate advertising media are always available if a company can afford them."

   Availability of media is an important consideration in the formulation of a promotion mix. Even given the large number of media vehicles available, it may be difficult to reach a target market. A small, highly specialized market is difficult to reach with any degree of certainty through mass media. In addition, some geographic areas may not be accessible through the use of media.

10. Explain the difference between a pull policy and a push policy. Under what conditions should each policy be used?

    A pull policy aims promotional efforts directly at consumers with the intention of developing a strong demand for the product. A push policy aims promotional efforts only at the next institution down the marketing channel. A pull policy is sometimes used to introduce convenience goods. A push policy often is used to promote items such as industrial goods and consumer durables.

11. Which criticisms of promotion do you believe to be the most valid? Why?

    This is an open-ended question, and students' opinions will vary. In any discussion of this question, it is important that you facilitate a balanced view of promotion, giving equal weight to criticisms as well as defenses.

12. Should organizations be allowed to promote offensive, violent, sexual, or unhealthy products and services that can be legally sold and purchased? Support your answer.

    This is an effective question for raising the issue of what is legal and what is ethical with regard to promotional activity. Some of the possible concerns students should consider: (a) Does restriction of advertising to appropriate audiences constitute censorship? (b) How does the age of the target market relate to how ethical or unethical promotions are? There is a difference between promoting products to children and promoting products to informed adults.

COMMENTS ON THE CASES

Case 17.1 National Pork Producers Promote "The Other White Meat"

The purpose of this case is to illustrate to students how an industry trade group can stimulate primary demand through a major long-term promotional program. This promotional program has been in place long enough that students should be familiar with some aspects of it and should have opinions about pork consumption.

The first question asks what types of promotional objectives the National Pork Producers Council is pursuing. One of the promotional objectives being pursued by NPPC is that of creating awareness. This organization is attempting to create product features awareness of pork with respect to fat content, cholesterol content, and product versatility. Another promotional objective pursued by NPPC is that of demand stimulation. Through its extensive promotional promotions, the NPPC is attempting to stimulate primary demand. Based on increases in per capita pork consumption, it appears that efforts to stimulate primary demand are working.

Question 2 asks which promotion mix elements NPPC is including in its promotion mix. The primary promotion mix elements being employed by the NPPC are advertising and sales promotion. To a lesser degree, the NPPC has used publicity also.

Question 3 asks students about the types of recommendations they might make to NPPC regarding its promotional programs. Students' recommendations are likely to vary considerably. The discussion of question 3 will probably be very lively if you show the video that accompanies this case.

Video Information

Video Title: The Retail Battle
Location: Tape 2, Segment 17
Length: 7:43
Video Overview: To improve the image of pork products in the minds of health-conscious American consumers, the National Pork Producers Council (NPPC) has launched an aggressive promotional campaign that includes introduction of leaner trademark cuts and advertising and sales promotion. Network and cable television commercials and radio, magazine, newspaper, and outdoor advertisements all promote pork as "the other white meat." Commercials inform consumers about lower-calorie cuts of pork and present them in appetizing dishes. Working in partnership with supermarkets, the NPPC operates sales promotions that include recipe cards, sampling, couponing, and tie-ins with other products. To encourage restaurants to include more pork on their menus, the council creates advertising, promotions, and public relations programs specifically for the food service industry. As a result of the NPPC's efforts, more consumers consider pork a healthy white meat alternative like chicken, and pork sales are increasing.

Multiple-Choice Questions About the Video

c   1. _____ is the name of the National Pork Producers Council promotional campaign to improve the image of pork products.
   a. "Today's Pork"
   b. "Pork: America's Healthy Alternative"
   c. "The Other White Meat"
   d. "The Future of America's Plate"
   e. "Pork: The Shape of Things to Come"

b   2. To strengthen consumer recognition of new, healthier cuts of pork, the NPPC
   a. advertises and promotes solely those leaner cuts.
   b. introduced trademark names for those cuts.
   c. encourages grocery stores to allot more space for pork in the meat case.
   d. spends about $1 million a year on promotional activities.
   e. eliminated all cuts of pork with more than 180 calories per serving.

e   3. Coupons offering cents off on both pork products and Bulls-Eye barbecue sauce or Shake-and-Bake coating mix when customers purchase these items at the same time is a type of _____ promotion.
        a. co-op
        b. cross-merchandising
        c. point-of-sale
        d. linkage
        e. tie-in

b   4. The National Pork Producers Council works closely with grocery retailers to increase sales of pork. Some of the council's retail tactics include introducing trademarks for cuts of pork, creating tie-in promotions, developing cooperative promotional programs, and
        a. developing spot television ads for individual retail grocery outlets.
        b. expanding distribution of boneless pork.
        c. forming the Pork Information Bureau, a service that provides consumers with a toll-free number to call for information about pork recipes, preparation, and meal planning.
        d. sponsoring consumer recipe contests.
        e. increasing advertising in major women's magazines and supermarket trade journals.

Case 17.2   Anheuser-Busch Tackles America's Alcohol-Related Problems

The objective of this case is to demonstrate how promotional efforts can be used for purposes other than simply stimulating demand for an organization's products. Before discussing this case specifically, you may wish to open with an initial discussion about any efforts taken by alcoholic beverage marketers in your local area to reduce underage drinking and alcohol abuse.

The first question asks why Anheuser-Busch engages in promotional efforts to reduce underage drinking and alcohol abuse. Without question, Anheuser-Busch is spending significant promotional dollars to exercise its social responsibility by discouraging underage drinking and alcohol abuse. An organization that makes products that are potentially harmful sometimes takes action to encourage proper and acceptable consumption of such products so as to reduce the negative consequences of improper consumption such as injuries, property damage, and fatalities. These companies do not want negative events associated with their products. In addition, such steps taken by these organizations, if effective, will also reduce the possibility of additional regulation and social sanctions against their marketing activities.

Question 2 asks students to identify major components of the promotion mix being used by Anheuser-Busch in its campaign to reduce alcohol abuse. Anheuser-Busch employs advertising, public service announcements, and educational videos, and the company develops and supports community-based alcohol awareness and educational programs.

The final question asks students to evaluate the effectiveness of Anheuser-Busch and other organizations in reducing underage drinking and alcohol abuse. Student evaluations will vary considerably. You may want to compare the evaluations of older students in the class regarding this issue with those of their younger classmates.

18

ADVERTISING
AND PUBLIC RELATIONS

TEACHING RESOURCES QUICK REFERENCE GUIDE

Resource	Location
Purpose and Perspective	IRM, p. 389
Guide for Using Color Transparencies	IRM, p. 389
Lecture Outline	IRM, p. 389
Class Exercises, Debate Issue, and Chapter Quiz	IRM, p. 401
Class Exercise 1	IRM, p. 403
Class Exercise 2	IRM, p. 404
Debate Issue: Is using celebrities in an ad campaign a good way to stimulate brand appeal?	IRM, p. 405
Chapter Quiz	IRM, p. 406
Answers to Discussion and Review Questions	IRM, p. 407
Comments on the Cases	IRM, p. 410
Case 18.1	IRM, p. 410
Video	Tape 3, Segment 18
Video Information	IRM, p. 411
Multiple-Choice Questions About the Video	IRM, p. 411
Case 18.2	IRM, p. 412
Transparency Acetates	Transparency package
Examination Questions: Essay	TB, p. 327
Examination Questions: Multiple-Choice	TB, p. 328
Examination Questions: True-False	TB, p. 343
Author-Selected Multiple-Choice Test Items	TB, p. 448

PURPOSE AND PERSPECTIVE

This chapter presents a detailed discussion of two promotion mix ingredients—advertising and public relations. First, we focus on the nature and types of advertising. Next, we analyze the major steps in developing an advertising campaign. Then, we discuss possible alternatives for determining the person responsible for developing advertising campaigns. In the second part of the chapter, we focus on the nature of public relations. We first examine a variety of public relations tools. We then focus on the specific public relations tools associated with publicity. Finally, we explore the requirements for using public relations effectively and dealing with unfavorable publicity.

GUIDE FOR USING COLOR TRANSPARENCIES

There are two groups of color transparencies. The transparencies identified by a double number are the same as the figures in the text. The transparencies labeled with a number and a letter are illustrations that do not appear in the text, but they can be used as additional examples of concepts discussed.

Figure 18.3 General steps for developing and implementing an advertising campaign
Figure 18.6 Geographic divisions for *Sports Illustrated* regional issues
Figure 18.7 Components of a print advertisement
Figure 18A Chapter 18 outline
Figure 18B Major types of advertising defined
Figure 18C Illustration techniques for advertisements
Figure 18D Major types of publicity-based public relations methods
Figure 18E Example of a reminder advertisement
Figure 18F The maker of Schick razors uses illustration techniques that include dramatizing a headline and emphasizing special features.
Figure 18G The Georgia Department of Revenue uses strong fear appeal in its advertising.

LECTURE OUTLINE

I. The nature and types of advertising

   A. **Advertising** is a paid form of nonpersonal communication that is transmitted through mass media, such as television, radio, newspapers, magazines, direct mail, mass transit vehicles, and outdoor displays. Advertising is used to promote goods, services, ideas, images, issues, people, and anything else advertisers want to publicize or foster.

   B. Institutional advertising

1.   **Institutional advertising** promotes organizational images, ideas, political issues, or socially approved behavior.

2.   **Advocacy advertising,** a type of institutional advertising, promotes a company's position on a public issue.

C.   Product advertising

1.   **Product advertising** promotes the uses, features, and benefits of products.

2.   The two types of product advertising are pioneer advertising and competitive advertising.

a.   **Pioneer advertising** focuses on stimulating demand for a product category (rather than for a specific product) by informing potential customers about the product's features, uses, and benefits, and is employed when the product is in its introductory stage.

b.   **Competitive advertising** attempts to stimulate demand for a specific brand by indicating a brand's features, uses, and advantages, sometimes through indirect or direct comparisons with competing brands.

(1)   **Reminder advertising** tells customers that an established brand is still around, and reminds consumers about the brand's uses, characteristics, and benefits.

(2)   **Reinforcement advertising** assures current users that they have made the right brand choice and tells them how to get the most satisfaction from it.

II.   Developing an advertising campaign

Several steps are required to develop an **advertising campaign,** which is the creation and execution of a series of advertisements to communicate with a particular target audience. The number of steps and the exact order in which they are carried out can vary according to the organization's resources, the nature of its products, and the types of audiences to be reached.

A.   Identifying and analyzing the target audience

1. The **target audience** is the group of people toward whom advertisements are aimed. A firm's target audience often includes everyone in the firm's target market. At times, however, marketers may wish to aim a campaign at only a portion of the target market.

2. Advertisers analyze target audiences to establish an information base for a campaign. Information commonly needed includes the location and geographic distribution of the target group; the distribution of age, income, race, sex, and education level; and consumer attitudes regarding the purchase and use of both the advertiser's products and competing products.

3. Generally, the more advertisers know about the target audience, the better able they are to develop an effective advertising campaign.

B. Defining the advertising objectives

1. Advertisers should consider what the firm hopes to accomplish with the campaign. To develop a campaign with direction and purpose, they must define their advertising objectives.

2. Because advertising objectives guide campaign development, advertisers should define them carefully to ensure that the campaign will accomplish what they desire.

3. Advertising objectives should be stated in clear, precise, and measurable terms.

   a. Precision and measurability allow advertisers to evaluate advertising success—to judge, at the campaign's end, whether the objectives have been met and, if so, how well.

      (1) A benchmark that states the current condition or position of the firm should be included in the statement of an advertising objective. The statement also should indicate how far and in what direction an advertiser wishes to move from the benchmark.

      (2) An advertising objective should specify a time frame so that advertisers know exactly how long they have to accomplish the objective.

   b. Advertising objectives usually are stated in terms of either sales or communication.

(1)   When an advertiser defines objectives in terms of sales, the objectives focus on raising absolute dollar sales, increasing sales by a certain percentage, or increasing the firm's market share.

(2)   When objectives are stated in terms of communication, they are designed to increase brand or product awareness, make consumers' attitudes more favorable, or increase consumers' knowledge of a product's features.

C.   Creating the advertising platform

1.   An **advertising platform** consists of the basic issues or selling points that an advertiser wishes to include in the advertising campaign.

2.   A marketer's advertising platform should consist of issues that are important to consumers.

a.   One of the best ways to determine what those issues are is to survey consumers about what they consider most important in the selection and use of the product involved.

b.   Research is the most effective method for determining the issues of an advertising platform, but it is expensive. As a result, the most common way to develop a platform is to base it on the opinions of personnel within the firm and individuals in the advertising agency if an agency is used.

3.   Because the advertising platform is a base on which to build the message, marketers should analyze this stage carefully in developing an advertising campaign. If the advertisements communicate information that consumers do not consider important when they select and use the product, the campaign can fail.

D.   Determining the advertising appropriation

1.   The **advertising appropriation** is the total amount of money a marketer allocates for advertising for a specific time period.

2.   Many factors affect the amount of the advertising appropriation, including size of geographic market, distribution of buyers within the market, type of product advertised, and the firm's sales volume relative to competitors'.

3.   Various techniques are used to determine the advertising appropriation.

   a.   In the **objective-and-task approach,** marketers initially determine the objectives that a campaign is to achieve and then attempt to list the tasks required to accomplish them. Once the tasks have been determined, their costs are added to ascertain the appropriation required to accomplish the objectives.

   b.   In the **percentage-of-sales approach,** marketers multiply a firm's past sales, plus a factor for planned sales growth or decline, by a standard percentage based on what the firm traditionally spends on advertising and what the industry averages.

   c.   In the **competition-matching approach,** marketers try to match their major competitors' appropriations in terms of absolute dollars or to allocate the same percentage of sales for advertising that competitors allocate.

   d.   In the **arbitrary approach,** a high-level executive in the firm states how much can be spent on advertising for a certain time period.

E.   Developing the media plan

1.   Advertisers spend tremendous amounts of money on advertising media. To derive the maximum results from media expenditures, a marketer must develop an effective media plan. A **media plan** sets forth the exact media vehicles to be used and the dates and times the advertisements will run.

2.   The media planner's primary goal is to reach the largest number of persons in the advertising target per dollar spent on media.

   a.   *Reach* refers to the percentage of consumers in the target audience actually exposed to a particular advertisement in a stated period of time.

   b.   *Frequency* is the number of times these targeted consumers are exposed to the advertisements.

3.   When selecting media, the planner must first decide which kinds of media to use.

a.   The major types of media are radio, television, newspapers, magazines, direct mail, outdoor displays, mass transit vehicles, or a combination of two or more of these.

b.   After choosing the major types of media to be used, the planner decides on the specific subclasses within each medium.

4.   Media planners must consider many factors when formulating the media plan.

a.   They should analyze the location and demographic characteristics of people in the advertising target because the various media appeal to particular demographic groups in particular locations.

b.   They should consider the sizes and types of audiences specific media reach.

5.   The cost of media is an important but troublesome consideration. Media planners should try to obtain the best coverage possible for each dollar spent.

6.   The message content sometimes affects the types of media used.

a.   Print media can be used more effectively than broadcast media to present many issues or numerous details.

b.   When colors, patterns, and textures are important, media that can yield high-quality reproduction, such as magazines or television, should be used.

7.   The variety of vehicles indicates the vast number of alternatives from which media planners may choose.

a.   The multitude of factors that affect media rates obviously add to the complexity of media planning.

b.   A **cost comparison indicator** lets an advertiser compare the cost of several vehicles within a specific medium relative to the number of persons reached by each vehicle.

F.   Creating the advertising message

1.   The basic content and form of an advertising message are a function of several factors.

   a.   The product's features, uses, and benefits affect the content of the message.

   b.   Characteristics of people in the advertising target, including sex, age, education, race, income, occupation, and other attributes, influence both the content and the form.

   c.   Objectives and platform of the advertising campaign

      (1)   If a firm's advertising objectives involve large sales increases, the message may have to be stated in hard-hitting, high-impact language and symbols; when campaign objectives aim at increasing brand awareness, the message may use repetition of the brand name and words and illustrations associated with it.

      (2)   The platform is the foundation on which campaign messages are built.

   d.   Type of media used

      (1)   Effective outdoor displays and short broadcast spot announcements require concise, simple messages.

      (2)   Magazine and newspaper advertisements can include numerous details and long explanations.

      (3)   Some magazine publishers print **regional issues,** in which advertisements and editorials are different in different geographic regions. A precise message content can be tailored to a particular geographic section of the advertising target.

2.   The basic components of a print advertising message are copy and artwork.

a.   **Copy** is the verbal portion of the advertisement and includes headlines, subheadlines, body copy, and the signature.

    (1)   The headline is critical because it is often the only part of the copy that people read. It should attract readers' attention and create enough interest to make them want to read the body copy.

    (2)   The subheadline links the headline to body copy and sometimes helps explain the headline.

    (3)   Body copy consists of an introductory statement or paragraph, several explanatory paragraphs, and a closing paragraph.

    (4)   The signature contains the firm's trademark, name, and address, identifying the sponsor. It should be attractive, legible, distinctive, and easy to identify in a variety of sizes.

    (5)   Radio copy should be informal and conversational and consist of short, familiar terms, to attract listeners' attention and result in greater impact.

    (6)   Television copy should neither overpower nor be overpowered by the visual material.

b.   **Artwork** consists of the illustration and the layout of the advertisement.

    (1)   Although **illustrations** are often photographs, they can also be presented in forms such as drawings, graphs, charts, and tables. Illustrations are used to attract attention, encourage the audience to read or listen to the copy, communicate an idea quickly, or communicate an idea that is difficult to put into words.

    (2)   The **layout** is the physical arrangement of the illustration, headline, subheadline, body copy, and signature.

c.   A **storyboard** is a mockup combining copy and visual material to show the sequence of major scenes in the commercial.

G. Executing the advertising campaign

1. The execution of an advertising campaign requires an extensive amount of planning and coordination.

2. Implementation requires detailed schedules to ensure that various phases of the work are completed on time. Advertising management personnel must evaluate the quality of work and take corrective action when necessary.

H. Evaluating advertising effectiveness

1. There are a variety of ways to test the effectiveness of advertising.

    a. Measuring achievement of advertising objectives

    b. Assessing the effectiveness of copy

    c. Evaluating certain media

2. Advertising can be evaluated before, during, and after the campaign.

    a. Evaluations performed before the campaign begins are called **pretests**. To pretest advertisements, marketers sometimes use a **consumer jury,** which consists of a number of persons who are actual or potential buyers of the advertised product. During such a test, jurors are asked to judge one or several dimensions of two or more advertisements. Such tests are based on the belief that consumers are more likely than advertising experts to know what will influence them.

    b. Measurement of effectiveness during a campaign usually is accomplished by using inquiries. In the initial stages of a campaign, an advertiser may use several advertisements simultaneously, each containing a coupon or form requesting information. The advertiser records the number of returned coupons and forms and determines which advertisement generated the most response.

    c. Evaluation of advertising effectiveness after the campaign is called a **posttest**. The type of advertising objectives set by the advertiser affects the kind of posttest used.

(1) If the advertiser sets objectives in terms of communication, the posttest should measure changes in dimensions such as product awareness, brand awareness, or attitude change.

(2) If the advertiser sets objectives in terms of sales, the posttest should measure changes in dimensions such as sales or market share.

(3) Posttest methods based on memory include recognition and recall tests.

    (a) In a **recognition test,** individual respondents are shown the actual advertisement and asked whether they recognize it.

    (b) Recall can be measured through either unaided or aided recall methods.

        (1) An **unaided recall test** is a posttest that asks subjects to identify recently seen ads but does not provide any clues.

        (2) An **aided recall test** is a posttest that asks subjects to identify recently seen ads and provides clues to jog their memory.

    (c) The major justification for using recognition and recall methods is that individuals are more likely to buy the product if they can remember an advertisement than if they cannot remember it.

III. Who develops the advertising campaign?

A. In very small firms, one or two individuals are responsible for performing advertising activities. Usually, these individuals depend heavily on personnel at local newspapers and broadcast stations for artwork, copywriting, and advice about scheduling media.

B. In certain types of large businesses, and especially in large retail organizations, advertising departments create and implement advertising campaigns. Depending on the size of the advertising program, an advertising department may consist of a few multiskilled persons or a sizable number of specialists such as copywriters, artists, media buyers, and technical production coordinators.

C. When an organization uses an advertising agency, the development of the advertising campaign is usually a joint effort of the agency and the firm.

1. The degree to which each participates in the campaign's total development depends on the working relationship between the firm and the agency. The firm ordinarily relies on the agency for copywriting, artwork, technical production, and formulation of the media plan.

2. An advertising agency can assist a business in several ways.

a. The agency, especially a large one, supplies the firm with the services of highly skilled specialists—not only copywriters, artists, and production coordinators but also media experts, researchers, and legal advisers.

b. Agency personnel are usually more objective than the firm's employees about the organization's products.

c. Agency personnel have broad experience in advertising. The services of an advertising agency can be obtained at a low or moderate cost because the agency usually receives its compensation through a 15 percent commission on media purchases.

IV. Public relations

Public relations is a broad set of communication efforts used to create and maintain favorable relationships between an organization and its publics, both internal and external.

A. Public relations tools

Companies use a variety of public relations tools to convey messages and create images.

1. Public relations material such as brochures, newsletters, company magazines, and annual reports reach and influence the various publics.

2. Corporate identity material such as logos, business cards, stationery, and signs are created to make a firm immediately recognizable.

3. Speeches can affect the organization's image.

4. Event sponsorship, in which a company pays for part or all of a special event, is an effective means of increasing brand recognition with relatively minimal investment.

5. **Publicity,** which is a part of public relations, is communication in news story form about an organization, its products, or both, that is transmitted through a mass medium at no charge.

   a. The most common publicity-based tool is the **news release,** or press release, which is usually a single page of typewritten copy containing fewer than 300 words.

   b. A **feature article** is a longer manuscript (up to 3,000 words) prepared for a specific publication.

   c. A **captioned photograph** is a photograph with a brief description explaining the picture's content.

   d. A **press conference** is a meeting called to announce major news events.

   e. Publicity-based public relations tools have several advantages including credibility, news value, significant word-of-mouth communications, and a perception of being endorsed by the media, as well as a relatively low cost.

B. Evaluating public relations effectiveness

   1. Because of the potential benefits of good public relations, it is essential that organizations evaluate the effectiveness of their public relations campaigns.

   2. A public relations audit is used to determine a corporate image among an organization's publics.

3. A communications audit can include a content analysis of messages, a reliability study, or a readership survey.

4. A social audit will determine the extent to which publics view the organization to be socially responsible.

C. Dealing with unfavorable public relations

1. A single negative event that produces unfavorable public relations can wipe out a company's favorable image and destroy positive consumer attitudes that took years to build through expensive advertising campaigns and other types of promotional efforts.

2. Organizations can directly reduce incidents and events through safety programs, inspections, and effective quality control procedures.

3. Because negative events can happen to even the most cautious firms, organizations should have predetermined plans in place to handle them when they occur so as to reduce the adverse impact.

4. By being forthright with the press and public and taking prompt action, firms may be able to convince the public of their honest attempts to deal with the situation, and news personnel might be more willing to help explain complex issues to the public.

CLASS EXERCISES, DEBATE ISSUE, AND CHAPTER QUIZ

On the following pages, you will find two class exercises, a debate issue, and a chapter quiz. These are formatted in large-size type so that you can use them as class handouts or for making transparencies. Below are the authors' comments on the class exercises, the debate topic, and the answers to the chapter quiz.

Class Exercise 1: The objective of this exercise is to recognize the purpose and uses of advertising and to evaluate the effectiveness of various advertisements.

You can present this exercise in various ways. One way is to bring in copies of magazines or newspapers. A second way is to show the class videotapes of commercials that you supply. Either approach makes for an interesting class discussion. Instructor flexibility is required because your students' answers depend on what medium you select.

Question 1. Review the advertisements and complete the following:

Identify ads that represent:

_____ a. Institutional advertising (promotes organizational images, ideas, or political issues)

_____ b. Product advertising (promotes the uses, features, images, and benefits of a selected product)

_____ c. Pioneer advertising (informs about a product's uses to stimulate primary demand without referring to specific brand)

_____ d. Competitive advertising (to stimulate selective demand, points out brand's uses, features, and advantages that benefit consumers)

_____ e. Comparative advertising (two or more specified brands are compared on the basis of one or more attributes)

_____ f. Reminder advertising (lets consumers know that brand is still around and has certain uses, characteristics, and benefits)

Question 2. Evaluate the effectiveness of the ads.

a. Local print or television ads are often cluttered, with jumbled attempts at several messages. These advertisers seem to think, "I'm paying for this space and I'm going to get as much in as I can!"

b. Students are quick to point out that some ads (particularly TV) have little relevance for them. Remind them that they might not be in the target audience.

Class Exercise 2: The purpose of this exercise is to assess the effectiveness of advertising slogans regarding what they communicate and how memorable they are. Answers:

1. "Aim high"	**U.S. Air Force**
2. "Just do it"	**Nike**
3. "Make a run for the border"	**Taco Bell**
4. "A mind is a terrible thing to waste"	**United Negro College Fund**
5. "Quality is job #1"	**Ford**
6. "You've got the right one, baby"	**Pepsi**
7. "It keeps on going and going"	**Energizer batteries**
8. "It just feels right"	**Mazda**
9. "Play hard"	**Reebok**
10. "Nothing beats the Copper Top"	**Duracell**
11. "The heartbeat of America"	**Chevrolet**
12. "Just for the taste of it"	**Diet Coke**
13. "Engineered like no other car in the world"	**Mercedes-Benz**
14. "If you don't look good, we don't look good"	**Vidal Sassoon**
15. "Your true voice"	**AT&T**

Debate Issue: Is using celebrities in an ad campaign a good way to stimulate brand appeal?

Chapter Quiz: Answers to multiple-choice questions are

1.	d	3.	a
2.	a	4.	a

CLASS EXERCISE 1

REVIEW THE ADVERTISEMENTS AND COMPLETE THE FOLLOWING:

1. Identify ads that represent:
   a. Institutional advertising (promotes organizational images, ideas, or political issues)
   b. Product advertising (promotes the uses, features, images, and benefits of a selected product)
   c. Pioneer advertising (informs about a product's uses to stimulate primary demand without referring to specific brand)
   d. Competitive advertising (to stimulate selective demand, points out brand's uses, features, and advantages that benefit consumers)
   e. Comparative advertising (two or more specified brands are compared on the basis of one or more attributes)
   f. Reminder advertising (lets consumers know that brand is still around and has certain uses, characteristics, and benefits)
   g. Reinforcement advertising (ensures current users that they have made the right choice)

2. Evaluate the effectiveness of the ads
   a. Does it have a clear objective?
   b. Are the issues or selling points important to the target audiences?

CLASS EXERCISE 2

IDENTIFY THE COMPANY OR BRAND THAT IS ASSOCIATED WITH EACH SLOGAN.

1. "Aim high"
2. "Just do it"
3. "Make a run for the border"
4. "A mind is a terrible thing to waste"
5. "Quality is job 1"
6. "You've got the right one, baby"
7. "It keeps on going and going"
8. "It just feels right"
9. "Play hard"
10. "Nothing beats the Copper Top"
11. "The heartbeat of America"
12. "Just for the taste of it"
13. "Engineered like no other car in the world"
14. "If you don't look good, we don't look good"
15. "Your true voice"

DEBATE ISSUE

IS USING CELEBRITIES IN AN AD CAMPAIGN A GOOD WAY TO STIMULATE BRAND APPEAL?

<u>YES</u>

- Reinforces and legitimizes use of the product

- Especially effective when celebrity is spokesperson over a long time period

- Breeds familiarity and trust between celebrity and customers

- Effective with children

<u>NO</u>

- Good at stimulating awareness but not brand appeal

- Celebrities are paid so consumers don't trust what they say

- Trust further dampened when celebrity endorses two different products

- Can backfire if truth of celebrity's lack of use of the product is made public

- Celebrity can develop a negative image which can rub off on the brand or organization

CHAPTER QUIZ

1. The incorrect assumption that sales create advertising is a disadvantage of which approach to setting the advertising budget?
   a. Arbitrary approach
   b. Objective-and-task approach
   c. Match competition approach
   d. Percent-of-sales approach
   e. Consumer-survey approach

2. Advertising campaign objectives that are aimed at making customers' attitudes more favorable are stated in
   a. communication terms.
   b. sales terms.
   c. demand terms.
   d. market terms.
   e. survey terms.

3. If Troy Products Company advertises a specific product very heavily, and Carbone Products Company wants to offset the effects of that advertisement, Carbone would most likely employ _____ advertising.
   a. competitive
   b. pioneer
   c. institutional
   d. primary
   e. target

4. Which of the following is the *most* commonly used type of publicity-based public relations tool?
   a. News release
   b. Captioned photograph
   c. Feature article
   d. Press conference
   e. Letter to the editor

ANSWERS TO DISCUSSION AND REVIEW QUESTIONS

1. What is the difference between institutional and product advertising?

    Institutional advertising promotes organizational images, ideas, and political issues. Product advertising promotes goods and services. It is used by businesses, governments, and private, nonbusiness organizations to promote the uses, features, images, and benefits of their goods and services.

2. When should advertising be used to stimulate primary demand? When should advertising be used to stimulate selective demand?

    In the introductory stage of the product life cycle, advertising is used to stimulate primary demand. This advertising generally is referred to as *pioneer* advertising because it stimulates demand for products in a general product category. When competitors enter the market, competitive advertising stimulates selective demand by pointing out each brand's uses, features, and advantages.

3. What are the major steps in creating an advertising campaign?

    The major steps in the creation of an advertising campaign are the following:
    a. Identify and analyze an advertising target.
    b. Define the advertising objectives.
    c. Create the advertising platform.
    d. Determine the advertising appropriation.
    e. Develop the media plan.
    f. Create the message.
    g. Evaluate the effectiveness of the advertising.

4. What is a target audience? How does a marketer analyze the target audience after it has been identified?

    The advertising target is the group of people toward whom the advertisements are aimed. After identifying the advertising target, the marketer generally analyzes it with regard to location and geographic distribution of persons; distribution of age, income, race, sex, and education; and consumers' attitudes regarding purchase and use of both the advertiser's products and competitors' products. The exact kind of information needed depends on the type of product being advertised, the characteristics of the target, and the type and amount of competition.

5. Why is it necessary to define advertising objectives?

    Advertising objectives must be defined to give the development of the campaign direction and purpose.

6. What is an advertising platform, and how is it used?

An advertising platform consists of the basic issues or selling points that an advertiser wishes to include in the advertising campaign. The advertising platform is used as the base from which to develop the message.

7. What factors affect the size of an advertising budget? What techniques are used to determine this budget?

The size of the geographic market and the distribution of the buyers within it influence the amount of an advertising budget. Also, the type of product—industrial, consumer durable, or consumer convenience item—affects the proportion of revenue appropriated for advertising.

Techniques used for determining the advertising budget include the objective-and-task approach, the percent-of-sales approach, the competition-matching approach, and the arbitrary approach. The objective-and-task approach involves determining the objectives of the advertising campaign and ascertaining the tasks necessary to accomplish them. After the tasks are determined, their costs are added to compute the amount of the total appropriation. In the percent-of-sales approach, the marketer simply multiplies the firm's past sales, forecasted sales, or a combination of the two by a standard percentage based on what the firm traditionally has spent on advertising or based on industry averages. In the competition-matching approach, the advertiser tries to match major competitors' appropriations in terms of absolute dollars or percent of sales. In the arbitrary approach, a high-level executive in the firm states how much can be spent on advertising for a certain period.

8. Describe the steps required in developing a media plan.

First, the planner decides which general kinds of media to use and selects specific subclasses within each medium. Then the planner selects the specific media vehicles to be used. Finally, the planner creates a time schedule showing the dates and/or times the advertisements will run.

9. What is the function of copy in an advertising message?

Copy is used to attract readers' attention and create interest. It also identifies a specific desire or problem of consumers, suggests the advertised product as the best way to solve that problem, states the advantages and benefits of the product, indicates why the advertised product is the best for the buyer's particular situation, substantiates the claims and advantages of the product, and asks the buyer to take action.

10. What role does an advertising agency play in developing an advertising campaign?

If a firm uses an advertising agency, the development of the advertising campaign is usually a joint effort, with the agency performing such functions as copywriting, artwork, technical production, and formulation of the media plan. The use of an agency provides a firm with highly skilled specialists who are generally more objective than the firm's employees and have more experience in advertising. In addition, the cost to the firm is generally low or moderate.

11. Discuss several ways to posttest the effectiveness of advertising.

Posttest evaluation of advertising may be performed in several ways, and the specific dimensions to be tested are determined by the advertising objectives. If the objectives are set in communication terms, posttests may include consumer surveys and experiments. If the objectives are stated in terms of sales, effectiveness can be determined by ascertaining changes in sales or in market share that are attributable to the advertising campaign. However, because of the expense associated with consumer surveys and experiments and the problems in determining the direct effects of advertising on sales, many advertisers use recognition and recall tests to evaluate advertising. In recognition tests, each respondent is shown the actual advertisement and asked if he or she recognizes it. In recall tests, the respondent is not shown the actual advertisement but instead is asked about what advertisements he or she has seen recently.

12. What is public relations? Whom can an organization reach through public relations?

Public relations is a broad set of communication efforts used to create and maintain favorable relationships between an organization and its publics. Through public relations, organizations can reach internal and external publics including customers, suppliers, employees, stockholders, the media, educators, potential investors, government officials, and society in general.

13. How do organizations use public relations tools? Give several examples that you observed recently.

Organizations can use public relations tools for a single purpose or for several purposes. Public relations tools are used by organizations to make people aware of its products, brands, or activities, but they are also used to create a specific company image. Public relations tools are also used to maintain an organization's positive visibility and to overcome negative images. On the second part of the question, students' answers will vary.

14. Explain the problems and limitations associated with publicity-based public relations.

Limitations of publicity-based public relations arise from requirements of media personnel that the messages be newsworthy, timely, and accurate. Many communications that a firm wishes to present through publicity-based public relations do not quality as newsworthy. Organizations have little control over the content or timing of publicity releases and no control over the locations in which the releases are presented. Therefore, messages sometimes appear in locations or at times that may not reach an organization's target audiences.

15. In what ways is the effectiveness of public relations evaluated?

Organizations evaluate the effectiveness of public relations in a variety of ways. Environmental monitoring, public relations audits, communications audits, and social audits are all research methods used to determine how effectively a firm is communicating its messages or images to its publics. Another approach to measuring the effectiveness of publicity-based public relations is to count the number of exposures in the media. Because counting the number of exposures doesn't reveal how many people actually receive the message, organizations also measure changes in product awareness, knowledge, and attitudes resulting from specific public relations campaigns.

15. What are some sources of negative public relations? How should an organization deal with negative public relations?

Although public relations is a planned activity, uncontrolled events can result in negative public relations. Some sources of negative public relations can include news stories about unsafe products, accidents involving an organization, such as a plane crash, or controversial actions taken by employees. One way to handle negative public relations is to avoid events (such as accidents) that generate negative publicity. An organization needs a definite set of policies and procedures to deal with coverage of negative events and to lessen their effects. In most situations, the best approach is to facilitate coverage rather than try to hide the event or reduce coverage. If the organization expedites coverage, less misinformation and fewer rumors are likely to result.

COMMENTS ON THE CASES

Case 18.1   The Advertising Council: Advertising for Good, Not for Gain

This case focuses on increasing students' awareness of the Advertising Council, its purposes, and its accomplishments. We hope this case will increase students' understanding of how a coalition of individuals and organizations in the advertising industry is attempting to deal with the social ills of our country.

The first question asks in what ways the process for developing the Ad Council's campaigns would differ from the process discussed in this chapter. While the manner in which the work gets done may vary, the overall process is similar to the process discussed in the text. Target audiences must be defined; advertising objectives and platforms must be established. Since public service announcements are used, only small budgets are required. Media must be selected and messages developed. Plans for implementation are developed and executed, and finally the campaigns are evaluated.

Question 2 asks who selects the topics for the Ad Council's campaigns and who creates the campaigns. Potential topics are suggested by a broad range of groups, including social organizations, advocacy groups, and government agencies. The Advertising Council's board of directors is advised by a committee called the Advisory Committee on Public Issues as to which issues or topics are to be included in Ad Council campaigns. The campaigns are created by a number of advertising industry personnel and ad agencies. The work is done on a volunteer basis.

The third question asks whether publicity plays a role in the Ad Council's campaigns. Publicity does play a small role in the Ad Council's campaigns. A number of news stories appear regarding the initiation of new campaigns as well as news stories about the impact of campaigns. In addition, other organizations at times get involved in promotional efforts that bring additional visibility to issues. These organizations sometimes sponsor student essay or poster contests.

The final question asks how the advertising effectiveness of the Ad Council's campaigns is measured. The issues on which the Ad Council focuses are major social problems for which change occurs slowly and for which measurement of change is often difficult. The advertising objectives established by the Ad Council typically are communication objectives aimed at attitude changes and behavioral changes. Effectiveness is thus measured in terms of changes in behavior and changes in people's awareness and attitudes.

Video Information

Video Title: The Advertising Council Historical Reel
Location: Tape 3, Segment 18
Length: 16:00
Video Overview: The Advertising Council is a nonprofit organization that develops advertising campaigns to inform and educate the public, change attitudes, and combat social problems. The council was created during World War II to motivate Americans to help with the war effort in a variety of ways. Its efforts were so successful that the word *war* was later dropped from the council's name as it began its efforts to educate and inform the public. Advertisements are created by volunteers, and the media donate space and time. Some of the Advertising Council's successful campaigns include ones to prevent drunk driving; to increase contributions to the United Negro College Fund; to encourage recycling and blood donation; to recruit new teachers; to help teenage runaways, child abuse victims, and rape victims; and to prevent AIDS and cancer. What the council's success reveals is that advertising is a powerful tool that can be used to sell more than merchandise.

Multiple-Choice Questions About the Video

c   1. The original name of the Advertising Council when it was created in 1942 was
       a. the United States Radio Bureau.
       b. the War Information Network.
       c. the War Advertising Council.
       d. the United States Information Bureau.
       e. the War Advertising Bureau.

d   2. Two of the Advertising Council's earliest well-known television commercials encouraged Americans to
       a. vote and prevent forest fires.
       b. stop littering and donate money to colleges and universities.
       c. carpool to work and donate blood.
       d. prevent forest fires and stop littering.
       e. attend church and stop littering.

b   3. During the 1970s, the Advertising Council faced difficulties because
       a. the media reduced the amount of time and space it donated to the council's advertising campaigns.
       b. the subjects of its advertising campaigns became more controversial.
       c. the federal government began exerting more control over the council's activities.
       d. its operating budget was greatly reduced.
       e. studies revealed that many of the council's campaigns were ineffective.

b   4. According to the video, since 1983 the Advertising Council's campaign to prevent drunk driving has reduced alcohol-related highway deaths by _____ percent.
       a. 15
       b. 11
       c. 50
       d. 25
       e. 31

Case 18.2   Marvel Entertainment's Public Relations Efforts to Keep Its Heroes Flying High

The objective of this case is to provide students with an example of how an organization uses public relations as a major part of its promotion mix. Many students will be familiar with this product and should participate enthusiastically in discussions regarding the Marvel Entertainment Company.

The first question asks what major public relations tools Marvel Entertainment uses. This organization is a heavy user of press releases. Marvel Entertainment also sponsors events to generate visibility for its characters and company. Because of its content and format, the annual report issued by Marvel Entertainment generates visibility for the organization.

Question 2 asks students to describe and evaluate Marvel Entertainment's use of its annual report as a public relations tool. Marvel Entertainment's annual report is in the form of a comic book, which is a significant departure from a normal corporation's annual report. This unique publication draws a great deal of interest from the media, which is translated into a number of news stories. Publicity regarding Marvel Entertainment's annual report appears in *USA Today,* the *Wall Street Journal,* on major television networks, and on radio talk shows.

Question 3 informs students that Marvel Entertainment's revelation that Peter Parker was a clone rather than a human resulted in negative public relations for the organization. Students are then asked to recommend actions that Marvel could take to turn this set of circumstances into a positive situation with the potential for favorable public relations. This question provides students with an opportunity to suggest very creative ideas to help Marvel Entertainment turn a negative situation into a positive one. Obviously, students' suggestions will vary considerably. During the discussion of this question, you have an opportunity to relate how other organizations have faced negative public relations and have taken courses of action that turned a problem around and treated it as an opportunity to generate favorable public relations.

19 PERSONAL SELLING AND SALES PROMOTION

TEACHING RESOURCES QUICK REFERENCE GUIDE

Resource	Location
Purpose and Perspective	IRM, p. 414
Guide for Using Color Transparencies	IRM, p. 414
Lecture Outline	IRM, p. 414
Class Exercises, Debate Issue, and Chapter Quiz	IRM, p. 429
Class Exercise 1	IRM, p. 431
Class Exercise 2	IRM, p. 432
Debate Issue: Do coupons make consumers more "brand loyal"?	IRM, p. 433
Chapter Quiz	IRM, p. 434
Answers to Discussion and Review Questions	IRM, p. 435
Comments on the Cases	IRM, p. 440
Case 19.1	IRM, p. 440
Video	Tape 3, Segment 19
Video Information	IRM, p. 440
Multiple-Choice Questions About the Video	IRM, p. 441
Case 19.2	IRM, p. 441
Transparency Acetates	Transparency package
Examination Questions: Essay	TB, p. 347
Examination Questions: Multiple-Choice	TB, p. 348
Examination Questions: True-False	TB, p. 361
Author-Selected Multiple-Choice Test Items	TB, p. 448

PURPOSE AND PERSPECTIVE

This chapter covers in detail two promotion mix elements—personal selling and sales promotion. To help students build a better understanding of the purposes and roles of salespeople, we initially discuss the basic elements of the personal selling process and the types of salespeople used in organizations. Because this book is based on a managerial framework, much of the section on personal selling is devoted to a discussion of sales management decisions and activities. The topics covered include establishing sales force objectives; determining the size of the sales force; and recruiting, selecting, training, compensating, motivating, routing, scheduling, and controlling salespeople.

Then we discuss how sales promotion activities are blended with other elements in a promotion mix. We also cover the objectives for which organizations use sales promotion. Finally, we classify and present major characteristics of a number of sales promotion methods.

GUIDE FOR USING COLOR TRANSPARENCIES

There are two groups of color transparencies. The transparencies identified by a double number are the same as the figures in the text. The transparencies labeled with a number and a letter are illustrations that do not appear in the text, but they can be used as additional examples of concepts discussed.

Figure 19.1	General steps in the personal selling process
Figure 19.6	Proportion of promotional expenditures allocated to advertising, consumer sales promotion, and trade sales promotion
Figure 19A	Chapter 19 outline
Figure 19B	Major sales management decision areas
Figure 19C	Percent of salespeople who meet or exceed their sales quotas
Figure 19D	Major types of sales force compensation methods
Figure 19E	Food, beverage, and beauty aid manufacturers' use of consumer sales promotion methods
Figure 19F	Example of sampling through physicians
Figure 19G	Hilton teams up with frequent flyer programs to build customer loyalty.
Figure 19H	Example of a manufacturer's coupon

LECTURE OUTLINE

I.   The nature of personal selling

Personal selling is personal, paid communication that attempts to inform customers and persuade them to purchase products in an exchange situation.

A.   There are two primary advantages of personal selling.

1. Personal selling provides marketers with their greatest freedom to adjust a message to satisfy customers' information needs.

2. Personal selling is precise; it enables marketers to focus on the most promising sales prospects.

B. A major disadvantage of personal selling is its cost. Generally, it is the most expensive element in the promotion mix.

C. Primary purposes of personal selling

1. Identifying potential buyers who are interested in an organization's products is a critical element in the personal selling process.

2. Convincing prospects to buy

   a. Because most potential buyers seek certain types of information before they make a purchase decision, salespersons must ascertain prospects' informational needs and then provide the relevant information.

   b. To achieve this purpose, sales personnel must be well trained in their products and the selling process in general.

3. Keeping customers satisfied

   a. Marketers depend on repeat sales for long-term survival. To obtain repeat purchases, a company must keep its customers satisfied.

   b. To accomplish this purpose, sales efforts often are directed toward providing buyers with information and service after the sale.

   c. Such activities allow a salesperson to evaluate the strengths and weaknesses of the company's product and other marketing mix ingredients. These observations can be used to develop and maintain a marketing mix that can better satisfy both customers and the firm.

II. Elements of the personal selling process

A.   Prospecting

1.   Developing a list of potential customers is called **prospecting,** and it is the first element in the selling process.

2.   A salesperson seeks the names of prospects from several sources, including company sales records, referrals, trade shows, public records, telephone directories, trade association directories, among others.

3.   After developing the prospect list, a salesperson evaluates prospects to determine if they are able, willing, and authorized to buy the product.

B.   Preapproach

1.   After developing a list of prospects, but before contacting them, a salesperson should find and analyze information regarding prospects' specific product needs, current use of brands, feelings about available brands, and personal characteristics.

2.   The more information about a prospect that a salesperson has, the better able he or she is to develop an approach and presentation that will precisely communicate with the prospect.

C.   Approach

1.   The **approach**—the manner in which a salesperson contacts a potential customer—is a critical step in the sales process because the prospect's first impression of the salesperson may be a lasting one with long-term consequences.

2.   Types of approaches

a.   In the referral approach, the salesperson explains to a prospect that an acquaintance, an associate, or a relative suggested the call.

b.   In the cold canvass technique, the salesperson calls on potential customers without their prior consent.

      c.   In the repeat contact approach, the salesperson mentions a prior meeting.

    3.   The type of approach used depends on the salesperson's preferences, the product being sold, the firm's resources, and the characteristics of the product.

D.   Making the presentation

    1.   During the sales presentation, the salesperson must attract and hold the prospect's attention to stimulate interest and develop desire for the product.

    2.   During the presentation, the salesperson must not only talk but also listen to gain information about the prospect's specific information needs.

E.   Overcoming objections

    1.   One of the best ways to overcome a prospect's objections is to anticipate and counter them before the prospect has an opportunity to raise them. This approach can be risky because the salesperson may mention some objections that the prospect would not have raised.

    2.   If possible, the salesperson should handle objections when they arise. An effective salesperson usually seeks out a prospect's objections to answer them because these may keep the prospect from buying.

F.   Closing the sale

    1.   **Closing** is the stage in the selling process when the salesperson asks the prospect to buy the product(s).

    2.   During the presentation, the salesperson may use a "trial close" by asking questions that assume the prospect will buy the product.

        a.   The reactions to such questions usually indicate how close the prospect is to buying.

        b.   The trial close allows prospects to indicate indirectly that they will buy the product without having to say the difficult words, "I'll take it."

3. Closing often serves as an important stimulus to uncover hidden objections.

G. Following up

1. If attempts to close the sale are successful, the salesperson must follow up the sale.

2. In the follow-up stage, the salesperson should determine if the order was delivered on time and was installed properly; should learn whether the customer has problems or questions about the product; and should determine the customer's future product needs.

III. Types of salespersons

A. Order getters

1. An **order getter** is the salesperson who sells to new customers and increases sales to present customers.

2. Order-getting activities are sometimes divided into two categories.

   a. Current-customer sales—sales personnel concentrate on current customers, calling on people and organizations that have purchased products from the firm at least once.

   b. New-business sales—sales personnel are responsible for locating prospects and converting them into buyers.

B. Order takers

1. An **order taker** is the salesperson who primarily seeks repeat sales. This repetitive task is necessary to perpetuate long-lasting, satisfying relationships with customers.

2. Order takers can be classified into two groups.

a. Inside order takers—salespersons located in sales offices who receive orders by mail and telephone. That does not mean, however, that inside order takers never communicate with customers face to face.

b. Field order takers—also referred to as outside order takers, salespersons who travel to customers. A customer and a field order taker often become interdependent.

C. Support personnel

1. **Support personnel** are sales staff members who facilitate the selling function but usually are involved with more than making sales. Activities support personnel perform include locating prospects, educating customers, building goodwill, and providing service after the sale.

2. There are three common types of support personnel.

   a. **Missionary salespersons,** usually employed by manufacturers, assist the producer's customers in selling to their own customers.

   b. **Trade salespersons** direct much of their efforts toward helping customers, especially retail stores, promote the products. Food producers and processors commonly use trade salespersons.

   c. **Technical salespersons** direct their efforts toward the organization's current customers by providing technical assistance regarding dimensions such as applications of the product, system designs, product characteristics, and installation procedures. Technical sales personnel frequently are employed to sell technical industrial products.

IV. Management of the sales force

Effective sales force management is an important determinant of a firm's success because the sales force is directly responsible for generating an organization's primary inputs—sales revenue.

A. Establishing sales force objectives

1. Sales objectives tell salespersons what they are to accomplish during a specified period. They give the sales force direction and purpose.

2. Sales objectives should be stated in precise, measurable terms and be specific about the time period and geographic areas involved.

3. Sales objectives usually are established for both the total sales force and individual salespersons.

   a. Objectives for the entire force are usually stated in terms of sales volume, market share, or profit.

   b. Sales objectives for individual salespersons are commonly stated in terms of dollars or unit sales volume.

B. Determining sales force size

1. The size of the sales force affects the firm's ability to generate sales and profits, the compensation methods used, salespersons' morale, and overall sales force management.

2. Several analytical methods are used to determine the size of the sales force.

C. Recruiting and selecting salespeople

1. **Recruiting** is a process by which the sales manager develops a list of qualified applicants for sales positions.

2. A set of required qualifications should be established by the sales manager before recruiting to ensure that the recruiting process results in a pool of qualified salespersons.

3. There is no set of general characteristics that a sales manager can use to ensure the recruitment of good sales personnel. A sales manager must develop a set of characteristics that is especially well suited for sales tasks in the particular company.

   a. The sales manager should prepare a job description that enumerates the specific tasks to be performed by salespersons.

   b. The sales manager should analyze the characteristics of the firm's successful as well as ineffective salespersons.

4. A sales manager usually recruits applicants from several sources: departments within the firm, other firms, employment agencies, educational institutions, respondents to advertisements, and individuals recommended by current employees.

5. The process for hiring a sales force varies from one company to another. Companies that are especially concerned about reducing sales force turnover are likely to have strict recruiting and selection procedures.

6. Recruitment should be a continuous activity aimed at reaching the best applicants. The selection process should be a systematic procedure that effectively matches applicants' characteristics and needs with the requirements of specific selling tasks.

D. Training sales personnel

Many organizations have formal training programs; others depend on informal on-the-job training.

1. Who should be trained?

   a. Training programs can be aimed at newly hired salespersons, experienced salespersons, or both.

   b. Training programs can be directed toward the entire sales force or toward one segment of it.

2. Where and when should training occur?

   a. Sales training may be performed in the field, at educational institutions, in company facilities, or in several of these locations.

   b. In some firms, recently hired salespersons receive the bulk of their training before being assigned to a specific sales position. Other business organizations put new recruits into the field immediately and provide formal training only after the new salesperson has gained some experience. Training programs can be as short as several days or as long as three years or more. Sales training often tends to be a series of recurring training efforts. Sales management must determine the frequency, sequencing, and duration of these activities.

E.   Compensating salespeople

1.   Desirable characteristics of a compensation plan

    a.   A compensation plan should attract, motivate, and retain the most effective individuals.

    b.   A compensation plan should be designed to give sales management the desired level of control and to provide sales personnel with acceptable levels of freedom, income, and incentive.

    c.   A compensation plan should be flexible, equitable, easy to administer, and easy to understand.

    d.   A good compensation program should facilitate and encourage proper treatment of customers.

2.   To create compensation programs, the developers must determine the level of compensation required and the most desirable method of calculating it.

    a.   In analyzing the required compensation level, a firm's sales management tries to ascertain a salesperson's value to the company on the basis of the tasks and responsibilities associated with the sales position. A salesperson's value to the firm is affected by several factors:

        (1)   Salaries of other types of personnel in the firm

        (2)   Competitors' compensation plans

        (3)   Cost of sales force turnover

        (4)   Size of nonsalary selling expenses

    b.   To deliver the required compensation, a firm may have one or more of three basic compensation methods.

       (1)   In a **straight salary compensation plan,** salespeople are paid a specified amount per time period, and this sum remains the same until they receive a pay increase or decrease.

       (2)   In a **straight commission compensation plan,** salespersons' compensation is determined solely by the amount of their sales for a given period. A commission may be based on a single percentage of sales or on a sliding scale that involves several sales levels and percentage rates.

       (3)   In a **combination compensation plan,** salespeople are paid a fixed salary and a commission based on sales volume.

F.   Motivating salespeople

   1.   A sales manager should develop a systematic approach for motivating salespersons to obtain high productivity.

   2.   Effective sales force motivation is achieved through an organized set of activities performed continuously by the company's sales management.

   3.   Although financial compensation is important, a motivational program must also satisfy salespersons' nonfinancial needs. Sales personnel, like other people, join organizations to satisfy personal needs and achieve personal goals. Positive motivational incentives (nonfinancial) include such things as enjoyable working conditions, power and authority, job security, and an opportunity to excel.

   4.   Sales contests and other incentive programs that offer an opportunity to earn additional rewards can be effective motivators.

G.   Managing sales territories

The effectiveness of a sales force that must travel to its customers depends on sales management's decisions regarding sales territories.

   1.   Creating sales territories

       a.   Territory size

(1)   Sales managers usually try to create territories that have similar sales potential or to develop territories that require about the same amount of work.

    (a)   Territories with equal sales potential usually will be unequal in geographic size. This causes salespersons with larger territories to have to work harder and longer to generate a specific sales volume.

    (b)   Territories that require equal amounts of work will cause salespersons who are compensated totally or partially by commissions to have unequal income potential.

(2)   Many sales managers try to balance territorial workloads and earning potential by using differential commission rates.

b.   Territory shape

(1)   The territories must be constructed so that sales potential can be measured.

(2)   The shape of territories should facilitate salespersons' activities to provide the best possible coverage of customers.

(3)   The territories should be designed to minimize selling costs.

(4)   The density and distribution of customers influence decisions regarding the shape of a territory.

2.   Routing and scheduling salespeople

a.   Several factors affect the routing and scheduling of sales personnel.

(1)   Major determinants are the geographic size and shape of a sales territory and the number and distribution of customers within it.

(2)   Frequency and duration of sales calls also affect routing and scheduling decisions.

b.   In routing and scheduling sales calls in the field, the planner must consider the sequence in which customers are called on, the specific roads or transportation schedules to be used, the number of calls to be made in a given period, and the time of day the calls will occur.

c.   Major goals of routing and scheduling should be to minimize nonselling time and maximize selling time.

H.   Controlling and evaluating sales force performance

1.   To control and evaluate sales force activities properly, sales management needs information. A sales manager gets information about salespersons from their call reports, customer feedback, and invoices.

2.   The dimensions used to measure a salesperson's performance are determined largely by the sales objectives that the sales manager sets. Indicators of performance used by sales managers include average number of calls per day, average sales per customer, actual sales relative to sales potential, number of new-customer orders, average cost per call, and average gross profit per customer.

3.   To evaluate a salesperson, a sales manager may compare one or more of these dimensions with a predetermined performance standard.

4.   After evaluating salespersons, sales managers must take corrective action when needed.

V.   The nature of sales promotion

A.   **Sales promotion** is an activity and/or material that acts as a direct inducement, offering added value or incentive for the product to resellers, salespersons, or consumers. It includes all promotional activities other than personal selling, advertising, and publicity.

B.   When an organization uses sales promotion activities, it usually intertwines them with other promotional efforts. Because the most effective sales promotion efforts usually are highly interrelated with other promotional efforts, decisions about sales promotion often affect advertising and personal selling decisions, and vice versa.

VI.   Sales promotion opportunities and limitations

A.   Sales promotion can increase sales by providing an incentive to purchase.

B.   However, excessive price-reduction sales promotion, such as couponing, can affect a brand's image.

C.   Marketers should ensure that the sales promotion objectives are consistent with the organization's overall objectives, marketing objectives, and promotional objectives.

VII. Sales promotion methods

A.   Marketers use a number of sales promotion methods. These can be grouped into two main categories: consumer and trade.

1.   **Consumer sales promotion methods** encourage or stimulate consumers to patronize a specific retail store or try a particular product.

2.   **Trade sales promotion methods** stimulate wholesalers and retailers to carry a producer's product and to market these products aggressively.

B.   A number of factors must be considered when deciding which sales promotion methods to use.

1.   The objectives of the sales promotion efforts

2.   The characteristics of the product (size, weight, costs, durability, uses, features, and hazards)

3.   The characteristics of the target market (age, sex, income, location, density, usage rate, and shopping patterns)

4.   How the product is distributed

5.   The number and types of resellers

6.   The state of the competitive environment and legal forces

C. Consumer sales promotion methods

1. **Coupons** are a written price reduction used to stimulate trial of a new or established product, to increase sales volume quickly, to attract repeat purchasers, or to introduce new package sizes or features; coupons usually reduce the purchase price of an item.

2. **Demonstrations** are a sales promotion method manufacturers use on a temporary basis to encourage trial use and purchase of the product or to show how the product actually works.

3. Frequent-user incentives such as frequent-flyer programs offered by most airlines reward consumers who engage in frequent (repeat) purchases, to foster customer loyalty to a specific company or group of cooperating companies that provide extra incentives for patronage.

4. **Point-of-purchase (P-O-P) materials** include such items as outside signs, window displays, counter pieces, display racks, and self-service cartons. These items are used to attract attention, inform customers, and encourage retailers to carry particular products.

5. **Free samples** are samples of a product given out to stimulate trial of a product, increase sales volume in the early stages of the product's life cycle, or obtain desirable distribution.

6. **Money refunds** offer consumers some money when they mail in a proof of purchase usually for multiple product purchases.

7. **Rebate** customers submit proof of purchase for a single product and are mailed a specific amount of money.

8. **Premiums** are items offered free or at a minimum cost as a bonus for purchasing a product. They can attract competitors' customers, introduce different sizes of established products, add variety to promotional efforts, and stimulate loyalty.

9. When a **cents-off offer** is used, buyers receive a certain amount off the regular price. This method is used to provide a strong incentive to try the product, stimulate product sales, yield short-lived sales increases, and promote products in off-seasons.

10.   **Consumer contests** are based on the analytical or creative skill of contestants who compete for prizes. This method is used to generate traffic at the retail level. The entrants in a **consumer sweepstakes** submit their names for inclusion in a drawing for prizes. Sweepstakes are used to stimulate lagging sales.

D.   Trade sales promotion methods

1.   A **buy-back allowance** is a certain sum of money that is given to a purchaser for each unit bought after an initial deal is over. This method is a secondary incentive in which the total amount of money that buyers can receive is proportional to their purchases during the initial trade deal.

2.   A **buying allowance** is a temporary price reduction to resellers for purchasing specified quantities of a product. Such offers are used to provide an incentive to handle a new product, achieve a temporary price reduction, or stimulate the purchase of an item in larger than normal quantities.

3.   A **scan-back allowance** is a manufacturer's reward to retailers based on the number of pieces moved through their scanners during a specific time period.

4.   The **count-and-recount** promotion method is based on the payment of a specific amount of money for each product unit moved from a reseller's warehouse in a given period. This method is used to reduce retail stockouts, clear distribution channels, and reduce warehouse inventories.

5.   **Free merchandise** sometimes is offered to resellers that purchase a stated quantity of the same or different products. Free merchandise sometimes is used in place of money as payment for allowances provided through other sales promotion methods.

6.   A **merchandise allowance** consists of a manufacturer's agreement to pay resellers certain amounts of money for providing special promotional efforts such as advertising or displays.

7.   **Cooperative advertising** is an arrangement in which a manufacturer agrees to pay a certain amount of a retailer's media costs for advertising the manufacturer's products. The amount usually allowed is based on the quantities purchased.

8. A **dealer listing** is an advertisement that promotes a product and identifies the names of participating retailers that sell the product. Dealer listings are used to influence retailers to carry the product, build traffic at the retail level, and encourage consumers to buy the product at participating dealers.

9. A **premium, or push, money,** is used in an incentive program to push a line of goods by providing additional compensation to salespeople.

10. A **sales contest** is used to motivate distributors, retailers, and sales personnel through the recognition of outstanding achievement.

11. A **dealer loader** is a gift given to a retailer that purchases a specified quantity of merchandise. Often dealer loaders are used to obtain special display efforts from retailers by offering essential display parts as premiums.

CLASS EXERCISES, DEBATE ISSUE, AND CHAPTER QUIZ

On the following pages, you will find two class exercises, a debate issue, and a chapter quiz. These are formatted in large-size type so that you can use them as class handouts or for making transparencies. Below are the authors' comments on the class exercises, the debate topic, and the answers to the chapter quiz.

Class Exercise 1: The objective for this class exercise is for students to understand and apply the steps used in personal selling.

Prospecting: developing a list of customers. After developing a list, evaluate each prospect on the basis of his/her ability, willingness, and authority to buy the product. Only such prospects (dates, teachers, parents) with potential are pursued further. Although prospecting helps salespeople be more efficient, they should be careful not to prejudge customers before getting adequate information (e.g., a poorly dressed customer may have the ability to buy).

Preapproach: find and analyze information about each prospect's specific product needs, current use of brands, feelings about available brands, and personal characteristics.

The approach: the manner in which a salesperson contacts a potential customer. The first contact is generally to assess buyers' needs and objectives. The prospect's first impression is usually a lasting one with long-run consequences. You might ask, "Why are these two stages so important?" One reason is that a customer-oriented salesperson will take the time to find out what the customer needs (satisfying those needs occurs in the presentation → application of the marketing concept). The second is the importance of the first impression. In most interviews, the company representative makes his/her mind up about the individual in the first few minutes (some say 30 seconds). Whether it is making a sale or getting a date or a job, how one first appears has a significant impact.

Making the presentation: the salesperson must attract and hold the prospect's attention to stimulate interest and stir up a desire for the product (AIDA). Product demonstrations, listening to comments, and observing responses are important.

Overcoming objections: seeking out a prospect's objections in order to address them. One of the best (though risky) ways is to anticipate and counter objections before the prospect has an opportunity to raise them. Otherwise, deal with objections when they occur or at the end of presentation.

Closing: asking the prospect to buy the product. Methods include "trial close" by asking questions that assume that prospect will buy the product. A salesperson should try to close at several points during the presentation because the prospect may be ready to buy. Although these steps generally follow this order, they are often intertwined. After students have discussed how they use these steps (with examples), you might ask, "Why is closing so important?" If given a chance to sell, most people can present and overcome objections but are hesitant to close since they are afraid of rejection. If they did a good job of preparing and listening, they should assume that the customer is ready to buy or that objections are only excuses to be overcome.

Follow-up: contacting the customer to learn what problems or questions have arisen. Follow-up may also be used to determine future needs. With the growing importance of relationship marketing, the follow-up is becoming as important as the other steps, if not more so. You might ask, "Why do some of you (or your parents) continue to buy cars from the same dealership?"

Class Exercise 2: This exercise is relatively straightforward. Almost every student will have had some contact with one or several of these salespeople. However, students usually do not think about the types of selling these people do.

Have your students classify each salesperson and then justify their answers. The most likely answers:

1. **Missionary salesperson**
2. **Order getter, new-business sales**
3. **Inside order taker**
4. **Order getter, new-business sales**
5. **Order getter, new-business sales**
6. **Order getter, new-business sales**
7. **Trade salesperson**
8. **Order getter/field order taker**
9. **Order getter, new-business sales**
10. **Field order taker**

Debate Issue: Do coupons make consumers more "brand loyal"?

Chapter Quiz: Answers to multiple-choice questions are

1.	a	3.	e
2.	e	4.	e

CLASS EXERCISE 1

EXPLAIN HOW YOU CAN USE THE SEVEN STEPS OF PERSONAL SELLING IN EVERYDAY ACTIVITIES SUCH AS DATING, ASKING PARENTS FOR MONEY, OFFERING EXCUSES TO PROFESSORS, GETTING A JOB, OR OTHER TASKS REQUIRING PERSUASION.

PROSPECTING: The salesperson must develop a list of customers.

PREAPPROACH: The salesperson must find and analyze information about each prospect's specific product needs, current use of brands, feelings about available brands, and personal characteristics.

THE APPROACH: The salesperson adopts a certain manner in contacting a potential customer. The first contact is generally to assess the buyer's needs and objectives. The prospect's first impression is usually a lasting one.

MAKING THE PRESENTATION: The salesperson must attract and hold the prospect's attention to stimulate interest. Product demonstrations, listening to comments, and observing responses are important.

OVERCOMING OBJECTIONS: One of the best ways is to anticipate and counter objections before the prospect has an opportunity to raise them. Otherwise, deal with objections when they occur.

CLOSING: The salesperson asks the prospect to buy the product. Attempt a "trial close" by asking questions that assume the prospect will buy the product. A salesperson should try to close at several points during the presentation.

FOLLOW-UP: The salesperson contacts the customer to learn what problems or questions have arisen. May also be used to determine future needs.

CLASS EXERCISE 2

SALESPERSONS ARE TYPICALLY CLASSIFIED AS ORDER GETTERS, ORDER TAKERS, AND SUPPORT PERSONNEL. HOW WOULD YOU CLASSIFY THE FOLLOWING SALESPEOPLE?

1. A pharmaceutical salesperson selling to doctors
2. A car salesperson
3. A retail store salesperson
4. A telemarketer soliciting donations for a charity
5. A real estate agent
6. A heavy equipment salesperson
7. An agent for a snack food distributor who only stocks shelves
8. A door-to-door cosmetics salesperson
9. An insurance salesperson
10. An agent for a snack food distributor who fills a retailer's orders

DEBATE ISSUE

DO COUPONS MAKE CONSUMERS MORE "BRAND LOYAL"?

<u>YES</u>	<u>NO</u>
• Good way to reward present users of a product	• Many manufacturers offer coupons; consumers will switch brands by buying those products for which they can find coupons
• Present users will use a particular brand more often	• Consumers have been trained not to buy without incentives
• Encourages consumers to purchase in larger quantities	• Truly brand-loyal consumers will buy a particular brand with or without a price incentive
• The larger the price reduction, the greater the number of consumers taking advantage of the promotion	• Temporary price reductions increase sales today at the expense of future sales

CHAPTER QUIZ

1. Suppose that to increase sales of its line of Chex cereals, Ralston Purina offered a free pound of bananas to customers who bought the large-size box. This form of sales promotion is called a
   a. premium.
   b. coupon.
   c. cents-off offer.
   d. free sample.
   e. money refund.

2. Which of the sales force compensation methods is easy to administer, yields more predictable selling expenses, and provides sales managers with a large degree of control over salespersons?
   a. Straight commission
   b. Salary plus bonus
   c. Salary and commission
   d. Straight commission and combination
   e. Straight salary

3. Which type of salespersons facilitate the selling function but are not strictly involved only with making sales?
   a. Field order takers
   b. Inside order takers
   c. Order getters who focus on current-customer sales
   d. Order getters who focus on new-business sales
   e. Support salespersons

4. Janetta Light tells her sales manager that she will be devoting more effort to _____ in the coming weeks, as her list of potential customers has dwindled below the level of thirty firms recommended by the selling plan.
   a. approaching customers
   b. preapproaching
   c. closing the sale
   d. following up
   e. prospecting

ANSWERS TO DISCUSSION AND REVIEW QUESTIONS

1. What is personal selling? How does personal selling differ from other types of promotional activities?

   Personal selling is a process of informing customers and persuading them to purchase products through personal communication in an exchange situation. It differs from other types of promotional activities in that it is the most precise method. It allows a marketer to adjust the message to satisfy a customer's information needs and to zero in on the most promising prospects instead of directing promotional efforts at a group of people.

2. What are the primary purposes of personal selling?

   The primary purposes of personal selling can be grouped into three general categories: (a) to find individuals and/or organizations that are prospective buyers; (b) to transform prospects into buyers; and (c) to maintain customer satisfaction.

3. Identify the elements of the personal selling process. Must a salesperson include all these elements when selling a product to a customer? Why or why not?

   The personal selling process consists of several elements or steps. The first step is prospecting and evaluating. This involves developing a list of potential customers. After developing a list of acceptable prospects, but before contacting a prospect, comes the preapproach step, in which the salesperson finds and analyzes information regarding the prospect's specific product needs, current brands being used, feelings about available brands, and personal characteristics. In the third step, the approach, the salesperson contacts the prospect. During the fourth step, making the presentation, the salesperson must attract and hold the prospect's attention, stimulate interest, and develop desire for the product. The fifth step is overcoming the prospect's objections. The sixth step is closing, in which the salesperson asks the prospect to buy the product or products. The seventh and final element in the selling process is the follow-up. In this stage, the salesperson contacts the buyer to see whether the order was delivered on time and was installed properly if installation was required, to see if the buyer has any problems or questions regarding the product, and to determine the buyer's future product needs. For personal selling to be effective, all seven elements should be included in the selling process.

4. How does a salesperson find and evaluate prospects? Do you consider any of these methods questionable ethically? Explain.

   A salesperson seeks the names of prospects from several sources, including company sales records, consumers' information requests from advertisements, other customers, newspaper announcements (marriages, births, deaths), public records, telephone directories, and trade association directories. After developing the prospect list, the salesperson evaluates each prospect to determine whether the prospect is able, willing, and authorized to buy the product. After this evaluation, some prospects may be deleted while others are deemed acceptable and are ranked according to their desirability or potential. The question about ethics will elicit varied responses. Some students may perceive the use of sources such as public records, directories, and announcements as unethical. Others may feel that this practice is ethical but that the sources of information are less satisfactory than are sales records and consumers' information requests.

5. Are order getters more aggressive or creative than order takers? Why or why not?

Order getters generally are considered more creative and aggressive than order takers because they are responsible for eliciting sales. These sales may be either new sales or sales to current customers. In either case, the salesperson is responsible for recognizing the potential buyer's needs and then providing the prospect with the necessary information. Order takers, on the other hand, engage in more repetitive tasks that involve perpetuating a long-lasting, satisfying relationship with customers.

6. Identify several characteristics of effective sales objectives.

Sales objectives should be stated in precise, measurable terms and be specific regarding the time period and the geographic areas involved. They are usually established for the total sales force and for each salesperson. These objectives inform salespersons about their accomplishments during a specified time period, provide the sales force with direction and purpose, and provide performance standards for the evaluation and control of sales personnel.

7. How should a sales manager establish criteria for selecting sales personnel? What do you think are the general characteristics of a good salesperson?

A sales manager must develop a set of characteristics that makes people especially well suited for the sales tasks in the particular company. To facilitate this function, the sales manager should (1) prepare a job description that enumerates the specific tasks to be performed by the salesperson and (2) analyze the characteristics of the firm's successful salespeople as well as the ineffective ones. Based on these two areas, the sales manager should be able to develop a set of specific requirements.

Although for years marketers have attempted to create a comprehensive set of traits that characterize effective salespeople in general, currently there is no such list.

8. What major issues or questions should management consider when developing a training program for the sales force?

The major issues or questions to consider when developing a sales force training program are the following:

a. Who should be trained? Training programs can be directed toward the total sales force or toward a segment of it.

b. When and where should the training occur? Sales training may be performed in the field, at educational institutions, in company facilities, or in several of these locations.

c. What should be taught? The content of sales training programs can deal with general company background, plans, policies, and procedures; product information regarding features, uses, advantages, problem areas, parts, service, warranties, packaging, sales terms, promotion, and distribution; and selling methods.

d. How should the information be taught? The specific methods and materials used in a particular sales training program depend on the type and number of trainees, program content, complexity, length of the training program, size of the training budget, location, number of teachers, and the teachers' preferences.

9. Explain the major advantages and disadvantages of the three basic methods of compensating sales personnel. In general, which method would you prefer? Why?

The straight salary method of compensation provides salespersons with maximum security, gives the sales manager a large degree of control over salespersons, is easy to administer, and yields predictable selling expenses. Its disadvantages include the lack of incentive, the necessity of close supervision of salespersons' activities, and the level of selling expenses during periods of sales decline. Advantages of the straight commission method of salesperson compensation include providing the maximum amount of incentive, the ability to encourage salespersons to sell certain items by increasing the commission rate on these items, and relating selling expenses directly to sales resources. Disadvantages of this method are the lack of control over the sales force, the possibility of inadequate service to smaller accounts, and the decreased predictability of selling expenses. The combination method of compensation provides a certain level of financial security to salespersons, provides some degree of incentive, and yields selling expenses that fluctuate with sales revenue. Unpredictable selling expenses and difficulties in administration are disadvantages of this method. The students' preferences for compensation methods will reflect individual attitudes toward each method. Because each method has advantages and disadvantages, arguments can be made for any of them.

10. What major factors should be taken into account in designing the size and shape of a sales territory?

In designing the size and shape of sales territories, the sales manager considers several major factors. First, the territories must be constructed so that sales potentials can be measured. Second, the shape of territories should facilitate salespersons' activities to provide the best possible coverage of the firm's customers. Third, the territories should be designed to minimize selling costs. Fourth, the density and distribution of customers influence the sales manager's decisions regarding territory size and shape. Fifth, topographical features may affect decisions about the size and shape of territories.

11. How does a sales manager—who cannot be with each salesperson in the field on a daily basis—control the performance of sales personnel?

Because a sales manager ordinarily does not travel with each salesperson, information is needed to control the performance of the sales force. This information can be supplied through salespersons' call reports, customer feedback, and invoices. Call reports and work schedules submitted by sales personnel provide the sales manager with detailed information about current interactions with clients and indicate salespersons' plans during a specific future period.

12. What is sales promotion? Why is it used?

Sales promotion is an activity and/or material that acts as a direct inducement, offering added value or incentive for the product to resellers, salespersons, or consumers. Sales promotion activities and materials are used to:

a. Identify and attract new customers

b. Introduce a new product

c. Increase the total number of users for an established brand

d. Encourage greater usage among users

e. Educate consumers regarding product improvements

f. Bring more customers into retail stores

g. Stabilize a fluctuating sales pattern

h. Increase reseller inventories

i. Combat or offset competitors' marketing efforts

j. Obtain more and better shelf space and displays

13. For each of the following, identify and describe three techniques and give several examples: (a) consumer sales promotion methods and (b) trade sales promotion methods.

a. Consumer sales promotion methods

(1) Retail coupons are used to build volume for a brand or product when price is an important purchasing determinant. These coupons may be for a specific brand or for a kind of product, and they may be distributed through retailers, as advertisements, or as throwaways. Clippings from newspapers or flyers distributed at shopping malls are examples of retail coupons.

(2) Demonstrations are supplied by the manufacturer and are good for attracting attention. They frequently show how a product works and sometimes involve the preparation and distribution of the product. An example is the demonstration of a product in an appliance store.

(3) Frequent user incentives reward customers who engage in repeat purchases. Examples of frequent user incentives include frequent flyer tickets and free food received after a number of food purchases are made at a specific restaurant.

(4) Point-of-purchase displays include outside signs, window displays, counter pieces, display racks, and self-service cartons. These are used to encourage retailers to carry a firm's product.

(5) Free samples may be distributed by mail, by door-to-door delivery, in stores, or on packages. This type of promotion is used to stimulate trial of a new or improved product, increase volume quickly in early life cycle stages, and aid in obtaining retail distribution of the product. Recent examples of free samples include soaps and toothpastes.

(6) Money refunds and rebates offer a specified amount of money to be sent to the consumer by mail after proof of purchase is established. These are used to promote trial of a product and to require multiple purchases to obtain proof of purchase. Such items as shampoos and razors have offered money refunds and rebates. Rebates have been offered even on automobiles.

(7) Premiums are items offered free or at minimal cost as a bonus for purchasing a particular product. They can be placed on or in the package or can be distributed in stores or through the mail. They are used to attract competitors' customers, introduce different sizes of current products, add variety to promotional efforts, and stimulate loyalty. Small toys offered in cereal boxes are examples of premiums.

(8) Cents-off offers entice the buyer to receive a certain amount off the regular price as shown on the label or package. These provide a strong incentive to try a product and are used to promote sales of lagging products. Such offers may appear on many convenience items, including toothpaste, detergent, and coffee.

(9) Consumer contests involve competition for prizes and usually are based on analytical or creative skills. An example of this technique would be to give $100 for writing a jingle for a new shampoo. Consumer sweepstakes require entrants to submit their names for inclusion in a drawing. Sweepstakes are often sponsored by cigarette manufacturers.

b. Trade sales promotion methods

(1) A buy-back allowance is a secondary sales promotion method used after a deal to stimulate repurchase. Such allowances are used to encourage cooperation in the initial transaction and in restocking.

(2) Buying allowances are temporary price reductions to resellers for the purchase of specified quantities. They are used as an incentive to handle new products, achieve temporary price reductions, or stimulate the purchase of an item in quantities larger than usual.

(3) A scan-back allowance is a manufacturer's reward to a retailer based on the pieces that move through the scanner during a given time period. They directly link trade spending to product movement.

(4) Count and recount involves the payment of a specific amount of money for each unit of product moved from the reseller's warehouse during a given period. This method is used to alleviate retail stockout and reduce warehouse inventory.

(5) Free merchandise may be offered to a reseller that purchases a stated quantity of the same or different products.

(6) Using merchandise allowances, the manufacturer agrees to compensate resellers with certain amounts of money for providing special reseller promotional efforts such as advertisements or displays. This technique is used for high-volume, high-profit, easily handled products.

(7) Cooperative advertising involves an agreement by a manufacturer to pay a certain amount of the retailer's media costs; the amount is based on the quantity of products purchased by the retailer.

(8) A dealer listing is dual-purpose advertising that announces a product or consumer promotion and contains names of participating retailers that carry the product.

(9) Premium, or push, money is used as an incentive to push a line of goods by providing additional compensation to salespeople.

(10) Sales contests use recognition of sales achievement to motivate resellers, retailers, and sales forces.

(11) Dealer loaders are premiums granted to a retailer for the purchase of specified quantities of merchandise.

14. What types of sales promotion methods have you observed recently? Comment on their effectiveness.

This is an open-ended question that will enable students to recall some sales promotion methods they have observed. Methods used to promote retail establishments, new products, or established products will probably be more familiar than those used to promote to resellers.

COMMENTS ON THE CASES

Case 19.1   Chili's Restaurants Take Training Seriously

This case focuses on the sales training efforts at Chili's Restaurants. The objective of the case is to provide students with an example of how a restaurant chain trains its wait staff. Prior to discussing this case, you may want to ask, "How many students work at restaurants or have worked at restaurants in the past?" Then, ask those students with food service experience to discuss the type of training they received for their restaurant employment.

Question 1 asks if Chili's servers are order getters, order takers, or support personnel. Well-trained Chili's wait persons fall into the category of order getters because they engage in suggestive selling rather than simply taking customers' orders. Rather than allowing customers simply to place an order, a well-trained Chili's server makes suggestions that often result in a higher ticket per customer.

Question 2 asks how Chili's motivates its server sales force. Chili's motivates its salespeople by showing them how to increase their sales, which in turn results in their earning higher tips. Also, Chili's has a recognition program that singles out highly effective wait persons to be honored.

For the third question, students must describe the role of training efforts at Chili's and assess the importance of training to Chili's success. Training efforts at Chili's are extremely important to Chili's success. Properly trained wait persons provide excellent customer service, which in turn leads to higher sales and greater customer satisfaction. Greater customer satisfaction builds long-term customer relationships. Long-term relationships result in future sales. In addition, Chili's training efforts help staff to be successful. Successful workers stay with Chili's for a longer time, which reduces employee turnover and helps keep Chili's costs lower.

Video Information

Video Title: Suggestive Selling
Location: Tape 3, Segment 19
Length: 12:22
Video Overview: Chili's Restaurants trains its staff extensively, convinced that excellent training leads to excellent customer service. Wait staff are trained to know menu items well, including how they taste and how they are prepared. They are also trained in the importance of making a good appearance. One of the sales techniques taught in Chili's training is called suggestive selling, a way of suggesting menu items that exposes customers to the best the restaurant has to offer. Suggestive selling includes upgrading the guest's original order, being very specific when suggesting menu items, assuming the guest wants to buy what you suggest, describing items in detail, and using props such as buttons and chalkboards to help describe items. Staff are also trained to respect the guest's decision and refrain from being pushy.

Multiple-Choice Questions About the Video

d 1. According to the video, what are the two most important qualities Chili's wait staff must possess in order to deliver excellent customer service?
a. A good appearance and sincerity
b. Knowledge of menu items and a positive attitude
c. Self-confidence and a good memory
d. Knowledge of menu items and a good appearance
e. Creativity and friendliness

b 2. Chili's calls its sales strategy for tastefully suggesting menu items to customers
a. "Sizzle Service."
b. "Suggestive Selling."
c. "Smart Selling."
d. "Suggestive Upgrading."
e. "Give the Guest the Best."

a 3. When waiting on customers' Chili's staff is expected to describe menu items thoroughly and
a. to assume the guest wants to buy.
b. not to accept no for an answer.
c. always to suggest an appetizer before taking the order.
d. never to make small talk with customers.
e. to keep guests from feeling rushed by waiting until they ask before bringing the bill.

c 4. Chili's service technique for encouraging customers to add menu items to their original orders is called
a. "Sizzle Selling."
b. "Order Enhancement."
c. "Upgradings."
d. "Suggestive Selling."
e. "P.P.A. (per person addition)."

Case 19.2   Nintendo Competes Through Sales Promotion Efforts

The purpose of this case is to demonstrate to students how an organization uses sales promotion to accomplish selected objectives that allow the organization to compete more effectively.

The first question asks students to identify the types of sales promotion methods employed by Nintendo. The major methods used by Nintendo include sampling, contests, sweepstakes, premiums, and coupons. Marketers at Nintendo are especially effective at integrating the use of several of these methods to gain significant benefits.

Question 2 asks in what ways Nintendo's specific sales promotion efforts benefit the company. Nintendo marketers are attempting to generate high awareness of new products and are providing multiple opportunities for customers to try the products. Providing hands-on opportunities through trial allows potential customers to gain experiences that are likely to influence future purchase decisions.

The third question asks students to evaluate Nintendo's practice of using product-specific sales promotion efforts rather than linking sales promotion efforts to a product line or the company's total product mix. Because one of the primary purposes of Nintendo's sales promotion efforts is product trial, promotions aimed at specific products more effectively achieve this purpose than sales promotion efforts aimed at a broad set of products. Also, product-specific sales promotion efforts are more effective at raising awareness of new products quickly than are sales promotion efforts linked to broader product groups.

20 PRICING CONCEPTS

TEACHING RESOURCES QUICK REFERENCE GUIDE

Resource	Location
Purpose and Perspective	IRM, p. 444
Guide for Using Color Transparencies	IRM, p. 444
Lecture Outline	IRM, p. 444
Class Exercises, Debate Issue, and Chapter Quiz	IRM, p. 453
Class Exercise 1	IRM, p. 455
Class Exercise 2	IRM, p. 456
Debate Issue: Is price competition more effective than nonprice competition?	IRM, p. 457
Chapter Quiz	IRM, p. 458
Answers to Discussion and Review Questions	IRM, p. 459
Comments on the Cases	IRM, p. 461
Case 20.1	IRM, p. 461
Video	Tape 3, Segment 20
Video Information	IRM, p. 461
Multiple-Choice Questions About the Video	IRM, p. 462
Case 20.2	IRM, p. 462
Transparency Acetates	Transparency package
Examination Questions: Essay	TB, p. 365
Examination Questions: Multiple-Choice	TB, p. 366
Examination Questions: True-False	TB, p. 378
Author-Selected Multiple-Choice Test Items	TB, p. 448

PURPOSE AND PERSPECTIVE

This chapter introduces basic pricing concepts and issues. First, we explore the nature and importance of pricing. Next, we discuss price and nonprice competition. Then, we discuss major pricing objectives such as survival, profit, return on investment, market share, cash flow, status quo, and product quality maintenance. We also identify and examine various factors that affect marketers' pricing decisions. We group these major factors into eight categories: organizational and marketing objectives, pricing objectives, costs, other marketing mix variables, channel members' expectations, buyers' perceptions, competition, and legal and regulatory issues. Finally, the chapter explores several issues associated with the pricing of products sold in organizational markets, focusing on price discounting, geographic pricing, and transfer pricing.

GUIDE FOR USING COLOR TRANSPARENCIES

There are two groups of color transparencies. The transparencies identified by a double number are the same as the figures and tables in the text. The transparencies labeled with a number and a letter are illustrations that do not appear in the text, but they can be used as additional examples of concepts discussed.

Part 6 Opener	Pricing decisions
Table 20.1	Pricing objectives and typical actions taken to achieve them
Figure 20.3	Factors that affect pricing decisions
Figure 20A	Chapter 20 outline
Figure 20B	Price versus nonprice competition
Figure 20C	Indicators of value consciousness, price consciousness, and prestige sensitivity
Figure 20D	Price-sensitive customers
Figure 20E	Forms of price discounts for organizational markets
Figure 20F	Buick focuses on value-conscious customer by emphasizing both quality and price in this Buick Regal advertisement.

LECTURE OUTLINE

I.   The nature of price

To a buyer, **price** is the value that is exchanged for products in a marketing transaction. Price is not always money or some other financial consideration. **Barter,** which is the trading of products, is the oldest form of exchange. Money may or may not be involved. Buyers' concern about price is related to their expectations about the satisfaction or utility associated with a product. Buyers must decide whether the utility gained in an exchange is worth the buying power sacrificed.

A.   Different terms can be used to describe price for different forms of exchange (see text for many examples).

B. The importance of price

1. Price plays an important role in efficient marketing because price is often the only marketing mix variable that can be changed quickly to respond to changes in demand or to competitors' actions.

2. Because price times quantity equals revenue, price is important in determining profits.

3. Because price has a psychological impact on customers, marketers can use it symbolically. A high price can emphasize the quality of a product; a low price can emphasize a bargain.

II. Price and nonprice competition

A product offering can compete on a price or nonprice basis.

A. With **price competition,** a marketer emphasizes price as an issue and matches or beats the prices of competitors that are also emphasizing low prices.

1. A major advantage of price competition is its inherent flexibility. Prices can be adjusted to compensate for an increase in the firm's operating costs, to offset changes in demand, or to counteract a competitor's pricing strategy.

2. A disadvantage of price competition is that competitors usually benefit from the flexibility to adjust prices by responding quickly and aggressively to price changes.

B. With **nonprice competition,** a seller emphasizes distinctive product features, service, quality, promotion, packaging, or other factors to distinguish its product from competing brands instead of focusing on price.

1. A major advantage of nonprice competition is that a firm can build customer loyalty toward its brand.

2. If customers prefer a brand because of nonprice issues, it is more difficult for competitors to lure these customers to their brands.

3. For nonprice competition to work, a company must be able to distinguish its brand through unique product features, higher product quality, promotion, packaging, or excellent customer service; further, buyers must view these product features as important, and the features must be difficult for competitors to imitate.

III. Pricing objectives

In setting a price, marketers should always begin by considering objectives. **Pricing objectives** are overall goals that describe what the firm wants to achieve through its pricing efforts. Because pricing objectives will influence decisions in most functional areas, the objectives must be consistent with the organization's overall mission and goals.

A. A fundamental pricing objective is survival.

   1. Most organizations will tolerate short-run losses, internal upheaval, and many other difficulties if these conditions are necessary for survival.

   2. Because price is such a flexible and convenient variable to adjust, it sometimes is used to increase sales volume to levels that match the organization's expenses.

B. Specific profit maximization objectives may be stated in terms of actual dollar amounts or in terms of percentage change relative to profits of a previous period. However, the objective of profit maximization is rarely operational because it is difficult to measure its achievement.

C. Pricing to attain a specified return on the company's investment is also a profit-related pricing objective. Unfortunately, most pricing objectives based on return on investment are achieved by trial and error because not all cost and revenue data needed to project the return on investment are available when prices are set.

D. Market share—a firm's sales in relation to total industry sales—is a very meaningful benchmark of success. Therefore, many firms establish pricing objectives to maintain or increase market share.

   1. Maintaining or increasing market share need not depend on growth or industry sales.

2. An organization's sales volume may increase while its market share within the industry decreases, if the overall market is growing. On the other hand, an organization's market share may increase even when sales for the industry are decreasing.

E. Some organizations set prices to recover cash as quickly as possible.

1. Financial managers are interested in quickly recovering capital that has been spent to develop products.

2. A possible disadvantage of this pricing objective is high prices, which might enable competitors with lower prices to gain a large share of the market.

F. In some instances, an organization may be in a favorable position and therefore set an objective of status quo.

1. Status quo objectives can focus on several dimensions, including maintaining a certain market share, meeting competitors' prices, achieving price stability, or maintaining a favorable public image.

2. A status quo pricing objective can reduce a firm's risks by helping stabilize demand for its products.

3. The use of status quo pricing objectives sometimes deemphasizes price as a competitive tool, which can lead to a climate of nonprice competition within an industry.

G. Another objective might be product quality leadership in the market. This effort results in charging a high price to cover the high product quality and high cost of research and development.

IV. Factors affecting pricing decisions

A. Organizational and marketing objectives

1. Marketers should set prices consistent with the organization's goals and mission.

2. Decision makers should make pricing decisions that align with the organization's marketing objectives.

B. Types of pricing objectives

The types of pricing objectives (discussed in the previous section) a marketer uses will have considerable bearing on the determination of prices.

C. Costs

Costs must be an issue when establishing price.

1. A firm may sell products below costs to match competition, to generate cash flow, or even to increase market share.

2. In the long run, an organization cannot endure by selling its products below cost.

D. Other marketing mix variables

Because of the interrelation of the marketing mix variables, price can affect product, distribution, and promotion decisions.

1. For many products, buyers associate better product quality with a high price and lower product quality with a low price.

2. Premium-priced products often are marketed through selective or exclusive distribution, whereas lower-priced products in the same product category may be sold through intensive distribution.

3. Bargain prices often are included in advertisements; premium prices are less likely to appear in advertising messages and are more likely to require personal selling efforts.

E. Channel member expectations

When making pricing decisions, a producer must consider what distribution channel members (e.g., wholesalers and retailers) expect.

1. Channel members often expect producers to give discounts for large orders and prompt payment.

2. At times, resellers expect producers to provide several support services such as sales training, service training, and cooperative advertising.

3. These discounts and support activities have associated costs, and the producer must consider these costs when determining prices.

F. Buyers' perceptions

Buyers' perceptions of the importance of price may vary depending on the target market.

1. Marketers should be aware of acceptable price ranges for particular product categories and of the effects of their pricing policies on company image.

2. Buyers' perceptions of a product may allow the firm to price its product or service differently from competitive products.

3. Buyers can be characterized according to their degree of value consciousness, price consciousness, and prestige sensitivity.

   a. **Value-conscious** customers are concerned about both price and quality aspects of a product.

   b. **Price-conscious** customers strive to pay low prices.

   c. **Prestige-sensitive** customers focus on purchasing products that satisfy prominence and status.

G. Competition

A marketer must remain aware of the prices competitors charge. This information helps the firm adjust its price in relation to competitors' prices.

1. When adjusting prices, a marketer must assess how competitors will respond.

2.   When an organization is a monopoly and unregulated, the firm can set prices at whatever the traffic will bear. If the monopoly is regulated, price flexibility is reduced and the regulatory body lets the organization set prices that generate a reasonable but not excessive rate of return.

3.   In an oligopolistic market, when one firm cuts price to gain a competitive edge, other firms are likely to cut prices, too, which means that very little is gained through price cuts.

4.   In a perfectly competitive market, there is no flexibility in setting prices. The price of the firm's product is determined by the going market price.

H.   Legal and regulatory issues

Government action at times strongly influences marketers' pricing decisions.

1.   The federal government may invoke price controls to curb inflation.

2.   The Sherman Act prohibits conspiracies to control prices. Marketers not only must refrain from fixing prices but also must develop independent pricing policies and set prices in ways that do not even suggest collusion.

3.   If price differentials tend to lessen or injure competition, they are ruled discriminatory and prohibited. The Robinson-Patman and Clayton acts limit the use of **price discrimination,** the practice of providing price differentials that injure competition by giving one or more buyers a competitive advantage.

V.   Pricing for organizational markets

Organizational markets consist of individuals and organizations that purchase products for the purpose of using them in their own operations or for producing other products. Establishing prices for this category of buyers is sometimes different from setting prices for consumers.

A.   When using price discounting, producers give intermediaries discounts off the list prices.

1. **Trade discounts** are reductions off the list price that a producer gives an intermediary for performing certain functions, such as selling, transporting, storing, processing, and providing credit services.

2. **Quantity discounts** are deductions from list price for purchasing in large quantities.

   a. **Cumulative discounts** are quantity discounts that are aggregated over a stated period.

   b. **Noncumulative discounts** are one-time reductions in price based on the number of units purchased, the dollar size of the order, or the product mix purchased.

3. A **cash discount** is a price reduction to the buyer for paying promptly or in cash.

4. A **seasonal discount** is a price reduction to buyers buying goods or services out of season.

5. **Allowances,** such as trade-in allowances and promotional allowances, are price reductions made to increase sales.

B. **Geographic pricing** involves reductions for transportation costs or other costs associated with the physical distance between the buyer and the seller.

   1. Prices may be quoted F.O.B. factory or F.O.B. destination, depending on who pays for the shipping costs.

      a. An **F.O.B. factory** price is the price of the merchandise at the factory, before the shipment; thus the buyer pays shipping costs.

      b. An **F.O.B. destination** price indicates that the producer is absorbing the shipping costs.

   2. **Uniform geographic pricing** involves charging all customers the same price, regardless of location; this strategy may be used to avoid problems involved with charging each customer a different price.

3. In **zone pricing,** regional prices are set to take advantage of a uniform pricing system; prices are adjusted for major geographic zones as transportation costs increase.

4. **Base-point pricing** is a geographic pricing policy that includes the price at the factory plus freight charges from the base point nearest the buyer. The legality of this approach has been questioned, so the method has been abandoned.

5. With **freight absorption pricing,** a seller absorbs all or part of the actual freight costs for a particular customer or geographic area.

C. **Transfer pricing** occurs when one unit in a company sells a product to another unit.

1. The price is determined by one of four methods: actual full cost, standard full cost, cost plus investment, or market-based cost.

    a. *Actual full cost* is calculated by dividing all fixed and variable expenses for a period into the number of units produced.

    b. *Standard full cost* is calculated on what it would cost to produce the goods at full plant capacity.

    c. *Cost plus investment* is calculated as full cost, plus the cost of portion of the selling unit's assets used for internal needs.

    d. *Market-based cost* is calculated at the market price less a small discount to reflect the lack of sales effort and other expenses.

2. The choice of method depends on the company's management strategy and the nature of the units' interaction.

3. An organization must ensure that transfer pricing is fair to all units that must purchase its goods or services.

CLASS EXERCISES, DEBATE ISSUE, AND CHAPTER QUIZ

On the following pages, you will find two class exercises, a debate issue, and a chapter quiz. These are formatted in large-size type so that you can use them as class handouts or for making transparencies. Below are the authors' comments on the class exercises, the debate topic, and the answers to the chapter quiz.

Class Exercise 1: This exercise examines price and nonprice competition, pricing objectives, and factors affecting price decisions.

Question 1. IBM is trying to keep within striking distance of the clone prices with price cuts. There are some reports that IBM may introduce its own low-end PCs, perhaps under a different name. At any rate, students should recognize that in the past IBM has not competed on a price basis, focusing instead on distinctive product features, service (for retailers and customers), product quality, and heavy promotion. This generally leads to increased customer loyalty. Unfortunately for IBM, its products have been successfully imitated by the clone manufacturers. This has forced IBM to compete on price since PCs have become fairly standardized products. IBM is not as flexible with its price changes as the clone makers, and the resulting price war has left IBM with its first unprofitable year on record.

Question 2. Product quality and cash flow objectives best fit IBM's position and past image. This conflicts with the price cuts necessary to maintain market share.

Question 3. Lower-priced products typically require more intense distribution. Ads may need to shift to emphasize price and value (you might check current *WSJ* ads to see if they are). Given the lower margins and more intense distribution, expect less personal selling and more self-service at the retail store.

Question 4. A visit to the local clone distributor will likely indicate a lack of sales training, repair service, cooperative ads, sales promotions, or willingness to return merchandise to the producer (who won't pay for it). This lack of support accounts for the low prices and explains why IBM's products are more expensive.

Question 5. Though not purely oligopolistic, this industry is characterized by matching price cuts.

Class Exercise 2: The purpose of this exercise is to demonstrate how different situations affect one's range of price acceptability. Although subjective, possible answers are as follows:

1. 12-oz. soft drink at a
   (a) vending machine $ 0.50
   (b) movie theater $ 1.25
   (c) supermarket $ 0.35

2. A steak dinner at a(n)
   (a) cafeteria-style restaurant $ 6.50
   (b) elegant restaurant $15.00
   (c) charity benefit dinner $75.00

3. A flat-tire repair
   (a) on a lonely stretch of highway $30.00
   (b) in a town where efficient public transportation is available $15.00
   (c) when schools and stores are within walking distance $ 8.00

4. A duplicate key
    (a) just to have an extra key around $ 0.75
    (b) at night in a mall parking lot when your keys are locked in your trunk $15.00
    (c) when your nonrefundable airline ticket is in your locked luggage and
        your flight leaves in 30 minutes $30.00

Debate Issue: Is price competition more effective than nonprice competition?

Chapter Quiz: Answers to multiple-choice questions are

1.	b	3.	c
2.	e	4.	d

CLASS EXERCISE 1

PRICES OF PERSONAL COMPUTERS RECENTLY DROPPED RAPIDLY BECAUSE OF (A) INCREASED COMPETITION FROM PC CLONE MAKERS, WHICH OPERATE ON NARROW MARGINS AND HIGH TURNOVER; (B) INCREASED CONSUMER KNOWLEDGE AND SOPHISTICATION, WHICH ENCOURAGES MORE CONSUMERS TO USE MAIL-ORDER DISCOUNT PC DISTRIBUTORS; AND (C) DECREASED DIFFERENCES IN QUALITY AND PERFORMANCE BETWEEN NAME BRAND AND CLONE PCS. ALTHOUGH IBM PRICES ARE STILL ABOVE THE PC CLONES, ALL PC MANUFACTURERS HAVE BEEN CUTTING PRICES TO MAINTAIN MARKET SHARE.

1. Do you think IBM should compete on a price or on a nonprice basis? What are the advantages and disadvantages of each approach?

2. IBM's leadership position requires financing high R&D expenses in addition to maintaining support services. What pricing objective(s) would best fit these needs and IBM's organizational image? Does this conflict with a market share objective?

3. If IBM were to continue competing on price, how might other marketing mix variables be affected?

4. What kind of support do dealers for IBM expect compared to dealers for AST, ALR, or Leading Edge? How do these expectations affect price.

5. If IBM drops its prices in the near future, what can you expect the clone makers to do? What kind of competitive situation is the PC industry (oligopoly, monopolistic, pure competition)? What does this imply for price setting?

CLASS EXERCISE 2

WHAT IS YOUR RANGE OF PRICE ACCEPTABILITY? EXPLAIN THE BREADTH IN YOUR RANGE OF PRICE ACCEPTABILITY.

1. How much would you pay for a 12-ounce soft drink at a
    *   vending machine?
    *   movie theater?
    *   supermarket?

2. How much would you pay for a steak dinner at a(n)
    *   cafeteria-style restaurant?
    *   elegant restaurant?
    *   charity benefit dinner?

3. How much would you pay to have a flat tire repaired
    *   on a lonely stretch of highway?
    *   in a town where efficient public transportation is available?
    *   when schools and stores are within walking distance?

4. How much would you pay for a duplicate car key
    *   just to have an extra key around?
    *   at night in a mall parking lot when your keys are locked in your car?
    *   when your nonrefundable airline ticket is in your locked car, your flight leaves in 30 minutes, and your car keys are lost?

DEBATE ISSUE

IS PRICE COMPETITION MORE EFFECTIVE THAN NONPRICE COMPETITION?

<u>YES</u>	<u>NO</u>
• Many customers today are very price conscious	• Price competition breeds price-sensitive customers with little brand loyalty
• With so many homogeneous products on the market, price is a major means of distinguishing a product from competitive brands	• Product features and quality are more distinguishing in setting a product apart from its competitors
• When price competition is used, firms attempt to keep their costs low	• Nonprice variables should be desirable to buyers as well as difficult to imitate

CHAPTER QUIZ

1. Which of the following prohibits price discrimination that lessens competition among wholesalers and retailers?
    a. Sherman Antitrust Act
    b. Robinson-Patman Act
    c. Lanham Trademark Act
    d. Federal Trade Commission Act
    e. Wheeler-Lea Act

2. If the terms of the exchange are 2/10 net 30, this means that the transaction
    a. involves a cumulative discount.
    b. involves a noncumulative discount.
    c. offers a discount if the buyer lives within a particular zone.
    d. price does not include the cost of freight.
    e. involves a cash discount if paid within 10 days.

3. _____ consumers are concerned about both the price and the quality aspects of a product.
    a. Price-conscious
    b. Prestige-sensitive
    c. Value-conscious
    d. Price-conscious and prestige-sensitive
    e. Quality-conscious

4. What type of pricing objective would an organization use if it were in a favorable position and desired nothing more?
    a. Return on investment
    b. Cash flow
    c. Profit
    d. Status quo
    e. Survival

ANSWERS TO DISCUSSION AND REVIEW QUESTIONS

1. Why are pricing decisions so important to an organization?

   Pricing decisions are important to a firm because they relate directly to the generation of total revenue. This ties price into the other elements of business, such as accounting and finance. A change or error in price will send repercussions throughout the company.

   Pricing is also important because it is indirectly related to quantities sold. As the most flexible aspect of the marketing mix, price plays another important role by affecting production and inventory levels. Price even more indirectly influences total costs through its effect on quantities sold.

2. Compare and contrast price and nonprice competition. Describe the conditions under which each form works best.

   Both price and nonprice competition are competitive means by which firms attempt to gain market share and profit. They can be used separately or in unison, depending on the situation.

   With price competition, a marketer emphasizes price as an issue and attempts to match or beat the prices of competitors that also are emphasizing low price. A seller that competes on the basis of price has a great deal of flexibility in adjusting to meet competitive pressures. A disadvantage is that the competition can do the same thing.

   Nonprice competition occurs when a seller elects to emphasize distinctive product features, service, quality, promotion, packaging, or other factors to distinguish its product from competing brands. One advantage to this competitive strategy is that a firm can build customer loyalty to its brand. A disadvantage is that it is fairly rigid and inflexible once applied.

3. How does a pricing objective of sales growth and expansion differ from an objective to increase market share?

   A pricing strategy of sales growth and expansion is much vaguer than the one for increased market share. A firm could have decreasing market share but increasing sales in a rapidly growing market. Conversely, a firm could maintain market share but lose sales volume in a deteriorating market. Market share takes a firm's competitors, environment, and personal effort into account and is thus a more accurate indicator of company performance.

4. Why must marketing objectives and pricing objectives be considered when making pricing decisions?

   It is important that consumers consider the firm consistent. The marketing objectives are set in conjunction with the organizational objectives that dictate the firm's course of action. To tie pricing decisions into this framework helps facilitate the continuity of the firm and contribute to ease of coordination.

5. In what ways do other marketing mix variables affect pricing decisions?

   The product marketing mix variable has an important influence on pricing decisions because price is the value placed on what is exchanged. If the product is perceived as being of very high quality, a high price will correspond with this image.

The place where a product is sold is also vital. It is important to keep the image of the outlet and the product within a similar range.

Promotion is also an important variable to coordinate with price. Price has a psychological impact on customers, as do different advertising media and approaches. It is important to try to coordinate this factor with price.

6. What types of expectations may channel members have about producers' prices, and how do these expectations affect pricing decisions?

A channel member expects to earn a profit. The amount of time required to handle the product is also a major consideration. Many resellers expect producers to provide several support activities, such as sales training, service training, repair advisory service, cooperative advertising, sales promotions, and perhaps a program for returning unsold merchandise. These activities affect pricing decisions because failure to price the product so that the producer can provide some of these activities may cause resellers to view the product less favorably.

7. How do legal and regulatory forces influence pricing decisions?

The state and federal governments can affect pricing decisions through price controls, freezing prices at certain levels, determining price increase rates, and so on. The Sherman, Clayton, and Robinson-Patman acts have a strong impact on pricing decisions by setting guidelines for pricing activities and making certain activities illegal.

8. Compare and contrast a trade discount and a quantity discount.

A trade discount is a reduction off of the list price that a producer gives an intermediary for performing certain functions: selling, transporting, storing, and so forth. It is usually given as a percentage or series of percentages off the list price. A quantity discount is a reduction for buying in quantity.

The two discounts are similar insofar as they are incentives to an intermediary from a producer. They help reward the intermediary for actions the producer feels are important. They are different because quantity discounts relate only to the size of the order placed, whereas trade discounts deal with compensation based on functions performed.

9. What is the reason for using the term F.O.B.?

This term relates to geographic pricing and stands for "free on board." It is used to indicate whether the price includes shipping charges. *F.O.B. factory* means that the price of the goods does not include shipping charges; *F.O.B. destination* means the producer pays for shipping.

10. What are the major methods used for transfer pricing?

Transfer price—incurred when one unit in an organization sells to another—is determined by one of four methods: actual full cost, standard full cost, cost plus investment, and market-based cost. Actual full cost is calculated by dividing all fixed and variable expenses for a period into the number of units produced. Standard full cost is calculated on what it would cost to produce the goods at full plant capacity. Cost plus investment is calculated as full cost, plus the cost of a portion of selling unit's assets used for internal needs. Market-based cost is calculated at the market price less a small discount to reflect the lack of sales effort and other expenses.

COMMENTS ON THE CASES

Case 20.1   Low Prices and Fun: The Winning Combination at Southwest Airlines

The primary objectives of this case are to illustrate (1) that low prices are not necessarily associated with low levels of customer service, and (2) how one company survived a period of fierce price competition through implementation of an unconventional, price-based marketing strategy. Specifically, the case illustrates how Southwest Airlines has combined an atmosphere of "fun and family" with an aggressive low-price strategy to succeed in a very competitive environment characterized by intense price competition.

Question 1 asks the student to consider reasons why Southwest has been able to implement a low-price strategy successfully while many of its competitors have failed with similar efforts. One reason is that Southwest's costs are generally lower than those of the competition as a result of, among other things, not giving customers more than they want. Southwest offers no-frills service and frequent, on-time flights, choosing not to offer extra benefits provided by many other passenger air carriers, such as fancy meals, individualized boarding passes, and other costly amenities. Another reason is the company's—i.e., Herb Kelleher's—unique ability to instill a sense of fun and family pride among not only company employees, but among members of its loyal passenger base as well.

The second question asks the reader to discuss Southwest's primary pricing objectives. Here, a strong case could be made for any of the objectives discussed in the text with the exception of "status quo." However, given the company's aggressive market-entry pricing philosophy and ability to remain successful while many of its competitors have gone bankrupt, "survival" and "market share" are of particular relevance. Another interesting perspective possibly taken would be to suggest that Southwest pursues "product quality" pricing objectives in that it seeks to give customers exactly what they want—and no more—at a low relative price.

Question 3 asks the student to discuss any possible negative aspects of the low market-entry pricing philosophy exhibited by Southwest. One potential drawback, although apparently not a major factor in actual practice, is that the low price may connote a low level of service quality to the customer, particularly someone not familiar with Southwest. From a more macro perspective, such practice may lead to low initial profits for the company and price wars that serve to increase the probability of continued low profits—if any can be realized at all. Also, such practices may invite charges of predatory pricing. It may be interesting to discuss how Southwest has been able to consistently overcome such potentially problematic issues while its competitors have failed to do so while following similar low-price strategies.

Video Information

Video Title: The Lone Star Flying Society's Good Time Band
Location: Tape 3, Segment 20
Length: 28:15
Video Overview: Southwest Airlines uniquely combines an aggressive low-price strategy with an atmosphere of "fun and family" to consistently succeed in a very competitive environment characterized by intense price competition. CEO Herb Kelleher has successfully cultivated this scenario over the last several decades, proving that low prices do not always necessarily connote

low levels of customer service. Southwest gives its loyal customers what they want—and no more—at the lowest possible price. The company has been able to operate effectively in this manner by instilling a sense of pride and family among both its customers and employees in a fashion not found at any other passenger carrier.

Multiple-Choice Questions About the Video

a   1. The example of Southwest Airlines illustrates the point that
      a. low prices do not necessarily connote low levels of customer service.
      b. the creation of a "fun atmosphere" is an expensive and frivolous undertaking in industries dominated by intense price competition.
      c. fun and low prices do not mix; successful companies must sacrifice one or the other.
      d. a company cannot successfully compete on the basis of price unless it has the lowest cost structure in the industry.
      e. customers are willing to pay extra for benefits they do not value.

c   2. Southwest has been able to develop a loyal base of satisfied customers by providing them with
      a. low-priced air travel.
      b. the highest level of customer service in thc industry at the lowest price.
      c. basic, reliable, and frequent service at low prices.
      d. lavish comedic extravaganzas on board all late-night flights.
      e. faster and safer air travel than competitors are able to offer.

Case 20.2   Denny's Competes Through Value Pricing

The objective of this case is to examine how Denny's uses value pricing as a major component in its marketing strategy. Denny's was one of the early users of value pricing. Before you discuss this case, ask students about their last visit to Denny's and why they went there. This restaurant chain should be very familiar to students.

The first question asks students to identify the major benefits and disadvantages of value pricing. The major benefit of using value pricing is to attract a large number of customers to your organization. Denny's serves over a million customers a day. Value pricing can encourage customer loyalty and frequent customer needs. Three disadvantages of value pricing are (a) it sometimes attracts primarily bargain-seeking customers, or it trains current customers to expect low prices all the time; (b) value pricing results in a lower revenue yield per customer; and (c) an organizations that uses value pricing must be extremely cautious to keep costs as low as possible so that it can survive when charging low prices.

Question 2 asks how Denny's marketers are assessing the chain's target market's evaluation of price. Denny's is measuring customers' reactions to the pricing of multiple breakfast meals for under $1.99 and several value price lunch meals that range between $2.99 and $4.99. If customers fail to purchase these value priced meals, Denny's will be forced to evaluate customers' perceptions of these prices relative to food quality.

The last question asks what pricing method Denny's uses. Prices for Denny's value priced meals are set based on the competition-oriented pricing method.

21 SETTING PRICES

TEACHING RESOURCES QUICK REFERENCE GUIDE

Resource	Location
Purpose and Perspective	IRM, p. 464
Guide for Using Color Transparencies	IRM, p. 464
Lecture Outline	IRM, p. 464
Class Exercises, Debate Issue, and Chapter Quiz	IRM, p. 472
Class Exercise 1	IRM, p. 475
Class Exercise 2	IRM, p. 476
Debate Issue: Is price differentiation ethical?	IRM, p. 477
Chapter Quiz	IRM, p. 478
Answers to Discussion and Review Questions	IRM, p. 479
Comments on the Cases	IRM, p. 481
Case 21.1	IRM, p. 481
Video	Tape 3, Segment 21
Video Information	IRM, p. 482
Multiple-Choice Questions About the Video	IRM, p. 482
Case 21.2	IRM, p. 482
Transparency Acetates	Transparency package
Examination Questions: Essay	TB, p. 383
Examination Questions: Multiple-Choice	TB, p. 384
Examination Questions: True-False	TB, p. 399
Author-Selected Multiple-Choice Test Items	TB, p. 448

PURPOSE AND PERSPECTIVE

This chapter describes an eight-stage price-setting process: (1) selecting pricing objectives; (2) assessing the target market's evaluation of price and its ability to purchase; (3) determining demand; (4) analyzing demand, cost, and profit relationships; (5) evaluating competitors' prices; (6) selecting a pricing policy; (7) developing a pricing method; and (8) determining a specific price. We point out that marketers do not always take all these steps; rather, the steps are guidelines that provide a logical sequence for establishing prices. In some situations, other stages should be included in the price-setting process; in others, some of these stages may not be required.

GUIDE FOR USING COLOR TRANSPARENCIES

There are two groups of color transparencies. The transparencies identified by a double number are the same as the figures in the text. The transparencies labeled with a number and a letter are illustrations that do not appear in the text, but they can be used as additional examples of concepts discussed.

Figure 21.1   Stages for establishing prices
Figure 21.3   Demand curve illustrating the price/quantity relationship and increase in demand
Figure 21.5   Demand curve illustrating the relationship between price and quantity for prestige products
Figure 21.6   Elasticity of demand
Figure 21.7   Typical marginal cost and average revenue relationships
Figure 21.8   Typical marginal revenue and average revenue relationships
Figure 21.9   Combining the marginal cost and marginal revenue concepts for optimum profit
Figure 21.10   Determining the break-even point
Figure 21.11   Price lining
Figure 21A   Chapter 21 outline
Figure 21B   Major pricing policies
Figure 21C   Major pricing methods
Figure 21D   Continental Airlines uses competition-oriented pricing by providing first class service for business fare.

LECTURE OUTLINE

The price-setting process involves eight steps that provide a logical way to analyze the effectiveness of price in the marketing mix and the contributions of price to the organization's objectives.

I.   Development of pricing objectives

Developing pricing objectives is an important task because pricing objectives form the basis for decisions about other stages of pricing.

    A.   Pricing objectives must be consistent with organizational and marketing objectives.

    B.   Organizations normally have multiple objectives, both short-term and long-term.

II.   Assessment of the target market's evaluation of price

    A.   The importance of price varies depending on the type of product, the type of target market, and the purchase situation. By assessing the target market's evaluation of price, a marketer is in a better position to know how much emphasis to place on price.

    B.   Buyers in the 1990s are looking for value. Value combines a product's price and quality attributes, which are used by consumers to differentiate competing brands.

    C.   Understanding the importance of a product to customers, as well as their expectations of quality, helps a marketer correctly assess the target market's evaluation of price.

III.   Determination of demand

The marketer must determine demand. Techniques to estimate sales potential—the quantity of a product that could be sold during a specific time period—are practical approaches to understanding demand. Sales estimates are helpful in establishing the relationship between a product's price and the quantity demanded.

    A.   The classic **demand curve** is a graph of the quantity of products expected to be sold at various prices, if other factors remain constant.

        1.   For most products, the quantity demanded goes up as the price goes down and goes down as the price goes up. Thus there is an inverse relationship between price and quantity demanded.

        2.   There are many types of demand, and not all assume the classic demand schedule. Prestige products, for example, sell better at high prices than at low ones.

B.   Changes in buyers' attitudes, other components of the marketing mix, and uncontrollable factors can influence demand. Although demand fluctuates unpredictably, some organizations adjust to demand fluctuations by correlating demand for a specific product to demand for the total industry or some other economic variable.

C.   After identifying the target market's evaluation of price and examining demand to learn whether price is related to quantity inversely or directly, the next step in pricing is to determine price elasticity of demand.

1.   **Price elasticity of demand** is the relative responsiveness of changes in quantity demanded to changes in price.

2.   If demand is elastic, a change in price causes an opposite change in total revenue; an increase in price will decrease total revenue, and a decrease in price will increase total revenue.

3.   An inelastic demand results in a parallel change in total revenue. An increase in price will increase total revenue, and a decrease in price will decrease total revenue.

IV.   Analysis of demand, cost, and profit relationships

A.   Marginal analysis

1.   Marginal analysis is the examination of what happens to a firm's costs and revenues when production is changed by one unit. To determine costs of production, it is necessary to distinguish among several types of cost.

a.   **Fixed costs** do not vary with changes in the number of units produced or sold. **Average fixed cost** is the fixed cost per unit produced.

b.   **Variable costs** do vary directly with changes in the number of units produced or sold. They are usually constant per unit. **Average variable cost** is the variable cost per unit produced.

c.   **Total cost** is the sum of fixed costs and variable costs. **Average total cost** is the sum of the average fixed cost and the average variable cost.

d.   **Marginal cost (MC)** is the extra cost a firm incurs when it produces one more unit of a product.

    e.   Average fixed cost declines as the output increases. Average total cost decreases as long as marginal cost is less than average total cost and increases when marginal cost rises above average total cost.

    2.   **Marginal revenue (MR)** is the change in total revenue that occurs when an additional unit of a product is sold. The point of maximum profit is the point at which marginal costs are equal to marginal revenues.

    3.   This economic concept gives the false impression that pricing can be highly precise. If revenue and cost remain constant, prices can be set for maximum profits. In practice, however, costs and revenues are constantly changing.

    4.   The economic approach is to be used only as a model; the marketer can benefit from understanding the relationship between marginal cost and marginal revenue.

  B.   Breakeven analysis

    1.   The **breakeven point** is the point at which costs of producing the product equal revenue from selling the product.

    2.   To use breakeven analysis effectively, a marketer should determine the breakeven point for each of several alternative prices. This comparative analysis will identify the highly undesirable price alternatives that definitely should not be used.

    3.   Breakeven analysis is simple and straightforward, but it assumes that the quantity demanded is basically fixed; the major task is to set prices to recover costs.

V.   Evaluation of competitors' prices

To set prices effectively, an organization must be aware of the prices competitors are charging.

  A.   Learning competitors' prices may be a regular function of marketing research.

  B.   A marketer in an industry in which nonprice competition prevails needs competitive price information to ensure that the organization's prices are the same as competitors' prices.

C.   An organization may set its prices slightly above the competition to give its products an exclusive image. Alternately, a company may use price as a tool and price its products below those of competitors to gain market share.

VI.   Selection of a pricing policy

The marketer must select a **pricing policy**—a guiding philosophy or course of action designed to influence and determine pricing decisions. Generally, pricing policies should answer the recurring question, How will price be used as a variable in the marketing mix?

A.   Pioneer pricing policies

Pioneer pricing is used when introducing new products. Setting the base price for a new product is a necessary part of formulating a marketing strategy and one of the most fundamental decisions in the marketing mix.

1.   **Price skimming** is charging the highest possible price that buyers who most desire the product will pay. Price skimming

   a.   Can generate revenues to help offset sizable development costs

   b.   Insures the marketer against the problems that arise when the price is set too low to cover costs

   c.   Can help keep demand consistent with the firm's production capabilities

2.   **Penetration pricing** is setting the price lower than competing brands to penetrate the market, thus giving the pioneer a larger unit sales volume; a marketer uses penetration pricing to gain a large market share quickly. Penetration pricing

   a.   Puts the marketer in a less flexible position because it is more difficult to raise a penetration price than to lower or discount a skimming price

   b.   Can be especially beneficial when a marketer suspects that competitors could enter the market easily

B.   Psychological pricing

Psychological pricing encourages purchases based on emotional reactions rather than rational responses.

1. **Odd-even pricing** influences the buyer's perceptions of the price or the product by ending the price with certain numbers. Odd-even pricing assumes that more of a product will be sold at $99.99 than at $100.00 because customers will think the product is a bargain.

    a. There are no substantial research findings to support the impact odd pricing has on sales.

    b. An even price supposedly will influence a customer to view the product as a high-quality, premium brand.

2. With **customary pricing,** certain goods are priced primarily on the basis of tradition.

3. With **prestige pricing,** prices are set artificially high to provide a prestige image.

4. With **price lining,** the organization sets a limited number of prices for selected groups or lines of merchandise. The basic assumption in price lining is that demand is inelastic for various groups or sets of products.

C. **Professional pricing** are fees set by persons who have great skill or experience in a particular field or activity.

    1. Professionals who provide certain services or products believe their professional fees should not relate directly to the time and involvement in specific cases; they charge a standard fee regardless of the problems involved in performing the job.

    2. Professional pricing carries the idea that professionals have an ethical responsibility to not overcharge unknowing customers.

D. Promotional pricing

    Promotional pricing is used to help promote the product.

1. Products priced below the usual markup, near cost or below cost are **price leaders;** management hopes to increase sales of regularly purchased merchandise by attracting consumers through an impression of low prices.

2. With **special-event pricing,** advertised sales or price cutting is used to increase sales volume and is linked to a holiday or special event.

3. **Superficial discounting,** sometimes called "was-is pricing," is fictitious comparative pricing. The Federal Trade Commission and the Better Business Bureau have attempted to discourage these deceptive markdowns.

E. **Experience curve pricing** lets a company fix a low price that high-cost competitors cannot match and thus expand its market share. This practice is possible when a firm gains cumulative production experience and is able to reduce its manufacturing costs at a predictable rate through improved methods, materials, skills, and machinery.

VII. Development of a pricing method

After selecting a pricing policy, the marketer must choose a **pricing method**—a mechanical procedure for setting pricing on a regular basis. The pricing method structures the calculation and determination of the actual price.

A. With **cost-oriented pricing,** a firm determines price by adding a dollar amount or a percentage to the cost of the product.

1. **Cost-plus pricing** is a method whereby the seller's costs are determined and then a specified dollar amount or percentage of the cost is added to the seller's cost to set the price.

   a. Used when production costs are predictable or a long production period is needed.

   b. One pitfall for the buyer is that the seller may increase costs to establish a larger profit base.

   c. For industries in which cost-plus pricing is common and sellers experience similar costs, price competition may not be especially intense.

   d. It is a very simple method.

2. Through **markup pricing,** a product's price is derived by adding a predetermined percentage of the cost, called a markup, to the cost of the product.

    a. Markups can be stated as a percentage of the cost or as a percentage of the selling price.

    b. Markups usually reflect expectations about operating costs, risks, and stock turnovers.

    c. To the extent that retailers use similar rigid markups for the same product category, price competition is reduced.

B. With **demand-oriented pricing,** marketers base the price of a product on the level of demand for the product rather than the product's cost.

1. This method results in using a high price if demand is strong and a low price if demand is weak; its effectiveness depends on the marketer's ability to make accurate demand estimates.

2. A marketer sometimes uses a demand-oriented pricing method called **price differentiation,** using more than one price on the marketing of a specific product.

3. Compared with cost-oriented pricing, demand-oriented pricing places a firm in a better position to reach higher profit levels assuming that buyers value the product at levels sufficiently above the product's cost.

C. With **competition-oriented pricing,** pricing is influenced more by competitors' prices than by costs and revenue.

1. The importance of this method increases if competing products are almost homogeneous and the organization is serving markets in which price is the key variable of the marketing strategy.

2. This pricing technique should help attain a pricing objective to increase sales or market share.

VIII. Determination of a specific price

Pricing methods (or a combination of them) will yield a certain price, However, this price is likely to need refinement.

A. Although a systematic approach to pricing is best, in practice prices are often finalized after only limited planning. Trial and error rather than planning may be used to set a price.

B. Because there are so many complex issues in establishing the right price, pricing is as much an art as a science.

C. Pricing is a flexible and convenient way to adjust the marketing mix.

CLASS EXERCISES, DEBATE ISSUE, AND CHAPTER QUIZ

On the following pages, you will find two class exercises, a debate issue, and a chapter quiz. These are formatted in large-size type so that you can use them as class handouts or for making transparencies. Below are the authors' comments on the class exercises, the debate topic, and the answers to the chapter quiz.

Class Exercise 1: The objective of this exercise is to understand how to set prices by using an orderly process.

You now own a new restaurant and are preparing to set the menu prices. Explain the type of restaurant that you will have. For students who need additional guidance, you might suggest that they use a familiar franchise concept, such as Bennigan's or Friday's. This exercise is application-oriented and stresses conceptualization of pricing techniques.

Question 1. Selecting pricing objectives: Remind students of the objectives described in Chapter 20. A new restaurant may have a short-term market share objective with penetration pricing for certain products but may have a product quality objective for the long term.

Question 2. Assessing target market: Upscale restaurant patrons will have greater purchasing power and be less concerned with price. Conversely, patrons of White Castle or Krystal's restaurants perceive price as the key element because of generally low purchasing power.

Question 3. Determining demand: Some students may be confused about elasticity of demand. Conceptually, if you raise your prices and good things happen, then demand is inelastic; if you raise prices and bad things happen, then demand is elastic. Quantitatively, consider the selling of pizzas:

Old price:	$8	Old quantity:	1,000/month
Total revenue:	$8,000		
New price:	$10	New quantity:	900/month
Total revenue:	$9,000		
Price elasticity of demand:	−10% (change in qty = −.4)		
	+25% (change in price)		

Demand is relatively inelastic (if e < 1.0), and good things happen when price goes up (see TR). Change the new quantity to 700 and e = 1.2, and bad things happen (TR = $7,000).

Question 4. Analyzing demand, cost, and profit: Students should recognize that some items they buy at restaurants cost a fraction of the price paid, such as drinks, side orders (fries), and desserts. Conversely, main entrees are priced much closer to their actual cost. The cost of soft drinks to a restaurant is usually pennies, with the cup costing almost as much as the syrup. Markups on side orders may be ten times the marginal cost. On the other hand, sandwiches and other main dishes may contribute very little to profit, if priced separately.

Breakeven: Assume that you are selling pizzas at $8. Your fixed costs (rent, salaries, utilities) are $4,800/month. The food cost and other variable costs are 50 percent of the selling price. What is your breakeven point?

$$\$4,800/8 - 4 = 1200 \text{ units or } \$9,600.$$

Question 5. Evaluating competitors' prices: To add emphasis, you might ask if students have been in a store recently where they decided to leave (or buy less) because the prices were higher than elsewhere. Retailers using traditional markup prices may fail to recognize the impact of competition.

Question 6. Selecting pricing policy:

- **New products: skimming or penetration** (introduction of a new entree usually requires a low penetration price to induce trial, although a new rich dessert might maintain a skimming policy).
- **Psychological: odd-even** ($1.79 for sandwiches or $15.00 for filet mignon).
- **Customary** (most drinks, such as beer, coffee, and sodas, are priced about the same no matter what restaurant).
- **Price lining** (most menus are formatted according to price lines: appetizers [$3–4], sandwiches [$4–6], chicken and pasta [$6–8], and steak [$10+]. This allows for meeting needs of different price segments).
- **Promotional: price leaders** (free drinks are often used as inducements that will lead to other purchases).
- **Special-event** (might include Super Bowl or Monday night football specials; special New Year's party).

Question 7. Choosing a pricing method: Using only a cost-oriented approach may result in pricing products too high relative to competition (particularly in international markets), too high relative to demand (when an economic recession creates more elastic demand), or too low (when demand is inelastic).

Class Exercise 2: The objective of this exercise is to help students become more familiar with different pricing policies by analyzing how they are applied to specific products. Answers:

1. **penetration**
2. **psychological, odd/even**
3. **professional**
4. **special event**
5. **customary**
6. **price leaders**
7. **experience curve**
8. **professional**

Debate Issue: Is price differentiation ethical?

Chapter Quiz: Answers to multiple-choice questions are

1.	d	3.	b
2.	e	4.	d

CLASS EXERCISE 1

YOU NOW OWN A NEW RESTAURANT AND ARE PREPARING TO SET THE MENU PRICES. EXPLAIN THE TYPE OF RESTAURANT THAT YOU WILL HAVE.

1. Select pricing objectives (short and long term)

2. Assess target market: How important is price to your target market?

3. Determine demand: How do consumers react to price changes? Are your products primarily elastic or inelastic?

4. Analyze demand, cost, and profit: Marginal costs must be covered. Which menu items could you afford to price close to, and which considerably above, marginal cost?

BREAKEVEN: ASSUME YOU ARE SELLING PIZZAS AT $8. YOUR FIXED COSTS (RENT, SALARIES, UTILITIES) ARE $4800/MONTH. THE FOOD COST AND OTHER VARIABLE COSTS ARE 50 PERCENT OF THE SELLING PRICE. WHAT IS YOUR BREAKEVEN POINT?

5. Evaluate competitors' prices: Who are your primary competitors? What prices are they charging? Do they engage in price or nonprice competition?

6. Select a pricing policy: Select the appropriate pricing policies and show examples of each:
   - New products: skimming or penetration
   - Psychological: odd-even, customary, prestige, price lining
   - Promotional: price leaders, special event

7. Develop a pricing method: What problems arise if you use only a cost-oriented pricing method?

CLASS EXERCISE 2

WHAT TYPE OF PRICING POLICY DOES EACH OF THE FOLLOWING DESCRIBE?

1. Hyundai prices the Excel lower than the price of competing brands.

2. A premium men's shirt has a suggested retail price of $32 instead of $31.95.

3. A doctor charges $35 for a routine office visit.

4. A restaurant lowers the price of its corned beef and cabbage plate during the week before St. Patrick's Day.

5. For years the price of a candy bar was 5 cents, and rarely did a manufacturer charge more.

6. A supermarket prices its eggs, bread, and milk below cost.

7. Because Texas Instruments gained cumulative production experience and reduced manufacturing costs, it was able to price its calculators below competitors' prices.

8. An attorney advertises a $199 fee for a divorce.

DEBATE ISSUE

IS PRICE DIFFERENTIATION ETHICAL?

YES

- Supply and demand dictate prices

- The type of customer, distribution channel, and time of purchase allow for pricing differences

- Customers are willing to pay different prices for the same product under different conditions

NO

- There is no difference in a product just because it's purchased in bulk, at a certain time, or by a person in a specific occupation

- Marketer prejudice is difficult to control but does not justify its use

- It simply is not fair for one person to pay more for a flight or hotel room than another person when both are receiving the same service at the same time

CHAPTER QUIZ

1. If Dayton's pays $16.50 for a six-ounce bottle of Anais Anais cologne and sells it for $25.95, its markup as a percentage of cost is _____ for this product.
    a. 64 percent
    b. 36 percent
    c. 18 percent
    d. 57 percent
    e. 45 percent

2. A price-skimming policy assumes that
    a. the initial demand is highly elastic.
    b. the product is efficient.
    c. it will be difficult to recoup development costs.
    d. all consumers have homogeneous tastes.
    e. the initial demand is highly inelastic.

3. If the product price is $100, average variable cost $40 per unit, and the total fixed costs are $120,000, what is the breakeven point?
    a. 500 units
    b. 2,000 units
    c. 1,200 units
    d. 300 units
    e. 3,000 units

4. When marketers at Consolidated Mustard Company tried to determine demand for their product, they found that at 50 cents, consumers wanted 2,000 jars; at $1.00, they wanted 6,000 jars; and at $1.50, they wanted 4,000 jars. What can Consolidated conclude?
    a. Somebody goofed up the research. No demand schedule looks like that.
    b. Consolidated has an elastic product.
    c. Consolidated has an inelastic product.
    d. Consolidated mustard is a prestige good.
    e. Consolidated mustard has a normal demand curve.

ANSWERS TO DISCUSSION AND REVIEW QUESTIONS

1. Identify the eight stages that make up the process of establishing prices.

   Stage 1 is developing a pricing objective that dovetails with the organization's overall objectives. Typical pricing objectives include survival, profit, return on investment, market share, cash flow, and maintaining the status quo. Stage 2 is identifying the target market's evaluation of price. Stage 3 is examining the nature and elasticity of demand. Marketers must learn what type of demand schedule characterizes the product, how demand fluctuates with changes in buyers' attitudes, other components of the marketing mix, uncontrollable environmental factors, and whether demand is elastic or inelastic. Stage 4, analyzing demand, cost, and profit relationships, is necessary to estimate the economic feasibility of alternative prices. The two approaches to understanding demand, cost, and profit relationships are marginal analysis and breakeven analysis. Stage 5, evaluating competitors' prices, is helpful in determining the role of price in the marketing strategy. Stage 6 is selecting a pricing policy to serve as a guiding philosophy designed to influence and determine pricing decisions. Among the most common pricing policies are pioneer pricing policies, psychological pricing, professional pricing, and promotional pricing. Stage 7 is choosing a method for calculating the price charged to customers. Three pricing methods are cost-oriented pricing (which includes cost-plus pricing and markup pricing), demand-oriented pricing, and competition-oriented pricing. Stage 8 is determining the final price.

2. Why do most demand curves demonstrate an inverse relationship between price and quantity?

   Most demand curves have an inverse relationship between price and quantity because the quantity demanded for most products goes up as the price goes down. This means that the demand for most products is elastic—a change in price causes an opposite change in total revenue.

3. List the characteristics of products that have inelastic demand. Give several examples of such products.

   Products typically have inelastic demand when people have strong needs and when there are very few substitutes for these products. Examples include many energy products and medicines.

4. Explain why optimum profits should occur when marginal cost equals marginal revenue.

   By producing and selling so that marginal costs equal marginal revenue, a firm should obtain optimum profits because at this point the production of one additional unit would result in greater cost than the revenue received from an additional unit. This approach to pricing blends the increasing costs and the inefficiencies of production with the price elasticity of the demand schedule.

   This economic concept gives the false impression that pricing can be highly precise. If revenue and cost remain constant, prices can be set for maximum profits. In practice, revenue and cost are constantly changing. In addition, this approach offers little help in pricing new products.

5. The Chambers Company has just gathered estimates for doing a breakeven analysis for a new product. Variable costs are $7 a unit. The additional plant will cost $48,000. The new product will be charged $18,000 a year for its share of general overhead. Advertising expenditures will be $80,000, and $55,000 will be spent on distribution. If the product sells for $12, what is the breakeven point in units? What is the breakeven point in dollar sales volume?

   The breakeven point equals 40,200 units, or $482,400 in sales.

6. Why should a marketer be aware of competitors' prices?

   A marketer needs to be aware of competitors' prices to set its own price slightly above, equal to, or below those prices.

7. For what type of products would a pioneer price-skimming policy be most appropriate? For what type of products would penetration pricing be more effective?

   A pioneer price-skimming policy would be most appropriate for products that have associated research and developmental costs, for example, cameras, computers, calculators, and many technical products. Products introduced with penetration pricing usually have few differentiated advantages. Market penetration is more typical for lower-cost items such as food products and small household items.

8. Why do customers associate price with quality? When should prestige pricing be used?

   Consumers associate price with quality because of experience and because they have been socialized to believe that the higher the price, the higher the quality. Symbolic pricing should be used when the marketer can determine that a higher price is consistent with buyers' attitudes toward the expected cost of a product.

9. Are price leaders a realistic approach to pricing?

   Price leaders should be used when competitive conditions and consumers' actions indicate that they are appropriate. In the long run, a firm must price at a level to achieve some degree of profit or at least to cover costs in the short run.

10. What are the benefits of cost-oriented pricing?

    Cost-oriented pricing is simple to calculate and easy to implement.

11. Under what conditions is cost-plus pricing most appropriate?

    Cost-plus pricing is most appropriate when actual production costs are difficult to estimate before the product is made.

12. A retailer purchases a can of soup for 24 cents and sells it for 36 cents. Calculate the markup as percentage of cost and as percentage of selling price.

    The markup is 50 percent of cost and 33.3 percent of selling price.

COMMENTS ON THE CASES

Case 21.1 Steinway: Price Supported by over 140 Years of Quality

The primary objective of this case is to illustrate how Steinway and Sons supports the setting of high product prices with a premium level of product quality. Steinway pianos, typically among the highest priced in the industry—up to $70,000 with an average price of $25,000—are backed by a rich tradition of craftsmanship dating back to the mid 1800s. Over the last two decades, the company has faced strong, lower-priced but high-quality competition, yet maintains its premium pricing structure. Although many of the latest competing pianos sound the same to the untrained ear, accomplished pianists claim that these largely machine-made instruments sound "shallow" compared to handcrafted Steinways, which take approximately two years apiece to produce from start to finish—no expenses are spared. Steinway pianos, which hold their value far better than competing instruments, are the choice of over 90 percent of the world's piano soloists performing in major orchestras.

The first question asks if the assumptions of the classic demand curve hold in the case of Steinway and Sons pianos. Further, from an elasticity of demand perspective, it also asks the student to describe what the demand curve for these products will look like if it does not conform to the classic demand curve model. The basic assumptions are not likely applicable to the case of Steinway and Sons' prestige products, since price is not inversely related to demand; the company could raise its prices—within some limits—at any time and not experience a significant drop in demand. Demand, then, would be described as inelastic. As regards what the demand curve would look like, although creative interpretations should be welcomed, it is likely to plateau at some high (industry) level of price and then decline at both higher and lower levels. Finally, it should be noted that although demand might rise if prices were dropped dramatically, the company would probably soon lose its reputation and loyal customer base and face the dire consequences of such activity.

The second question asks the reader to consider why Steinway and Sons has not lowered its prices in the face of low-priced, high-quality competition. Further, it asks for identification of factors that might serve to justify the high relative price of the company's pianos. First, as stated above, a price reduction would likely lead to the loss of the company's long-standing tradition as the crafter of the finest pianos in the world, which would then lead to the loss of its loyal customer base. Second, factors that serve to justify the high prices charged for Steinways include the company's painstaking production process, the use of only the finest materials, patented technologies, high resale values, and the company's reputation as the producer and marketer of only the finest musical instruments.

The third and final question asks the student to speculate, from a pricing method and policy perspective, on what Steinway and Sons should do in regard to low-priced, high-tech competition such as the Yamaha Disklavier. As hinted at in the last paragraph of the case text, the continuation of current pricing efforts is recommended, since it appears that a significantly large segment of piano consumers appreciates the quality built into Steinways enough to pay the price asked by the company for them. Specifically, in terms of pricing policy, the company should maintain its practice of *price skimming*. With regard to pricing method, incomplete information makes the answer less clear. However, one might speculate that the company should maintain its current methods, with the *markup* method of *cost-oriented pricing* appearing to be the most logical choice.

Video Information

Video Title: It's a Steinway
Location: Tape 3, Segment 21
Length: 15:12
Video Overview: The high relative prices set by Steinway and Sons are justified on the basis of the premium level of quality and craftsmanship painstakingly built into each instrument produced. Based on the company's ongoing success, it appears that there is a large enough segment of piano consumers perceiving the high prices to be justified for the company to continue its pricing policies, even in the face of increased low-price, high-quality competition. As stated in the case text, "Even in the sterile, high-tech frenzy of modern life, it seems that the old world traditions of quality and workmanship still have considerable appeal." Steinway and Sons pianos are one of but a select few products for which such a claim could justifiably be made.

Multiple-Choice Questions About the Video

c   1.   The high prices of Steinway and Sons pianos are
    a.   not justified given the comparable quality of competing products.
    b.   justified due to the fact that there appear to be some people willing and able to pay for them.
    c.   justified on the basis of the premium level of quality and craftsmanship painstakingly built into each instrument produced.
    d.   not justified given that customers feel that the quality differences between Steinway pianos and competing instruments do not warrant such disparity in price.
    e.   justified on the basis of the high prices of some competing products.

e   2.   What would most likely *not* happen if Steinway and Sons were to drastically reduce the prices of its pianos while not otherwise altering its marketing and production philosophies?
    a.   The company's long-standing, high-quality reputation would suffer.
    b.   The company would lose its loyal, quality-conscious customer base.
    c.   The company's quality-oriented marketing claims would lose effectiveness.
    d.   Short-term sales would increase.
    e.   The company would enjoy unparalleled long-term prosperity based on increased demand from current customers.

Case 21.2   Back Yard Burgers: Fresh Gourmet Food at a Competitive Price

Question 1 asks what type of psychological pricing is most evident in the fast-service food industry in this case, and how this situation might present possible problems for Back Yard Burgers, given the company's pricing objectives. In this case, the fast-food industry was using the odd-even pricing type of psychological pricing, with its value menu priced at .99. In Taco Bell's case, the 59-, 79-, and 99-cent pricing schemes might be considered price lining, with several products available at the same price within a price line. Back Yard Burgers prices its standard line of burgers and chicken sandwiches to be competitive with other restaurants' premium offerings, and has another group of value-priced items. If the fast-food industry continues its trend toward value pricing all items, Back Yard Burgers may find that its gourmet product will be too expensive when compared to similar burgers and chicken sandwiches, and that its costs will prohibit reduction of prices in order to be competitive.

Question 2 asks the student to discuss the effects of both fixed and variable costs on Back Yard Burgers' ability to compete successfully on price with other fast-food establishments. Back Yard Burgers has an advantage over Wendy's, McDonald's, and Burger King with regard to fixed costs. Since Back Yard Burgers requires one-third to one-half the land of typical fast-food chains, its fixed capital costs are less. Additionally, the franchise fees, another fixed cost, are just slightly higher than McDonald's (by $2,500) but are considerably less than those required at Burger King ($15,000 difference). Back Yard Burgers may be in a position to compete more aggressively with a lower breakeven point due to lower fixed costs. Variable costs at Back Yard Burgers reflect the gourmet nature of the food and the larger number of ounces per burger (1/3 lb) versus the industry standard (1/4 lb). However, these variable costs vary with the number of units sold and are easily adaptable.

Question 3 asks how demand factors might figure into the prices set at Back Yard Burgers and whether the resulting individual demand curves for the various products are likely to differ. The fact that many of the fast-food restaurants are price-competitive with their use of value pricing on a regular basis may force all fast-food establishments to lower their prices on similar items. This price-competitive activity would have different effects on the demand curves of the regular-priced items at Back Yard Burgers than on the value-priced menu items. If prices at competitors' restaurants are lower on similar items, the demand for regular-priced items at Back Yard Burgers would likely decrease. However, if Back Yard products are perceived as prestige or gourmet items, the demand could increase rather than decrease, reflecting an inelastic price-demand curve. The demand curve for the value-priced items at Back Yard Burgers would be more elastic.

22 STRATEGIC MARKET PLANNING

TEACHING RESOURCES QUICK REFERENCE GUIDE

Resource	Location
Purpose and Perspective	IRM, p. 485
Guide for Using Color Transparencies	IRM, p. 485
Lecture Outline	IRM, p. 485
Class Exercises, Debate Issue, and Chapter Quiz	IRM, p. 496
Class Exercise 1	IRM, p. 498
Class Exercise 2	IRM, p. 499
Debate Issue: Is the Boston Consulting Group's product-portfolio analysis (PPA) technique a good strategic planning tool?	IRM, p. 500
Chapter Quiz	IRM, p. 501
Answers to Discussion and Review Questions	IRM, p. 502
Comments on the Cases	IRM, p. 504
Case 22.1	IRM, p. 504
Video	Tape 3, Segment 22
Video Information	IRM, p. 505
Multiple-Choice Questions About the Video	IRM, p. 505
Case 22.2	IRM, p. 506
Transparency Acetates	Transparency package
Examination Questions: Essay	TB, p. 405
Examination Questions: Multiple-Choice	TB, p. 405
Examination Questions: True-False	TB, p. 422
Author-Selected Multiple-Choice Test Items	TB, p. 448

PURPOSE AND PERSPECTIVE

This chapter focuses on strategic market planning. First, we examine the strategic market planning process, including the development of a mission statement and organizational goals. We also examine the role of organizational opportunities and resources in strategic market planning. We discuss the development of corporate and business unit strategy and then explore the nature of marketing strategy and the creation of the marketing plan.

GUIDE FOR USING COLOR TRANSPARENCIES

There are two groups of color transparencies. The transparencies identified by a double number are the same as the figures and tables in the text. The transparencies labeled with a number and a letter are illustrations that do not appear in the text, but they can be used as additional examples of concepts discussed.

Part 7 Opener	Marketing management
Figure 22.1	Components of strategic market planning
Figure 22.5	Levels of strategic market planning
Figure 22.6	Illustrative growth-share matrix developed by the Boston Consulting Group
Figure 22.8	Intensive growth strategies
Figure 22.10	Diversified growth strategies
Figure 22.12	The marketing planning cycle
Table 22.2	Components of a marketing plan
Figure 22.14	The four-cell SWOT matrix
Figure 22A	Chapter 22 outline
Figure 22B	Marketing strategy
Figure 22C	Anheuser-Busch celebrates diversity by recognizing the artistic achievements of Carmen Lomas Garza.
Figure 22D	3M stands for innovation.
Figure 22E	America's dairy farmers develop a strategy for promoting the consumption of cheese.

LECTURE OUTLINE

I. Defining strategic market planning

    A. A **strategic market plan** is an outline of the methods and resources required to achieve an organization's goals within a specific target market. It takes into account not only marketing, but also all functional aspects of a business unit that must be coordinated, including production, finance, and human resources, as well as environmental issues.

    B. The strategic business unit is used to define areas for consideration in a specific strategic market plan.

1. A **strategic business unit (SBU)** is a division, product line, or other profit center within a parent company.

2. Each SBU's revenues, costs, investments, and strategic plans can be separated from those of the parent company and evaluated.

C. The process of **strategic market planning** yields a marketing strategy that is the framework for a marketing plan, which is a written document that specifies the activities to be performed to implement and control an organization's marketing activities.

D. The set of marketing strategies that are implemented and used at the same time is referred to as the organization's **marketing program.**

1. Marketing strategy is best formulated when it reflects the overall direction of the organization and is coordinated with all of the firm's functional areas.

2. The process of strategic market planning helps an organization to develop marketing strategies that, when properly implemented and controlled, will contribute to the achievement of its marketing objectives and overall goals.

E. The strategic market planning process is based on an analysis of the environment.

1. Marketers differ in their viewpoints about the effect of environmental variables on marketing planning strategy.

2. When environmental variables affect an organization's overall goals, resources, opportunities, or marketing objectives, they also affect its marketing strategies, which are based on these factors.

II. Establishing an organizational mission and goals

A. The goals of an organization should be derived from its mission. The **mission statement** describes the long-term view, or vision, of what the organization wants to become.

1. A mission answers two questions.

a. What is our business?

b.   What should our business be?

2.   Having a mission statement can benefit the organization by

a.   Giving the organization a clear purpose and direction

b.   Describing the unique focus of the organization that helps to differentiate it from competitors

c.   Keeping the organization focused on customer needs rather than its own abilities

d.   Providing specific direction and guidelines to top managers for selecting from among alternative courses of action

e.   Providing guidance to all employees and managers of an organization, even if they work in different parts of the world

3.   A mission statement should include a firm's **distinctive competency,** which is something that it does extremely well, sometimes so well that it gives the company an advantage over its competition.

B.   An organization's goals, which are derived from its mission, guide the remainder of its planning efforts.

1.   Goals focus on the end results sought by the organization.

2.   Organizations can have short-term and long-term goals.

III.   Making the most of organizational opportunities and resources

A.   Environmental scanning is the process of collecting information about the marketing environment, which helps marketers identify opportunities and assists in planning.

B.   Market opportunities are the right combination of circumstances and timing that permit an organization to take action toward reaching a target market.

1. They are often called **strategic windows,** or temporary periods of optimum fit between the key requirements of a market and the particular capabilities of a firm competing in that market.

2. The attractiveness of market opportunities is determined by market factors, such as size and growth rate, as well as competitive, economic, political, legal and regulatory, technological, and sociocultural factors.

3. **Market requirements** relate to customers' needs or desired benefits. They are satisfied by components of the marketing mix that provide buyers with these benefits.

C. Capabilities and resources

1. A firm's capabilities relate to distinctive competencies that it has developed to do something well and efficiently.

2. A **competitive advantage** is created when a company matches its distinctive competency to the opportunities it has discovered in the market.

IV. Developing corporate and business-unit strategies

In any organization there are essentially three levels of strategic market planning: corporate strategy, business-unit strategy, and marketing strategy. The outcomes of each planning stage must be consistent with the stage that precedes it.

A. **Corporate strategy** determines the means for utilizing resources in the areas of production, finance, research and development, human resources, and marketing to reach the organization's goals.

1. It determines the scope of the business, its resource deployment, and competitive advantages, and overall marketing coordination of production, finance, marketing, and other functional areas.

2. It applies to all organizations, not just corporations.

3. Corporate strategy planners are concerned with

a.   Issues such as diversification, competition, differentiation, interrelationships between business units, and environmental issues

b.   Attempting to match the resources of the organization with the opportunities and risks in the environment

c.   Defining the scope and role of the strategic business units of the firm so that they are coordinated to reach the ends desired

4.   One of the most helpful tools proposed to aid corporate managers in their planning efforts is **product-portfolio analysis,** the Boston Consulting Group (BCG) approach, which is based on the philosophy that a product's market growth rate and its relative market share are important considerations in determining marketing strategy.

a.   The BCG approach integrates all the firm's products into a single, overall matrix and evaluates them to determine appropriate strategies for individual SBUs and the overall portfolio strategies.

b.   Managers can classify the firm's products into four basic types (Figure 22.6).

(1)   Stars are products with a dominant share of the market and good prospects for growth, but they use more cash than they generate to finance growth, add capacity, and increase market share.

(2)   Cash cows have a dominant share of the market but are low prospects for growth; they typically generate more cash than is required to maintain market share.

(3)   Dogs have a subordinate share of the market and are low prospects for growth.

(4)   Problem children or question marks have a small share of a growing market and generally require a large amount of cash to build share.

c.   The long-term health of an organization depends on having some products that generate cash and acceptable profits and others that use cash to support growth.

B.   Business-unit strategy

1.   The next step in strategic market planning is to determine business directions and develop business-unit strategies.

2.   A business may choose one or more competitive strategies, including intensive growth or diversified growth.

    a.   **Intensive growth** can take place when current products and current markets have the potential for increasing sales.

        (1)   *Market penetration* is a strategy of increasing sales in current markets with current products.

        (2)   *Market development* is a strategy of increasing sales of current products in new markets.

        (3)   *Product development* is a strategy of increasing sales by improving present products or developing new products for current markets.

    b.   **Diversified growth** occurs when new products are developed to be sold in new markets.

        (1)   *Horizontal diversification* results when new products that are not technologically related to current products are introduced into current markets.

        (2)   *Concentric diversification* occurs when the marketing and technology of new products are related to current products, but the new ones are introduced into new markets.

        (3)   *Conglomerate diversification* results when new products are unrelated to current technology, products, or markets and are introduced into markets new to the firm.

        (4)   *Integrated diversification* typically occurs within the same industry or product market when one company buys or merges with another.

V.   Developing a marketing strategy

A marketing strategy is a detailed explanation of how an organization will achieve its marketing objectives. It includes two components: selection of a target market and the creation of a marketing mix that will satisfy the needs of the chosen target market.

A.   Target market selection

Selecting an appropriate target market may be the most important decision a company has to make in the planning process.

1.   Should the company select the wrong target market, all other marketing decisions will be a waste of time.

2.   An organization must examine whether it possesses the necessary resources and skills to create a marketing mix that will satisfy the needs of its target market.

3.   Organizations must also choose their target markets carefully because of the changes taking place in the U.S. population.

B.   Creating the marketing mix

1.   The elements of the market mix—product, distribution, promotion, and price—are sometimes referred to as marketing mix variables because each can be varied or changed to accommodate the needs of the target market.

2.   The decisions made in creating a marketing mix are only as good as the organization's understanding of the target market.

3.   Marketing mix decisions must also have consistency and flexibility.

4.   Different elements of the marketing mix can be changed to accommodate different marketing strategies.

VI.   Creating the marketing plan

A.   **Marketing planning** is the systematic process of assessing marketing opportunities and resources, determining marketing objectives, defining marketing strategies, and establishing guidelines for implementation and control of a marketing plan.

B.   The **marketing planning cycle** is a circular process, with feedback used to coordinate and synchronize all stages of the planning cycle.

C.   The duration of marketing plans varies.

  1.   **Short-term plans** cover a period of one year or less.

  2.   **Medium-range plans** cover two to five years.

  3.   **Long-range plans** extend beyond five years.

D.   The extent to which marketing managers develop and use plans also varies.

  1.   A firm should have a plan for each marketing strategy it develops.

  2.   Because such plans must be changed as forces in the firm and in the environment change, marketing planning is a continuous process.

  3.   Although planning provides numerous benefits, some managers do not use formal marketing plans because they spend almost all their time dealing with daily problems, many of which would be eliminated by adequate planning.

E.   Components of the marketing plan

  1.   The executive summary is a brief synopsis of the entire report, including an introduction, an explanation of the major aspects of the marketing plan, and a statement about the costs of implementing the plan.

  2.   Environmental analysis provides information about the company's current situation with respect to the marketing environment; this information is obtained from both internal and external environments, usually through the firm's marketing information system or marketing research.

a. It assesses the marketing environment—the competitive, economic, political, legal and regulatory, technological, and sociocultural factors external to the firm.

b. It examines the current situation with respect to the target market.

c. It critically evaluates the firm's current marketing objectives and performance.

3. Strengths and weaknesses (first half of the SWOT analysis)

a. The analysis of strengths and weaknesses focuses on internal factors that give the organization certain advantages and disadvantages in meeting the needs of its target markets.

b. **Strengths** refer to competitive advantages or distinctive competencies that give the firm an advantage in meeting the needs of its target markets.

c. **Weaknesses** refer to any limitations that a company might face in marketing strategy development or implementation.

4. Opportunities and threats (second half of SWOT analysis)

a. This section focuses on factors that are external to the organization that can greatly affect its operations.

b. **Opportunities** are favorable conditions in the environment that could produce rewards for the organization if acted upon properly.

c. **Threats** refer to conditions or barriers that may prevent the firm from reaching its objectives.

d. When internal strengths are matched to external opportunities, the organization creates capabilities that can be used to create competitive advantages in meeting the needs of customers.

e. Internal weaknesses should be converted into strengths and external threats into opportunities.

5. Marketing objectives

    a. A **marketing objective** states what is to be accomplished through marketing activities.

    b. Marketing objectives should possess certain characteristics.

        (1) They should be expressed in clear, simple terms so that all marketing personnel understand exactly what they are trying to achieve.

        (2) They should be written so that they can be measured accurately.

        (3) They should specify a time frame for accomplishment.

6. Marketing strategies

    a. Marketing strategy refers to how the firm will manage its relationships with customers so that it gains an advantage over the competition.

    b. It is at the marketing mix level that the firm will detail how it will achieve a competitive advantage.

        (1) To gain an advantage, the firm must do something better than the competition.

        (2) A **sustainable competitive advantage** is one that cannot be copied by the competition.

7. Marketing implementation

    a. **Marketing implementation** is the process of putting marketing strategies into action.

    b. This section of the marketing plan answers questions about marketing activities.

        (1) What specific actions will be taken?

(2)   How long will these activities be performed?

(3)   Who is responsible for the completion of these activities?

(4)   How much will these activities cost?

c.   Without a workable implementation plan, the success of the marketing strategy is in jeopardy.

8.   Evaluation and control

a.   The final section of the marketing plan details how the results of the plan will be measured and evaluated.

b.   It includes the actions that can be taken to reduce the differences between planned and actual performance.

(1)   Standards for assessing the actual performance need to be established.

(2)   The plan needs to address the financial data used to evaluate whether the plan is working.

(3)   The firm can use a number of monitoring procedures to pinpoint causes for any discrepancies.

F.   Using the marketing plan

1.   The creation and implementation of a complete marketing plan will allow the organization to achieve not only its marketing objectives, but also its business-unit and corporate objectives.

2.   The marketing plan is only as good as the information it contains and the effort and creativity that went into its development.

3.   Every marketing plan is and should be unique to the organization for which it was created.

4.   The marketing plan should be flexible enough so that it can be adjusted on a daily basis.

CLASS EXERCISES, DEBATE ISSUE, AND CHAPTER QUIZ

On the following pages, you will find two class exercises, a debate issue, and a chapter quiz. These are formatted in large-size type so that you can use them as class handouts or for making transparencies. Below are the authors' comments on the class exercises, the debate topic, and the answers to the chapter quiz.

Class Exercise 1: The objective of this exercise is to understand the importance of strategic market planning by applying product portfolio planning tools.

Market share information was not available for all products, but for new products like PowerAde, Mocha Cooler, and H20h, market share is negligible. Judging from distribution intensity, one might estimate that Minute Maid holds a dominant position in the juice market. It's also interesting to note that although Pepsi continues to invest heavily in producing the most popular ads (first place on Video Storyboard Tests for 1990 and 1991), Coke maintains its market share.

Question 1. The increased interest in "New Age" drinks, which are fruity, clear beverages often sold in glass bottles, may offer the opportunity to invest resources in the familiar brand name of Fresca (which Coke is doing). The opportunity, in terms of growth, looks good for cold coffee in a can, but one might doubt the chances for sustaining growth because it appears unappealing to many consumers (i.e., doesn't meet market requirements). Mocha Cooler tastes more like a coffee-flavored milk shake, and cold coffee is very popular in other countries (Japan).

Question 2. Social forces moving toward more health consciousness should increase demand for clear sodas and juices. (Pepsi and Coke may soon enter the market with clear colas.) This surely influenced the acquisitions of Minute Maid and Ocean Spray. The aging of America and increasing time pressures may enhance demand for coffee in cans. Economic pressures may increase the sale of private label brands.

Question 3. You might use the overhead of Figure 22.6 to plot these on the matrix. Because of the lack of complete information, you might want to instruct students simply to classify the products:

Coca-Cola	*Pepsi-Cola*
Coke (cash cow)	Pepsi (cash cow)
Diet Coke (cash cow)	Diet Pepsi (cash cow)
Fresca (was dog, now ?)	H20h (?)
PowerAde (?)	Possible jv w/Lipton (?)
Minute Maid juices (star)	Ocean Spray juices (? or star)

Both companies have basically imbalanced portfolios with a need for new stars to take the place of the diet drinks, which grew at double-digit rates in the 1980s.

Question 4. Figure 22.7 suggests that if the product is not divested, harvested, or abandoned, then three building options exist. Coca-Cola is investing millions of dollars in Fresca in repackaging, increased distribution, and new promotional campaigns. Coke acquired Minute Maid to gain share in a growth market and attempted to develop a cooperative distribution agreement with Gatorade (which failed). It would seem logical that

Mocha Cooler might be able to focus on a definable niche where dominance can be achieved. Cash cows such as Coke and diet Coke can produce the cash necessary to support these efforts.

Sources for much of the information in this exercise came from Allison Fahey, "Fresca Freshens Up: Diet Soft Drink Gets New Frosted Packaging," *Advertising News,* January 6, 1992, p. 57; Richard Gibson, "Gatorade Unit to Sweat Out Global Rivalry," *Wall Street Journal,* April 28, 1992, B1; Laurie M. Grossman, "Slimmer Diet Cola Sales Growth Prompts Beverage Firms to Seek New Smash Drink," *Wall Street Journal,* November 19, 1991, B1.

Class Exercise 2: Because market shares and market growth potential are constantly changing, the products listed in this exercise could be classified very differently today than they might have been when this tenth edition was in production.

1.	Chrysler/Dodge minivans	**cash cow**
2.	LP records	**dog**
3.	Levi's blue jeans	**cash cow**
4.	ValuJet	**problem child**
5.	Windows 95	**star/cash cow**
6.	Pizza Hut Pan Pizza	**cash cow**
7.	Miller Light	**cash cow**
8.	Tampa Bay Buccaneers	**problem child**
9.	Laser discs	**star**
10.	Black and white televisions	**dog**

Debate Issue: Is the Boston Consulting Group's product-portfolio analysis (PPA) technique a good strategic planning tool?

Chapter Quiz: Answers to multiple-choice questions are

1.	a	3.	a
2.	b	4.	c

CLASS EXERCISE 1

ANSWER THE FOLLOWING QUESTIONS USING THE INFORMATION SHOWN BELOW:

1. Which of the newer products look like good market opportunities and appear to meet target market requirements?

2. What environmental forces might affect the growth of some of these segments?

3. Place the products for one of the two companies in the BCG growth-share matrix. Is it a balanced portfolio?

4. For those products that you classified as problem children, what do you suggest be done? What purpose do cash cows serve?

SEGMENTS	GROWTH (%)	SALES (BILLION $)
Colas	–	$30+
Diet colas	3	$11
All-natural sodas	5	*
Sparkling juices	7	*
Sports drinks	11	$1
Single-serving teas	18	*
Single-serving coffees	23	*
Total		$46 (approx.)
Fruit drinks and juices	10	$12

* less than $1 billion

COCA-COLA (market share)	PEPSI-COLA (market share)
Coke (41%)	Pepsi (33%)
Diet Coke (7.5%)	Diet Pepsi (5.8%)
Fresca (diet grapefruit)	H2Oh (flavored bottled water)
PowerAde	All Sport
Mocha Cooler and Ice Breaker (joint venture with Nescafe)	Possible joint venture with Lipton
Minute Maid juices	Ocean Spray juices

CLASS EXERCISE 2

USING BCG'S PRODUCT-PORTFOLIO ANALYSIS, HOW WOULD YOU CLASSIFY THE FOLLOWING PRODUCTS?

1. Chrysler/Dodge minivans

2. LP records

3. Levi's blue jeans

4. ValuJet

5. Windows 95

6. Pizza Hut Pan pizza

7. Miller Light

8. Tampa Bay Buccaneers

9. Laser discs

10. Black and white televisions

DEBATE ISSUE

IS THE BOSTON CONSULTING GROUP'S PRODUCT-PORTFOLIO ANALYSIS (PPA) TECHNIQUE A GOOD STRATEGIC PLANNING TOOL?

YES

- Allows a firm to examine its existing products to determine the overall configuration of its offering

- Uncovers strengths and weaknesses of firm's product offering

- Suggests areas where examination of the product should take place

NO

- Reporting tool that highlights past business practice

- Detrimental when used alone

- Improper philosophy can be tagged to a given category within the matrix

- Provides a general overview but no specific directions for strategy

CHAPTER QUIZ

1. Collins Copiers currently produces a color copier that has several outstanding features. Collins is aware of the intense competition in the copier industry and decides to lower its price compared to other color copiers in order to increase sales and market share. Collins is using which type of strategy?
   a. Market penetration
   b. Market development
   c. Product development
   d. Horizontal diversification
   e. Integrated diversification

2. When Mitlin Computer enters into the final stage of strategic market planning, it develops a marketing plan that will cover the next three years. Which type of market planning is this considered to be?
   a. Long-range market planning
   b. Medium-range market planning
   c. Short-range market planning
   d. Intensive market planning
   e. Integrated market planning

3. Toyota has decided to aggressively go after luxury car buyers to attempt to convert BMW buyers over to the Lexus automobile. This strategy would be classified as which one of the following growth categories?
   a. Intensive
   b. Diversified
   c. Integrated
   d. Horizontal
   e. Vertical

4. The Berkdorf Shoe Company is currently writing its marketing plan. Berkdorf is aware of possible new legislation that will limit the amount of glue that can be used in shoes that are marketed as "genuine leather," and considers this in its marketing plan. Which component of the marketing plan does this information most likely fit into?
   a. Executive summary
   b. Marketing strategies
   c. Opportunities and threats
   d. Strengths and weaknesses
   e. Marketing objectives

ANSWERS TO DISCUSSION AND REVIEW QUESTIONS

1. Identify the major components of strategic market planning, and explain how they are interrelated.

   The major components of strategic market planning include the establishment of organizational goals, organizational opportunities, organizational resources, and marketing strategies (selection and analysis of target markets/development of marketing mixes). Once goals are determined, opportunity can be assessed and marketing objectives developed. Marketing objectives must help achieve the overall organizational goals.

2. Describe the characteristics of a good mission statement. What role does the mission statement play in strategic market planning?

   A good mission statement should have some form of the following:
   - A clear purpose and direction for the organization, to keep it on track
   - A description of the unique attributes of the organization that help set it apart from others
   - A focus on customers' needs rather than the abilities of the organization
   - Specific guidelines and direction for top managers—to help them make appropriate strategic decisions
   - Guidance to all employees and managers, even those around the world, that will solidify the organization

   The mission statement is a foundation for the organization in developing its overall business strategies that, in turn, serve as the foundation for developing its marketing strategies. An organization's goals should be developed from its mission statement as well.

3. What are some of the issues that must be considered in analyzing a firm's opportunities and resources? How do these issues affect marketing opportunities and market strategy?

   There are three major considerations in assessing opportunities and resources: environmental forces must be monitored, market opportunity must be assessed, and the firm's capabilities must be understood. Marketing strategy and objectives must be viewed in light of these constraints.

4. Why is market opportunity analysis necessary? What are the determinants of market opportunity?

   Managers must undertake market opportunity analysis to determine when the right combination of circumstances allows them to take action toward a target market. The opportunity could provide a favorable chance for the firm to generate sales from markets (strategic window). Market opportunity determinants are market size, market growth rate, market requirements, and the actions of other firms.

5. In relation to resource constraints, how can environmental scanning affect a firm's long-term strategic market planning?

Monitoring the outside environment helps the company avoid crisis management. An environmental change can suddenly alter the firm's opportunities or resources, and new, effective strategies may be needed to guide the total marketing effort.

6. Explain how an organization can create a competitive advantage at the corporate, business-unit, and marketing strategy levels.

At the corporate level, a competitive advantage can be created through corporate mergers. The talents and abilities that one corporation possesses can be combined with different competencies of another organization, to be matched to opportunities in the marketplace.

At the business-unit level, a competitive advantage can be developed by intensifying growth in those products or services that a company has mastered and that also have great potential customer markets. A competitive advantage would also be created when a company has the foresight to diversify into other markets and/or products that capitalize on its current skills and knowledge.

At the marketing strategy level, a competitive advantage can be created by careful analysis of customers and their needs, and then selecting the appropriate target market. The selection of the target market should not only meet an anticipated customer need, but should also be appropriate for the distinctive competencies that an organization holds.

7. Give examples of intensive and diversified growth strategies that are being used by today's firms. Which strategy appears to be the most effective in today's environment? Why?

Intensive growth takes place when current products have the potential for increasing sales. Rockport Shoes, long known for its walking and athletic shoe comfort and quality, has introduced new lines of dress pumps for women—who represent a large share of the work force.

Diversified growth occurs when new products or services are developed to be sold in new markets. The Promus Corporation has diversified its business of hospitality (Holiday Inns) by moving into the casino industry.

In an environment that is dynamic, diversification can protect a corporation by spreading risks over several markets.

8. Describe the role of the marketing plan in developing marketing strategy. How important is the SWOT analysis to the marketing planning process?

The process of developing a marketing strategy provides a framework for the marketing plan, which is a more detailed blueprint for the activities that are to be performed. The plan then becomes instructions for implementing and controlling the strategy, providing a benchmark against which the actual performance can be measured and evaluated.

One of the components of the marketing plan is the environmental analysis, which provides information about the company's current situation with respect to the market environment, the target market, and the firm's current objectives and performance. A SWOT analysis outlines the internal strengths and weaknesses of a firm and the external opportunities and threats. This information is a synopsis of the market environment and is used to develop the environmental analysis.

9. How should an organization establish marketing objectives?

Marketing objectives must be consistent with the organization's goals. They should be clear, measurable, and quantifiable, and should state what is to be accomplished and in what time frame.

10. Refer to question 6. How can an organization take these competitive advantages and make them sustainable over time? How difficult is it to create sustainable competitive advantages?

A sustainable competitive advantage is developed by capitalizing on a firm's strengths and developing an expertise in an area that cannot be copied by the competition. Rather than attempting to be all things to all customers, a firm might choose a specific area of concentration and then focus on becoming the best in that area.

The degree of difficulty in maintaining a sustainable competitive advantage would depend on the specific area of expertise, and the ease of entry by the competitor. For example, store location is one sustainable competitive advantage that would present some degree of difficulty for the competitor to challenge. However, a sustainable competitive advantage of lowest price would be more easily copied by the competition.

11. What benefits do marketing managers gain from planning? Is planning necessary for long-run survival? Why or why not?

Planning helps marketing managers define their strategy in light of resources and opportunities. Planning forces the marketing manager to determine the difference between objectives and current performance. Specifying expected results, identifying the resources needed, describing the activities, and monitoring the activities allow the firm to achieve its long-term goals and survive.

COMMENTS ON THE CASES

Case 22.1   PETsMART: Looking to Be Man's Best Friend

This case focuses on strategic market planning and implementation at PETsMART. The case describes the market for pet supplies, traces the development of the pet-supply superstore, and provides a brief history of PETsMART as well as its marketing strategy.

The first question asks students to describe PETsMART's target market and marketing mix. PETsMART's target market obviously includes all pet owners in the United States. The product variable includes the firm's nearly 200 superstores, which stock more than 12,000 different products, including pet foods, toys, collars, and other pet supplies, as well as pet-related services such as grooming, obedience classes, and veterinary care, to satisfy the pet supply needs of its target market. As a category-killer retailer, PETsMART stores provide time, place, and possession utility by making a wide selection of products available. As to the price variable, PETsMART competes against supermarkets with low prices. PETsMART uses promotion, particularly advertising, to educate pet owners about its products, prices, and social activities.

Question 2 asks what general type of strategy PETsMART used in its first and second year of operation and what strategy it should employ next. During its first year of operation, PETsMART's strategy focused on the promotion variable of the marketing mix, using advertising to introduce and create an awareness of the firm in consumers' minds. Advertising informed consumers about the firm's wide selection of products and low prices. During its second year, PETsMART shifted to a branding strategy by focusing on identification of its trademark, recall of its commercials, and encouraging repeat customer visits. Student answers with regard to the second half of the question will vary but should consider PETsMART's increasing competition from Petco, as well as from traditional retailers of pet foods—supermarkets and discount stores. PETsMART should probably continue to emphasize its wide product mix, low prices, and Adopt-a-Pet programs to differentiate itself from the competition.

The third question asks whether PETsMART's advertising seems to be consistent with its overall strategies and objectives. Based on the material presented in the case, PETsMART's advertising does seem consistent with its strategies. Many of its advertising messages appeal to pet owners' emotions and the bond they share with their pets.

Video Information

Video Title: Where Pets are Family
Location: Tape 3, Segment 22
Length: 7:00
Video Overview: PETsMART superstores offer more than 12,000 different products, including pet foods, colognes, shampoos and conditioners, and health-related items. PETsMART encourages owners to bring their pets to the stores to "shop together." With 180 superstores in the Midwest, West, and South, PETsMART dominates the pet store industry with sales over $1 billion. PETsMART also promotes its Adopt-a-Pet program, which makes available dogs and cats from local shelters for potential pet owners to adopt, with the advertising slogan, "We don't sell pets, but we help save thousands of them each year."

Multiple-Choice Questions About the Video

a   1. PETsMART's closest rival in terms of market share is
     a. Wal-Mart/Sam's Clubs.
     b. Petco.
     c. Albertsons.
     d. Petzazz.

d   2. PETsMART wants to be for pet lovers what _____ is to homeowners.
     a. Petco
     b. Wal-Mart/Sam's Clubs
     c. Builder's Square
     d. The Home Depot

c   3. The United States has an estimated _____ million companion pets, which PETsMART caters to with a strong marketing strategy.
     a. 10
     b. 25
     c. 50
     d. 100

Case 22.2   Anheuser-Busch Returns to Its Roots

This case looks at strategic market planning from the perspective of a major brewery, Anheuser-Busch Cos. It gives students an opportunity to think about the differences between corporate, business-unit, and marketing-level strategies. Students may be particularly interested to learn about the history of a firm they are likely to be familiar with because of its highly visible advertising and corporate sponsorships.

Question 1 asks why Anheuser-Busch abandoned its diversification strategy. The brewer retrenched from its diversification program primarily because the expected synergies from its diverse units never materialized; declining beer sales and market share suggested that the firm had lost its focus. By refocusing on beer and entertainment, areas where the firm has competitive advantages (e.g., the well-known Budweiser name), the firm has bounced back.

The second question asks students to describe Anheuser-Busch's corporate strategy for growth. The firm's most recent corporate strategy has been divestment and abandonment of the "dogs" (e.g., Campbell Taggart, Eagle Snacks, the St. Louis Cardinals) in its product mix and a refocusing on its stars, cash cows, and problem children. The firm is also engaging in a market development business-unit strategy by trying to expand globally.

Question 3 asks students to discuss the firm's current marketing strategy for developing various brands to compete with popular regional brews. Anheuser-Busch's development of new brands, such as Red Wolf, Crossroads, and ZiegenBoch, to compete with popular regional brews is an example of a product-development strategy. With domestic beer sales flat and regional beers taking market share, Anheuser-Busch is adopting a market segmentation approach by customizing products to appeal to smaller geographic-based target market segments. Although these new brands may cannibalize market share from the firm's flagship Budweiser brand, the firm will lose fewer customers and sales dollars to competitors.

23

MARKETING IMPLEMENTATION AND CONTROL

TEACHING RESOURCES QUICK REFERENCE GUIDE

Resource	Location
Purpose and Perspective	IRM, p. 508
Guide for Using Color Transparencies	IRM, p. 508
Lecture Outline	IRM, p. 508
Class Exercises, Debate Issue, and Chapter Quiz	IRM, p. 520
Class Exercise 1	IRM, p. 522
Class Exercise 2	IRM, p. 523
Debate Issue: Is cost analysis more important than sales analysis?	IRM, p. 524
Chapter Quiz	IRM, p. 525
Answers to Discussion and Review Questions	IRM, p. 526
Comments on the Cases	IRM, p. 529
Case 23.1	IRM, p. 529
Video	Tape 3, Segment 23
Video Information	IRM, p. 529
Multiple-Choice Questions About the Video	IRM, p. 529
Casc 23.2	IRM, p. 530
Transparency Acetates	Transparency package
Examination Questions: Essay	TB, p. 427
Examination Questions: Multiple-Choice	TB, p. 428
Examination Questions: True-False	TB, p. 444
Author-Selected Multiple-Choice Test Items	TB, p. 448

PURPOSE AND PERSPECTIVE

This chapter continues the discussion of marketing management issues. First, we consider the place of marketing in an organization because it influences the extent of a marketing manager's authority and management style and methods. We also discuss the bases on which marketing units can be organized. In our discussion of implementation, we focus on the importance of coordinating marketing activities, motivating the personnel who perform those activities, and establishing effective communication within the marketing unit and with top management. Our analysis of the marketing control process deals with establishing performance standards, evaluating actual performance by comparing it with established standards, and reducing the differences between desired and actual performance. We also look at the problems that arise when attempting to control marketing efforts. Then we explore sales and cost analyses, the two major categories of analysis used to evaluate the actual performance of marketing strategies. The chapter ends with a focus on a comprehensive form of marketing control: the marketing audit.

GUIDE FOR USING COLOR TRANSPARENCIES

There are two groups of color transparencies. The transparencies identified by a double number are the same as the figures in the text. The transparencies labeled with a number and a letter are illustrations that do not appear in the text, but they can be used as additional examples of concepts discussed.

LECTURE OUTLINE

I.   The marketing implementation process

A. Marketing strategies almost always turn out differently than expected. In essence, organizations have two types of strategy.

   1. **Intended strategy** is the strategy that the organization decided on during the planning phase and wants to use.

   2. **Realized strategy** is the strategy that actually takes place. It comes about during the process of implementing the intended strategy.

B. Problems in implementing marketing activities

   1. Managers fail to realize that marketing implementation is just as important as marketing strategy.

   2. Marketing strategy and implementation are related.

   3. Marketing strategy and implementation are constantly evolving.

   4. The responsibility for marketing strategy and implementation is separated.

C. Components of marketing implementation

   The marketing implementation process has several components—organizational resources, marketing strategy, marketing structure, systems, leadership, and people—which must mesh if implementation is to succeed.

   1. Systems refer to work processes, procedures, and the way that information is structured.

   2. The people component refers to the importance of employees in the implementation process.

   3. Leadership is the art of managing people and involves issues such as employee motivation, communication, and reward policies.

   4. Shared goals draw the entire organization together into a single, functioning unit.

D. Approaches to marketing implementation

1. Internal marketing

    a. **External customers** are the individuals who patronize a business.

    b. **Internal customers** are the employees who work for a company.

    c. The needs of both sets of customers must be satisfied through marketing activities if implementation is to be successful.

    d. **Internal marketing** is a management philosophy that coordinates internal exchanges between the organization and its employees to better achieve successful external exchanges between the organization and its customers.

    e. Internal marketing refers to the managerial actions necessary to make all members of the marketing organization understand and accept their roles in implementing the marketing strategy.

    f. Internal marketing may involve market segmentation, product development, research, distribution, and public relations and sales promotion.

2. **Total quality management (TQM)** is a philosophy that uniform commitment to quality in all areas of the organization will promote a culture that meets customers' perceptions of quality.

    a. It involves coordinating efforts directed at improving customer satisfaction, increasing employee participation and empowerment, forming and strengthening supplier partnerships, and facilitating an organizational culture of continuous quality improvement.

    b. TQM is founded on three basic principles.

        (1) Continuous quality improvement is built around the notion that quality is free and involves building in quality from the very beginning. An important tool is **benchmarking,** the measuring and evaluating of the quality of an organization's goods, services, or

processes as compared with the best-performing companies in the industry.

    (2)   **Empowerment** gives frontline employees the authority and responsibility to make marketing decisions without seeking the approval of their supervisors.

    (3)   Quality-improvement teams bring together the best and brightest people from a wide variety of perspectives to work on a quality-improvement issue.

  c.   Benefits of total quality management include lower operating costs, higher returns on sales and investment, an improved ability to use premium rather than competitive pricing, as well as faster development of innovations, improved access to global markets, higher levels of customer retention, and enhanced reputation.

  d.   However, few companies are using TQM because it requires a substantial investment of time, effort, money, and patience.

II.   Organizing marketing activities

  A.   The role of marketing in an organization's structure

    1.   Companies using the marketing concept begin with an orientation toward their customers' needs and desires, and they are able to closely coordinate the marketing unit with other functional areas.

    2.   A **marketing-oriented organization** concentrates on discovering what buyers want and providing it in such a way that it achieves its objectives. It focuses on customer analysis, competitor analysis, and the integration of the firm's resources to provide customer value and satisfaction, as well as long-term profits.

    3.   A true marketing orientation takes a different perspective on a firm's structure.

      a.   In the traditional hierarchy, top management or the CEO is the pinnacle of authority, and every level of the organization is under the authority of the levels above it.

b. The marketing-oriented approach inverts this pyramid, placing customers at the top, and every action within the organization is directed at serving customer needs. Each level must answer to the levels above it, but answering to the next level means taking actions necessary to ensure that each level performs its job well.

B. Alternatives for organizing the marketing unit

1. Centralization versus decentralization

a. A **centralized organization** is one in which the top-level managers delegate very little authority to lower levels of the organization.

b. A **decentralized organization** delegates authority as far down the chain of command as possible.

2. The best approach to organizing a marketing unit depends on the number and diversity of the firm's products, the characteristics and needs of the people in the target market, and many other factors.

3. A marketing unit can be organized according to function, products, regions, or types of customers, or a combination.

a. Organizing by functions

(1) Is fairly common because it works well for some businesses with centralized marketing operations

(2) Can cause serious coordination problems in more decentralized firms

b. Organizing by products

(1) Is appropriate for firms that produce and market diverse products

(2) Gives a firm the flexibility to develop special marketing mixes for different products

           (3)   Can be expensive because of the layers of management and employees that it creates

    c.   Organizing by regions

           (1)   Is appropriate for large firms that market products nationally or internationally

           (2)   Is effective for firms whose customers' characteristics and needs vary greatly from one region to another

    d.   Organizing by types of customers is appropriate for a firm that has several groups of customers whose needs and problems differ significantly.

III.   Implementing marketing activities

    A.   Motivating marketing personnel

       1.   To motivate marketing personnel, managers must discover their physical, psychological, and social needs, and then develop motivational methods that help employees satisfy those needs.

       2.   Plans to motivate employees must be fair, ethical, and well understood, and rewards must be tied to organizational goals.

       3.   A firm can motivate its workers by directly linking pay with performance and by informing workers how their performance affects department and corporate results.

       4.   Selecting effective motivational tools has become more complex because of greater differences among workers due to race, ethnicity, gender, and age.

    B.   Communicating within the marketing unit

       1.   Good communication helps marketing managers motivate personnel and coordinate their efforts.

2. Communication with top-level executives keeps marketing managers aware of the company's overall goals and plans, guides the marketing unit's activities, and indicates how they are to be integrated with those of other departments.

3. An important type of communication is communication that flows upward from the frontline of the marketing unit to higher-level marketing managers.

4. Marketing managers should establish an information system within the marketing unit to make it easy for marketing managers, sales managers, and sales personnel to communicate with one another.

C. Coordinating marketing activities

1. Marketing managers must synchronize individuals' actions to achieve marketing objectives and work closely with managers in research and development, production, finance, accounting, and human resources to see that marketing activities mesh with other functions of the firm.

2. Marketing managers must coordinate the activities of marketing staff within the firm and integrate those activities with the marketing efforts of external organizations.

3. Marketing managers can improve coordination by using internal marketing activities to make each employee aware of how his or her job relates to others and how his or her actions contribute to the achievement of marketing objectives.

D. Establishing a timetable for implementation

1. Successful marketing implementation requires that employees know the specific activities for which they are responsible and the timetable for completing each activity.

2. Establishing an implementation timetable requires

a. Identifying the activities to be performed

b. Determining the time required to complete each activity

  c.   Separating the activities that must be performed in sequence from those that can be performed simultaneously

  d.   Organizing the activities in the proper order

  e.   Assigning the responsibility for completing each activity to one or more employees, teams, or managers

IV. Controlling marketing activities

The formal **marketing control process** consists of establishing performance standards, evaluating actual performance by comparing it with established standards, and reducing the differences between desired and actual performance.

  A.   Establishing performance standards

    1. Planning and controlling are closely linked because plans include statements about what is to be accomplished.

    2. A **performance standard** is an expected level of performance against which actual performance can be compared.

    3. Performance standards should be tied to organizational goals.

  B.   Evaluating actual performance

    1. Marketing managers must know what employees are doing and have information about the activities of external organizations that provide the firm with marketing assistance.

    2. Records of actual performance are compared with performance standards to determine whether and how much of a discrepancy exists.

  C.   Taking corrective action

    1. Marketing managers have several options for reducing a discrepancy between performance standards and actual performance.

      a.   Improve actual performance

      b.   Reduce or totally change the performance standard

      c.   Do both

  2.   Improving performance may require better methods of motivating marketing personnel or more effective techniques for coordinating marketing efforts.

  3.   Sometimes performance standards are unrealistic as written, and sometimes changes in the marketing environment make them unrealistic.

D.   Problems in controlling marketing activities

  1.   The information required to control marketing activities may be unavailable or available only at a high cost.

  2.   The frequency, intensity, and unpredictability of environmental changes may hamper control.

  3.   The time lag between marketing activities and their results limits a marketer's ability to measure the effectiveness of specific marketing activities.

  4.   Because marketing and other business activities overlap, marketing managers cannot determine the precise cost of marketing activities, which makes it difficult to know if the outcome of marketing activities is worth the expense.

  5.   It is very hard to develop exact performance standards for marketing personnel.

V.   Methods of evaluating performance

A.   **Sales analysis** uses sales figures to evaluate a firm's current performance.

  1.   Sales analysis is probably the most common method of evaluation because sales data partially reflect the target market's reactions to a marketing mix and are readily available.

2. To provide useful analyses, current sales data must be compared with fore-casted sales, industry sales, specific competitors' sales, or the costs incurred to achieve the sales volume.

3. The basic unit of measurement is the sales transaction, which results in a customer order for a specified quantity of an organization's product sold under specified terms by a particular salesperson or sales group on a certain date.

4. Firms frequently use dollar volume sales analysis because the dollar is a common denominator of sales, costs, and profits. However, price increases and decreases affect total sales figures.

5. Market-share analysis lets a company compare its marketing strategy with competitors' strategies. The primary reason for using market-share analysis is to estimate whether sales changes have resulted from the firm's marketing strategy or from uncontrollable environmental forces.

B. **Marketing cost analysis** breaks down and classifies costs to determine which are associated with specific marketing activities.

1. Marketing cost analysis lets a company evaluate the effectiveness of an ongoing or recent marketing strategy by comparing sales achieved and costs incurred.

2. Four broad categories of costs are used in marketing cost analysis.

    a. **Fixed costs**—such as rent, salaries, office supplies, and utilities—are based on how the money was actually spent. However, they often do not explain what marketing functions were performed through the expenditure of the funds.

    b. **Variable costs** are directly attributable to production and selling volume.

    c. **Traceable common costs** can be allocated indirectly, using one or several criteria, to the functions they support.

    d. **Nontraceable common costs** cannot be assigned according to any logical criteria and thus are assignable only on an arbitrary basis.

3.   Approaches to marketing cost analysis

    a.   In a **full-cost approach,** cost analysis includes variable costs, traceable common costs, and nontraceable common costs.

        (1)   Proponents of this approach claim that if an accurate profit picture is desired, all costs must be included in the analysis.

        (2)   Opponents contend that full costing does not yield actual costs because nontraceable common costs are determined by arbitrary criteria.

    b.   The **direct-cost approach** includes variable costs and traceable costs, but not nontraceable common costs. Critics argue that this approach is not accurate because it omits one cost category.

C.   The **marketing audit** is a systematic examination of the marketing group's objectives.

    1.   Its primary purpose is to identify weaknesses in ongoing marketing operations and plan the necessary improvements to correct these weaknesses.

    2.   A marketing audit may be specific and focus on one or a few marketing activities, or it may be comprehensive and encompass all of a company's marketing activities.

        a.   A specialized type of audit is the **customer-service audit,** in which specific customer-service activities are analyzed and service goals and standards are compared with actual performance.

        b.   Specialized audits could also be performed for product development, pricing, sales, or advertising and other promotional activities.

        c.   The scope of any audit depends on the costs involved, the target markets served, the structure of the marketing mix, and environmental conditions.

    3.   The marketing audit should

    a.   Describe current activities and results related to sales, costs, prices, profits, and other performance feedback

    b.   Gather information about customers, competition, and environmental developments that may affect the marketing strategy

    c.   Explore opportunities and alternatives for improving the marketing strategy

    d.   Provide an overall database to be used in evaluating the attainment of organizational goals and marketing objectives

4.   Marketing audits can be performed internally or externally, formally or informally.

5.   There is no single set of procedures for all marketing audits, but some guidelines should be adhered to.

    a.   Questionnaires should be developed carefully to ensure that the audit focuses on the right issues.

    b.   Auditors should develop and follow a step-by-step plan to guarantee that the audit is systematic.

    c.   The auditors should strive to talk with a diverse group of people from many parts of the company.

6.   Problems with audits

    a.   They can be expensive and time-consuming.

    b.   Selecting auditors may be difficult because objective, qualified personnel may not be available.

    c.   Audits can be extremely disruptive because employees sometimes fear comprehensive evaluations, especially by outsiders.

CLASS EXERCISES, DEBATE ISSUE, AND CHAPTER QUIZ

On the following pages, you will find two class exercises, a debate issue, and a chapter quiz. These are formatted in large-size type so that you can use them as class handouts or for making transparencies. Below are the authors' comments on the class exercises, the debate topic, and the answers to the chapter quiz.

Class Exercise 1: The purpose of this exercise is to apply organizational structure principles to multinational corporations marketing in the European Union.

Question 1. A centralized organization avoids confusion among the marketing staff, vagueness in marketing strategy, and autonomous decision makers who are out of control. The down side is that they may be too dependent on a few top managers and too slow to respond to market changes. Decentralized organizations may foster innovation and greater responsiveness to customers but may be inefficient and have blurred strategies (as seen in the next question). You might ask if any students have visited EU countries and ask them if there seem to be many differences or similarities among the countries. Most will indicate some significant differences exist, which would indicate a need for a decentralized organization. You might then ask if they saw some products (McDonald's, Coke, or Pepsi) almost everywhere in Europe, which might indicate some similarity of needs.

There is really no correct answer for the second question, since research (Samiee and Roth 1992) has so far found that no differences exist in performance between centralized/standardized and decentralized/adaptation organizations.

Question 2. A marketing-oriented organization is one that concentrates on discovering what buyers want and providing it in a way that lets it achieve its objectives. Just as U.S. consumers have different preferences (and thus different segments), Europeans do as well: Germans want a product that's gentle on lakes and rivers and will pay more for it. Spaniards want cheaper products that get shirts white and soft. Greeks want smaller packages that allow them to hold down the cost of each store visit. Trying to find a product that meets everyone's needs or preferences has been difficult for Lever.

Question 3. Decentralized organizations with different target markets and products might be more likely to organize by regions that have similar needs. Centralized organizations (as P&G has become in the EU) may be more prone to organize by functions. However, even though they are attempting to market pan-European products, the breadth of Procter & Gamble product lines may require organizing according to product.

Question 4. Formal controls involve performance standards, evaluation of actual performance, and corrective action to remedy shortfalls (see Figure 23.10). Informal controls include self-control, social or group control, and cultural control through acceptance of a firm's value system. Centralized control systems, seeking to achieve unified strategic performance, would likely emphasize formal controls. Autonomous units in decentralized organizations may depend on more informal controls.

Additional information: Mars renamed its big-selling Marathon chocolate bar in Britain Snickers; renamed Europe's most successful candy bar, Raider chocolate biscuit, Twix; changed the name of Bonitos in France to M&Ms and changed color, coatings, and formula. However, difficulties arose in changing Milky Way and Mars bars. In the EU, a Mars bar is caramel and chocolate, which is the Milky Way in the United States. Milky Way bars exist in Europe, but they don't have any caramel. Mars bars in the United States contain almonds. Product changes such as these (and in Lever's situation) may result in loss in market share.

Sources for company information: E. S. Browning, "In Pursuit of the Elusive Euroconsumer," *Wall Street Journal,* April 23, 1992, B1; Saeed Samiee and Kendall Roth, "The Influence of Global Marketing Standardization on Performance," *Journal of Marketing,* April 1992, 1–17.

Class Exercise 2: This exercise is relatively easy and is meant to bring out the organization portion of the chapter. A possible follow-up exercise might be to ask students to give examples of where a marketing unit can be organized according to a combination of functions. Answers:

	Classification	*Organized by*
1.	District	**region**
2.	Sales	**function**
3.	Research	**function**
4.	Southern	**region**
5.	Product manager	**product**
6.	Retail buyers	**type of customer**
7.	Institutional sales	**type of customer**
8.	Brand	**product**
9.	Advertising	**function**
10.	International sales	**region/type of customer**

Debate Issue: Is cost analysis more important than sales analysis?

Chapter Quiz: Answers to multiple-choice questions are

1. a	3. b
2. e	4. e

CLASS EXERCISE 1

MULTINATIONAL CORPORATIONS (MNCs) COMPETING ON A GLOBAL BASIS HAVE APPROACHED ORGANIZATIONAL STRUCTURE AND STRATEGIC CONTROL WITH TWO BASIC METHODS. SOME FIRMS, SUCH AS MARS, INC., AND PROCTER & GAMBLE, HAVE BECOME HIGHLY CENTRALIZED AND ATTEMPT TO PRODUCE STANDARDIZED PRODUCTS WORLDWIDE. OTHERS, SUCH AS UNILEVER AND NESTLÉ SA, HAVE TRADITIONALLY BEEN MORE DECENTRALIZED BUT ARE NOW MOVING TOWARD GREATER CENTRALIZATION. THESE COMPANIES ARE ALL TRYING TO MARKET THEIR PRODUCTS TO EUROPE IN SEARCH OF COMMON NEEDS AND PERCEPTIONS SHARED BY ALL EUROPEANS.

1. What are the advantages of a centralized organization and of a decentralized organization? Which do you think would better suit organizations marketing to the European Union (EU)?

2. Lever, the EU subsidiary of Unilever, has sold Snuggle fabric softener in ten EU countries under seven names, with different bottles, different strategies and sometimes different formulas. Lever is slowly trying to change to a single brand name. What problems might a marketing-oriented organization encounter in doing so?

3. Considering the number and diversity of the firm's products and the characteristics and needs of the target market(s), should a firm such as Lever be organized by function, products, regions, or types of customers in Europe? What about a firm such as Procter & Gamble, which is introducing standardized products with standardized names across Europe?

4. The type of marketing control process that is employed by these MNCs is dependent on the internal and external environment. If a MNC is highly centralized, would you expect the control process to be primarily formal or informal?

CLASS EXERCISE 2

A MARKETING UNIT CAN BE ORGANIZED ACCORDING TO FUNCTIONS, PRODUCTS, REGIONS, OR TYPES OF CUSTOMERS. WITH WHICH OF THESE CLASSIFICATIONS ARE THE FOLLOWING TERMS MOST CLOSELY ASSOCIATED?

1. **District**

2. **Sales**

3. **Research**

4. **Southern**

5. **Product manager**

6. **Retail buyers**

7. **Institutional sales**

8. **Brand**

9. **Advertising**

10. **International sales**

DEBATE ISSUE

IS COST ANALYSIS MORE IMPORTANT THAN SALES ANALYSIS?

YES

- Knowing the cost of specific resources allows management to allocate resources more precisely

- Cost analysis is the cornerstone of cost control

- In a price-competitive industry, the firms with low costs, relative to competitors, are likely to be the long-term survivors

NO

- Cost analysis tells management very little about customers' reactions to the firm's marketing strategies

- Sales analysis helps marketers to understand which products are selling and which customer groups are buying

- Sales analysis aids marketers in measuring the performance of marketing resources and marketing strategies

CHAPTER QUIZ

1. Kate is upset because the bank did not credit her account with a deposit, which resulted in a returned check to Kate's mortgage company. When she was told the branch manager was on vacation, she expected to have to wait two weeks to have the matter resolved. Kate was surprised when the receptionist apologized for the error, and drafted a letter to the mortgage company while Kate waited. The bank was engaging in which type of decision-making strategy?
    a.   Employee empowerment
    b.   Centralized management
    c.   Structured
    d.   Immediate-focused
    e.   Product-focused

2. Sam's employer is currently developing a new marketing strategy. The top managers have developed the marketing strategy and have given it to Sam so that he can now develop an implementation plan. Sam's company will most likely end up with which type of strategy?
    a.   Decentralized
    b.   Rigid
    c.   Intended
    d.   Centralized
    e.   Realized

3. Stratford Manufacturing is interested in total quality management and wants to learn more about its principles. Which of the following elements will Stratford *not* address in its investigation of TQM?
    a.   Improving customer satisfaction
    b.   Purchasing lowest-cost materials
    c.   Increasing employee participation
    d.   Strengthening supplier partnerships
    e.   Continuous product improvements

4. Sara's company has developed an excellent marketing plan and implementation strategy. All managers of the company have been involved and have been notified of the timetable for implementation. Sara and her coworkers have heard only rumors about their responsibilities, and the implementation is due to begin at the end of this week. Sara's firm needs to devote more attention to
    a.   internal marketing.
    b.   motivating personnel.
    c.   establishing performance standards.
    d.   strategy implementation.
    e.   developing a realistic timetable.

ANSWERS TO DISCUSSION AND REVIEW QUESTIONS

1. Why does an organization's intended strategy often differ from its realized strategy?

    There are several possibilities for explaining why the intended strategy, developed in the planning phase, often does not get implemented exactly as planned. Since the environment is constantly changing, the intended strategy must also change. Therefore, it becomes the realized strategy—that which actually gets implemented. Another reason that the intended strategy differs from the realized strategy is that the managers often develop the intended strategy separately from the plans for its implementation; therefore, it may not work the way they envisioned, due to changes required for actual operation.

2. Discuss the three problems associated with implementing marketing activities. How are these problems related to the differences between intended and realized marketing strategies?

    a. Managers sometimes fail to remember that marketing strategy and implementation are related. Companies sometimes assume that strategic planning always comes first, when in fact it should be developed concurrently with the implementation plan. Actual implementation requirements can change the intended strategy to the realized strategy.

    b. Marketing strategy and implementation are not static—they are constantly changing due to the fluctuating environment. This fluctuation would cause the intended strategy to be modified to the realized strategy.

    c. Another problem is that in many organizations, the responsibilities for marketing strategy and its implementation are separated. This could cause differing opinions on importance of tasks and resource allocation, and internal political friction. The intended strategy as outlined by those responsible for strategy could be altered by those who are actually implementing it.

3. What is internal marketing? Why is it important in implementing strategies?

    Internal marketing involves applying traditional marketing activities to employees within the organization to encourage them to carry out the firm's marketing strategy. Internal marketing involves getting employees to understand the role of marketing in the organization and the specific role they play in implementing the marketing strategy. Marketing strategies do not exist in a vacuum. People in the organization are necessary to communicate with customers and to carry out the many activities required to produce the desired products. An example of internal marketing would be educating employees concerning the importance of customer service and then giving them some freedom in customizing some dimension of service that would increase customer satisfaction.

4. How does the total quality management approach relate to marketing implementation? For what types of marketing strategies might TQM be best suited?

    The principles of TQM include empowered employees, continuous quality improvement, and quality-improvement teams. The implementation of marketing activities requires the cooperation of employees, as well as their empowerment. Employees, especially frontline employees, are the direct link between the organization and its customers. To better achieve successful exchange between the employee and the customer, employee empowerment should occur. Since it has been suggested that plans for both marketing strategy and its implementation should be developed simultaneously, use of TQM's quality-improvement teams would be helpful. Teams made up of individuals from varying backgrounds and responsibilities would bring necessary perspectives to the planning process. And TQM's principle of continuous quality improvement could be related to the required flexibility of marketing implementation, due to changes in the environment.

TQM might be best suited for business-unit strategies such as intensified growth, due to the need to focus on customers' needs and wants and to modify products as required to meet those needs.

5. What determines the place of marketing within an organization? Which type of organization is best suited to the marketing concept? Why?

The place of marketing is determined by whether the firm is production-, sales-, or marketing-oriented. The marketing-oriented firm is best suited to practice the marketing concept because a number of the firm's activities are coordinated through the marketing unit. Marketing encompasses a large number of business functions when a firm is marketing-oriented.

6. What factors can be used to organize the decision-making authority of a marketing unit? Discuss the benefits of each type of organization.

The factors that can be used for organizing a marketing unit's internal organization include:

a. *Function*—This form of organization may be useful in large, centralized firms whose products and types of customers are not numerous or diverse.

b. *Product*—A business that produces diverse products sometimes organizes according to product group. This gives the firm flexibility to develop special marketing mixes for different products. A company with this organization can hire specialists to market specific types of products.

c. *Region*—This type of organization is effective for a firm whose customers' characteristics and needs vary greatly from one region to another. This may help companies that try to penetrate the national market.

d. *Types of customers*—This form of organization can work well for a firm with several groups of customers whose needs and problems are quite different.

7. Why might an organization use multiple bases for organizing its marketing unit?

Product features may dictate that the marketing unit be structured by product, and customer characteristics may require that the unit be organized by region or customer type. The use of multiple bases allows the firm to acquire the benefits from several approaches. The primary benefit is flexibility.

8. Why is the motivation of marketing personnel important in implementing marketing plans?

Proper motivation helps personnel perform their activities effectively and in a manner that helps accomplish marketing plans. The degree to which a marketing manager can motivate marketing personnel strongly determines the ultimate success of the firm's marketing efforts.

9. How does communication help in implementing marketing plans?

    Communication is necessary to motivate and coordinate personnel and their efforts. Further, communication with higher-level management helps the marketing manager stay informed about other departments' activities, which helps the manager in coordinating marketing activities with those of other departments.

10. What are the major steps of the marketing control process?

    The major steps in the marketing control process are (a) establishing performance standards, (b) evaluating actual performance by comparing it with performance standards, and (c) reducing the differences between desired and actual performance.

11. Discuss the major problems in controlling marketing activities.

    In controlling marketing activities, several problems arise. Often the information needed to control the activities is not available or is too costly to obtain. In addition, marketing controls should be flexible because of the unpredictability of the environment, which hampers control. Also, the time lag between the performance and the effects of marketing activities limits measurement of effectiveness and control. Marketing activities and costs overlap with other areas within the firm, making it difficult to identify the cost of marketing activities and compare marketing activities on a performance basis. Finally, the development of performance standards may be difficult because of the multitude of uncontrollable factors associated with accomplishing marketing tasks.

12. What is a sales analysis? What makes it an effective control tool?

    In a sales analysis, sales figures are used to evaluate the firm's current performance, and the fundamental unit of measurement is the sales transaction. A company can analyze sales in terms of dollar volume or market share. Current sales data alone are not enough. Such information must be compared with forecasted sales, industry sales, specific competitors' sales, or the costs incurred to achieve the sales volume.

13. Identify and describe two cost analysis methods.

    Direct costing includes only variable costs and traceable common costs. Full costing includes variable costs, traceable common costs, and nontraceable common costs. Proponents of full costing claim that all costs must be included in analysis. Opponents say full costing does not yield actual costs because nontraceable common costs are determined by arbitrary criteria.

14. How is the marketing audit used to control marketing program performance?

    The marketing audit is the feedback phase of the evaluating process. It is the intelligence system used to gather information needed to determine whether the strategy is working.

COMMENTS ON THE CASES

Case 23.1   Marketing Casual Clothes at Work: Dressing Down, Productivity Up

This case focuses on how the workplace trend of dressing more casually is affecting employee motivation and productivity, and how several firms are taking advantage of the trend by modifying their marketing strategies. Discussion of this case might be initiated by asking students if any of their employers have implemented casual days and what the result has been.

The first question asks how casual-dress days help companies implement marketing strategies. Research indicates that casual-dress days boost employee motivation and productivity, which may help employees be more efficient and effective in their roles in implementing marketing strategy. Highly motivated and productive employees do their jobs more effectively and provide better customer service, which improves exchanges with customers.

Question 2 asks how Levi Strauss & Co. is taking advantage of the trend to dress down in the workplace. Levi Strauss has modified its marketing strategy by expanding its product mix to include more clothing items appropriate to the casual-yet-professional workplace. The company has also developed promotional materials (toll-free number, videos, fashion shows) designed to help other companies communicate to their employees what casual dress is appropriate for their particular workplaces.

The third question asks how dress-down policies can contribute to more satisfying exchanges for both internal and external customers. Casual-dress days are an internal marketing technique companies can use to help their employees get greater satisfaction and enjoyment out of their jobs. By allowing employees to dress more comfortably at work, companies improve internal exchanges because their employees are more motivated and productive.

Video Information

Video Title: Levi's Casual Business Wear
Location: Tape 3, Segment 23
Length: 4:35
Video Overview: Companies are quickly embracing the benefits of allowing their employees to dress casually certain days of the week, in large part because casual dress has been related to increased productivity and satisfaction in the workplace. Apparel manufacturers are realigning their marketing strategies and product lines to adapt to this new style of work dress. Manufacturers are developing new lines such as Haggar Clothing Company's City Casual line and Levi's Dockers line. Levi's has even developed a video and sent it to companies explaining "How to Put Casual Businesswear to Work."

Multiple-Choice Questions About the Video

b   1. What percentage of U.S. companies have at least one day when employees can dress for comfort?
   a. 100
   b. 70
   c. 50
   d. 30

c   2. Which of the following is *not* a benefit of casual days?
        a. Employee comfort
        b. Greater productivity
        c. Higher employee turnover
        d. Cost savings on clothing and dry cleaning

a   3. The dress-down trend has become the linchpin of the marketing strategy of
        a. Levi Strauss & Co.
        b. Hartmarx.
        c. Talbots.
        d. Haggar Clothing Cos.

Case 23.2   Implementing a New Culture at Denny's

This case briefly profiles Denny's problems with allegations of racial discrimination and examines how the firm is trying to rebound through effective marketing implementation. Because of the content, discussion may become heated, but students should be reminded that the purpose of this case is to discuss implementation issues.

Question 1 asks how Denny's realized strategy differed from its intended strategy in serving racially diverse customers. Denny's intended strategy was to serve all customers and to maintain a workplace environment for employees with high morale and quality service. It was not realized due to a failure to achieve proper implementation, especially in the area of human resources management. The realized strategy resulted in accusations and legal settlements related to racial discrimination, as well as negative publicity and lost sales because of boycotts by some interest groups over the allegations.

The second question asks whether there were problems in implementing the marketing strategy based on the separation of top and midlevel managers and frontline management. Obviously there were. Top management did not want to create legal and public relations problems through operations in the management of employees at different levels. Denny's previous structure and corporate culture permitted decentralized decision making in the area of hiring that presented opportunities for discrimination. As a result, new CEO Adamson has reduced the layers of management and centralized much of the firm's decision making to bring consistency to restaurant operations and minimize the potential for future racial issues.

Question 3 asks students to explain how Denny's could use total quality management and internal marketing to improve its service to all customers. Adopting a mindset of total quality management could help Denny's coordinate efforts directed at improving customer satisfaction, increasing employee participation and empowerment, forming and strengthening supplier partnerships, and facilitating an organizational culture of continuous quality improvement. Adopting a philosophy of internal marketing would require that Denny's treat its employees like its customers and make them aware of what the company is trying to achieve through its operations and marketing activities. An internal marketing approach would help Denny's coordinate internal exchanges between the organization and its employees to better achieve successful external exchanges between the organization and its customers. If employees are given the opportunity to discriminate and mistreat any customers, the overall objectives of the firm will not be achieved.

APPENDIX A

CASE COMMENTS ON STRATEGIC PART-ENDING CASES

STRATEGIC CASE 1
KENTUCKY FRIED CHICKEN EXPANDS GLOBALLY

The objective of this first strategic case is to allow students to examine how a familiar organization has identified a target market in the fast-food industry and developed a marketing mix to satisfy consumers' need on a global basis. Students should feel comfortable discussing this case because KFC and its restaurants are familiar to them.

Question 1 asks students to focus on KFC's greatest marketing challenges in the domestic fast-food market. KFC has been well positioned in the rapid-growth franchise fast-food business over the last forty years. The target market for fried chicken is large and provides excellent differentiation from other fast-food giants such as McDonald's. Between Colonel Sanders, Heublein, and more recently, PepsiCo, KFC has obtained 49 percent of the 7.7 billion U.S. fast-food chicken market. The greatest challenge is competition from Hardee's and McDonald's adding fried chicken as well as the growth of Mexican and pizza fast-food markets. Perhaps one of the greatest challenges is the trend away from fried foods to restaurant chains that feature roasted chicken. Finally, the U.S. fast-food market is near saturation.

Question 2 asks students to define the role of globalization of marketing in KFC's plans to expand sales. The key concern focuses on the possible use of the same marketing strategies worldwide. Many countries have strong culinary customs and traditions that do not represent easy target markets to penetrate. KFC has had difficulty in Germany, for example, but has been more successful in Asian markets, where chicken is a staple dish. Japan, Australia, China, and Europe all offer opportunities with some modification of the marketing strategy. Although there is economic risk, Mexico is KFC's most important foreign market. KFC's strategy works there, and the company enjoys enormous popularity.

Question 3 asks why environmental forces are so important to KFC's sales success in Latin America and Mexico. Franchising was not possible in Mexico until 1990. Until then, the legal environment prevented growth through its direct investment franchise system. Now franchising can be profitable, but economic instability in prices, wages, and exchange rates threatens profits. Continued devaluation of the peso has resulted in higher import prices, runaway inflation, and exorbitant interest rates. Until greater economic and political stability can be achieved, KFC plans to be conservative.

STRATEGIC CASE 2

BLACK & DECKER GOES AFTER SERIOUS DO-IT-YOURSELFERS

This case allows students to examine how a familiar organization identified a target market and analyzed its power tool needs in order to develop a marketing mix that satisfies these needs. Students should feel comfortable discussing this case because the organization and its products are familiar to them.

Question 1 asks students to describe the approach that Black & Decker management has taken in selecting and analyzing the target market toward which Quantum tools are aimed. Black & Decker management is using a differentiated targeting strategy. While Black & Decker aims Quantum tools at serious do-it-yourselfers, it also produces other lines of power tools aimed at different market segments.

The second question asks about the types of information that Black & Decker acquired and how management used this information. When Black & Decker did consumer research, it went directly to customers to find out what they wanted. Through an independent research firm, Black & Decker established a "living laboratory" consisting of fifty male home owners aged 25 to 54 years. Over a three-month period the company gathered considerable information about how these people use power tools and why they choose specific brands. Black & Decker's own executives visited the homes of these group members, watched them use tools, and questioned them about their use of tools. Marketers at Black & Decker also went with group members when the do-it-yourselfers were purchasing tools and building supplies. Black & Decker used this information to isolate the specific product features and product benefits desired by serious do-it-yourselfers. These features and benefits were the ones on which Black & Decker focused as the Quantum tool line was developed.

Question 3 asks students to identify the specific customer needs that Black & Decker attempted to satisfy with the Quantum tool line. Examples of specific needs:

a. A cordless drill that has enough power to finish the job without being recharged

b. An electric saw that has a blade which stops immediately as soon as the saw switch is turned off

c. Power tools that also vacuum sawdust as they are being used because do-it-yourselfers do not like cleaning up piles of sawdust

The fourth question asks students which factors are most likely to influence the consumer buying decision process for Black & Decker Quantum tools. Demographic characteristics represent an important personal factor that would likely influence the consumer buying decision process. Among the psychological factors, perception and consumer attitudes are likely to be very important factors influencing the purchase of power tools. Role and family influences and reference group influences are social factors that are likely to affect do-it-yourselfers' purchases of Quantum power tools.

STRATEGIC CASE 3

MATTEL TOYS SINGS, "OH, YOU BEAUTIFUL DOLL!"

In 1959 Mattel introduced the Barbie doll. Today Barbie is a $1.4 billion business and accounts for over 37 percent of Mattel's annual sales volume. The objective of this case is to examine how Mattel has developed Barbie into a world leader in the toy industry and how it continues to manage this product to maintain its leadership.

The first question asks what actions Mattel marketers have taken to extend the life of Barbie and to make this product successful. Mattel has extended Barbie's life by introducing variations on the doll that range from varying hair lengths and colors to changing facial features. In addition Mattel has continued to produce a stream of Barbie extras such as houses, cars, furniture, clothing, and accessories to help maintain interest in this product. Mattel has also created a social system for Barbie that includes friends and relatives. Through the use of designers, Mattel has attempted to keep Barbie a contemporary figure who changes to reflect our culture. As the lifestyles of women have changed, Mattel has transformed Barbie's occupational roles and leisure time pursuits as well to reflect these changes.

The second question asks students to describe the product positioning of Barbie. Barbie is positioned in the minds of buyers as being a friend of girls. While Mattel produces clothing and accessories to place Barbie in certain roles, it also provides considerable latitude to allow girls to make Barbie whatever they want Barbie to be. Barbie is positioned in the minds of buyers as being the number one doll within its subcategory of the doll product category. Occasionally, imitators attempt to challenge Barbie but usually are unsuccessful.

The third question asks students to evaluate the brand equity of the Barbie brand. To consider the brand equity of the Barbie brand, we need to examine the four major elements of the concept.

- *Brand awareness.* A recent study indicates that 98 percent of American households recognize the Barbie name.

- *Brand loyalty.* Loyalty for the Barbie is so significant that challengers in this part of the product category have been unsuccessful for a number of years.

- *Perceived brand quality.* The fact that Mattel sells $1.4 billion worth of Barbie-related products annually is strong evidence that customers hold favorable impressions about the brand quality. The average three-to-ten-year-old American girl buys two to three Barbies a year.

- *Brand associations.* Brand associations for Barbie are created both by the doll and by the accessories provided by Mattel. Customers associate Barbie with "contemporary," able to take on many occupations to represent the many potential roles of women in our culture.

In summary the Barbie brand, given its strength in all four aspects, has very strong equity.

STRATEGIC CASE 4
GOODYEAR BREAKS WITH TRADITION

The objective of this case is to provide students with a learning experience acquired by examining an organization that is changing its marketing channels and attempting to cope with the problems created by these changes.

In the initial question students are asked to identify the major sources of channel conflict between Goodyear and its franchised dealers. The major sources of conflict are as follows:

a. Goodyear is allowing a number of large retailers to sell Goodyear tires. Prior to this shift in channels, Goodyear distributed its replacement tires only through franchised dealers.

b. Goodyear is not restricting the selling of its most popular tires to just Goodyear franchise dealers but instead is allowing all dealers to sell these tires, such as the Aqua Tread.

c. Some of the large competitive retailers are selling tires at prices lower than what franchise dealers actually pay in acquiring tires from Goodyear.

Question 2 asks students to explain the steps that Goodyear could take to reduce the conflict with its franchise dealers. Goodyear could price its tires to its franchise dealers at levels that would allow them to be competitive with the larger retailers. Goodyear could create lines of tires specifically for franchise dealers that are not available through the major retailers. For larger franchise dealers, Goodyear could produce private-branded tires.

The third question asks about the major benefits to Goodyear of marketing its tires through retailers such as Sears, Wal-Mart, Discount Tire, and Kmart. One major benefit is that Goodyear achieves much broader distribution by distributing through large retailers with hundreds of retail outlets. This broader distribution will clearly allow Goodyear to sell a larger number of replacement tires. Broader distribution should help Goodyear achieve a greater market share.

Question 4 asks students to identify the channel leader and the channel leader's sources of power. The channel leader is the Goodyear tire manufacturing organization. The economic sources of power derive from the fact that this producer has control over the product and who will distribute it. This firm's size also gives it economic power. As a manufacturer Goodyear also has expert power, reward power, and coercive power to some extent. Since Goodyear continues to distribute its tires through major retailers, channel leadership may change because these retail organizations are very powerful. It can be expected that these retail organizations will eventually influence which tires they purchase, how much they will pay for the tires, how warranties will be managed, and other details.

The final question asks students to provide recommendations to a Goodyear franchise dealer regarding possible approaches to remaining a competitive and profitable retailer. Some of the following recommendations are likely to be voiced:

a. Stop marketing Goodyear tires if their costs to the independent retailer are higher than the prices charged by large retailers.

b. Consider selling privately branded tires.

c. Carry a larger number of tire brands.

d. Provide services and store warranties that large retailers cannot provide.

e. Market special-use tires and tires in sizes and designs that are not traditionally carried by large retailers.

STRATEGIC CASE 5
THE AMERICAN DAIRY INDUSTRY: GOT PROMOTION?

For many years various trade groups in the American dairy industry have spent considerable money and exerted major marketing efforts to promote milk and milk-related products. Yet total milk consumption in the United States has remained fairly flat over the last decade. The purpose of this case is to examine the promotional tools and efforts currently being employed by several groups that are a part of the American dairy industry.

The first question asks what types of promotional objectives the American dairy industry is attempting to achieve. The groups making up the American dairy industry are attempting to stimulate primary demand for milk. These groups are not promoting specific brands of milk (which would be selective demand); they are attempting to increase overall milk consumption.

In addition, the promotional efforts are aimed at retaining customers and encouraging them to consume a larger amount of milk by reminding them of the various traditional uses of milk.

The second question asks students to assess the dairy industry approach of advertising milk as an accompaniment to foods that traditionally go with milk, such as brownies and cereal. Some students will take the position that reminding milk drinkers about how great milk tastes with certain types of products will in fact stimulate demand by increasing consumption among current milk drinkers. Other students are likely to argue that this tactic will not increase consumption because these individuals are already buying and drinking milk and will do so without being reminded. The students who take this position may go further and indicate that to increase the overall consumption of milk, milk drinkers should be shown new or less conventional ways of consuming milk.

Question 3 asks why the milk mustache and Got Milk? campaigns have generated significant publicity. These campaigns have generated significant publicity because they are creative, direct, and employ celebrity endorsers. These advertisements also have achieved widespread visibility and awareness, which makes them more likely to be used by television personalities.

The last question asks, "Do you believe that the American dairy industry's current promotional efforts will increase long-term milk consumption?" Clearly, students' opinions will vary. Some of the positions taken in the answers to question 2 may resurface here. For the discussion of this question, you may wish to use transparency 6E regarding long-term milk consumption patterns. Some students may also take the position that long-term milk consumption can be increased if certain milk products—such as reduced fat milk and skim milk—are emphasized.

STRATEGIC CASE 6
UNITED STATES POSTAL SERVICE COMPETES THROUGH PRICING

The United States Postal Service as a government-owned corporation faces a number of challenging pricing issues as it attempts to compete with aggressive private enterprises such as Federal Express and United Parcel Service. This case focuses on the Postal Service's attempts to price its products in order to compete more effectively with other providers of overnight delivery services.

The first question asks students to discuss how buyers' perceptions affect the pricing of Priority Mail Service. Buyers' perceptions of the Postal Service are likely to lean toward viewing it as being generally reliable but not especially fast. Thus, the Postal Service's strategy of pricing Priority Mail Service at a low price is a reasonable approach. Some users of overnight services are concerned about speed, some are concerned about security, and still others are concerned about both. For persons concerned primarily about security rather than speed, Priority Mail Service provides a secure alternative at a low price. Another perception that buyers have is that the Postal Service is supposed to be a low-price service provider because, traditionally, the organization has not provided premium services at premium prices. These perceptions suggest that the Postal Service should be providing Priority Mail Service at a reasonably low price.

Question 2 asks whether USPS and Federal Express have similar pricing objectives when pricing their similar services. Federal Express's pricing objective is primarily based on product quality. This organization prefers to price its product at a premium level and to provide a very high-quality overnight delivery service. The Postal Service is pursuing a pricing objective of gaining market share. It provides Priority Mail Services at only a fraction of what Federal Express charges.

The third question asks students to identify which pricing method is being used by USPS. The Postal Service is using a competition-oriented pricing method. It clearly wants to be a low-price competitor relative to both Federal Express and United Parcel Service.

The final question asks what types of issues face USPS officials as they make future pricing decisions. A major issue that the Postal Service officials face is that they lack flexibility in setting prices and changing them quickly. While its competitors can change prices relatively fast, the Postal Service is burdened with long waiting periods regarding pricing decisions. Another major issue for the Postal Service is that its costs traditionally have been extremely high as a government organization. Organizations that can most effectively compete on the basis of price in the long term are those that have low costs. Thus cost control will be a significant factor for the Postal Service to consider.

STRATEGIC CASE 7
APPLE COMPUTERS

The objective of this case is to allow students to examine the problems facing an organization and the company's response to those problems. Although Apple has been one of the most innovative businesses in the computer industry, it has had major difficulties in the area of marketing strategy and implementation. Students should feel comfortable discussing this case because of their familiarity with the computer maker; many will also have used Apple products at home, school, or work. By the time students read this case, events at Apple will most certainly have changed. You may wish to provide a brief update on the company, or assign students to update the case themselves as an additional exercise for this case.

Question 1 asks students to describe how Apple's unique culture contributed to its present situation and to put themselves in the shoes of Apple's new CEO and explain how they would deal with the culture. From its inception, Apple thrived as a rebel. Accordingly, it developed an organizational culture based on thumbing its nose at the Establishment, even scorning dress codes, formal meetings, and other traditional business trappings. More importantly, Apple developed a culture of consensus, as indicated by the internal joke, "a vote can be 15,000 to 1 and still be a tie." Although this culture fueled phenomenal innovation and fostered the development of many successful products, most notably the Apple Macintosh and its operating system, it also created difficulties for Apple executives trying to develop and implement effective marketing strategies for the firm. Although consensus decision making has been the norm in Japanese firms, strong leadership and tough decision making is necessary in the volatile U.S. computer industry. As to the second half of the question, new CEO Gilbert Amerlio has a definite challenge in walking the fine line between using Apple's culture to motivate employees and fuel future innovation while taking command and making tough decisions to turn those innovations into successful products in the marketplace. Students will have a variety of answers as to how to deal with Apple's unique culture, but their answers should consider employee motivation, coordination, communication, and decision making.

The second question asks how Apple's frequent strategy changes brought it where it is today and what is the single most costly error made by executives. Apple's frequent strategy changes may be confusing consumers as to what exactly an Apple computer is and how it differs from the competition. The result has been declining sales and market share. Many industry analysts believe Apple's single most costly error was failure to license the Mac operating system to other computer makers in order to create a "clone" industry that could increase market share for the Mac platform.

Question 3 asks students to describe Apple's current strategy. As of the writing of the case, Apple's strategy was to refocus itself with an intensive growth strategy in market segments where it already had a solid presence, as well as diversified growth by developing new products for the rapidly growing Internet.

The final question asks students to propose a strategy to take Apple into the twenty-first century, keeping in mind such factors as Microsoft's Windows and the Internet. It also asks students to describe how they would implement their proposed strategies. This question requires students to think creatively and strategically and to incorporate all that they have learned in this course. Students could even be required to complete a marketing plan (including a SWOT analysis) for Apple to be turned in for a grade, either individually or as a group project. Responses to this question will vary based on students' understanding of the material and their own creativity. All responses should include an analysis of Apple's strengths, weaknesses, opportunities, and threats; indicate appropriate marketing strategies (target markets, marketing mixes) for capitalizing on Apple's strengths and opportunities and minimizing its weaknesses and threats; and indicate methods of implementation for Apple.

APPENDIX B

FINANCIAL ANALYSIS IN MARKETING: ANSWERS TO DISCUSSION AND REVIEW QUESTIONS

1. How does a manufacturer's income statement differ from a retailer's income statement?

   A manufacturer's income statement contains a "cost of goods manufactured" entry in the Cost of Goods Sold column, instead of the "purchases" entry used by retailers.

2. Use the following information to answer questions a through c:

   Company TEA
   Fiscal year ended June 30, 1997

Net sales	$500,000
Cost of goods sold	300,000
Net income	50,000
Average inventory at cost	100,000
Total assets (total investment)	200,000

   a. What is the inventory turnover rate for TEA Company? From what sources will the marketing manager determine the significance of the inventory turnover rate?

   $$\text{Inventory} = \frac{\text{Cost of goods sold}}{\text{Average inventory at cost}}$$

   $$= \frac{\$300,000}{\$100,000}$$

   $$= 3 \text{ times}$$

   The marketing manager must compare the inventory turnover rate with historical turnover rates and industry turnover rates.

538

b. What is the capital turnover ratio for fiscal year 1997? What is the net income ratio? What is the return on investment (ROI)?

Capital turnover rate $\quad = \quad \dfrac{\text{Net sales}}{\text{Total investment}}$

$$= \quad \dfrac{\$500,000}{\$200,000}$$

$$= \quad 2.5 \text{ times}$$

Net income ratio $\quad = \quad \dfrac{\text{Net income}}{\text{Net sales}}$

$$= \quad \dfrac{\$50,000}{\$500,000}$$

$$= \quad .1 \text{ or } 10\%$$

Return on investment (ROI) $\quad = \quad \dfrac{\text{Net income}}{\text{Total investment}}$

$$= \quad \dfrac{\$50,000}{\$200,000}$$

$$= \quad .25 \text{ or } 25\%$$

c. How many dollars of sales did each dollar of investment produce for TEA Company in fiscal year 1997?

Capital turnover $\quad = \quad \dfrac{\text{Net sales}}{\text{Total investment}}$

$$= \quad \dfrac{\$500,000}{\$200,000}$$

$$= \quad \$2.50 \text{ of sales for each dollar invested}$$

3. Product A has a markup percentage on cost of 40 percent. What is the markup percentage on selling price?

Markup percentage on selling price $\quad = \quad \dfrac{\text{Markup percentage on cost}}{100\% + \text{markup \% on cost}}$

$$= \quad \dfrac{40}{100 + 40}$$

$$= \quad .286 \text{ or } 28.6\%$$

4. Product B has a markup percentage on selling price of 30 percent. What is the markup percentage on cost?

$$\text{Markup percentage on cost} = \frac{\text{Markup percentage on selling price}}{100\% - \text{markup \% on selling price}}$$

$$= \frac{30}{100 - 30}$$

$$= .429 \text{ or } 42.9\%$$

5. Product C has a cost of $60 and a usual markup percentage of 25 percent on selling price. What price should be placed on this item?

100% = 25% of selling price + cost
X = price
.75X = $60
X = $80

6. Apex Appliance Company sells twenty units of product Q for $100 each and ten units for $80 each. What is the markdown percentage for product Q?

$$\text{Markdown percentage} = \frac{\text{Dollar markdowns}}{\text{Net sales in dollars}}$$

$$= \frac{10 \text{ units } (\$20)}{20(\$100) + .10(\$80)}$$

$$= \frac{\$200}{\$2,000 + \$800}$$

$$= .071 \text{ or } 7.1\%$$